D0875180

BRITAIN'S INDUSTRIAL FUTURE

being the Report of the
Liberal Industrial Inquiry
of 1928

With a Foreword by
DAVID STEEL, M.P.

ERNEST BENN LIMITED
LONDON & TONBRIDGE

Published by Ernest Benn Limited
25 New Street Square, Fleet Street, London EC4A 3JA
& Sovereign Way, Tonbridge, Kent TN9 1RW

First published 1928
Second impression 1977

Distributed in Canada by
The General Publishing Company Limited, Toronto

ISBN 0 510-02300-2
0 510-02301-0 *paperback*

FOREWORD

THROUGHOUT history, politicians and economists have endeavoured to peer into the future and promulgate courses of action to better the lot of mankind. Few have been so accurate in their analyses and forecasts as the authors of "The Yellow Book".

Their creed was simple and fundamental: "We believe with a passionate faith that the end of all political and economic action is not the perfecting or the perpetuation of this or that piece of mechanism or organisation, but that individual men and women may have life, and that they may have it more abundantly." That tenet is as valid for Liberals in the seventies as it was in the twenties.

Originally "Britain's Industrial Future" was subtitled "the Report of the Liberal Industrial Enquiry" but, sensitive to the unfortunate implication in the initials, Enquiry was altered to Inquiry. However, formal titles were academic; "The Yellow Book" is the name by which it will always be known.

Lloyd George funded the inquiry, Asquith dictated the preface to the report almost from his death-bed, and the book sold in enormous numbers. Of course, sections of it are out of date now, nearly fifty years later. But it is perhaps only with hindsight that we are able to assess the crucial impact which the report could have had on the condition of Britain, had more heed been paid to its conclusions and recommendations. If acted upon at the time the course of the twentieth century in Britain would have been very different.

Much of the inquiry is still—alas—very relevant. It recognises "a fungoid growth of unnecessary intermediary operations," so there was a burgeoning bureaucracy even in the twenties, "and a decline in genuine productive effort." It presses for the clearance of the waterways to develop "this cheap method of transport", for an increase in exports, reform of the rating system, for minimum wages, industrial partnership, profit sharing and works councils. These issues are the stuff of Liberal politics today.

There are two special themes to which I commend your attention.

Firstly, the committee urges a totally different approach to industrial relations based on the idea of partnership. Modern Liberal industrial policy, whose provenance can be found in the pages of "The Yellow Book", accepts the view that a positive psychological approach is required to bring all sides of industry together. This was then a new untried idea. It is now an old untried idea; it should be implemented.

Secondly, the committee asserts that government cannot and should not initiate everything and control everything, as it is trying to do at the present time. This accelerating trend has led to a centralisation of the power of institutions throughout the gamut of public life. Both these require urgent attention today.

To us it is a commonplace to read about forecasting units' computer predictions on the economy and industry. These rely on enormously complicated mathematical calculations. They often contradict one another, because men and women of vision cannot be replaced by machines: where there is no vision the people perish.

We, the heirs of the "Liberal Industrial Inquiry", can look back and judge that it was and is right.

House of Commons,
25 October 1976

DAVID STEEL, M.P.

PREFACE

IT was felt by many of those who attended year by year the meetings of the Liberal Summer School that there was need for fresh investigation of the economic and social problems by which the nation is now faced, and for the formulation of a policy to deal with them, starting from the Liberal standpoint and aiming at the application of Liberal ideas. With these objects in view, the Summer School Committee, which was fortunate in securing the active co-operation of Mr. Lloyd George, took the initiative in getting together the men and women who have collaborated in this Inquiry. These include not only some of the leading members of the Liberal Party, but also business men, trade unionists and others, some of whom have no formal connection with it. The material of this Report has been prepared by special Committees dealing with various divisions of the wide field which has been under investigation, while a large number of persons qualified by their experience to speak with authority have given evidence, supplied information, written reports on British or foreign conditions, and assisted with advice and counsel.

For the final form in which the Report appears the Executive Committee is alone responsible. It will not be expected, when a Report such as this is presented, that every member of the Committee from which it emanates will concur in every detailed recommendation or consider himself bound by every phrase. Nor can our conclusions and recommendations be more than suggestions, offered for the consideration of the Liberal Party as a whole by the methods of its established procedure. But on the broad policy and the general proposals we are unanimous, and we trust that the measures we suggest, as the outcome of long consideration, may in substance meet with the acceptance of the Party, and through it, in due course, of the electorate.

The problems of British industry are so many and their ramifications so wide that we have been bound to set strict limits to the field of our investigation. We have not forgotten that the temperance question and the standard of national education have a close bearing upon industry; that the structure of our system of local government touches industrial questions at many points; that the issue between Free Trade and Protection is of fundamental importance. If we make little reference to these matters, it is because their problems are special, the considerations that arise are many, and any adequate examination of them would stretch too far the length of this Report.

On all the subjects which we have included within our scope we have tried to offer specific recommendations. Not all of them relate to action by the State. Our proposals would have been incomplete if we had limited ourselves to those that would fall definitely within the political sphere as usually understood. Although the greater part will be found to demand legislation or administrative action from Parliament or the Government of the day, there are many which depend for their adoption upon the approval and the action of those who are themselves engaged in industry.

The problems are urgent. The solutions cannot be easy or simple. To find the solutions and to apply them must be the principal object of the politics of our time.

The Executive Committee desire to express their warm appreciation of the work done by the members of the special committees who, though taking no general responsibility for the recommendations of this report, provided the drafts and memoranda on which it is based.

They are also grateful for the invaluable assistance of all those who gave evidence, supplied criticisms, or in other ways assisted in carrying out the investigation.

The very warm thanks of the Committee are also due to Mr. Eagar and the members of the staff for their efficient, loyal, and untiring collaboration, without which this report could not possibly have been completed.

Finally they wish to record their sense of the profound loss which not only this investigation but the cause of Liberalism generally has suffered in the early death of Mr. C. F. G. Masterman. The members of the Committee mourn a vigorous, inspiring, and loyal colleague and friend.

MEMBERSHIP OF LIBERAL INDUSTRIAL INQUIRY

EXECUTIVE COMMITTEE

W. T. Layton, C.H. (*Chairman*)
E. D. Simon (*Vice-Chairman*)
Rt. Hon. D. Lloyd George, O.M., M.P.
E. H. Gilpin
H. D. Henderson
Philip Kerr, C.H.
J. M. Keynes, C.B.
Rt. Hon. C. F. G. Masterman *
Ramsay Muir
Major H. L. Nathan
B. S. Rowntree
Rt. Hon. Sir Herbert Samuel, G.C.B., G.B.E.
Rt. Hon. Sir John Simon, K.C.V.O., K.C., M.P.

* Died November 17th, 1927.

Secretary: W. McG. Eagar
Assistant Secretary: J. Menken
Economic Adviser: Hubert Phillips
Statistician: A. R. Burnett-Hurst

In addition to the members of the Executive Committee, the following served on one or more of the Special Committees which have sat during the past eighteen months:

Mrs. Corbett Ashby
Hon. R. H. Brand, C.M.G.
Ernest Brown, M.P.
Lawrence Cadbury
S. Russell Cooke

E. O. Fordham, J.P.
G. M. Garro-Jones, M.P.
Philip Guedalla
Professor L. T. Hobhouse
Stuart Hodgson
Mrs. E. M. Hubback
W. A. Jowitt, K.C.
Mrs. Layton
Rt. Hon. C. A. McCurdy, K.C.
Arnold D. McNair, LL.D.
Rt. Hon. T. J. Macnamara, LL.D.
Frank Murrell
C. G. Renold
D. H. Robertson
Sir Archibald Sinclair, Bt., C.M.G., M.P.
Sir Josiah Stamp, G.B.E.
W. Stonestreet
Miss L. W. Taylor
Major L. F. Urwick
William Wareing

CONTENTS

BOOK 1

THE CONDITION OF BRITISH INDUSTRY

BOOK 2

THE ORGANISATION OF BUSINESS

BOOK 3
INDUSTRIAL RELATIONS
(*a*) SURVEY

(*b*) PROPOSALS FOR REFORM

BOOK 4
NATIONAL DEVELOPMENT

BOOK 5
NATIONAL FINANCE

LIST OF TABLES

BOOK 1

BOOK 2

BOOK 3

BOOK 4

BOOK 5

INTRODUCTION

INTRODUCTION

DEMOCRACY has been established as the ruling principle in the State, through the efforts of the Liberals of the past, in order that the people may have the means of remedying grievances, of creating the conditions that are necessary for their welfare, of securing that no member of the community shall be denied the opportunity to live a full and free life. The task of the Liberals of the present is to frame, and to carry, such measures as will bring us nearer to that goal—still so distant—and so enable democracy to fulfil its essential purpose.

1. Defects of the Industrial System

The grievances of to-day are mainly economic. No impartial man would contend that our industrial system has yet attained an adequate standard either of justice or of efficiency. In its progress it has reached a point where it provides, it is true, a fair level of comfort for a large proportion of our population, but it still allows a mass of great poverty at the one end, at the other an ostentatious luxury which is bitterly, and rightly, resented. For several years a million of our working people have been unemployed; a large additional number have been living as best they could on the low earnings of short time and intermittent work. In spite of the building of numbers of new houses, the slums of the great cities remain almost as they were; from overcrowding, and the ill-health and degradation that come from it, millions of the people are still powerless to escape. Yet all the time, individuals accumulate or inherit great fortunes, and it is clear in all men's sight that, more often than not, the prizes are awarded capriciously, with little regard either to economic service or to personal desert.

So there is discontent widespread among the people. And this discontent is itself a further cause of inefficiency. It sometimes leads to restrictive practices among the workers, which in the long run further worsen their own conditions. It gives rise constantly to friction within the industrial system, and not seldom to open and destructive conflict. Those who should be working together in the closest co-operation for common ends waste their energies on mutual quarrels. Much of the driving force of public-spirited men, urgently needed for the tasks of construction and improvement, is diverted to criticism, to antagonism, sometimes to revolutionary schemes of upheaval. All this hinders British industry and lessens its success. Efficiency depends upon contentment; and there can be no lasting contentment where a sense of injustice prevails.

Every motive, then, forbids a silent acceptance of things as they are. The call of human sympathy with those who are in distress, the sense of fair dealing between man and man, between class and class, the realisation that injustice in the long run means inefficiency—all these prevent an acquiescence in existing conditions, forbid an attitude of mere Conservatism.

2. Merits of the Industrial System

But to say that evils attach to the present industrial system, is not to say that it is without merits and should be destroyed. We are not driven, as the only alternatives, to the crude theories of the Communists, or to the sweeping, and, as we think, ill-considered, proposals of the Socialists.

Private enterprise has achieved great results. If present economic conditions are often bad, it is incontestable that past conditions have been very much worse. The nineteenth century was an age of unequalled material progress. The average level of real wages to-day is four times what it was in 1800; the money-wage has doubled and its purchasing power has doubled also. There has been, and there still is, an energy and resourcefulness in our industry and commerce which it would be harmful to impair and fatal to destroy. The problem is how to cure what is unhealthy in the economic body without injuring the organs which are sound.

3. Scope of State Action

When it is asked how far it is the business of the State to attempt to set things right, we hold that the answer cannot be given in a phrase or a sentence. We are not with those who say that, whatever may be our present difficulties, the intervention of the State would only increase them. Nor do we share the views of the dwindling band who think that the right course is to hand over to the State the maximum of productive activity and industrial control. We have no love for State intervention in itself. On the contrary, we attach the greatest importance to the initiative of individuals and to their opportunity to back their opinion against that of the majority and to prove themselves right. But the methods of production have been subject of late to great changes. The theory that private competition, unregulated and unaided, will work out, with certainty, to the greatest advantage of the community is found by experience to be far from the truth. The scope of useful intervention by the whole Society, whether by constructive action of its own or by regulating or assisting private action, is seen to be much larger than was formerly supposed. We have no intention of writing a treatise on political philosophy, but before going further we think it well to define more closely, though briefly, the political ideas which run through all our chapters and connect into a whole our various proposals.

4. The Liberal Point of View

Liberalism stands for Liberty; but it is an error to think that a policy of liberty must be always negative, that the State can help liberty only by abstaining from action, that invariably men are freest when their Government does least. Withdraw the police from the streets of the towns, and you will, it is true, cease to interfere with the liberty of the criminal, but the law-abiding citizens will soon find that they are less free than before. Abolish compulsory education: the child, and perhaps his parent, will no longer be forced to do what they may perhaps not wish to do; but the adults of the next generation will be denied the power to read, to think, to succeed, which is essential to a real freedom. Repeal, to take one more example, the Shops Acts: short-sighted shopkeepers will be allowed to trade for longer hours, but other shopkeepers and the whole class of shop-assistants will be robbed of their proper share of the leisure without which life is a servitude. Often more law may mean more liberty.

But not of course always. The principle may be pushed too far. There is such a thing as a meddlesome, unjustified officious interference, against which we have to be on our guard. The fact remains that there is much positive work that the State can do which is not merely consistent with liberty, but essential to it. The idea of the extreme individualist, that in proportion as State action expands freedom contracts, is false.

Equally false is the idea that because State action on the widest scale is favoured by Socialists, those who are not Socialists must oppose any and every extension of State action. It will lead, it is said, to Socialism in the long run. It is a partial surrender to false and flimsy theories.

True that the Socialist is inclined to welcome extensions of State activity for their own sakes; he regards them all as stages on the road to an ideal which he cherishes. But the fact that we do not share his ideal, and do not favour particular measures merely because they might be steps towards it, is no reason why, out of prejudice, we should close our eyes to whatever merits those measures may possess in themselves. If no one had ever generalised about Socialism, or used the word, or made it the rallying cry for a party, these measures might have been universally welcomed. It would be folly to reject what is right because some would have it lead to what is wrong.

We refuse therefore to spend time or energy over the controversy between Individualism and Socialism, which has raged so long and with so lavish an expenditure of breath and ink and temper. While the controversialists have exhausted themselves in struggling for theoretical objectives, work-a-day industry and political practice have moved far away from that issue; if it ever were a real issue, it is certainly now obsolete. To us those stalwarts of controversy seem to resemble the two knights in the story, who engaged in deadly combat in order to determine whether the shield which hung from a tree between them was gold or silver, only to discover that in fact it was gold on one side and silver on the other. Or perhaps it would be truer to say that they resemble two armies, each equipped with obsolete maps, and battling fiercely for the possession of fortifications which have long since been razed to the ground.

In the last hundred years, in this and every other industrial country, the State has progressively assumed a vast range of functions that closely affect industry and commerce. No one would now propose to repeal them. What would the conditions of employment in Great Britain have been if the Factory Acts and Mines Regulation Acts and Trade Boards Acts had never been passed? What would be the death-rate in our towns, and the infant mortality in particular, if the sanitary authorities had never been set up? To what petty dimensions would our national industry be now restricted if the Limited Liability Company had never come into being, the offspring of wise commercial laws? And what would be the extent of our merchant shipping without the help of the controlling hand of the Board of Trade?

No doubt there are some who will criticise our proposals as a whole on the ground that they would carry fresh interventions too far. We would remind such critics that there has hardly been one of the forms of State action that we have mentioned, proved by experience to have been beneficent, which was not hotly opposed at its inception as an unwarrantable invasion of individual liberty. The fact does not prove, of course, that every new proposal is right. But it does at least suggest that it is wise to keep an open mind. And it would be absurd to assume that precisely the right limit had now been reached, that last year had seen the final instance of useful Government intervention, that next year and the years to come will find nothing left to do.

Almost the whole of the modern system of regulation and assistance—and we have given but a few examples out of a long list of such measures—has been due to Liberal statesmanship; there is scarcely one of the reforms which has not either been carried or initiated by the Liberal Party. We believe that the Party will not be slow to take up the new duties which belong to a new age.

5. The Changing Economic Order

The economic order in which the doctrine of *laissez-faire* had its origin has already in large measure passed away. The typical unit of production used to be the small firm, built up within a generation or two by its owner, and financed by his savings or those of his immediate connections. Very many such businesses of course still remain. But the industrial unit which is now predominant is different. The ownership of businesses has passed, and is passing in ever-increasing degree, into the hands of scattered multitudes of shareholders, who have no real opportunity of forming any judgment as to the problems or prospects of the undertakings, and no effective method of making their opinions felt were they able to form any. Management is in the hands of salaried persons; decisions of policy are left to men who are not staking their fortunes on being right, as did the founder of a one-man business. One consequence of these changes is that the inefficient producer is no longer speedily eliminated. An established business is frequently too strong to be supplanted, although a new one may be better managed. Bankruptcy has gone out of fashion; at the worst "capital reorganisation" has taken its place.

And the increase in the scale of the producing unit has of late been very rapid. In some industries, amalgamations and absorptions have created businesses ten, twenty, or fifty times as vast, in their capital resources, in their labour force, in the dimensions of their trade, as any that would have been thought possible half a century ago.

Whole tracts of industrial enterprise, again, have already passed, by common consent, out of the sphere of purely private enterprise. We shall analyse the many intermediate forms of management which have sprung up, almost unnoticed, between the business under purely private control and the business under direct State or municipal control. We shall draw attention to the remarkable proportion of British large-scale industry which has come, in greater or less degree, under social authority.

A further great change, that goes far to decide the character of the modern world, is the establishment of political democracy. When individualism took its rise, political rights were still confined to a comparatively narrow class, so that there was no glaring contrast between the industrial status of the manual worker and his political status, between the economic autocracy exercised by the individual employer in farm or factory and the political oligarchy of the "privileged classes" in the government of the State. Universal franchise and the democratisation of political parties have changed all that. There is now felt to be something inconsistent between the industrial status of the worker as a factory "hand," subject to strict discipline and holding his employment on the most precarious of tenures, and his political status as a free and equal citizen and a maker and unmaker of governments. To a certain extent this inconsistency is inherent in the necessities of industrial organisation. No good can come, as even the controllers of Soviet Russia have had to recognise, of blurring the distinction between those whose function is to conceive and to plan and those whose function is to execute their plans. Nor is there anything to be gained by applying blindly the political devices of the public meeting and the ballot-box to the quite different problems of industrial life. It would, we think, be wrong and dishonest to hold out hopes to the ordinary man that he will ever be in a position to choose at each moment of the day whether he will do this thing or that, or even to take a direct part in the election or dismissal of those from whom he receives his immediate instructions. But it is not unreasonable to hope and to plan both that he shall take a direct part in framing and administering the code of discipline under which his daily work must be done, and also that, through the organisations which he has built and the leaders in whom he has confidence, he shall come to exercise an increasing influence on the wider government both of the business unit and of the whole industry of which he forms part.

The State here, from the nature of the case, can do little; but it can do something, and the nation should resolve that something shall be done. In the main, however, we must look, on the one hand, to a spread of the statesmanlike and pioneering spirit which has already found expression in the best practice of individual firms; on the other, to a growing determination on the part of the great Labour organisations to do their share in promoting, and indeed enforcing, efficiency in the conduct of business enterprise—to make their weight felt as powerfully in the constructive work of organising industry for the tasks of peace as they have made it felt on occasions in the conduct of industrial warfare.

6. The Aim of an Industrial Policy

Our conclusion, then, is not the rough-and-ready rule that, since so much already has been done in the direction of State action, the simple course is to do the rest and to nationalise everything. Individual management and the competition on which it is based still work reasonably well within a wide range of miscellaneous industries. They are an unrivalled method for ensuring the decentralisation of management—that is, for securing that power and responsibility should be exercised as near as possible to the act to be performed, and not through a long line of intermediaries. They are an excellent means for securing a variety of experiment, and for trying out the comparative efficiency both of methods and of men. They provide, though with some friction and inequality, the only practicable method which has yet been suggested of evaluating the various goods and services which it is the function of industry to supply. We regard, therefore, the direct management of industries by Departments of State, or agencies analogous to them, as prima facie undesirable and likely to remain the exception rather than the rule.

Faced by these conditions in modern industry, convinced that our present social order denies a real liberty to a great proportion of the population, anxious to effect the reforms that are necessary without at the same time injuring the springs of such efficiency (and it is not small) as that order retains, we have framed the constructive proposals, touching the many parts of the one great problem, which this book contains. Financial and industrial reforms, international trade and national development, the juster distribution of wealth, the worker's right to be a citizen, and not merely a subject, in the world of production—the measures we advocate in relation to all these things spring from one clear purpose. We believe with a passionate faith that the end of all political and economic action is not the perfecting or the perpetuation of this or that piece of mechanism or organisation, but that individual men and women may have life, and that they may have it more abundantly.

BOOK I

THE CONDITION OF BRITISH INDUSTRY

ARGUMENT OF BOOK I

The Nineteenth Century in Great Britain was an age of commercial and industrial progress, marked towards its close by a rising sense of social injustice and the growth of Trade Unionism, while foreign competition had begun to challenge British supremacy. The economic consequences of the War were, broadly, shrunken markets, expanded shipping and contracted trade for it to carry, and reduced demands for coal, cotton, iron, and steel. It left Britain with an increased population, wages at pre-war level (though supplemented by other benefits), reduced hours of work, and a set-back in national savings. Britain retained her pre-war share of the world's trade; but as that trade was smaller, her exports were reduced. Hence unemployment, which centred in the exporting industries. Some of these may be permanently threatened from other causes. It follows that the problem of industrial revival may require a migration of labour from the threatened industries and the diversion to home development of capital normally devoted to foreign investment, while an international policy of political and commercial peace is essential.

CHAPTER I

BEFORE AND AFTER THE WAR

THE simple explanation that attributes our troubles to the War is obviously some part of the truth. But it is far from being the whole truth. Certainly it is unsound to suppose either that we shall drift comfortably back into the situation of 1913 if only we have patience, or that all would have been well if there had been no war. Indeed, many of the acutest difficulties which the War has thrust upon us were not created by it. They are rather the result of developments which had begun much earlier, but were very greatly speeded up by the economic upheaval of 1914–18. Moreover, the pre-war situation is only idealised in retrospect by those who have forgotten that the decade before the War was one of greater industrial strife than ever before, and that poverty, overcrowding, sweating, and many other social evils were the occasion of serious and justified discontent. We cannot hope to prescribe remedies until we have decided how far the problems we have set out to solve are new, how far they are due to temporary and passing causes, and how far they have deep-seated roots in the past. It will also help us if, in passing, we can note how far our difficulties are peculiar to Great Britain and how far they are shared with other countries. We propose, therefore, first to mention very briefly some of the main tendencies in the economic history of Britain during the last hundred years; secondly, to give a picture of the economic conditions of the country at the present time; thirdly, to direct attention to the black spots and note how they affect the whole economic life of the community; and finally, to see what answer we can give to the questions we have posed.

1. Economic Progress in the Last Century

The Victorian Age was for Western Europe in general, and for Britain in particular, an age of amazing material progress.

The productivity of industry grew with unprecedented rapidity; and a population which expanded enormously in numbers was enabled to enjoy a standard of living and comfort which was incomparably higher than had been known before.

Sir Josiah Stamp has calculated that the average level of real wages to-day is no less than four times as high as it was at the beginning of the nineteenth century; that is to say, the average wage-earner to-day can buy four times as much in goods —food, clothing, house-rent, etc.—as his ancestor of a hundred years ago. Other incomes have risen in similar proportion. Yet this advance has taken place in spite of the fact that the population has increased fivefold.

The technical foundations of this progress were the utilisation of power derived from coal, the development of railways and steamships, and the revolutionising of one branch of manufacture after another by the application of engineering methods. It was an age of coal and iron. Its commercial foundations were laid by the opening up of the undeveloped quarters of the globe by the people and the capital of Western Europe, and the reliance in an altogether new degree on an international "division of labour," which enabled Britain to exchange her textiles and metallurgical products for the foodstuffs and raw materials of other lands. It was an age of emigration, foreign investment, and Free Trade. The social foundations of progress were the liberation of the energies of the middle classes, the scope offered to their enterprise, their talents, and their thrift, and the honour paid to success in business life. It was the age of Samuel Smiles and the self-made man, of the dominance of the *bourgeoisie*. Its political foundations were the general abstention of the State from attempts to control the course of industrial development and the reliance on the initiative and unrestricted competition of independent business concerns. It was the age of *laissez-faire*.

The material success which attended the Victorian era was dazzling to those who first witnessed it, and particularly to those who enjoyed the lion's share of its fruits. And for most of the period accordingly the predominant mood was an uncritical business complacency. From the repeal of the Corn Laws in 1846 to the London Dock Strike in 1889 Britain enjoyed a freedom from fundamental economic controversy such as has been by no means common in the history of human society. Politicians were preoccupied with such questions as the reform of the Parliamentary franchise, the government of Ireland, the growth of nationality in Europe and Imperial Development, and, though public spirit and reforming ardour were plentiful enough, they raised no challenge to the fundamental structure of society.

2. The Growth of Discontent

Towards the end of the century, however, a change began to manifest itself. The working classes, whom popular education had made, for the first time, articulate, became increasingly discontented with their lot. The glamour faded from the material progress which had seemed such an inestimable blessing to their fathers. They came to take this progress for granted, and to turn questioning eyes on the gross inequalities which progress had done nothing to diminish. The more prosperous society as a whole became, the more indefensible did it seem that the great mass of the people should be condemned to live lives which, even though they represented a real improvement on preceding generations in elementary physical standards, were none the less narrow stunted lives, unillumined by hopes, and haunted by the constant terror of a plunge into extreme destitution in the event of accident, sickness, or unemployment.

This growing sense of the fundamental injustice of society was accompanied by a growth in the power of the industrial organisation of the working classes—the Trade Unions—and this led not unnaturally to a tendency to look to the Trade Unions to transform the structure of society. This was the more natural inasmuch as the rise of Trade Unionism met at first with the bitter hostility of employers. It took many years and many conflicts to induce employers to recognise Trade Unions and to bargain with them, and a longer time still to induce them to cultivate friendly relations with Trade Unions and to conceive them as a desirable element in the industrial structure. Having had thus to struggle for its existence, Trade Unionism developed a belligerent psychology which became increasingly identified with the growing feelings of social discontent. Accordingly the development of Trade Unionism proceeded along militant lines: the dominant motive became that of increasing the striking strength of organised labour. With this end in view, local Trade Unions were absorbed in national federations and amalgamations; and some of the most powerful of the national organisations sought to increase their power still further by alliances with one another. The notion of an essential community of interests between Capital and Labour in the prosperity of industry faded, until the more militant section of wage-earners came to speak as though Capital and Labour had no common interests at all. The idea of the Class War took its place, and began more and more to permeate Trade Union thought and policy.

These tendencies were very prominent in the last decade before the War. It became evident that Labour unrest constituted a serious menace to the stability and progress of British industry. The loss and waste caused by strikes and lock-outs increased greatly as the scope of industrial conflicts was enlarged; and the spirit of antagonism not only gave rise to strikes and lock-outs, but in various ways impaired the efficiency of the normal conduct of industry. To establish better relations between employers and employed had become one of the paramount needs of British industry before the War; but though, to this end, various steps were taken to establish machinery of industrial conciliation, it cannot be said that we were approaching a satisfactory solution.

3. The Challenge to British Industrial Supremacy

There were also signs before the War of a change in the other conditions on which our Victorian progress had been based. From the late seventies onwards there was a marked tendency towards higher tariffs abroad. There was a weakening of the general complaisance towards free immigration, reflected in our own Aliens Act. The coming of oil indicated a challenge to the monopoly of coal as the source of fuel. Moreover, there were disquieting signs that Britain was losing ground in the relative efficiency of her manufacturing and business technique, and that in some respects we were falling behind the United States and Germany. There was reason to doubt whether we were not relying too much on casual, rule-of-thumb competitive enterprise, and too little upon scientific research and deliberate organisation. However, our world-wide commercial connections, the position of

London as the financial centre of the world, our overwhelming preponderance in shipping, the wide extent of the British Empire and the advantages derived from Empire markets, and the fact that we were the chief suppliers of capital to overseas countries, stood us in good stead. In face of the rapid opening up of distant countries, the increasing industrialisation in Europe and America, and the economic awakening of the Far East, it was impossible that we should retain the same high percentage of the world's total international commerce that we had held half a century before, and our proportion dropped from 21.6 per cent. in 1871-5 to 15.3 per cent. in 1913. But though the challenge to our supremacy was becoming more insistent, we were still able to maintain our leadership in international commerce, and the volume of our foreign trade continued to increase rapidly right up to 1913, in which extension the basic industries, coal, textiles, and metals, still played the major part.

4. Consequences of the War

The War, and the pressure of war needs, produced a great industrial shake-up in this and in other countries. For the time being, the impulse to pull together in a common cause outweighed the deep-rooted instinct of class antagonism, and the Trade Unions acquiesced more or less willingly in the suspension of restrictive practices and in the dilution of labour on the promise that pre-war conditions in these matters would be restored after the War. Great progress was made in technique and management in the War industries. Under Government direction, processes hitherto kept secret by particular firms were enforced throughout industry, cost accounting was taught to and imposed upon firms both great and small, while inventive ingenuity was stimulated to the utmost. Non-war industries, on the other hand, were atrophied, their personnel drawn away for the Forces or for munition industries, and they were denied fresh capital. It was thus a period of great industrial movement. In England and Wales between the censuses of 1911 and 1921 the building trade lost 103,000 workers, agriculture 106,000, the cotton trade 32,000, and domestic service nearly 300,000. On the other hand, 162,000 were drawn into the mines, 323,000 into the engineering, shipbuilding, and iron and steel trades, 65,000 into the chemical trades (an increase of nearly 50 per cent.), while the Central Government increased the number of its employees by 233,000. Some of these movements were in accordance with the drift indicated by previous censuses, but subsequent information shows that, so far as the main munition industries are concerned, workers have had to be slowly and painfully squeezed out of these war-swollen occupations. In short, the War caused a very lopsided development of the employment and economic activity of the nation.

On the other hand, the fact that there was a scarcity of everything meant that competition was dormant and that, as everyone in war industries was making easy profits, waste was rampant.

One further effect of the War which must be noted was the breakdown of the monetary system and the use, not only by this country but by all the belligerents, except the United States, of systems of *fiat* money—a change which produced an unprecedented rise in prices and in money rates of wages.

5. The Post-War Position

When the War ended and the short-lived post-war boom was over, Great Britain found herself faced not merely with internal dislocation, but with her pre-war international difficulties so gravely increased as to create a completely new situation. The War had produced not only in Europe but even in far-distant countries a condition of extreme economic isolation. Our customers in the Empire, the East, and elsewhere had been compelled to provide, either at home or from some alternative source, the goods and services which we had formerly furnished. Our European markets were impoverished, credit in a state of chaos, and transport disorganised. Considerable time was needed before political hatred began to die down, and in the meantime nations, not merely in Europe but elsewhere, which had experienced the artificial protection of war hesitated to open their frontiers and permit trade with their neighbours. It is impossible here to give a general picture of the economic condition of the world after the War or to detail other nations' troubles. We may, however, shortly enumerate the elements in the situation which particularly affected Great Britain.

(i) The volume of the world's commerce, which increased fourfold in the forty years before the War, remained for several years far below the level of 1913. As Great Britain is more dependent on foreign trade than any other nation in the world, this was an especially heavy blow to us.

(ii) The shipping position had been rendered quite abnormal by the German submarine campaign, which compelled the Allies as well as neutral countries to extend their shipbuilding activities to the utmost. To-day, with the volume of the world's seaborne trade little more than in 1913, the world's mercantile fleet is 50 per cent. larger than before the War, and its capacity for transporting goods even larger still owing to the greater carrying capacity of oil-burning ships of a given tonnage, the increased speed of merchant ships, and better port facilities which enable ships to turn round more quickly. It is little wonder that the freight market has suffered a prolonged depression, and that shipyards and shipbuilding workers all over the world have been unemployed.

(iii) Among the industries the normal activity of which was most disorganised by the War was the coal trade. Both during and immediately after the War there was the utmost incentive to economise in the use of coal and to find substitutes. To-day we are faced with the fact that increased industrial activity as a whole does not involve anything like a proportionate increase in the demand for coal.

(iv) The insufficiency of capital in the world generally, and in particular in those countries where economic life was most seriously disorganised by the War and by the chaos that succeeded it, has meant that the demand for the products of the iron and steel and the engineering trades, which are largely concerned with providing capital goods, is subnormal outside America, whereas the equipment of these industries was greatly inflated by the War.

(v) The growth of industrialisation in the East has resulted in a rapidly growing output of coarse standard cotton goods, and has reduced the demand from the old-established centres of cotton manufacture, of which Lancashire is the chief.

(vi) The rise of prices, which continued until the wholesale index number rose to over 300 in 1920 and was accompanied by an all-round reduction in the hours of labour, was followed by a fall of unprecedented rapidity and extent. This involved a corresponding readjustment of wage-rates. The wide use of the cost of living index number, improved machinery of wage negotiation, and the prevention of distress by a wide extension of Unemployment Insurance enabled us to weather the severest economic storm of the last hundred years without a social upheaval. But the fall of money wages, which inevitably involved a certain amount of friction, did not take place as rapidly in trades "sheltered" from foreign competition as in those which had to face the direct effects of adverse international conditions. A disparity of wages in these two groups of trades continues to the present day and gives rise to many economic difficulties, especially for the export industries.

(vii) These troubles of readjustment, the frustration of the hopes entertained at the end of the War, and the survival from pre-war days of the dissatisfaction with the existing order of things, which was dormant during but not removed by the War, have combined to produce—particularly in the coal-fields and the railways—a series of bitter industrial disputes which have repeatedly set back the process of industrial reconstruction.

In view of these facts it is not surprising that ever since the brief boom which followed the Armistice, the great basic exporting industries of Great Britain—coal, metallurgy, and textiles—have been in a bad way. Instead of expanding rapidly as they used to do, they have been now for some seven years in a more or less stagnant condition. Instead of leading the way in wages and hours and standards of livelihood, they now, for the most part, contrast unfavourably with other occupations. Instead of being the chief providers of employment for a rapidly growing population, they are now the chief contributors to our obstinate post-war unemployment.

These great groups of industries stand out so prominently in our economic life and played so preponderant a part in our development during the last century that they are apt to monopolise attention. It is common, accordingly, to speak of the post-war " trade depression " as though British trade and industry as a whole were experiencing the same misfortunes as the basic trades. This, however, is far from being true. There is not to-day, and there has not been for several years, a general trade depression in the sense in which economists are accustomed to use the term. In many directions, on the contrary, there has been remarkable expansion. New industries have sprung up, or have grown from small beginnings, which have provided compensation, in no small degree as regards both employment and the national income, for the decline in the basic trades. Meanwhile there has been a steady expansion in a great variety of miscellaneous occupations, catering mainly for the home market. For these and other reasons our economic position as a people is not so unfavourable as would be concluded from considering only the state of the basic export trades. But before proceeding farther it is desirable to sum up the general economic situation, as far as the data permit.

CHAPTER II

A SUMMARY OF THE PRESENT POSITION

1. National Income and Production

THE first test of the condition of the country is its annual production of goods and services. Various authoritative attempts have been made to estimate this aggregate national income in recent years; for example, by the Colwyn Committee, and by Professor Bowley and Sir Josiah Stamp. The general conclusion of such computations is that our national income is now (or was in 1924) about the same, in terms of real value, as it was before the War; but, as the population has increased by nearly 7 per cent., it is appreciably lower per head. Professor Bowley and Sir Josiah Stamp, for example, estimate that the aggregate net social income was £1,988,000,000 in 1911 and £3,803,000,000 in 1924; which, on the assumption of a rise in the price-level of 88½ per cent., gives a real national income about as large in the aggregate, but about 5 per cent. less per head. The figure of 88½ per cent. is, however, a liberal allowance for the rise in the general level of prices, so that the final conclusion is cautious and more likely to err on the side of pessimism than on that of optimism. Indeed, it seems likely that, in spite of unemployment, short time, etc., the real income per head of the country is only a little lower than before the War. In contrast with the progress of the nineteenth century, however, it must be counted a poor achievement that after fifteen years of startling scientific advance we have scarcely maintained the real income per head of 1911.

The conclusion of the last paragraph as to the national income, which is based on wage, tax, and other statistics, is confirmed by statistics which throw light on the physical volume of production. We select for these purposes two sets of figures which are not ordinarily regarded as encouraging, and are indeed far from encouraging to the industries primarily concerned. We refer to the statistics of coal consumption and of railway traffic.

The coal consumed *at home* in the three years 1923–5 averaged 178,000,000 tons against 181,000,000 in the five years from 1909 to 1913. Thus we consumed as a people in the three years before the coal stoppage over 98 per cent, of the consumption in the last five pre-war years. These figures, as we have said, are not encouraging to the coal industry. But when we take into account the immense growth in the use of oil in multifarious ways, and—still more important perhaps—the great progress which has been made in economical methods of coal consumption, the figures suggest an expansion rather than a decline in the aggregate volume of our industrial activity. It is worth noting in this connection that the consumption of coal by the United States was 479,000,000 tons in 1913, and increased only to 499,000,000 tons in 1925, though aggregate industrial activity must have increased by more than 50 per cent. in the interval.

The figures of railway traffic suggest the same conclusion. The general merchandise (excluding livestock) carried on the British railways was 60.9 million tons in 1924 and 59.7 million tons in 1925, as against 67.8 million tons in 1913, a drop of from 10 to 12 per cent. When, however, we take account of the enormous strides that have been made by road transport, these figures are easier to reconcile with a growth than with a decline of the total volume of production.

2. Wages and Earnings

The figures relating to the position of the manual workers tell a slightly better story than those for the country as a whole. At the date to which the post-war estimates of the national income refer—namely, 1924—there had been a very slight increase in the numbers employed as compared with 1914. The Balfour Committee estimated that in that year the extra unemployed amounted to 800,000, while the employable population had increased by some 900,000. That is to say, only 100,000 of the increased employable population had been added to the numbers at work, the rest being added to the numbers unemployed.

With this large mass of additional unemployed seeking work, it might have been expected that rates of wages would be depressed. The provision of Unemployment Insurance, however, has been an important factor in creating a situation in which the Trade Unions have been able to maintain wage-rates.

The conclusion of the Balfour and Colwyn Committees on this matter is that in 1925 real rates of wages for adults in full-time employment were about the same as before the War, these figures being based upon estimates of wage-rates by the Ministry of Labour, compared with the cost of living index numbers compiled by the same authority. Sir Josiah Stamp and Professor Bowley make more optimistic calculations. They explain the difference between their estimate and that of the Ministry of Labour on the ground that there is definite evidence that in some of the greater industries earnings have increased much more rapidly than piece or time rates; secondly, that there has been some changing over from time to piece rates which yield higher earnings; thirdly, that there has been some shift of numbers in favour of the better-paid occupations and industries. They estimate that in 1924 the average man in full work earned 60*s.* per week as compared with 32*s.* in 1914, while the average earnings of all wage-earners (including women and juveniles) for a full working week increased about 94 per cent., in spite of a fall of about 10 per cent. in the average number of hours worked. Using the Ministry of Labour's cost of living index—though there is reason to think that this index exaggerates the rise in the cost of living—these estimates would show an increase in real weekly wages of 11 per cent. for those in full work. Annual real earnings, which are affected by the extent of unemployment, show an average rise of about 5 per cent. In other words, the wage-earner has come off better than the figures for average incomes for the nation as a whole would indicate. Indeed, Sir Josiah Stamp and Professor Bowley, in building up their total estimate of the national income, reach the conclusion that wage-earners received as wages 44 per cent. of the national income in 1924, as against 43 per cent. in 1911.

Even this figure under-estimates the position of the wage-earning class, which has benefited through employers' contributions to the Insurance Fund, and through the great increase in the Government's contribution towards various other forms of social expenditure of which they chiefly draw the benefit—for example, old-age pensions and education. In this connection also should be mentioned the great progress in health standards, of which the fall in infant mortality is perhaps the most significant illustration.

It is, however, notorious that improvement in the average position of the wage-earner does not apply to all uniformly. The Balfour Committee estimates that unskilled rates of wages per week have risen from 80 to 90 per cent., while skilled wages on the average have risen only from 60 to 70 per cent. Again, there is a great difference between the increase in sheltered and unsheltered industries. The same authority estimates that in industries subject to foreign competition average wages have risen from 45 to 75 per cent., with an average of about 60 per cent., whilst in sheltered trades the increase has been from 80 to 120 per cent., with an average of about 100 per cent. In money terms, this means that in sheltered trades skilled workers earn 73*s.* and labourers 50*s.* In unsheltered trades skilled workers earn 58*s.* and labourers 45*s.* per week.

3. Standard of Living

We may take it, therefore, as reasonably certain that our aggregate real income is at least as high as it was before the War, though there may have been some decline in the average income per head. It seems equally certain that the average standard of living of the mass of the population has improved, though different sections have, of course, fared very differently. Figures relating to the consumption of staple commodities indicate that the consumption per head of commodities such as bread, meat, etc., is about the same as before the War, that the consumption of tea and sugar has risen, and that the consumption of alcohol has fallen (though the money spent on it has increased). There has also been a great increase in expenditure on amusements, etc. Moreover, though the accumulated shortage of house accommodation has not yet been made good, and no impression has been made on the slum problem, the housing effort which is in progress should result before long in a definitely higher standard of housing accommodation.

4. Hours and Output

In considering these facts, it is important to bear in mind that our productive power has not only been impaired by the great waste implied in an unemployment figure which has never during the last seven years fallen appreciably below a million, but that the weekly hours of work have been substantially reduced. Professor Bowley estimates that the reduction in hours since the Armistice amounts on the average to about 10 per cent. The maintenance of the aggregate national income despite this change indicates a considerable increase in the output per hour per head of those employed, as a result of improvements in administration and technique and of hard work. Indeed the reduction in working hours without a reduction in real wages represents the main achievement since the War of British manufacturing organisation and of the skill and industry of the workers, and one which must not be overlooked by critics of our technical efficiency.

5. Wages at Home and Abroad

The International Labour Office has worked out a means of broadly comparing real wages in various cities. Their object has been to show the relative purchasing power (the cost of house room being taken into account) of certain fairly comparable wage-rates in different countries. A comparison of labour costs in the several cities has not been attempted. The results of any such inquiry are necessarily rough approximations, but the following table, which has been compiled from the International Labour Office figures, gives a fair impression of the relative position of real wages in certain occupations during 1927. The following are the occupations upon which the data are based: building, engineering, furniture trades, printing, and bookbinding. The wages of both skilled and unskilled labour are taken into account:

TABLE 1

RELATIVE REAL WAGES IN VARIOUS CITIES—1927

(General Average Index number, including allowance for rent, London = 100)

Philadelphia	175–180
Ottawa	150–155
Copenhagen	105–110
London	100
Amsterdam	85–90
Stockholm	85–90
Berlin	65–70
Paris	55–60
Brussels	50–55
Prague	50–55
Madrid*	50–55
Rome	45–50
Vienna	45–50
Lodz	45–50

* Excluding allowance for rent.

Compiled from the Ministry of Labour Gazette.

Real wages in Britain have for many decades been substantially above those of our European competitors. But the events of the years since the War have tended in some cases to increase the difference, and as methods of organisation, technical processes, etc., tend to become general, the maintenance of these standards sets a very severe task to British employers who have to compete with employers in France, Belgium, or Germany. Evidently the organisation and general ability of our employers and workers must be superior to those of their continental competitors if in such circumstances they are to be able to sell at a profit in world-markets. Employers in the engineering industry in particular, whom we have consulted, emphasise the severity of their competitive problem in view of the disparity of wage-rates. The difficulties of our employers must not be overlooked when in certain sections of this Report we venture, in the interests of a still higher efficiency, to advance certain criticisms.

6. National Savings

In view of the likelihood that there has been some decline in the real national income per head, the maintenance or improvement in working-class standards implies some reduction in the real incomes of other classes, at all events in the net incomes remaining after taxation has been paid. It is doubtful, however, whether there has been a reduction in the standards of living or expenditure of the middle classes, except in certain limited circles in which the pressure has been felt severely. It appears rather that the standard of living has been maintained at the expense of a substantial reduction in the volume of savings. The Colwyn Committee estimated that the total national savings were in 1924 about £500 millions, as against, say, £375 millions before the War. Allowing for the fall in the value of money, savings on the pre-war scale would have amounted in 1924 to £650 millions. Thus there was a decline in the real value of savings of about one-quarter. This has not entailed any reduction in the volume of new capital available for British industry, for we were accustomed before the War to invest nearly half our savings abroad. Indeed, the Colwyn Committee's estimate suggests that savings invested at home in 1924 amounted to some £400 millions compared with £200 millions before the War—which would have been equivalent to about £300 millions at present prices. But the change means a big reduction in the margin available for foreign investment, after the capital needs of British industry have been first supplied. The figures of our balance of trade suggest that our *net* foreign investment has in fact been in recent years on a much smaller scale than it used to be before the War.

But while our economic condition is by no means one of unrelieved depression, nevertheless the state of our export trade and in particular the persistent troubles of our basic industries justify the most serious concern. The continued depression of these industries entails the unemployment, on a large scale, of many of our most highly skilled and highly specialised workers whom it is peculiarly difficult to transfer to other occupations, and raises acute problems in a number of distressed areas; whilst the diminished purchasing power of those engaged in them spreads throughout the country, and acts as a brake on the advance of all other activities. To this question we turn in the next chapter.

CHAPTER III

THE EXPORT TRADE

1. Changes in Foreign Trade

SINCE the Armistice the volume of British exports has never exceeded about 80 per cent. of what it used to be before the War. Moreover, whereas in pre-war days our exports used to expand rapidly and steadily (the average rate of expansion between 1880 and 1913 was about 3 per cent. per annum), they have been obstinately stagnant in the post-war period and show no clear signs of any big recovery in the near future. While the volume of our exports has declined, the volume of our imports has materially increased. We are now importing a quantity of food, drink, and tobacco more than 20 per cent. larger than in 1913, a year when the quantity of imports in this class was at the highest level of the pre-war period.

We are also importing a larger volume of manufactured goods than formerly. Indeed, it is significant and disquietening that the only class of imports that we are importing in smaller quantities is raw materials. These changes are shown in Table 2.

The depression in exports [1] is closely related to the changes indicated in Chapter I, and is centred in the trades mentioned there. Indeed, the five industries—coal, iron and steel, cotton, wool, and machinery—account for substantially more than half the total exports of Great Britain.

The figures suggest, however, that the difficulties from which these trades are suffering are not entirely difficulties peculiar to them; for the compensating development of export business in other industries has not been very substantial—a relative decrease of 10 per cent. in the importance of the five trades and increase of 10 per cent. in other trades. This is shown in Table 3 on p. 23.

[1] Following an estimate of the Balfour Committee, the index for the volume of exports in 1925 should be 81 instead of 76, owing to improvements in quality.

TABLE 2

VOLUME OF BRITISH FOREIGN TRADE—PRE-WAR AND POST-WAR

	1913	1924	1925
Class I.—Food, Drink, and Tobacco.			
Net Imports . . .	100	125·2	123·0
British Exports . . .	100	85·7	82·8
Re-exports . . .	100	132·7	138·6
Class II.—Raw Materials and Articles Mainly Unmanufactured			
Net Imports . . .	100	90·0	96·9
British Exports . . .	100	89·4	80·1
Re-exports . . .	100	93·4	92·0
Class III.—Articles Wholly or Mainly Manufactured			
Net Imports . . .	100	105·0	117·9
British Exports . . .	100	78·6	79·7
Re-exports . . .	100	84·0	77·8
Total Foreign Trade			
Net Imports . . .	100	109·2	113·6
British Exports . . .	100	80·1	80·0
Re-exports . . .	100	96·9	95·1

The establishment of the Irish Free State slightly distorts the comparison here shown. In the following figures an attempt has been made to calculate for 1924 and 1925 and compare with 1913 the total volume of the foreign trade of the old United Kingdom:

Total Foreign Trade	1913	1924	1925
Net Imports . . .	100	106·6	111·8
British Exports . . .	100	76·1	76·0
Re-exports . . .	100	88·4	87·8

Compiled from the Report of the Committee on Industry and Trade, Survey of Overseas Markets, and from Board of Trade Journal.

The figures in Table 3 represent values, not quantities. In the case of the cotton trade the figures for 1925 would have been lower if it had not been for the high price of raw cotton—whereas among the newer trades prices have in some cases fallen very greatly owing to improvements in production. But even when allowance is made for price changes, it is remarkable that the old staple trades still account for so large a percentage of the total of our exports. It is evident, therefore, that when we come to look for causes we must be prepared to deal not only with those relating to the special industries, but also with causes affecting the whole of our exports.

TABLE 3

STAPLE TRADES—THEIR PROPORTION OF TOTAL EXPORTS

	1913	1925	1927
	Per cent.	*Per cent.*	*Per cent.*
Coal, Coke, and Manufactured Fuel .	10·2	7·0	6·9
Iron and Steel	10·5	8·8	9·8
Cotton	24·1	25·8	21·0
Wool	6·8	7·6	8·0
Machinery	6·4	6·3	7·0
Total of Five Trades . . .	58·0	55·5	52·7
Other Export Trades . . .	42·0	44·5	47·3
Grand Total	100·0	100·0	100·0

Compiled from Annual and Monthly Trade Returns.

2. Exports and Unemployment

The decline in the volume of exports and the consequent stagnation of the industries which are mainly associated with export is the principal explanation of our formidable post-war unemployment. Coal, iron and steel, engineering, shipbuilding, cotton, and wool, are our great exporting industries, and the following table shows what a large proportion of our unemployment is attributable to these industries:

TABLE 4

GREAT BRITAIN AND NORTHERN IRELAND—UNEMPLOYMENT IN STAPLE INDUSTRIES

	MALES			*FEMALES*		
	Estimated Number of Insured Workers at July 1927	*Unemployed November 1927*	*Per cent.*	*Estimated Number of Insured Workers at July 1927*	*Unemployed November 1927*	*Per cent.*
Coal Mining . .	1,192,190	220,520	18·5	6,800	1,234	18·2
Metal Manufacture .	326,390	61,682	18·9	16,910	1,293	7·6
Engineering . .	703,120	69,700	9·9	61,160	2,204	3·6
Shipbuilding and Ship Repairing .	212,660	46,659	21·9	3,370	163	4·8
Cotton and Wool .	311,950	33,804	10·8	507,340	53,591	10·6
Total of Five Groups	2,746,310	432,365	15·8	595,580	58,485	9·8
Other Trades .	6,152,690	570,774	9·3	2,636,420	148,062	5·6
GRAND TOTAL .	8,899,000	1,003,139	11·3	3,232,000	206,547	6·4

Compiled from The Ministry of Labour Gazette for December 1927.

It will be observed that the five groups of industries here specified employ roughly one-third of all the insured persons in the country. Among their male employees the rate of unemployment is almost 16 per cent. In the remaining two-thirds of insured male employees it is only 9.3 per cent. For women the figures are 9.8 per cent. and 5.6 per cent. respectively. Taking the period June 1923 to April 1926, unemployment has averaged 34.5 per cent. in shipbuilding, 22.3 per cent. in iron and steel, 15 per cent. in engineering, 12.3 per cent. in cotton (where in addition there has been much short time), 10.7 per cent. in wool textiles.

An examination of unemployment in different parts of the country brings out a further interesting point, namely, that whereas the figure (for men) in the second half of 1927 was about 12½ per cent. in the North of England and in Scotland, over 22½ per cent. in Wales, and nearly 14½ per cent. in Northern Ireland, it was less than 8½ per cent. in the Midlands, and less than 6½ per cent. in London and the South of England. This discrepancy in the severity of unemployment as between the North and the South of the country has been fairly constant for some years, and is particularly significant because the North has been predominantly the industrial area of the country ever since the Industrial Revolution. Figures of unemployment in the engineering trade illustrate the point even more closely. At the beginning of 1924 the unemployment figure for London and the South was 11.2 per cent., but in the Midlands and North 19.6 per cent.; at the beginning of 1925 it was 7.3 per cent. in the South and 14.3 per cent. in the Midlands and North; at the beginning of 1926 it was 5.6 per cent. in the South, and 14.2 per cent. in the Midlands and North; in January 1927 it was 6.2 per cent. in the South, and 16.0 in the Midlands and North.

The Chief Factory Inspector in his last two Annual Reports has called attention to the great industrial development in Greater London, in Coventry and its neighbourhood, and, more generally, in the district lying east of a line drawn from Portsmouth to the Wash. It is inaccurate, therefore, to speak of Great Britain being generally depressed. Our industrial difficulties are essentially the difficulties of a limited group of exceedingly important industries which are largely dependent upon foreign trade and concentrated to an important degree in particular localities.

3. Comparison with other Countries

The very elaborate documentation prepared for the World Economic Conference at Geneva and other recent estimates of world trade enables this to be put shortly and with certainty. The chief points are as follows:

(i) According to the Balfour Committee, the exports of the United Kingdom were, in 1913, 13 per cent. of the world's total exports, and this figure rose to 14 per cent. in 1923. Mr. Flux puts it at approximately 12 per cent. in 1925, while the League of Nations gives it as 12.7 per cent. for the two years. In either case the percentage is not materially different to what it was before the War. It is doubtful, however, whether the comparative figures for 1926-7, if they were available, would prove equally satisfactory.

(ii) Other countries, according to the calculations of the League of Nations, have fared in accordance with the following table:

TABLE 5

SHARE OF VARIOUS COUNTRIES IN WORLD'S EXPORT TRADE

	1913.	1924.	1925.
	Per cent.	*Per cent.*	*Per cent.*
United Kingdom *	13·93	13·01	12·43
United States	13·34	16·54	16·04
Germany *	13·09	5·73	6·97
France *	7·23	7·98	7·21
India	4·21	4·34	4·79
Canada	2·35	3·94	4·43
Japan	1·72	2·68	3·03
Italy *	2·64	2·30	2·42
Argentine	2·73	2·92	2·65
Belgium *	3·82	2·37	2·29
Australia †	2·04	2·31	2·48
China	1·60	2·30	2·17
Brazil	1·73	1·54	1·65
Switzerland	1·44	1·34	1·31
Sweden	1·19	1·23	1·22
South Africa †	1·73	1·37	1·40
Russia *	4·22	0·99	0·97

* Changes in territory. In these cases the 1913 figures refer to the pre-war customs area and the 1924 and 1925 figures to the post-war customs area; in other cases the customs area was the same both before and since the War.

† Including bullion and small amounts of specie.

Extracted from League of Nations Memorandum on Balance of Payments, etc., 1911–25.

It is evident from the complete table from which these figures are extracted that we have lost ground in company with most of the countries of Europe except France; that our position is good compared with Germany and Russia, but bad compared with the United States and the East. In the case of Japan, China, and Canada, the proportionate increases are very substantial, but they are still small trading nations compared with Great Britain and the United States.

(iii) The proportion of our exports which goes to the Empire has been somewhat increased, the proportion to Europe is about stationary, that to foreign countries outside Europe has fallen. But the impression made by these figures is rather different when looked at from the point of view of the buyer from what it is when considered from the point of view of ourselves as sellers. Empire purchases, for example, from other countries have expanded even faster than their purchases from Great Britain, which are therefore a diminishing percentage of Empire trade. In Europe, on the other hand, our sales, though reduced, have maintained their position in proportion to the trade available. In other words, our trade with the Empire is doing well because the dominions and colonies are prosperous—not because we are proving to be successful competitors. On the contrary, America, Japan, and other competitors are, if anything, beating us in spite of the preferences we enjoy. In Europe, on the other hand, our low exports are partly due to impoverishment of our customers and partly to new tariff obstacles. So far as competition goes, we have not apparently been beaten, for our chief competitors in this field have been labouring under similar, and in some cases much worse, handicaps than ourselves.

4. Exports and the Balance of Trade

A further unsatisfactory result of our low level of exports is that the balance of trade is thrown out of gear, for the increased volume of imports, together with a diminished volume of exports, has made the visible trade balance much less favourable than it used to be. It is true that this effect has been somewhat mitigated by the changes in the relative prices of the goods which we import and export respectively. Our exports have risen in price to an appreciably greater extent than have our imports, so that a given quantity of exports goes further than it used to do in purchasing foodstuffs and raw materials. None the less, after allowing for this the adverse balance of trade in terms of money values has been swollen to very large dimensions. The trade figures and the balance in terms of money are as follows:

TABLE 6

IMPORTS, EXPORTS, AND VISIBLE TRADE BALANCE

(In millions of £s)

Annual Averages.	*Net Imports of Merchandise.*	*British Exports of Merchandise.*	*Excess of Imports of Merchandise.*	*Excess of Imports (−) or Exports (+) of Bullion and Specie.*	*Total Visible Adverse Trade Balance.*
1900–4	466	289	177	− 4	181
1905–9	522	377	145	− 3	148
1910–13	611	474	137	− 7	144
1920	1,710	1,334	376	+ 44	332
1921	979	703	276	+ 12	264
1922	899	720	179	+ 14	165
1923	978	767	211	+ 16	195
1924	1,137	801	336	+ 12	324
1925	1,167	773	394	+ 10	384
1926	1,116	653	463	− 12	475
1927	1,096	709	387	− 4	391

Compiled from the Statistical Abstract of the U.K., and Annual and Monthly Statements of Trade.

The unfavourable movement in the merchandise trade balance, revealed by the above tables, has not been fully compensated by the improvement in our non-merchandise foreign earnings (e.g. interest, freights, commissions, and profits abroad, etc.). On the contrary, our shipping trade, which is one of the most important contributors to the non-merchandise services by which we square our foreign trade account, has experienced the same adversity as has overtaken our basic industries, and our total net income from shipping, though somewhat larger in money values than before the War, has certainly not risen proportionately to the general level of prices.

Again, our income from overseas investments, the other great item in our non-merchandise foreign earnings, was seriously impaired by the inroads which were made in these investments during the War in order to pay for munitions and necessary supplies from overseas. Accordingly, although the income from overseas investments is now larger in terms of money than it used to be, it also represents a smaller real value than the pre-war figure. Moreover, a new item in the account of international payments has been created by the system of inter-governmental debts which the War has left behind, and under this heading we have a debit account, having to pay more every year to the United States than we obtain in reparation from Germany or debt payments from France or other countries.

The net result of all these factors is that the margin which remains available for making fresh investments abroad is materially lower than it used to be. An estimate of the international balance sheet for recent years in comparison with the position in 1913 is given in Table 7 opposite.

It shows that in the last four years our surplus for foreign investment has been fully £100 millions per annum less, not only than it was before the War, but also than it was so lately as 1922–3. This surplus is the true measure of the net increase of our ownership of capital abroad. As the table shows, however, it differs materially from the amount of money which has been invested in new foreign issues on the London market. Such a difference may be accounted for by an equivalent import either of long-term or of short-term capital. It is exceedingly difficult to disentangle all the movements of long-term investments, for, in addition to new issues, a great number of transactions are constantly taking place in securities and other forms of permanent investment. Sales and purchases of British securities by foreigners (such as those which took place during the flight from the mark, the franc, and other Continental currencies), sales and purchases by British owners of existing foreign securities, and the repayment by sinking funds or otherwise of previous foreign loans—none of these items can easily be traced. If, on balance, the net effect of these transactions were a continuous return flow from overseas of formerly invested capital or of foreign-owned capital seeking refuge in Britain, we could use the proceeds to issue new foreign loans. In such circumstances we could continue indefinitely to float new foreign issues in London in excess of the surplus shown on current items of income and outgo, just as a private individual who owns maturing mortgages can make a fresh investment with the proceeds without drawing on his current income. It is, however, highly improbable that a large part of the difference between our true

TABLE 7

THE INTERNATIONAL BALANCE SHEET

(In millions of £s)

	1913.	1922.	1923.	1924.	1925.	1926.	1927.†
			I. *Income Account*				
Estimated Net Income from Overseas Investments .	210	175*	200*	220	250	270	270
Estimated Net National Shipping Income . . .	94	133*	133*	140	124	120	120
Estimated Receipts from Short Interest and Commissions	25	40*	50*	60	60	60	60
Estimated Receipts from other Services. . .	10	12*	15*	15	15	15	15
Total . . .	339	360*	398*	435	449	465	465
Deduct Estimated Excess of Government Payments made Overseas . .	—	?	25	25	11	—	?
Net Non-Merchandise Surplus	339	360*	373*	410	438	465	465
Net Merchandise Deficiency (i.e. excess of Imports of goods and bullion over Exports) . . .	158	171	195	324	384	477	391
Net surplus on Income account	181	189	178	86	54	−12	74
			II. *Capital Account*				
New Foreign Issues of Capital in London . . .	198	135	136	134	88	112	139
Bank of France repayments to Bank of England ‡ .		5	5	5	6	7	37
Assumed Increase (+) or Decrease (−) of other Capital Items required to Balance the Account .	−17	+49	+37	−53	−40	−131	−102
Total of Capital Account .	181	189	178	86	54	−12	74

* Board of Trade original estimates (*Board of Trade Journal,* January 31, 1924, p. 152) revised to harmonise with the official revision of their original estimates for 1924 and 1925.

† Non-merchandise surplus assumed to be the same as in 1926.

‡ Estimates.

Compiled from the Board of Trade Journal, January 31, 1924, p. 152, *January* 27, 1927, p. 93; *Midland Bank Review.*

surplus and our foreign issues can be accounted for by these movements of long-term capital. Indeed, we are of opinion that during the last four years not less than £150 millions of our new issues must have been balanced by an increase in foreign short-term investments in the London market in the form of deposits by foreigners in British banks and of sterling bills carried with foreign money. This process, if carried beyond a certain point, must create an uncomfortable and anxious situation. In any case it cannot continue indefinitely, and we must ultimately confine our new overseas investments to our true surplus plus the funds accruing to us from the repayment of the principal of existing foreign loans. This total cannot be expected to equal the pre-war total plus the 50 per cent. increase which would be needed to allow for the general rise of prices.

We argue later in this Report that certain types of foreign investment—e.g. to Governments, to Public Utility concerns, to Local Authorities—are not as economically advantageous to this country as investment in similar forms at home, which would contribute to the efficiency of the British industrial system as a whole. At the same time, there are other forms of foreign investment which it is highly desirable for a trading nation like Great Britain to maintain. For example, investment in the production of important raw materials overseas has been in the past, and should be in the future, highly lucrative. Moreover, the granting of credit and the financing of big orders establishes commercial connections which mean trade not merely for the moment, but in the future. Our present surplus on income account of at least £70 millions per annum should be adequate for these purposes. Nevertheless the state of our trade balance must be regarded with some anxiety.

5. Staple Trades

Before drawing conclusions from these facts, we will deal with the position of certain special industries.

(a) *Coal*

Of these the most important is coal. For a number of reasons there is a lack of resiliency in the world's demand for coal. The League of Nations' Report on the world's coal trade, however, brings out the fact that British coal production was a slightly diminishing percentage of the whole before the coal dispute, even if we exclude America. But an explanation of this decrease may be found in the fact that Britain has been the chief provider of coal for the world's mercantile marine, and it is precisely in this field that oil has made its greatest inroads into the province of the coal trade. Taking a very long view, the world supplies of oil are small compared with its supplies of coal, and the latter should come into its own again, particularly when means have been found for converting coal into liquid fuel. But in the meantime the reign of oil has partly dispossessed the sea-borne coal of Britain.

This, however, is not the sole explanation. It is very difficult to make international comparisons in a trade which has had such violent ups and downs as the coal industry in recent years. But the broad fact remains that the output per man in the Ruhr (which produced in 1913 three-fifths of the total output of coal of pre-war Germany and in 1925 three-quarters of the coal output of post-war Germany) fell between 1913 and 1925 from 284 tons per annum to 275 tons per annum, whereas the output per man in Britain fell between 1913 and 1925 from 260 tons per annum to 217 tons per annum. These figures show a much heavier fall in the case of Great Britain than in that of the Ruhr. They are to some extent the result of reduced hours of labour in Great Britain; but this is only a partial explanation. They are no doubt to be accounted for on the one hand by the intermittent working of an industry which is producing below its normal capacity, and on the other by the small-scale and unco-ordinated organisation of the British mining industry, which has kept in being pits and, indeed, whole districts in which very poor mines are still being worked. We deal with the coal question more fully in Chapter XXV of Book 4.

(b) *Shipbuilding*

For the last seven years, during which the demand for new ships has been reduced to very small dimensions, British builders have had to compete against very severe competition, three features of which may be particularly mentioned.

The first is the granting of subsidies by foreign Governments to their own shipyards and preferential treatment in the placing of orders.

The second is the slowness with which British shipyards have taken up the motor-ship as compared with Germany and Italy. British shipbuilders have felt that design was immature, that depreciation and other costs of working were unknown, and that the motor-ship was at the mercy of the price of oil, whereas ships burning oil under steam boilers can be readily converted to coal if oil prices rise too high. The result is that while British shipyards have built some of the largest ships in the world driven by Diesel engines, they have not had as much experience in building motor-ships as other countries. British yards, for example, in the quarter ended September 30, 1927, were building roughly three-fifths of the world's steam tonnage, but only about two-fifths of the world's motor tonnage. It is impossible for non-experts to say whether this is a course of wisdom or the result of simple conservatism on our part, but so long as the motor-ship is still in the ascendant as it is at present, we have given foreign competitors a long start which we are only slowly overhauling.

There remains the question of cost. Wages are higher in Britain than in competitive countries, but this has always been the case, and our supremacy has hitherto been based upon the efficiency of the workpeople, of technicians, designers, and organisers of the industry. An important handicap of the industry has been the restrictive policy of Trade Unions, and in this trade in particular the unnecessary multiplication and overlapping of the Unions themselves. A notable step forward, however, has been taken in the joint conferences held in recent years, which have decided to abolish practices which are proved to be obstacles to efficiency. Britain's percentage of the new world tonnage is at the moment rising, and there is no reason why it should not reach its pre-war proportion. But we cannot expect the world demand to return to its old level until the surplus built during the War has disappeared. The scrapping process is taking place, but it does not look as if it will be finished for some years to come. The outlook for the shipbuilding industry is a very moderate one, but we may by now have passed the worst point and the situation should slowly improve.

(c) *Iron and Steel*

The depression of our iron and steel industry and our inability to market abroad as large a quantity of iron and steel manufactures as before the War are also partly the result of a growth in the iron and steel industry in foreign countries. In this case, however, the situation is materially different from that of coal or cotton. It is pre-eminently a case of lop-sided productive capacity in which potential supply has greatly outrun demand. Largely as the result of the artificial stimulus given to this industry by the demand for munitions, the world's capacity for production is greater than ever before, while the steady growth of consumption which marked the pre-war period has not been maintained. Stagnant consumption outside the U.S.A., coupled with an excessive capacity for production, is mainly responsible for the fact that steel prices have recently been less than 20 per cent. above pre-war level, whereas prices in general have been 50 per cent. higher. The production figures for the world are shown in the following table:

TABLE 8

WORLD PRODUCTION OF STEEL

(*In millions of metric tons*)

	1909–13 (*pre-war boundaries*).	1913 (*post-war boundaries*).	1924.	1925.	1926.	1927.*
Great Britain	6·7	7·8	8·3	7·5	3·7	9·2
Germany	14·5	12·2	9·8	12·2	12·3	16·3
France	3·9	7·0	6·9	7·4	8·4	8·2
Rest of Europe	11·3	16·4	12·6	14·5	16·3	17·8
Total Europe	36·4	43·4	37·6	41·6	40·7	51·5
North America	28·5	32·9	39·2	46·9	49·9	46·0
Rest of the World	·3	·3	2·0	2·3	2·6	2·8
Total World	65·2	76·6	78·8	90·8	93·2	100·3

* Provisional figures.

Compiled from League of Nations Memorandum on the Iron and Steel Industry and "The Economist."

The consumption of iron and steel depends in a considerable degree on the rate of capital investment in new industrial plant, railways, ships, etc. The paucity of capital since the War is responsible for a diminished demand for the products of the iron and steel industry, except in America, and the preceding table shows that the demand is only now recovering. Our industry has been handicapped in a special degree in the last few years by the very heavy depression in our shipbuilding industry, which is the chief consumer of British iron and steel, and in 1926 by the prolonged coal dispute.

The facts that we have excellent coking coal near the seaboard and that we are excellently placed to import the world's best ores at low rates of freight are permanent influences in favour of this country as a steel producer. But we cannot maintain a large steel industry except on an export basis, for nearly half our present output is directly exported, while of the remainder almost a half is worked up in manufactures which we sell abroad.

Our plant is not, as a whole, so up-to-date as that of Germany and Lorraine. Thus, General Sir Herbert Lawrence, the Chairman of Vickers Ltd., recently declared (according to *The Times* of November 2, 1927) "that it was a matter common knowledge . . . that there was a very large percentage of the steel and engineering businesses which for one reason or another are ill-adapted for modern production." Moreover, the extensions made during the War were not located with an eye to foreign trade or post-war competition, but were designed to make the best use of our then existing resources. The industry, therefore, is in need of concentration and a better balancing of plant available for smelting pig-iron and making steel respectively. It has to be remembered that we have to do an export business which must necessarily be of a rather miscellaneous character and cannot effectively be turned out by giant plants such as those of Luxemburg and the United States. Such plants can only be effectively employed in producing a standard product for an immense market. But even for miscellaneous export business, orders should be as concentrated as possible if the cheapest production is to be achieved. It is universally admitted that if our national advantages are to be exploited successfully, our industry must take measures to concentrate output in the plants best fitted for production.

In the meantime, with currency fluctuations to contend against, the British steel industry has failed to maintain its hold upon foreign trade. In the following table the British export figures would look considerably better but for the large reduction in our export of pig-iron, which was an important item before the War, but is now reduced to small proportions:

TABLE 9

IRON AND STEEL—IMPORTS AND EXPORTS

(In millions of metric tons)

	1913.	1923.	1924.	1925.
Imports				
United Kingdom *	2·27	1·34	2·47	2·76
Germany	·31†	1·76	1·29	1·20
France‡	·17	·39	·26	·17
Belgium‖	·89	·56	·57	·54
United States	·26	·59	·51	·78
Exports				
United Kingdom*	5·05	4·39	3·92	3·79
Germany	6·31†	1·33	1·56	3·26
France‡	·63	2·29	2·94	3·88
Belgium‖	1·58	2·53	3·31	3·11
United States	2·96	1·98	1·74	1·71

* 1913 including Ireland; 1923–5 excluding Irish Free State.

† Pre-war territory, including Luxemburg.

‡ The Official Trade Statistics of France include the Saar in 1925. In the above table the figures for 1923 and 1924 have also been adjusted in accordance with available figures for the iron and steel trade of France and Germany with the Saar in order to make them directly comparable with the figures for 1925.

‖ 1913 Belgium alone; 1923 and thereafter, the Belgo-Luxemburg Customs Union.

Extracted from League of Nations Memorandum on the Iron and Steel Industry, Geneva, 1927, p. 66.

This Table shows clearly the increase of British imports and the decline of British exports of iron and steel, the gain in French and Belgian exports, largely at the expense of those of Germany, and the decline of exports from the United States. The value of our exports of iron and steel, however, still greatly exceeds that of our imports, owing to our exports being chiefly highly manufactured goods, whereas our imports are mainly semi-products.

(*d*) *Cotton*

Up to about 1890 Great Britain was accustomed to spin more than 40 per cent. of the output of American cotton. This predominant position was already impaired before the War, when our share had fallen to about 25 per cent. Since the War there has been a further sharp decline to about 15 per cent., and in the year just ended (1926–7) the figure fell to 13.48 per cent. Our percentage of the world's consumption of all kinds of cotton has followed a similar course, being 11.6 per cent. in 1926-7 compared with 18.7 per cent. in 1912-13. As a result of this loss of business our equipment is greatly in excess of the business we are at present able to command, in spite of the fact that the number of spindles in Great Britain has been almost stationary since 1913, whereas the spindles in other countries have considerably increased. This may be illustrated by the following table, which shows that, although we consume only about 12 per cent. of the world's cotton, we still own 35 per cent. of the world's spindles. In this table a column has been added showing the percentage growth in the number of cotton spindles since 1913:

TABLE 10

COTTON SPINDLES OF THE WORLD

Countries.	*At August* 31, 1913.	*At January* 31, 1927.	*At August* 31, 1913.	*At January* 31, 1927.	1927 *as per cent. of* 1913.
	(*In thousands.*)		*Per cent.*	*Per cent.*	*Per cent.*
Great Britain	55,652	57,548	38·8	35·0	103·4
Rest of Europe	43,853	46,105	30·6	28·0	105·2
United States	31,505	37,374	22·0	22·7	118·6
Asia	9,384	17,827	6·5	10·8	190·0
Other Countries	3,055	5,762	2·1	3·5	188·6
Total	143,449	164,616	100·0	100·0	114·8

Compiled from the League of Nations Memorandum on Cotton and from the Statistics of the International Cotton Federation.

The disparity between our ownership of spindles and our consumption of cotton is partly explained by our greater output of the finer counts of yarn which use a less weight of cotton per spindle employed, but mainly by the fact that, whereas we have been working not much more than half-time, many of our competitors have been using their machinery on double shifts. The greatest progress has been made in the Southern States of America, partly at the expense of New England, whose cotton industry has been faced with problems not unlike those of Manchester, and in Japan, whose spindles have been worked in recent times 4 to 5 times as intensively as those of Lancashire.

The result is that Lancashire has lost about one-third of her pre-war export trade. In the best post-war year the export of piece-goods has never reached two-thirds of the 1913 figure, and in 1926 was only 54 per cent. of what it was in 1913:

TABLE 11

BRITISH EXPORTS OF COTTON PIECE GOODS

1913	7,075 million linear yards
1922	4,184 ,, square* ,,
1923	4,140 ,, ,, ,,
1924	4,444 ,, ,, ,,
1925	4,436 ,, ,, ,,
1926	3,834 ,, ,, ,,
1927	4,118 ,, ,, ,,

* One square yard was equivalent to ·970 linear yards in 1922, to ·958 linear yards in 1923, to ·969 linear yards in 1924, to ·957 linear yards in 1925, to ·977 linear yards in 1926, and to ·966 linear yards on the average of 1922–6.

Extracted from the Annual Statement of the Trade of the United Kingdom for 1922, *ib. for* 1926, *and from Accounts relating to Trade and Navigation of the United Kingdom for November* 1927.

Thus our decline has been not only relative but absolute. Indeed we have to go back nearly fifty years (to 1875-80) before we find a pre-war quinquennial period in which our exports were so low as during the last five years. It is particularly discouraging that in 1926 and 1927, a period of abnormally cheap cotton and of record world consumption, our exports should have shown a further severe decline even compared with the immediately preceding years.

The trade includes, however, one important branch in which we are fully holding our own, namely, the most skilled branch which produces the fine counts from Egyptian and similar cottons. Some 22,000,000 spindles out of Lancashire's total of 57,000,000 are satisfactorily employed on the production of fine goods—which casts into deeper shadow the gloomy position of the remaining 35,000,000.

When we remember that cotton textiles still account for 21.0 per cent. of our total export trade, the seriousness of the above figures is obvious. It is evident that Lancashire's present methods are becoming less and less capable of producing the coarser goods on a competitive basis with the rest of the world. How far this inability is due to unsound finance, how far to her failure hitherto to deal satisfactorily with the acute problem of surplus capacity, how far to the competition of labour with low standards of life, how far to the growth of tariffs, and how far to the imperfections of the excessively individualistic lines on which the industry is now organised, opinions differ.

CHAPTER IV

THE NATURE OF THE PROBLEM

THE broad conclusions which emerge from the preceding survey are the following:

1. Output and Wages

In spite of the recovery that has taken place from the post-war depression and of the great technical and scientific advances that have been made in industry here and throughout the world, real wages in Britain are little if any higher than before the War, and we have not yet succeeded in reducing the numbers of the unemployed to anything like the pre-war level. This is very far from being a satisfactory state of affairs. How much it falls short of the possibilities is shown by a comparison with the United States where factory output per head was no less than 40 per cent. greater and real wages at least 30 per cent. greater in 1925 than in 1919. Allowing for the shortening of hours, British manufacturing efficiency would seem to have increased by not more than 15 per cent. in the last fifteen years. Whatever the explanation of our comparatively poor rate of progress and in whatever proportions responsibility should be shared between Great Britain's leaders in business, in the Trade Unions and in Government respectively, the standard of life in this country would unquestionably be materially higher if the existing resources of nature and of science were being exploited with maximum efficiency by all concerned. This in itself is sufficient reason for an up-to-date and better considered policy towards industrial affairs.

2. Depression in Staple Industries

Certain industries in particular are proving unable to provide the established standards of life for their workers, with results reflected either in low wages, in unemployment, or in both. Yet these industries occupy a position of exceptional importance in our national life. They are the chief contributors to our export trade; and their expansion in the last century was the basis of our national development as a foreign-trading, foreign-investing country. They represent a very high degree of specialisation of plant and skill. They are concentrated very largely in particular localities. For these reasons the unsatisfactory condition of these industries must be a matter of peculiar concern. It would be impossible to view their decline with the same comparative equanimity with which we have been able in the past to view the decline of other industries against which the tide of fashion or economic opportunity has turned. The coach-building industry might go down before the advent of the motor-car; the saddlery and harness trades might suffer from the same cause. Such changes might involve minor hardship, but they did not spell dislocation on a big scale, or a change in the fundamental nature of our economic equilibrium. The same concern which found its market falling for horse-drawn vehicles might set itself to the production of bodies for motor-cars, or an increase in the output of leather trunks might compensate the same industry for a falling demand for saddles. But it is only necessary to ask to what alternative purposes a coal-mine or blast-furnace could be converted in order to realise that the decline of our basic industries would confront us with an altogether more formidable problem. We have only to reflect how the economic life of the Clyde, the Tyne, South Wales, East Lancashire, and the mining areas centres round these industries in order to realise the magnitude of the social issues which are involved.

To improve the condition of the basic industries, to remove every removable obstacle which at present hampers them, and to assist them to overcome their difficulties, must therefore be one of our principal objects. For this reason we place in the forefront an international policy calculated to promote the commercial intercourse of nations, and in particular a single-minded support of the policy outlined by the World Economic Conference at Geneva. This Report is not a suitable place for an extended treatment of the question of Fiscal Policy. But we have summarised our views in the following chapter. It is for this reason, again, that we lay great stress on reducing the burden of local rates, which at present fall most heavily on the distressed industries and areas (*vide* Book 5), and make many recommendations scattered through the Report directed to the assistance and rejuvenation of some of our basic industries.

But there are two conclusions which, in our view, the extreme desirability of the recovery of our basic industries does not entitle us to draw. The first is that because this recovery would be so desirable it can therefore be taken for granted. The geographical position of these islands, together with the possession of ample coal resources located in spots convenient for economical development, has been, perhaps, the most fundamental reason why we have been a great trading nation. In the past our freedom from external aggression and our political stability enabled us to develop these advantages and secure a long lead in the world's commerce and industry. These natural conditions remain. We stand between the new world and the old—economically, politically, and financially. We are at the door of Europe, which is still the largest market in the world, and we enjoy the trading connections which come from being first in the field in almost every overseas market. These are assets which make it difficult for other countries to displace us in world-commerce. At the same time, our long-established position may lead to lethargy and conservatism, and in any case we have had in recent years to fight against hostile tariffs, fluctuating exchanges, the effect of the coming of oil, and the general diffusion of industrial knowledge. While, therefore, we have every reason to suppose that we shall remain in the front rank of the world's industrial nations, we cannot be sure that our staple trades will revive to their old dimensions. We must, therefore, be ready to meet any contingencies—however unpleasant—which seem likely, and to grapple with the problems—however formidable—which they may entail.

The second illegitimate conclusion is of a different kind. The policy, which some advocate, of relieving the situation by reducing the standard of life all round, and in particular by reducing it decidedly below the pre-war level in the distressed industries, is one which should, in our opinion, be decisively rejected, on the ground that it should not be necessary in face of the technical improvements of recent years. It would be a confession of failure and a good reason for drastic changes in the personnel of our industrial leadership if we were to declare ourselves unable to maintain the very moderate standards of life which now prevail. We feel convinced that with proper organisation and a proper distribution of the national resources of capital and men, no reduction of real wages should be necessary and an early increase should be aimed at.

3. External Forces and Internal Efficiency

It is, therefore, a vital question how far the troubles of the basic industries are due to remediable causes and how far they are due to changes—whether of an enduring or of a temporary character—which lie outside the control of those running these industries.

We think that there is in some cases a certain amount of remediable inefficiency within the industries themselves. In certain sections of the coal, textile, and steel industries those upon whom responsibility lies seem to outside observers to have proved themselves unequal to dealing with the new problems which confront them. For example, a failure year after year to deal with the problem of surplus capacity and a continued acquiescence in the wastes of working many plants partially instead of securing the economies of concentration does not seem creditable to the powers of initiative and adaptation of those controlling them. Though there are striking exceptions, coalowners as a class are becoming a proverbial type of conservative obstinacy in the face of changing facts. Even in these cases, however, the inefficiency often lies not in the technical equipment and management of the individual enterprise, but in the policy and statesmanship of the industry as a whole in the face of changing circumstances. This is probably in some degree a natural consequence of diminished vitality in industries which were in their prime and in the forefront of progress two or three generations ago. Then the leaders of these industries were nearly all pioneers; now few of them have reached their present position by their own unaided abilities, but partly at least because they are the sons of their fathers or the grandsons of their grandfathers. Furthermore, the problems of surplus capacity in the face of stagnant or declining demand are of an essentially different character from those of a period of rapid and continuous expansion.

This is not intended as a criticism of individuals. But the changes which are being made by our competitors, notably in Germany and America, warn us that the organisation of business must develop on new lines, that the relations of great stock enterprises—run by salaried officials—to the public and to their workers must be put on a satisfactory footing, and that new vitality must be breathed into the system of private enterprise.

Moreover, throughout industry our competing strength has been undermined by industrial strife. A belligerent policy by labour organisations has in the past often been the only means by which they could obtain the wages which subsequent experience proved that the industry could pay, and this experience has had the unfortunate effect of instilling into the minds of many workers the false doctrine that the interests of owners, managers, and workers are fundamentally opposed. Until this idea of the class war is eliminated we cannot expect British industry to regain its full potential efficiency. Efficient business organisation and management and the effective co-operation of the partners in industry are the foundations of economic prosperity, and the solution of these twin problems is the main theme of this report.

Nevertheless, when full allowance has been made for such factors, we think that there remain substantial depressing influences of a different kind. Some of these industries are no longer of the same relative importance in the world's economy that they used to be, and are in distress not only in this country but everywhere. Some of them have inevitably lost the precarious monopoly which this country used to enjoy, and find their former customers, often behind tariff walls, making the goods for themselves. Some of them could operate effectively on a suitable scale, but, as the result of abnormal stimulus received during the War or afterwards, are trying to maintain an inflated equipment of plant and workers. In some of them there are branches which formerly yielded a large return per head of the labour employed and were therefore relatively high-wage occupations, but owing to subsequent developments it has become possible to carry them on with less-skilled and lower-paid labour. Unless this tendency is reversed by new inventions or methods, where the advantages of skill and experience can make themselves felt, such processes of production must inevitably tend in course of time to become the business of nations which do not aim at so high a standard of life as ours. Whilst, therefore, we should do everything possible to extend our foreign markets, we think that it would be unsafe to take it for granted that our troubles will be solved by the recovery of these industries to their former pre-eminence.

4. Need for Mobility of Labour

If this diagnosis is correct, it follows that considerable numbers of workers may have to be transferred from the localities and trades in which they have been brought up to new places and engage in fresh occupations which produce either new classes of exports or goods for the home market. This is indeed occurring already on a considerable scale under the pressure of natural economic forces. But the obstacles to its taking place fast enough are very great. The housing shortage, trade-union restrictions, unemployment benefit, the miscellaneous character of the new openings, and the failure even of the prosperous industries to go ahead fast enough to draw the surplus labour out of declining industries stand in the way of smooth or easy transference.

5. The Direction of Investment

The necessity of restricting our foreign investments, the high total of which was formerly a reflection of our large favourable balance of trade, to a scale commensurate with our present diminished balance is the financial facet of the same problem. So long as there is an insufficient outlet at profitable rates of interest for the investment of savings at home, these savings will continue to seek an outlet abroad, and any attempt to maintain foreign investment at the old rate must, in present circumstances, greatly aggravate the difficulty of the Bank of England's task in maintaining the exchanges, cause a stringency of credit, and set up a vicious circle by retarding or preventing further developments at home. On the other hand, the setting up of new industries, the modernisation of old ones, the revolution in the modes of transport and in forms of power, the need to house our increased population, and to rebuild a great part of our towns in accordance with modern standards of health and decency, all call for a large expenditure of capital at home. Without it we cannot hope to equal the efficiency of our leading industrial competitors. Moreover, a greater employment of labour in home trades can only take place if there is a greater investment of our savings at home. If it be true—as we are convinced that it is—that the capital equipment of this country is by no means complete, and that great developments and improvements are possible, it follows that an increase in the proportion of our savings which is invested at home at the expense of the share which goes abroad, so far from being a mere temporary expedient, might be very desirable in itself.

It is clearly imperative to maintain our export trades at a level which with our other earnings will pay for our imports and furnish some surplus every year to finance British enterprise abroad. We do not doubt that in part by the recovery of our older industries and in part by the development of new ones this objective will be reached. But this is a much less ambitious task than that of raising them to their former level. So long, however, as we can attain this limited objective, there is no reason for despondency or for the fear that our national economic life is in peril merely because our exports are not large enough to maintain our pre-war scale of foreign investment. It is a fallacy to assume that the national wealth is more truly increased if the fruits of British savings embodied in British labour are used to embellish the city of Rio de Janeiro than if they are employed to demolish the slums of South London or to build motor-roads through the Midlands.

6. Development of National Resources

It will now be evident to the reader where our argument is leading us. We feel no assurance that a restoration of our old export industries to the same position of relative importance in the economic life of the nation which they held before the War is possible without a reduction of wages or a lengthening of hours or a lowering of the standard of life in some other way. The hope for our export trade generally must lie rather in the development of the newer trades. Moreover, a return to the pre-war ratio between imports and exports is not necessary unless we wish to increase our foreign investment to its pre-war dimensions, a course for which at present the national savings provide no sufficient margin after providing for home needs. Nor is there any reason in the nature of things why the national interest should require indefinitely the exportation of wealth on so great a scale. It seems to us, therefore, that the time is now ripe for a bolder programme of home development which will absorb and employ the national resources of capital and labour in new ways. Such a programme, which we develop in Book 4, seems to us to be not only recommended in the national interest as a means of exploiting the technical developments of the modern age, but also as the best available method to break the vicious circle of unemployment. We believe that alternative plans, however they may wrap themselves up, whether under the names of Protection, of wage adjustments, or of economy on social services, all amount in effect to an assault on the standard of life of the mass of the population. The alternative policy to ours—one indeed avowed by many industrialists—aims at restoring the past situation by lowering standards instead of boldly exploring the possibility of raising standards by encouraging new developments, new methods, new ideas.

CHAPTER V

INTERNATIONAL POLICY AND COMMERCE

THE cardinal principles of the international economic policy of a country so densely populated as Great Britain must be to encourage the utmost freedom of commerce between the nations and to ensure that Great Britain has the freest possible entry into all the markets of the world. The methods by which these aims are to be achieved are so well established as to seem almost axiomatic. But, as they are so often disregarded, they will bear brief repetition.

1. Conditions Essential for International Trade

The first condition of international trade is peace. It is not enough that we should maintain a condition of restless and uneasy peace by skilfully escaping from crisis after crisis. If trade is to expand on the basis of the economic interdependence of nations, it is essential that there should be an international sense of security. One of the motives for the prohibitions and restrictions imposed by certain European nations is the desire to foster war industries within their borders. Political suspicion is too readily translated into economic rivalry and attempts to injure other nations by the use of economic weapons. An essential step, therefore, in the recovery of world trade is to strengthen the League of Nations, in the hope not only of avoiding war but of creating and fostering a sense of security.

In particular it is essential to recognise that the present unsatisfactory relations between Russia and the rest of the world are not merely preventing us from carrying on trade which would help very much to lift us out of depression, but are one of the chief causes that prevent the spread in Europe of an atmosphere of real and prolonged peace.

A second condition is monetary stability. Monetary chaos

was a symptom of the economic disorders which caused the low level of international trade in the years which have followed the War. It seems probable that the worst of these difficulties are now past. But even in normal times currency plays a highly important part in economic life, and under present conditions new problems and difficulties are constantly arising which will call for the most careful handling for many years to come. Our views on this matter are briefly set out in Chapter XXVIII.

Finally, international trade can only expand freely if nations refrain from imposing deliberate obstructions to the movement of goods, of money, and of persons. Unfortunately this condition is far from existing to-day. In particular the expansion of international commerce is most persistently obstructed by the almost universal practice of imposing tariffs and other barriers to trade. The rest of this chapter is concerned with this problem, first, from the world point of view, and, second, from that of Great Britain.

2. Tariffs and International Trade

In the world of to-day it is as impossible for the nations to live and to grow in prosperity if they try to maintain themselves as detached and independent economic units as it would be for scientific attainment and knowledge generally to be confined within the bounds of a political frontier. On the contrary, civilisation implies that the nations will become economically interdependent to an ever-increasing degree. Countries which pursue an ideal of self-sufficiency for which nature has not fitted them are merely handicapping their own natural progress.

These truths are beginning to be realised by the world at large. Prior to the War—thanks to the revolution in transport and in spite of tariffs which were sometimes high and sometimes low—the natural tendency for nations to trade with one another overcame all obstacles and caused an unexampled increase in world commerce which grew in volume fourfold in forty years. The War put an abrupt end to this development, and shut up many countries within an economic Chinese wall. When the War ended, the nations were unwilling to resume immediately the old and comparatively free conditions of trading. In the last eight years they have in fact been indulging in an orgy of protection. Not content with imposing heavy fines—in the shape of high customs duties—upon trade, it has been the practice of many countries to take the simple course of bluntly prohibiting trade in certain commodities altogether. There has recently been a tendency for these extreme measures to be relaxed; but in the words of the recent World Economic Conference, held at Geneva in May 1927, the tariffs of the world, "which in recent years have shown a tendency to rise, are for the most part higher than before the War, and at present are one of the chief barriers to trade."

It has become increasingly clear that no one was benefiting from this folly, and it was a remarkable sign of this change of view that the Conference, which contained some Free Traders but consisted to an overwhelming extent of Protectionists (including a substantial number of the world's actual tariff builders), unanimously agreed that the tendency had gone much too far and should be checked. Indeed, this Conference of fifty nations—including the United States and Russia—agreed [1] that the world's great need was that international commerce should resume "the general upward movement, which is at once a sign of the world's economic health and the necessary condition for the development of civilisation."

They pointed out that in Europe the position was complicated by the creation of new customs units in 1919, the number of which had increased from twenty to twenty-seven, and that the harmful effects of these tariffs were considerably increased by their constant changes, which make it impossible for business people to enter into long-term engagements or to lay plans for a considerable period ahead.

The Conference disclaimed the intention of delivering a final judgment on the question of Free Trade or Protection, but they were so impressed with the harmful effects that have resulted from the way in which the Protectionist system has run to extremes since the War that they declared in emphatic terms for a greater measure of freedom of trade. After making the significant declaration that "tariffs, though within the sovereign jurisdiction of separate States, are not a matter of purely domestic interest, but greatly influence the trade of the world," they state

[1] The Report was approved by all members of the Conference except those from Russia and from Turkey, who abstained from voting.

categorically that "the time has come to put an end to the increase in tariffs and to move in the opposite direction." This declaration, which was amplified by specific proposals to be referred to shortly, is very significant, for it shows a widespread recognition of the fact that under the nationalistic policies which have been in vogue since the War, countries are suffering more damage from one another's tariffs than they could possibly hope to gain from their own.

The way tariffs have been used in recent years shows the continued existence of a war spirit. The Conference, for example, pointed out that "fighting tariffs" have been ostensibly imposed for the purpose of negotiations, but that instead of negotiating first and imposing the tariffs afterwards, as was the prewar practice, countries have imposed their fighting tariffs in advance of negotiations. In too many cases these negotiations have never been undertaken, or if undertaken have not come to successful results, as the vested interests which have grown up behind these high tariffs have resisted any attempt to lower them. Everyone is suffering from this state of affairs, but no one is willing to take the first step; and the Conference therefore realised that if anything is to be done, action must be concerted. They proposed that the system of commercial treaties, which in practice substantially reduced the obstacles created by the prewar tariff system, should be revived. But they went further and made the important suggestion that the Economic Organisation of the League should endeavour to organise a concerted move for lower tariffs among the nations.

The Conference also dealt with some other aspects of commerce. They urged the framing and adoption of a convention for abolishing import and export restrictions of all kinds, and agreement has already been reached on the terms of such a convention. They pointed out the disadvantages of indirect methods of Protection, such as subsidies, flag discrimination, differential treatment of traders, and other similar devices. They showed that the practice of dumping demoralises the world-market to the ultimate disadvantage of all concerned. In arriving at these conclusions, the Conference was clearly impressed by the contrast between the progress of the United States, which is much the largest Free Trade area in the world, and the situation in Europe, which has been split up into a number of economic units too small to furnish an adequate home market or to permit production on the largest and most economical scale.

These recommendations are entirely in line with what we have defined as Britain's interest in international economic affairs. Indeed, it has frequently been stated by publicists in Europe that the Report of the Conference was a victory for British economic diplomacy in contrast to that of certain other countries which hoped to see a stimulus given by the Conference to the idea of international industrial agreements. A moment's consideration of British commercial policy in recent years shows, however, the inadequacy of this theory. The significance of the Conference lies in the fact that its Report, which we have briefly summarised, represents the spontaneous view of people of all nations who have suffered from what has been going on in recent years. It creates a great opportunity for British statesmanship, for there can be no doubt whatever that a strong backing of the Conference's Resolutions by Great Britain would enormously increase the prospect of their being carried into practice.

3. Britain's Fiscal Policy

But whether we shall make full use of this opportunity is still uncertain, owing to the departures which we have made from our free trade system in recent years. During the War the shortage of shipping and the difficulty in obtaining the means of paying for our foreign purchases made it desirable to restrict as far as possible the importation of all but essential commodities. One of the means employed to effect this was the imposition of the "McKenna duties" on certain luxury goods. Again, while the issue of the War was in doubt, the fear was entertained that the physical conflict might be followed by a fierce and organised economic struggle on the largest scale, and preparations were made for meeting that contingency if it arose. This danger did not materialise. But the economic disorganisation which prevailed after the War, coupled with the almost complete monetary collapse of many countries, had the effect of making our trading position exceedingly precarious, and Great Britain, in company with every other country in the world, attempted by means of temporary expedients to minimise the disturbing effect of the rapid and incalculable changes that were taking place.

With the passing of these abnormal conditions, the justification for exceptional measures has disappeared, whereas the case for restoring the utmost freedom of trade has become perhaps more urgent than ever before.

Sir Austen Chamberlain realised this need as long ago as 1922 when he made the following pronouncement on the general subject of tariff reform:

> "It would seem to me perfect madness to think that in a world so altered from that in which we were acting before the War—in a world where what you want is not to defend yourself against competition, but to find anyone who is in a position to purchase your goods, and to place orders with you—and with a country that has smarted, and very naturally smarted, under the evil effects of those Government controls and interferences in industry unavoidable in war, but have proved a great source of difficulty to us both in their existence, and in the necessity to get rid of them since the War concluded—in such a world and in such a country to go out with the old programme of Tariff Reform at this time seems to me perfect madness."

If this view was sound in 1922, when the currencies of our competitors were producing fantastic and disturbing effects on international trade, it is far more cogent to-day when currencies are practically stable.

Clearly Sir Austen Chamberlain had in mind the fundamental truth that international trade is a process of exchange of goods and services, and that if a country is not prepared to buy from its customers, it cannot continue to sell abroad. It is true that for a time it may supply its goods on credit by making large and continuous loans to countries overseas; but even in this case the interest must be paid and the principal ultimately returned in the shape of imports of goods and services.[1]

While therefore it is true that a particular trade may benefit by protection, a country cannot restrict imports without restricting exports or increasing its foreign investments. In other words, tariffs are not a device for increasing the employment

[1] This general argument is not invalidated by the international movement of gold, which is a bagatelle in comparison with international commerce in general. Such movements have important monetary effects. But in the international balance of payments they only settle small balances.

and production of a country, but are rather a means of diverting it from one direction to another. And as this usually means a stimulus to the less successful industries of a country at the expense of those for which the country is better fitted, the result is that it is poorer than under a system of Free Trade. It is not a mere accident that European countries with the highest standard of living are those with the lowest tariffs. (See Tables, pp. 18, 55.)

Such arguments are of special force for Great Britain, which, as we have seen, depends for its existence on imported food and raw material. But it is also pertinent to point out that in spite of the fact that our population is much smaller than that of Germany or the United States and our resources of coal, ore, and other materials are incomparably less, we remain by far the world's largest exporter of manufactures. In this connection the British delegates to the Geneva Conference reported the result of an analysis of the trade returns of Britain, America, Germany, and France, in accordance with the international classification of foreign trade laid down at Brussels. This enables a direct comparison to be made of the exports of the manufactures of the four countries. The figures for 1913 and 1925 are shown in Table 12.

Other countries are beginning to export significant quantities of manufactured goods; but these four nations are still responsible for over 70 per cent. of the total. Great Britain was therefore in 1925 the source of more than a quarter of the world's exports of manufactured commodities.

Our proportion in 1926 was undoubtedly smaller, owing to the coal dispute, and in 1927 the recovery was by no means complete. But it is evident from the table that under our Free Trade system we have built up and continue to hold a long lead in precisely those categories of commodities in which international competition has become world-wide and against which barriers have been most generally erected.

A similar consideration is the fact that under Free Trade we established so strong an economic position that we were able to bear the main financial burden of the War on the Allied side. In the light of such facts, it would indeed be "perfect madness" to attempt to reverse the evolution of the last century and enter upon a policy of protection tending towards the illusory and unattainable ideal of self-sufficiency.

TABLE 12

EXPORTS OF MANUFACTURED GOODS

Countries.	1913.		1925.	
	In Millions of £.	*Per cent.*	*In Millions of £.*	*Per cent.*
From United Kingdom . .	398·2	37·7	589·3	38·4
,, United States . .	159·2	15·1	356·6	23·2
,, Germany . . .	330·6	31·3	326·6	21·3
,, France . . .	167·3	15·9	262·7	17·1
Total from four countries .	1,055·3	100·0	1,535·2	100·0

Per head.

	1913.	1925.
	£ s. d.	£ s. d.
United Kingdom	8 14 6	13 1 8
United States	1 14 4	3 1 10
Germany	4 18 4	5 4 8
France	4 4 1	6 9 1

The figures of trade and population from which this table is compiled refer to the respective customs areas in 1913 and 1925.

Compiled from "The Economist."

Unfortunately, instead of returning to Free Trade, we have been drifting in the opposite direction, for though Protection has been emphatically condemned by the electorate on the only occasion on which its opinion has been asked, the Government has been quietly introducing small doses of protection under the euphemistic disguises of "safeguarding," "luxury taxes," etc.

Our market is still in the main free, for less than 3 per cent. of our imports are subject to protective duties. The balance is, however, subjected to a variety of safeguarding duties which constitute the most crazy tariff in the world outside Bedlam. These are extremely high as tariffs go. The ad valorem level of present-day tariffs is shown in the following table, which gives the results of an elaborate investigation carried out in connection with the World Economic Conference. The measure chosen for this table is the average of the percentages which the duties imposed by any given country constitute of the values of the commodities which go to compose the range of manufactured goods normally entering into international trade:

TABLE 13

THE LEVEL OF TARIFFS ON MANUFACTURED ARTICLES

Countries outside Europe.		*New States of Central Europe.*		*Great Powers of Europe.*		*Scandinavian and other Low-tariff Countries.*	
U.S.A.	37	Poland	32	Spain	41	Sweden	16
Argentine	29	Hungary	27	Italy	22	Belgum	15
Australia	27	Czecho-Slovakia	27	France	21	Switzerland	14
Canada	23	Jugo-Slavia	23	Germany	20	Denmark	10
India	16	Austria	16	Great Britain	5	Holland	6

Compiled from League of Nations Memorandum on Tariff Level Indices

Even Mr. Joseph Chamberlain's plan of 1903 was a 10 per cent. tariff on manufactures and 5 per cent. on semi-manufactures. Our present " standard rate " is 33⅓ per cent. Our " average " is, of course, still very low; but if our " standard " tariff became general it would at once place us among the most highly protectionist countries in the world. It has been well said by a foreign observer that no one can measure the height of the British tariff wall, for in reality we have no wall at all, but a few scattered and exceedingly high spiked railings.

Again, the device of having every small item studied by a separate Committee ensures that no duty shall have any relation whatever to any other duty, while the fixing of rates—which is one of the most highly complex economic problems in the world—is carried out by people selected because they have no knowledge either of the trade in question or of tariff making.

Moreover, our rates of duty are sacrosanct. Other countries may at all events make a show of using their duties for bargaining purposes. Our duties are the minimum which the Committee consider necessary to " safeguard " industries which it is considered essential to retain in this country. There are many in England who think that there is something to be said for duties imposed in the hope of beating down the other fellow's tariff. This plan very rarely succeeds and, as we have seen, the Geneva Conference recognised that the attempt of countries since the War to get into a good bargaining position had merely had the effect of raising tariffs all round and of creating vested interests which made it more difficult than ever to reduce them. But even if there were anything to be gained by this policy of bargaining, our system is carefully devised so that it cannot be used for this purpose. High duties in a particular trade can, of course, increase employment in it—at the expense of others—provided there are not too many protected trades. Our present plan of giving a bonus here and a little artificial stimulus there would have caused an angry outcry from other industries and from the public generally if it had not been confined to such small dimensions.

We are not, however, so much concerned to point out here the defects of our crude and confused methods as to show their bearing on the general tariff situation. It must be evident to everyone that the effects of our safeguarding duties, whether for good or evil, are of insignificant proportions in comparison with the results that would be obtained by a general lowering of tariffs and by securing freer markets for our exports. Our present policy is, however, extremely detrimental from this point of view. The fact that Great Britain has abandoned her traditional Free Trade standpoint and adopted the Protectionist thesis in its crudest possible form—even though it be only for a few articles—has weakened the forces making for a more liberal commercial policy in every country of the world. The arguments now used for "safeguarding" and implicitly embodied in the famous White Paper which governs the procedure of the various Committees are arguments which can be used to justify the highest tariffs in the world. If competition is "unfair" when a country has lower costs of production than ourselves, and if duties were always imposed at a rate calculated to balance the difference in the cost of production at home and the lower costs of production abroad, foreign trade would cease.

Our policy has weakened the position of friends of international trade abroad and strengthened the hands of those who would put obstacles in the way. There have been periods in modern history when tariffs have moved downwards in Europe—notably in the twenty years following the Cobden Treaty of 1860—and during those decades the world's commerce advanced to a notable degree. There is good reason to think that we are approaching another period of comparative fiscal sanity. But if this is to happen, it is imperatively necessary that Great Britain should forswear further experiments in Protection and should throw her full weight into the task of drawing other nations in the direction of the policy under which our commercial greatness has been built up. Britain's policy in the economic, as in the political, affairs of the world is still very influential, and we could embark on this crusade with high prospects of success. At the least we should be able to ensure that the recent upward tendency of tariffs should cease.

Apart, however, from the action of foreign countries, the present situation is anomalous and full of danger. Without any clear guiding principle we are conferring special privileges on trade after trade, most of which are too unimportant in themselves to arouse the active hostility of the trading community or of the consuming public. But a system created to meet temporary conditions which are passing away is in danger of encouraging a growing distortion of our economic activities.

It is, perhaps, worth adding one further word. If the protection of small industries is a handicap in pursuing our chief objective of increasing trade, the protection of our great export industries would be suicidal. We have already mentioned that the iron and steel industry exports in normal times half its products and that nearly half the remainder is exported in the form of other goods or is used for building ships which thrive upon foreign trade. There is no possibility of building up a thriving iron and steel industry on home trade; and to protect the industry—with the inevitable effect of raising prices here and lowering them in neutral markets where our competitors would sell their surplus output—would handicap all our steel-using industries in world-competition. The same is true of engineering, shipbuilding, the textile trades, and many others. Our export trades must find the means to compete in the world or perish. The Chairman of Vickers went to the root of the matter when he remarked in a recent speech to the shareholders that " we are not going to find our salvation by advocating a policy of tariffs. . . . I believe a system of tariffs is simply another word for subsidising inefficiency. It is a harmful policy for the country to adopt as a whole."

In short, nothing which has happened during and since the War serves to diminish the overwhelming force of the Free

Trade argument. In present conditions, as in past conditions, Protection may snatch a temporary advantage for special interests and trades. But Protection cannot help our export industries or our shipping and must aggravate their problems and increase their costs. Protection cannot increase our efficiency or raise the standard of life. On the other hand, it is a surreptitious method of raising the cost of living and lowering the standard of life. Protection diverts the resources of the nation into the wrong directions, encourages unhealthy and precarious developments, and poisons the springs of business enterprise and the probity of Government. Our policy must be to return as rapidly as possible to the system of Free Trade on which our industrial life and our world-wide commercial activities have been built up.

BOOK 2

THE ORGANISATION OF BUSINESS

ARGUMENT OF BOOK 2

A large area of British enterprise is already, directly or indirectly, under public control, since it is worked by Public Concerns, viz. bodies operated, controlled, or limited by public authorities or enactment. No general extension of this area is recommended. But these bodies should be modified in the direction of greater efficiency by the transfer of public undertakings to specialised bodies responsible to the public authorities concerned, and by the adoption of more practical methods of recruitment for their staff and members.

The rest of the field of large-scale enterprise is worked by Joint Stock Companies. Where these have outgrown the effective control of their members or the healthy influences of competition, full publicity as to their operations should be secured by new and stringent requirements as to their audit and published accounts, and various measures are suggested for ensuring greater efficiency in the directorate. Vast undertakings controlling monopolies should be subjected, by special registration as Public Corporations, to the obligations of public investigation and control recommended by the Committee on Trusts, including in the last resort price-fixing by public authority. Trade Associations, where sufficiently representative, should assume similar obligations of publicity, with power, subject to Government approval, to enforce their decisions on small minorities.

The stream of national investment, which is at present chaotically controlled by a multiplicity of public authorities and private interests, should be canalised by a Board of National Investment, with power to issue bonds and to finance all capital expenditure by public bodies. It should also have power to finance other capital outlay of national importance, to approve the classification of new Dominion and Colonial loans as trustee securities, and, in emergency, to control the issue of foreign Government loans.

An Economic General Staff should be established for the continuous survey of national problems and for advising Ministers, in conjunction with a standing Cabinet Committee of Economic Policy. Economic information should be improved by the co-ordination and rapid publication of all available material and a continuous Census of Production; while business efficiency should be stimulated by collaboration between industrialists, labour organisations, and the State in the application of research to industry and in fostering standardisation, technical instruction, and vocational selection and training.

CHAPTER VI

THE PUBLIC CONCERN

I. "Individualism" and "Socialism"

THE choice between "Individualism" and "Socialism" in the form in which it occupies the controversialists of the Conservative and Labour Parties is, in the main, a distorted, and indeed an obsolete, issue, based on a picture of the financial and industrial world of England as it was fifty or more years ago. As we shall attempt to show quantitatively, the evolution from these conditions is already far advanced. Change has been going on at a great rate. It is not a choice between nailing to the mast the Jolly Roger of piratical, cut-throat individualism, each man for himself and the devil take the rest, or, on the other hand, the Servile Society of a comprehensive State Socialism. Nor is the alternative between standing still and violent change. The world moves on anyhow at a smart pace; it is only the ideas of Conservatives and Socialists which remain where they were. The task is one of guiding existing tendencies into a right direction and getting the best of all worlds, harmonising individual liberty with the general good, and personal initiative with a common plan—of constructing a society where action is individual and knowledge and opportunity are general, and each is able to make his contribution to the efficiency and diversity of the whole in an atmosphere of publicity, mutual trust, and economic justice.

When we come to look at the facts of the modern world, no sensible person can doubt that in a modern community many services must be run by a Public Concern—meaning by this a form of organisation which departs in one way or another from the principles of unrestricted private profit, and is operated or regulated in the public interest. On the other hand, most people would agree that there is a wide field of business enterprise which is much better left to private concerns and can be left to them without the least danger to the public interest.

Now in endeavouring to settle the right division between the Public Concern and the private concern respectively, the first thing to understand is the part already played by the former. We shall give below a fairly detailed statement of this, because we think that anyone who fully appreciates the existing position will be led inevitably to our conclusion that the immediate practical problem is not a great extension of the field of Public Concerns, except in one or two special cases, but a thorough overhauling of the methods of running the Public Concerns which already exist, with the object of making them lively and efficient enterprises. It is a consequence of the gradual and haphazard way in which Public Concerns have grown up in Great Britain that we have never deliberately considered the problems of managing and financing them.

Individualism has been strongest, in our opinion, and Socialism weakest, on the purely practical side, namely, in devising a satisfactory and efficient technique for the actual conduct of business.

This strength of individualism as a technique for efficient production has in the main depended on three features:

(i) It is an unrivalled method for the decentralisation of decisions, that is, for providing that the power and responsibility should lie as near as possible to the act and not at the end of a long chain of intermediaries. By this means time and trouble are saved, the power of judgment is not submerged by the necessity for explanations, and decisions can be made on a small scale and with reference to particular cases so as not to tax unduly the capacity of human wits. Moreover, the average result of decisions taken by a number of individuals, judging independently, may get nearer the truth, or at least run less risk of wide divergence from it, than one comprehensive decision, taken by a single individual, who may know more than any of the crowd and yet not so much as the average of the crowd.

(ii) It is an unrivalled method of arriving at the right result by trial or error. When a number of individuals are each attempting to solve much the same problem, independently, it may be possible to discover the solution by comparing the success of alternative methods. The mediocrity of attainment in the art of war and of government may be partly attributable not only to the complexity of the problem, but also to the absence of competition between policies as a method of discovering the most effective from amongst the possible alternatives.

(iii) It is an unrivalled method of "scoring," that is, of measuring the comparative efficiency not only of methods but of individuals. This may be as necessary for the satisfaction of the individual as for the selection of the fittest. How often must a Civil Servant, or any bureaucrat, lament the absence of an objective measure of the degree of his success if only for his own personal satisfaction, as compared with the business man, who can be judged, or thinks he can be judged, by the test of money profit! Without desiring the profit for himself, he may reasonably desire it as a test of his methods and of his capacity. Moreover, "scoring" contributes an important element of efficiency in the automatic penalty which it provides for failure and in the elimination of the unfit, though not always as quickly as is desirable, from the higher directing personnel. Human nature may require the spur of a penalty to keep effort at its highest pitch of intensity, just as much as, if not more than, the lure of exceptional rewards.

These three valuable devices for the successful attainment of our economic objects are what we are most in danger of losing whenever State action, or any form of highly centralised action, intervenes; and it is these losses which we must endeavour to minimise whenever we are impelled for other good reasons to extend the functions of the State. On the other hand, the pooling of knowledge, the elimination of the wastes of competition (which are very great), the deliberate aiming at the general advantage, instead of trusting that the separate pursuits of private advantage will tend the right way on the whole and on the average, are real advantages in central control and ownership.

As to the necessity in all cases of the unrestricted private-profit motive, such as exists in the highest degree in a one-man business, as an incentive to effort and efficiency, we are more doubtful. The notion that the only way to get enough effort out of the brain-worker is to offer him unfettered opportunities of making an unlimited fortune is as baseless as the companion notion that the only way of getting enough effort out of the manual worker is to hold over him the perpetual threat of starvation and misery for himself and those he loves. It has never been even supposed to be true, at all events in England, of the soldier, the statesman, the civil servant, the teacher, the scientist, the technical expert. It is only the "business man" who, with a certain rather engaging cynicism, has insisted that it is and always must be true of himself. It is not certain that he was ever entirely right. Even in the old-fashioned one-man business, the efficacy of the unrestricted private-profit motive as an incentive to effort and efficiency is liable to exaggeration: for many temperaments, the "worry" involved and the too habitual presence of subconscious financial calculation may be big factors of inefficiency. A certain salary, plus the hope of promotion or of a bonus, is what the generality of mankind prefers. Indeed, it is what the vast majority of those who manage our affairs enjoy already, with varying degrees of certainty and hope. In this respect the performance of functions by Public Concerns in place of by privately owned Companies and Corporations would make but little difference to the ordinary man.

We have said enough to indicate the general point of view from which we approach these problems. We are content that the practical suggestions which follow should be judged by the above criteria. We think that the balance of advantage requires some extension of the functions of the State, but above all a consolidation and reorganisation of those which it already performs. We appreciate the real advantages of the decentralised society of the pure Individualist's dreams; and wherever force of circumstances compels a departure from pure individualism, we have endeavoured so to frame our proposals as to retain as many as possible of its advantages.

2. Survey of Existing Public Concerns

We give below a catalogue of the various types of socialised, semi-socialised, and other State-regulated enterprises which are already in existence. We think that most readers will be astonished by their magnitude and their importance and the large proportion of the total capital of the nation which they already control.

A. National Undertakings operated by the Central Government itself.

These are few in number in this country. The leading examples are, of course, the Post Office, the Telegraphs, and the Telephones. A considerable amount of capital has been sunk in these three enterprises, which, after writing off depreciation, now stands in the national books at about £100,000,000, of which about three-quarters is attributable to the telephone system. The land and buildings of the Post Offices of the whole country stand at £16,500,000, which appears a very moderate figure.

There are, of course, certain other Government Productive Services which ought to be mentioned in this place, for example:

(*a*) The dockyards and other manufacturing establishments of the War Departments.

(*b*) The Office of Works.

(*c*) The Royal Mint.

(*d*) The Commissioners of Crown Lands.

(*e*) The Stationery Office.

(*f*) The State Management Districts under the Licensing Act, 1921.

(*g*) The Roads Department (which is at present part of the Ministry of Transport).

The capital plant of most of these undertakings is relatively small, but the roads are an exception, of which the replacement cost must exceed £1,300,000,000.

B. National Undertakings operated by officially appointed ad hoc Bodies.

The two leading examples of this type are very recent creations, established in fact by the present Conservative Government —the British Broadcasting Corporation and the Central Electricity Board. Possibly the Forestry Commission should be classified here also.

C. Local Undertakings operated by the Local Authority itself

Local Authorities are now responsible for operating nearly £700,000,000 worth of revenue-earning capital plant:

TABLE 14

PUBLIC UTILITY UNDERTAKINGS OWNED BY LOCAL AUTHORITIES

	Total Number of Public Undertakings.	*Number of these in Hands of Local Authorities.*	*Value of Capital Plant.*	
			No. Included.	*Value.*
				£
(*a*) Gas . .	782	317	317	62,650,000
(*b*) Electricity .	563	338	338	125,310,000
(*c*) Tramways, etc.	235	168	168	81,780,000
(*d*) Water * .	1,236	977	977	148,060,000
(*e*) Housing * .	?	1,568	1,568	219,490,000
(*f*) Miscellaneous	?	?	79	38,200,000

* England and Wales only.

These particulars are taken partly from the *Stock Exchange Official Intelligence*, partly from the *Eighth Annual Report of the Ministry of Health*, partly from information supplied directly by the Ministry of Health, partly from other official returns, and partly from *Public Administration*, vol. iv, p. 289. The latter, which is the Journal of the Institute of Public Administration, contains much material bearing on the subject-matter of this chapter.

In the case of Public Utility Undertakings, such as gas, water, electricity, and tramways, which are run by local authorities, profits are restricted by limiting the amount which can be used in relief of local rates.

D. Local Undertakings operated by officially appointed ad hoc Authorities.

(i) *Docks and Harbours.*—Out of 177 Harbour Undertakings, 10 are worked by Government Departments, 43 by Local Authorities, and 60 by *ad hoc* bodies not trading for profit. The twenty largest out of the last-named category have an aggregate capital of about £100,000,000. The Port of London Authority, the Mersey Docks and Harbour Board, the Clyde Navigation Trust, and the Tyne Improvement Commission are the most important. Generally speaking, these are non-dividend-paying bodies which are expected to earn a sufficient income to pay the interest on their outstanding bonds, annuities, and debenture stocks. An interesting example, not included in the above, is the Manchester Ship Canal Company (with a capital of £9,000,000), which is a parliamentary company organised under various Acts of Parliament with the object of gain, but in part municipally owned, and with a Board of Directors on which the Corporation of Manchester must always have a majority of one.

The constitutions of the controlling bodies are very varied. They have been summarised as follows by Sir Joseph Broodbank (formerly of the Port of London Authority):

" The Ports of London and Liverpool are governed by mixed bodies of traders and representatives of Government and public bodies, but their respective powers and jurisdictions differ widely in important details. Bristol and Preston are municipally operated. Southampton and Hull Dock undertakings are owned and worked by Railway Companies, but Harbour Boards have jurisdiction in the water approaches. Manchester Docks and Canal are owned by a private company where the Corporation has secured a majority on the Board through financial assistance in their early days of struggle. The Tyne Docks are divided between the London and North-Eastern Railway Company and the Tyne Commissioners. The South Wales Ports were originally operated by different methods, but are now amalgamated under the control of the Great Western Railway Company. Dover is administered by its Harbour Board, but the Southern Railway Company occupy the important piers and guarantee a part of the debenture interest. The Board of Trade are in control at Ramsgate, but think of handing the harbour over to the town. A Dock Company are the owners of the Sharpness Dock and the Gloucester Docks and the Ship Canal connecting them, whilst there is a Harbour Authority installed as well."

(ii) *Water Boards.*—These Boards are established by special Act of Parliament, and their members are generally appointed by the Local Authorities interested in their activities. Their funds, as a rule, are raised by the issue of debentures or other forms of loan capital, and rates and charges are designed to provide only the service of the outstanding loans together with a fair margin of safety. The Metropolitan Water Board, with an outstanding capital debt of £53,000,000, is a leading example of this type of body. The number of such Boards is not less than fourteen, having an aggregate capital of £69,730,000. There are also at least seven other Public Boards of various kinds of some importance, with a capital of £4,670,000.

(iii) *Public Authorities in London.*—Bodies of this kind have been developed particularly in the London area, where the indirectly elected *ad hoc* authorities include the following:

(*a*) The Metropolitan Water Board.
(*b*) The Metropolitan Asylums Board.
(*c*) The Port of London Authority.
(*d*) The Thames Conservancy and the Lee Conservancy Board.
(*e*) The London and Home Counties Traffic Advisory Committee.
(*f*) The London and Home Counties Joint Electricity Authority.

E. Companies under the Building Societies Acts and the Industrial and Provident Societies Acts.

So far we have been dealing with non-profit-making undertakings. We now come to another category, where profit enters in, but either not on the usual capitalistic lines (e.g. Co-operative Societies) or not without some measure of regulation or restriction of profit.

Societies may be established under the Building Societies Acts, 1874–94, provided that their object is:

> " to assist their members in acquiring dwelling-houses, business premises, or other freehold, copyhold, or leasehold property, for occupation or investment. Members' subscriptions are accumulated in a fund which may be augmented by deposits and loans, and advances are made from the fund to assist members in the purchase of properties. Security for advances is given by a mortgage upon the property purchased."

Building Societies, which are distinct from the Land and Housing Societies mentioned below, numbered about 1,000 in 1926 with over 1,250,000 members. The magnitude of their financial transactions is shown in the fact that in 1926 new advances amounted to over £50,000,000, mortgage assets were over

£170,000,000, and total assets more than £190,000,000. Assets have been increasing recently by about £25,000,000 a year and new advances have averaged about £50,000,000 a year. Thus these Societies are now administering something like 10 per cent. of the total savings of the country.

A society established to carry on any industry, business, or trade may be registered under the Industrial and Provident Societies Acts, and may obtain the privilege of incorporation with limited liability, "provided that it restricts the interest which any member may have or claim in its shares to £200, and, if it carries on the business of banking, that its share capital is not withdrawable."

Practically all co-operative organisations have availed themselves of this method of incorporation, but it is not essential that societies should be co-operative in character in order to obtain registration. The Co-operative Wholesale and Retail Societies are, however, the most important. In 1925 the total membership of Retail Societies was nearly 5,000,000, and the total assets of Retail and Wholesale Societies together was £153,500,000. The following table shows, in respect of three classes of Co-operative Trading Societies, viz. (1) General Productive Societies, (2) General Distributive Trading Societies—Wholesale, (3) General Distributive Trading Societies—Retail, the total share and loan capital, reserves, and insurance funds, and their annual increases.

TABLE 15

CO-OPERATIVE TRADING SOCIETIES—FUNDS

	Total Share and Loan Capital, Reserves and Insurance Funds.	*Annual Increase.*
	£	£
1920	123,266,553	—
1921	125,599,254	2,332,701
1922	128,094,676	2,495,422
1923	135,328,004	7,233,328
1924	146,580,315	11,252,311
1925	153,495,103	6,914,788

Compiled from the Statistical Abstract for the U.K.

These figures exclude Agricultural Productive and Distributive Societies, of which the share and loan capital, reserves, and insurance funds, and the changes therein, in the years for which statistics are available are as follows:

TABLE 16

AGRICULTURAL CO-OPERATIVE SOCIETIES—FUNDS

	Total Share and Loan Capital, Reserves and Insurance Funds.	*Annual Increase (+) or Decrease (−).*
	£	£
1920	3,182,839	—
1921	3,534,581	+ 351,742
1922	3,426,064	− 108,517
1923	3,349,928	− 76,136
1924	3,047,579	− 302,349

Compiled from the Statistical Abstract for the U.K.

The table given below relates to all classes of Industrial and Provident Societies:

TABLE 17

INDUSTRIAL AND PROVIDENT SOCIETIES IN GREAT BRITAIN—MEMBERSHIP AND ASSETS

General Summary 1924

Class of Society.	*Number of Returns Received.*	*Members.*	*Assets.**
			£
Agricultural and Fishing . .	1,631	298,401	4,540,246
Retail Distributive Trading (Co-operative)	1,403	4,662,795	110,568,786
Wholesale Trading (Co-operative) .	6	2,229	37,411,963†
Productive Trading . . .	160	45,501	4,203,135
Clubs	2,116	589,001	4,141,557
Other Businesses (Services) . .	170	42,238	30,063,648‡
Land and Housing . . .	301	34,683	10,669,213
Development	14	9,346	776,878
	5,801	5,684,194	202,375,426

* The Assets include investments by some Societies in other Co-operative Societies, also Societies' balances at C.W.S. Bank, which together in 1920 approximated £33,000,000.

† Excluding Trading Department Balance at C.W.S. Bank £9,535,396 included in C.W.S. Bank Assets against "Other Businesses."

‡ Excludes English and Scottish Joint Co-operative Wholesale Society's Overdraft on C.W.S. Bank, £1,382,918.

Extracted from the Report of the Chief Registrar of Friendly Societies for the year 1925, *Part* 3, *Industrial and Provident Societies, London,* 1927.

F. *Parliamentary Companies*

These companies are formed under Private Acts of Parliament and Provisional or Special Orders. The leading categories are as follows:

TABLE 18

PARLIAMENTARY COMPANIES—CAPITAL

		£
(*a*) Railways	87 undertakings	1,151,747,000
(*b*) Tramways	67 ,,	19,967,000
(*c*) Gas	465 ,,	109,336,000
(*d*) Water	86 ,,	26,100,000
(*e*) Electricity	225 ,,	68,707,000

Compiled from official returns and from the Stock Exchange Official Intelligence.

The statutory regulations as to the profits to be earned or rates to be charged by these undertakings have assumed a great variety of forms.

Both the charges and the profits of the railways are regulated by the Railways Act of 1921. The Act provides that rates and charges and conditions of service are to be so controlled and regulated by the Railway Rates Tribunal—a statutory body set up by the Act—as to yield to the company a " standard revenue." This " standard revenue " is to be " equivalent to the aggregate net revenues in the year 1913 " together with certain additional allowances.

In the case of local authority or company electricity undertakings maximum charges for electricity (which are subject under certain conditions to revision at triennial periods) are fixed for each undertaking in the Order which authorises it. For " power companies " (which are in the nature of wholesalers and have a special position *vis-à-vis* their several local authorities) a sliding scale comes into operation when dividends amount to 8 per cent. (or sometimes to 10 per cent.); in other cases profits are subject to sliding-scale conditions which in certain circumstances may be reviewed by the appropriate authority; moreover, sliding scales may be imposed in certain circumstances under the Electricity (Supply) Acts, 1922 and 1926.

Under Acts of 1847 the dividends of Gas and Water Companies were restricted either to the rate fixed in the Special Act constituting the company or, failing such limitation, to 10 per cent. Since about 1875 dividends of Gas Companies have generally been regulated under a sliding scale which provides that they may increase beyond a standard figure on consideration that a reduction in the price of gas below a fixed standard price. Conversely, prices may rise if dividends fall.

The Bank of England is the most prominent example of a miscellaneous group falling within this category. Theoretically, there is no limitation to the profits which can be earned and distributed to the Bank's private shareholders. But in practice the shareholders' dividends have been fixed for a long time past, and any additional profits are either retained within the institution or (as was the case in respect of part of the exceptional profits arising out of the War) returned to the Treasury.

Thus productive undertakings, mainly transport and public utilities, representing a capital in the neighbourhood of £2,750,000,000, or £4,000,000,000 if we include roads, are already administered according to a variety of methods, all of which depart in some respect from the principles of private capitalism and unrestricted individualism. The transport undertakings and other public utilities included in this total, measured by the amount of capital involved, must comprise at least two-thirds of what could be called the large-scale undertakings of the country, though it would be a smaller proportion, measured in terms of the number of workmen employed.

G. Independent Undertakings not run for Profit

There are numerous charitable undertakings, etc., not run for profit, as follows:

(*a*) The Ecclesiastical Commission.

This body administers, for Church purposes, estates and securities having an aggregate value of about £50,000,000.

(*b*) The Universities, Schools, and City Companies.

Whilst no exact figures are available, we estimate that in the aggregate the Colleges, Universities, and Public Schools of the country administer property and buildings having a capital value of more than £100,000,000.

(*c*) Charities, about 49,000 in number, under the supervision of the Charity Commissioners, held at the end of

1926 securities aggregating £68,000,000, of which two-thirds were British Funds, in addition to an unstated value of real estate.

The total property administered by bodies of this type cannot be less than £250,000,000.

These formidable totals—amounting to over £4,000,000,000 under all heads—demonstrate what we have said above as to the unreal character of the supposed antithesis between Socialism and Individualism. What does the Socialist think he could gain by assimilating all this valuable diversity, developed by experience to meet real problems and actual situations, to a single theoretical model? Are not the abuses of private capitalism and unrestricted individualism capable of being reformed, in so far as they are still to be found in these mixed types, by a further evolution along the lines already set? On the other hand, is the individualist really prepared to scrap all this elaborate special legislation enacted by Governments of every political complexion under pressure of actual circumstances, and hand over the vast capital of our public utilities and railway system to the operation of uncontrolled individualism? If not, then there is no question of principle at stake but only one of degree, of expediency, of method.

3. The Nature and Function of Public Concerns

When we seek to analyse in the light of experience the characteristics of the types of enterprises which tend to become Public Concerns, it is fairly clear what they are. They comprise undertakings of great national importance; which require large amounts of capital, yet may fail to attract private enterprise on an adequate scale, either because of the necessity of limiting profits or for some other reason; where unavoidable conditions of monopoly would render unregulated private enterprise dangerous; or where the private shareholder has ceased to perform a useful function. These characteristics are not only explanations, but justifications of public ownership or of regulation in the appropriate conditions.

It follows that there is a necessary and important place for the Public Concern in the national economic system. The problem is to evolve an efficient business organisation for such concerns, to find room for various types intermediate between the Public and the Private Concern, and to define in the right way the field of operation appropriate to each type.

State Trading

As regards the mode of operating a Public Concern, we see no great advantage, and some substantial disadvantages, in direct State trading of type A (see p. 67 above).

If "the Nationalisation of Industry" means this, we are decidedly opposed to it. We think that Ministers should be directly responsible for commercial operations and the employment of labour to the least possible extent, and that the financial side of these operations should be kept separate from the State Budget to the greatest possible extent. The great Departments of State are not organised for business administration. Nor are Ministers selected for their business capacity. So far, therefore, from recommending any additions to the list of State trading concerns operated by the Central Government, we are inclined to think that it would have been better if in the first instance the Post Office, Telephones, and Telegraphs had been in the hands of an *ad hoc* administrative body detached from the Central Administration. There are weighty arguments for requiring Government undertakings to be conducted in a form analogous to that of joint-stock companies, the capital of which is owned and the Directors appointed by the State. This is the present method of administering, for example, the Belgian and German Railways and the German Post Office. Amongst its advantages are a greater detachment from politics and from political influence.

Municipal Trading

We are in favour of municipal trading in the sense of local public ownership of local public utilities. But we are doubtful whether the right form of organisation and the right geographical unit have yet been attained. As regards organisation, there are often objections to direct administration by Committees of Local Authorities. As in the case of State enterprises, the right model seems to us to be one which borrows some of the machinery of large-scale private enterprise. Generally speaking, an *ad hoc* body should be set up, the executive and administrative Board of which would correspond to the Board of Directors of private concerns (though freed, we hope, from some of the grave faults of these Boards as at present constituted, to which we shall advert in the next chapter), the Local Authorities themselves corresponding to the shareholders. We elaborate this idea in further detail below. As regards the choice of geographical unit, there is no presumption that this will coincide with the boundaries of local government areas. It is a defect of many existing municipal undertakings that their operations are confined to an area too small to be worked to the best advantage. Hence existing municipal and local enterprises should be overhauled so as to ensure for each enterprise the optimum area. This task would be facilitated by a form of organisation analogous to that of a public company in that a single executive could be responsible to more than one local authority as shareholders.

4. The Line of Evolution

Thus we are of opinion that, for the administrative and executive management of public concerns, the *ad hoc* Public Board points to the right line of evolution. We think that a Board of this kind, appointed by and ultimately responsible to some public authority, national or local—but only in the sense in which a company is responsible to its shareholders—is a better model to follow than that of direct public trading, whether national or local. We see no inherent reason why such Boards, merely because they have no private shareholders and are functioning entirely in the public interest, need be any less efficient than the Boards of large public companies, which are managed by salaried directors and officials subject to no real or effective control by their shareholders.

But it is quite another question whether the existing examples of Public Boards ought to be imitated, or are incapable of improvement. We have allowed Public Boards to creep into our economic system, without enough preliminary criticism or deliberate reconsideration of their efficiency in the light of experience. They have not come into the limelight of public discussion. Parliament and the Press since the War have been almost oblivious of them.

How many people, for example, have any clear idea of the constitution of the Metropolitan Water Board, that vast undertaking to the expenses of which every inhabitant of London makes his contribution? Do either the Socialists or the Individualists seek to understand, to improve, or to correct the huge socialised undertakings which we already have? Not they. They exchange their phrases without relation to the world of established fact. The great researches of Mr. and Mrs. Sidney Webb into the slow, historical process by which the Public Concerns of Great Britain have crept unnoticed into existence have produced almost as little effect on the controversialists of their own party as on the academic individualists. It will serve to illustrate what follows if we sketch in a few words the constitution of the Metropolitan Water Board. We should add that we choose this body merely as an example, without our having any reason to suppose that its officials are otherwise than zealous and efficient within the limitations which its constitution and its organisation impose on them.

The Metropolitan Water Board was established by Act of Parliament in 1902 to take over nine water companies which were then separately supplying the London area, and it began to function in 1904. The Board has an outstanding capital debt of £53,000,000 in bonds and debentures. It supplies 563 square miles and an estimated population of 7,000,000. The number of its separate services is 1,180,000. The Board itself consists of sixty-six individuals appointed by the London County Council, the Common Council of the City, the Council of the City of Westminster, and various other municipal councils connected with the area of supply, together with the Conservators of the River Thames and the Lee Conservancy Board. The Chairman and Vice-Chairman are appointed by the members of the Board and are unpaid. The chief executive officials consist of the Chief Engineer (salary £2,500), the Director of Water Examination (£1,750), the Accountant (£1,250), the Clerk of the Board (£1,000), the Solicitor (£900), the Supervisor (£900), and the Surveyor (£700). Yet it is said to be "one of the largest, if not the largest municipal authority in the world." At any rate, no one can accuse the Board of extravagance in salaries, compared with private concerns. The Board has not raised any additional capital by public issue since 1920. Any deficit, which cannot be met by raising charges within the maxima allowed by the Act, is chargeable against the rating authorities represented on it. Nevertheless, Metropolitan Water stock is not a trustee security.

Now, it may be that the business of supplying water to the Metropolis has been reduced so completely to routine and that further technical improvements or economies are so improbable, that it is not necessary to furnish the Board with a proper business management. However this may be, it is scarcely possible that a body constituted as above can be fit to conduct with efficiency or enterprise any important large-scale productive operations. The Board is much too large. The Chairman should be a well-paid whole-time expert instead of an unpaid volunteer. The chief executive officials should belong to a regular Civil Service with high traditions and considerable prizes for efficiency. The facilities for raising new capital should be the best possible. Would not anyone be reluctant to hand over a living industry, as, for example, electricity supply, to a body constituted like the Metropolitan Water Board?

We emphasise these criticisms precisely because we think that *ad hoc* bodies like the Metropolitan Water Board and the Port of London Authority may provide, with due amendments and improvements, the best model for the Public Concerns of the future. But before we seek to extend their functions further, surely it is a prior duty to stir the dead leaves beneath which these bodies are now slumbering unnoticed, and to evolve a sound system of management. The problem is a practical one, not an abstract one to be debated on high philosophical apriorities. The long list of semi-socialised and regulated undertakings enumerated above are all alike in one respect, namely, that they are controlled and managed by salaried, or in some cases unpaid, individuals, and not under the stimulus of personal profit. It may well be that they are already open—the Railway Companies not less than the Water Boards or the Municipal Gas Works—to the charges levelled against State Socialism, namely, of being fossilised, unenterprising, or extravagant. As a first step towards greater efficiency, we must become much more conscious about what is going on around us. Variety is valuable, but it may have been carried in this case to the point of disorder.

5. Proposals

Our suggestions for the future organisation of Public Boards may be formulated as follows:

(i) The method of appointing the executive authority of Public Boards should be reformed, particularly in the case of some of the older established bodies. Business and technical efficiency should be aimed at in choosing the personnel rather than the representation of "interests," consumers' or other. We see no objection to some powers of co-option by the executive authority itself—which is, in practice, the method by which the Boards of most public companies are filled. Above all, large Boards, half composed of dead-heads or ex-officio members who never attend, are to be avoided. We doubt if it is in the interests of efficiency that, for example, the Chairman and Vice-Chairman of a vast undertaking like the Metropolitan Water Board should be unpaid. We think that the appropriate Ministry should be given powers, subject to proper safeguards, to overhaul the membership of the governing bodies of Public Boards and the mode of their appointment.

(ii) We need to build up an attractive career for business administration of this type open to all the talents. A regular service should be recruited for Public Concerns with a cadre and a pension scheme, with room for the rapid promotion of exceptionally efficient officials and with satisfactory prizes for those who reach the top. We should like to see the maximum amount of interchange of the officials between different undertakings, and a practice of moving such officials about at different stages of their career from one concern to another—and not leaving them as at present to vegetate in one job for thirty years or more—wherever the requirement of special technical qualifications does not stand in the way of transfer.

(iii) In the case of concerns ultimately subject to municipal and other local authorities, it might be advisable to set up a body representative of such authorities from all parts of the country with functions covering those now performed for the Civil Service by the Civil Service Commission and the Establishments Division of the Treasury. By these means the prospects and attractions of a business and administrative service for local bodies might be, as they need to be, greatly improved.

(iv) Whenever possible, there should be several Public Boards, in any given type of undertaking, operating in different parts of the country in circumstances sufficiently similar to give value to comparisons between their respective results.

(v) We attach a great importance to a proper system of accounting which distinguishes on sound principles between expenditure on capital and on current account. The system should be as uniform as possible, so as to facilitate comparisons. We ought to know exactly how much new capital is being put into these enterprises year by year and how much is being written off the old capital; we ought to be able to compare the prices charged and the profits earned by Public Concerns of a similar kind in different parts of the country. It should be added that existing State-run concerns (of type A above), whether or not they continue as they are, should also show their financial results in a proper shape, keeping business accounts and presenting clear balance sheets which distinguish expenditure on capital account and make allowance for interest and depreciation. The charge on the National Budget for the year, or, where there is a trading profit, the contribution to the Budget, should then be the net balance on income account properly chargeable to the year in question.

6. The Future of the Public Concern

We do not wish, at the present stage, greatly to enlarge the scope of operation of Public Concerns. The first step is to put those which exist on a more up-to-date basis, to improve the position and prospects of their officials, to get their capital accounts into order, to ascertain whether they are expending on capital account as much as they should for efficiency and progress, and then to watch the measure of their success. Nor do we wish at any time to hand over business to such bodies merely for the sake of doing so. Our object must be to work out, more consciously than hitherto, the best type of organisation for the great body of public services which have already crept half-unnoticed out of private hands, and to recruit a class of officials for running them as capable as the General Managers of great industrial companies.

Some further extensions of the field of Public Concerns will, however, become indicated as necessary and desirable year by year in the future as in the past. For example, so far from curtailing the activities of the Road Fund, we should like to see a Road Board set up with wider jurisdiction, fuller responsibility, and larger resources. We are also in favour of a single Public Board which should control every section of the transport system of the London area. We do not yet know whether the voluntary amalgamation of interests proposed by the recent Committee on this subject will be carried into effect or not; and in any case the method by which the common management is to be introduced has not yet been defined. In our view the problem is precisely one of those for which the formation of a Public Board with statutory powers would afford the most satisfactory solution.

The most important development of the Public Concern during the next decade is likely to be in connection with electricity. We hope that neither thought nor money will be spared to furnish this country with a publicly-owned system of electrical supply, which will be at least the equal of that of any other country in cheapness and efficiency.

In the case of the Railway Companies, we do not consider that the recent Railway Act provides a satisfactory solution. Nevertheless, in view of the recency of the change, we think that there would be some advantage in gaining further experience of its operation before making definite proposals for the next stage. If the Railways are successful in earning their standard revenues as a regular thing, the functions of the private shareholders will have atrophied as much as those of the shareholders of the Bank of England. It will then need but a very slight change to convert all the shares into fixed-interest shares and to assimilate the Companies, if it seems desirable hereafter, to Public Boards. This is the natural line of evolution rather than the useless and unprofitable proposal to nationalise the Railways on the lines of the Post Office. Indeed, on the Continent, the previous tendency towards State-managed systems is being replaced by a movement towards management by Public Boards in the sense in which we are here using this term.

Generally speaking, the functions of private shareholders must tend to atrophy as soon as it has proved necessary to adopt the principle of limiting or of fixing profits. The choice between a Public Concern and a Private Concern then resolves itself, or should resolve itself if Public Boards could learn to borrow all they might from the experience of private enterprise, into a question, not of the methods of internal management and administration, for which in either case salaried staffs will be wholly responsible, but of the manner of appointment of the Directors and of the right to the residual profits after payment of the current rate of interest on the capital employed. The shareholders in old-established industries of diffused ownership, above all in industries where there is a legal limitation of profit, perform no function beyond that of supplying the fruit of savings, the appropriate reward for which is to be found in the current rate of interest rather than in residual profit. The residual profit may be much better employed in such cases in strengthening the financial position of the industry to give better and cheaper service in future, and, very rarely, in furnishing a contribution to national or local expenditure, rather than in precarious and fortuitous windfalls to shareholders, who are remote from the operations of the business and know next to nothing about it.

We believe that there will be even more room in the future than in the past for the type of Public Concern represented by Building Societies and Co-operative Societies. But whilst these are in certain important respects Public, rather than Private, Concerns, it is of their essence that they should be based on the free association of individuals. We think that the action of the State in respect to them should generally be limited to securing publicity, standard forms of accounts, and honesty of management, and, in some cases, facilitating the supply of some part of the capital which they require.

CHAPTER VII

THE JOINT STOCK COMPANY

WE come next to the Joint Stock Companies which now operate practically the whole of the large-scale business of the country which lies outside the scope of the Public Concern. As regards ordinary small-scale business, operated by partnerships, private firms, and individuals, we have nothing to say, and see no occasion for any change. The most important existing legal distinction is between Public Companies, of which there are about 10,000, and Private Companies, limited to not more than 50 shareholders, of which there are about 90,000 in operation—no less than half of these having been founded since 1914. But within the category of Private Companies there are those which are commonly known as "one-man" Companies, namely, those the shareholding control of which is vested in five hands or less.

It is not always recognised how recent a development the Joint Stock Company is as the dominant and characteristic type of business organisation. The whole system is less than a hundred years old, and its present all-embracing growth has been an affair of the last twenty years consequent on the new legislation of 1908. This particular form of incorporation furnishes to those who participate in it very great privileges and advantages, the practical value of which is indicated by the general eagerness to take advantage of them. It is reasonable, therefore, that these privileges and advantages should be accompanied by proper safeguards for the public and for the State. We believe that the amendments of Company Law which we propose below may prove to be the framework within which joint-stock enterprise may extend its developments still further to the general advantage. It has been, in fact, after each of the successive legislative changes of 1862 and 1908 that the big leaps forward have been made.

The important distinctions for practical purposes are:

(i) Between those companies which have passed out of the effective control of their shareholders, and those which are still managed or effectively controlled by their proprietors or by the friends and relations of these, though the method of distinguishing the one from the other must necessarily be a rough-and-ready one; and

(ii) Between those companies which have attained for one reason or another to something of a monopoly position and where free competition from newcomers is ineffective, and those which are still subject to normal competitive conditions and to the elimination of the unfit established firm by the more fit newcomer.

Where neither diffused ownership nor monopolistic tendencies are present, our object should be not to interfere with the existing state of affairs, but to establish an environment in which normal competitive conditions can flourish with the greatest efficiency and the least possible waste.

Our proposals are as follows:

1. Publicity of Accounts and Responsibility of Auditors

In large companies of diffused ownership, where the shares are mainly held by the general public and not by interests represented by the directors, abuses are increasingly frequent, for which the secrecy of accounts is at least partly responsible. The common practice of publishing balance sheets which convey entirely inadequate information to the shareholders themselves or can only mislead them, facilitates the continuance of gross mismanagement, and is the cause of loss and deception for the investing public by placing a premium on "inside information," gossip, and breach of confidence. It is hardly an exaggeration to say that half the business of successful investment to-day in industrial shares consists in getting hold, in one way or another, of private information not available to the general body of shareholders or investors. The honest financier spends his time in getting hold of true information to which he is not entitled, and the less honest in spreading false information for which, under the cover of general darkness, he can obtain credence.

Thus the actual proprietors of a concern are frequently at a serious disadvantage with " outsiders " who can obtain access to " inside " information, with the result that they may part with their property for less than its real value, owing to their ignorance of the actual facts. At the same time, the knowledge by the public that there is such a thing as valuable " inside " information often puts them at the mercy of alleged " inside " information which is only intended to deceive, and of market tips which are part of a scheme of manipulation. The newspapers are full of a flood of gossip, advice, and suggestion, in which items of real and of spurious " inside " information are inextricably confused and intermingled. We think that this scandal is graver than has been admitted hitherto, and that the only remedy is to be found in compulsory publicity.

A further abuse, namely, the growing practice of directors dealing directly or indirectly in the shares of their own companies, is closely connected with the above. It is not easy to correct it except by raising business standards in this respect or re-establishing old-fashioned standards. Directors can always take great advantage over other shareholders through their knowledge of the exact position of their concern. It ought to be considered bad practice to do this, as it is already in some business circles, but not in all. We propose below an increase of publicity in this matter, by which any change in a director's holding will become known to the shareholders at the end of the year. But we think that in addition to this, no director of a Public Company should be permitted to buy or sell the securities of his own company (either in his own name or in that of nominees or in that of a company which he controls) without first disclosing his intention to the Board as a whole and obtaining their assent.

The misleading nature of the published balance sheets of Public Companies is, indeed, the subject of general adverse comment. It is widely felt that matters are getting worse rather than better, and public opinion is in favour of a change. Nevertheless, many of those who are in favour of publicity in principle do not go nearly far enough in their actual proposals. For there is very little to be said in favour of the instinctive secrecy of the British business man. The high standard of publicity which prevails (in some quarters, but not in all) in the United States has shown how unnecessary it is. Moreover, even when the compulsory disclosure of particular facts discomforts an individual, the occasions are very rare when such disclosure is not to the interest of the business world as a whole. We think, therefore, that this is a case for decided action, disregardful of established prejudices. We do not hope to protect the born gull from the born crook; but we think that the drastic proposals for the publicity of accounts which we set forth below may do something to help forward sound methods of investment, through Investment Companies and otherwise, based on skilled professional advice and on the guidance of really competent stockbrokers. For some radical change from the present state of affairs is essential if the general public are to be encouraged for the future to engage their savings in joint-stock enterprises with which they are not themselves concerned.

It is difficult to lay down cut-and-dried rules as to what particulars shall be made public which will be appropriate to all types of companies. Our proposals fall, therefore, into two parts —the one laying down the general character of the information to be given, and the other proposing an enlargement of the responsibilities of the Auditor, with a view to ensuring that he shall consider it his duty to see that these requirements are satisfied in substance as well as in the letter.

A. The Nature of a Company's Assets

(i) Land and buildings, plant, stocks of raw materials, stocks of finished products, value of patents, value of good-will, loans, advances and deposits, shares in other companies, and any other important items which it is practicable to separate, should be shown separately.

(ii) The basis of valuation should be stated, including the cost price and the amount of depreciation written off.

(iii) A complete list should be published of shares held in other companies, together with the current market quotation where this exists.

(iv) In any case in which a company holds a controlling interest in another company, there should be circulated a composite balance sheet, or the balance sheet of the subsidiary should be circulated along with the balance sheet of the holding company covering the same period.

B. The Nature of a Company's Liabilities

(i) Internal reserves, provision for bad or doubtful debts, pension reserves, and income-tax reserve should be stated as separate items.

(ii) The Auditor should be required to certify that there are no concealed reserves in excess of (say) 10 per cent. of the share capital, apart from such undervaluation of assets as may be indicated in his Report.

C. Publication of Profits

(i) Every company shall publish, in addition to the balance-sheet profit, the profit on which the company has been assessed to income tax in respect of the preceding income-tax year, with comments by the Auditors on any important difference between the balance-sheet profit and the profit assessed to income tax.

(ii) The statement of revenue should give separately trading profits, dividends, interest, profits on the sale of capital assets, and sums brought in from reserves; and it should be obligatory to show separately any exceptional receipts (or payments) of a non-recurring nature.

D. Date of Issue of Balance Sheet

A balance sheet should be issued to shareholders within four months of the close of the period covered by it, unless the Auditors certify that this is impracticable from some sufficient and unavoidable cause. The balance sheet of subsidiary companies, circulated simultaneously, should relate to the same period as that of the parent company.

E. The Directors

(i) The annual report to the shareholders should give the total payments received by each director from the company and from its subsidiaries.

(ii) Each director should declare at the end of each year the number of shares in which he has sole or joint beneficial interest and the number which he holds as a sole or joint nominee; and these particulars should be included in the annual report to the shareholders.

F. The Auditors

As regards duties of Auditors, we think that the now existing societies of Chartered Accountants and of Incorporated Accountants might, perhaps, be amalgamated under a Charter, that the Auditors of Public Companies should be required to be members of this united body, and that its Council should be given the duty of maintaining the highest professional standards together with strong disciplinary powers for enforcing them.

It should be part of the duties of Auditors to see that the publicity provisions of the revised company law are fully satisfied, to keep an eye on under-valuation of assets, as well as on over-valuation, to call the attention of the shareholders to any matters of importance which it would be in their interest to know, and to elucidate in their report any item in the balance sheet as published which might, in their opinion, mislead a competent person as to the true position of the company's affairs.

If these new and onerous duties are placed on Auditors, it would be desirable that their tenure and their independence should be more fully protected. It must be remembered that, whilst they are acting for the shareholders, they are chiefly brought into contact with the Management and the Directors, with whom they may necessarily be, at times, in conflict. In particular it should be illegal for Directors to solicit proxies or to vote as regards the appointment or removal of Auditors, who should be given a statutory right to attend and speak at all general meetings of the company.

We believe that these provisions would be, on balance, overwhelmingly in the interest of the investor and also of the public. We do not propose that they should be applied to private companies, except such as are controlled by public companies.

2. Directorships in Concerns where Ownership is Diffused

A large part of our company system has grown up quite recently out of conditions in which the directors, or at any rate the governing group of the Board, were either themselves the proprietors of the concern or the direct and responsible representatives of the proprietors. We have carried on practices which would be reasonable and proper on such assumptions into conditions in which frequently these assumptions are no longer satisfied. Consequently the method of appointing Boards of Directors and the qualifications necessary now require in many cases serious reconsideration.

In practice vacancies on Boards of Directors are filled in the vast majority of cases by co-option. In point of form, of course, the appointments must be approved by the shareholders. But the shareholders are so scattered and disorganised that it is seldom or never practicable for them to dispute the nominations of the Board, unless there is a serious dissension within the Board itself or there is a special reason to suspect an abuse. Thus the power of shareholders is really available only in the last resort; and the vast majority of appointments to Boards of Directors are made in effect, as stated above, by co-option by the existing directors.

Partly as a result of this, a director once appointed, though nominally requiring re-election every few years, considers himself entitled to the office for life, unless he chooses to retire. We are speaking, the reader must bear in mind, mainly of large companies of diffused ownership. Sometimes, there may be a chairman or a group within the Board strong enough to drop a useless director. But generally speaking, a director would consider himself greatly aggrieved if he were to be dropped merely because he was elderly, useless, or without special qualifications for the work. It would even be considered bad form to propose such a thing. Since the duties are indefinite and the privileges agreeable, the way is open to various kinds of jobbery. The pay is often high in relation to the work done; though for directors who take their duties and responsibilities seriously, it may often be too low. Some individuals hold dozens of directorships. A director on resigning frequently expects to be succeeded by his son. A directorship is, therefore, too often considered as a pleasant semi-sinecure and a desirable vested interest for the loss of which compensation is expected as a matter of course. Directorships are, in fact, the "pocket boroughs" of the present day.

A directorship in a great Public Company, such as a Bank or an Insurance Office or a Railway, is apt to be awarded to influential people who bring business or lend to the concern a colour of respectability and social distinction in the eyes of the public, but are without technical qualifications for the management of the business. The four big Railway Companies, for example, though the position has been much improved by the recent amalgamations, still have between them about a hundred directors, many of whom cannot be accused of having either leisure or qualifications for tackling the problems of a railway.

We do not think that the Boards, as at present constituted, of Public Companies of diffused ownership are one of the strong points of private enterprise. There is here an important actual and potential element of inefficiency and conservatism in the more old-established British businesses. We understand that both the American and the German corresponding institutions are, in some respects, superior to ours. Nevertheless, we fear that this is a matter with which it is difficult or impossible to deal by legislation. We think that something could be done, as is proposed above, by increased publicity. We should like to see a provision in Company Law for the compulsory retirement of directors at seventy. But in the main we must depend on the leaders of the business world becoming more alive to the dangers of present methods and to the importance of increased efficiency in this respect. The truth is that a strong and possibly efficient management rather likes to have an ineffective Board which will know too little to have views or to interfere; and the ineffective Board enjoys its fees. If the names of the Board also serve to impress the shareholders, there is much temptation to everyone to let sleeping dogs lie.

The right line of evolution, in our opinion, is towards the system now commonly established in Public Companies in Germany, namely, that of having in addition to the Board of Directors a Council of Supervision. As adapted to the requirements of British industry the Board of Directors of a Public Company would be composed of the Chairman, the Managing Directors, and in some cases the most responsible departmental heads of the concern, together perhaps with a few outside persons with special qualifications; whilst the Supervisory Council would consist of members directly representing the shareholders and, in some cases, the employees. The Supervisory Council would meet quarterly or half-yearly to hear detailed reports, to cross-examine and criticise the Board of Directors, and to be the ultimate authority over the higher appointments, including those of Directors themselves. The same principles should apply *mutatis mutandis* (i.e. with Public Authorities in place of the shareholders) to Public Concerns. It would be an incidental advantage of this system that it would be possible in certain cases to make provision for the representation of the employees on exactly the same footing (though not necessarily with an equal voting power) as the shareholders, without allowing to either the employees or the shareholders any undue or inconvenient powers of interference with the daily management of the concern. We propose that the law should be modified so as to provide optional arrangements along these lines for the representation on a Supervisory Council either of the shareholders or of the shareholders and the employees.

CHAPTER VIII

TRUSTS AND TRADE ASSOCIATIONS

THE instinctive public distrust of monopolies is a natural and well-founded one, for in general it is competition which has passed on to the consuming public the results of industrial and economic progress in the form of low prices. Even under conditions of normal competition, every producer endeavours to obtain for himself the highest possible return for his efforts in whatever field he may be engaged. The grant of patent rights is a recognition by the State that some special return may in the long run be an advantage to the community by encouraging enterprise and initiative. Goodwill, widely advertised trade names, etc., are among the many other means by which individual producers endeavour to put themselves ahead of their rivals. But it is competition which keeps these efforts within bounds, and in the end assures to the consumer the advantage of obtaining goods at the lowest practicable price; if, therefore, competition is in one way or another—whether by the power of great aggregations of capital or otherwise—rendered ineffectual, and monopolistic or semi-monopolistic conditions are created, the public naturally becomes suspicious and looks for some means of protecting what it conceives to be its interests.

But in our view this very proper objective is not to be secured in these days by mere attempts to restore the old conditions of competition, which often involve waste and effort, the uneconomic duplication of plant or equipment, and the impossibility of adopting the full advantages of large-scale production.

In modern conditions a tendency towards some degree of monopoly in an increasing number of industries is, in our opinion, inevitable and even, quite often, desirable in the interests of efficiency. It is, therefore, no longer useful to treat trusts, cartels, combinations, holding companies, and trade associations as inexpedient abnormalities in the economic system to be prevented, checked, and harried. The progression from purely private individualistic enterprises to the Public Concern is one of endless gradations and intermediate stages. We believe that there is still room at one of these intermediate stages for large-scale enterprises of a semi-monopolistic character which are run for private profit and controlled by individuals. We must find a place for such enterprises within our national economic system and create an environment for them in which they can function to the public advantage.

Semi-monopolistic positions are the consequence partly of tariffs, partly of technical economies, partly of the risk of over-production if competition were to be left entirely unregulated, but most of all, perhaps, of marketing advantages created by established goodwill, advertisement, patents, or a control over retailing and other links in the chain of distribution. Partial monopoly of the latter kind is governed by the consideration that it is extremely valuable, that a change in the attitude of the public may destroy it, and that, if it is destroyed, a large amount of money which has been spent in building it up will be totally lost. Thus we have to-day a considerable number of semi-monopolies, built up on the possession of markets, which are held, so to speak, subject to good behaviour. A monopoly thus held in check by its inherent vulnerability may often serve the public well and offer many of the advantages of free competition simultaneously with the economies of concentration.

Now, the necessary condition for the right use by the consumer of his ultimate weapon against this type of combine, namely, his power in the last resort to carry his custom elsewhere, calling into being, if necessary, an elsewhere to carry it to, is *Publicity.* Publicity will protect the combine from unfair criticism on the part of the public and from blackmail by other powerful interests (by the Press, for example), and it will protect the public by keeping them informed of any case where there is occasion for them to put forth their ultimate weapons of reprisal.

1. Public Corporations

For the control, therefore, of large-scale concerns, other than transport and public utilities, it is on Publicity that we propose mainly to rely. With this object, we suggest a further differentiation within the category of Public Companies, which may also assist the solution of some of the problems arising from diffusion of ownership as well as those of monopoly.

We propose that within the category of registered Public Companies there should exist a special class of Company to be designated Public Corporations.

The distinction between ordinary Public Companies and Public Corporations should depend partly on their size, partly on the degree of diffusion of their ownership, but mainly on their preponderant position in their own industry or trade. Our suggestion is that at the discretion of the Board of Trade (which should not be exercised as a rule in the case of companies operating mainly abroad) a Public Company may be required to register as a Public Corporation provided:

(1) Its balance-sheet assets exceed (say) £1,000,000; and

(2) It controls, directly or indirectly, more than (say) 50 per cent. of the output or of the marketing of a product within Great Britain.

Whilst it would be difficult to estimate the total number of companies satisfying these two conditions, we should be surprised if the Board of Trade would find reason to exercise its discretion in the case of so many as 50 concerns at the outside.

We should add that a Private Company, controlling or controlled by a Public Company or Corporation, should have the same status as the Public Company or Corporation, and that large Private Companies and other concerns possessing assets in excess of a stated amount should be subject to the same provisions as Public Companies in respect of publicity.

A Public Corporation should be required to conform to conditions appropriate to what is in fact a semi-public concern. It should be subject to inspection at intervals under direction of the Board of Trade, with powers to the latter to investigate and to publish a report on its rate of profit on the capital employed, its rate of profit on turnover, its provision for depreciation, the amount of profit placed to reserve, the remuneration of its higher officials, the extent, if any, of its monopoly, and the terms of any agreements as to prices or rates of output with kindred concerns. Further, it might be required, at the discretion of the Board of

Trade, to prepare approved schemes of profit-sharing or of workers' representation.

We consider that, in the event of abuses coming to light, the procedure of investigation and control recommended by the Committee on Trusts in their Report, published in 1919, should be followed. In the opinion of this Committee, the Board of Trade should be charged with the duty of obtaining from all available sources information as to the extent and development of combines, associations, and agreements having for their purpose or effect the regulation of prices or output, particularly in so far as such organisations tend to create monopolies or bring about the restraint of trade. If the activities of these organisations lead to complaints, the Board of Trade is to make a preliminary investigation; if the Board finds it impossible to secure the necessary information, or if a *prima facie* case is made out against such organisations, the Board is to refer the matter to a Trust Tribunal. Such a Tribunal will be set up for purposes connected with the investigation and control of combines and associations; and after making an inquiry, and, if necessary, compelling the production of books and taking evidence on oath, shall publish such facts, if any, as prove that acts injurious to the public have been committed. It will then be the duty of the Board of Trade to make recommendations as to State action for the remedying of any grievances which the Tribunal may find to be established. In our opinion, the recommendations made by the Board might, in exceptional circumstances, include the control of prices.

2. International Cartels and Combines

There has been a tendency in the last two or three years in foreign countries to take the view that while fighting for trade by means of tariffs is admittedly a failure and a damage to everybody, it is not enough to leave the sharing of the world trade merely to competition. In a few cases, notably the iron and steel industry, the abnormal development of plant means that in open competition there must be a keen rivalry and cutting of prices for many years to come before equilibrium is re-established between production and demand, and that in the meantime temporary and adventitious circumstances, such as exchange fluctuations, may in fact determine who it is that gets the trade.

It is claimed that a rational division of trade between nations will conduce to efficiency and cheap production by getting rid of violent fluctuations in output and by making possible specialisation of plant. There is a strong case to be made on paper for this move, but recent experience has shown that international industrial agreements are very difficult to make, that they are readily broken, and that they are only practicable in a limited number of industries with comparatively simple products. Moreover, there is always a danger that agreements of this kind may be designed to restrict production and raise prices rather than to produce a large output efficiently at low prices. The Labour representatives at the Economic Conference (Geneva, 1927) were ready to accept the development of international agreements, but were anxious to set up some form of international control. In practice these agreements are too indeterminate, the law of different countries on monopolies is too varied, and the machinery of international control too cumbersome to make it practical at this stage to set up such an organisation. In our judgment, agreements of this kind might be helpful in preventing industrial fluctuations, and should not be indiscriminately attacked. But they are capable of developing into dangerous monopolies, and should be closely watched. The best remedy against the abuse of such agreements is, as in the case of national agreements, full publicity.

3. Trade Associations

Quite apart, however, from combinations within the Companies Acts with which we have been dealing above, Trade Associations are assuming an increasingly important place in the economic system. We think that in many ways this movement is to be welcomed, and that the Trade Association developed on sound lines may play an important part in improving the efficiency of private enterprise.

But it will be impossible to deal adequately with the practical problem of monopoly, as it actually presents itself in modern conditions, unless we take express account of these Associations. For probably, the majority of cartels and price rings fall under the category of Trade Associations, in the sense in which we are about to define the latter, and not under that of Public Companies or Corporations. It is important, therefore, that these Associations should be brought forth from the privacy in which many of them flourish at present, and should be given a definite status.

Trade Associations are Associations of Traders, Producers, or Employers formed for any of the purposes of—

(1) Scientific research and the co-operative supply of information to its members;

(2) The collection of trade statistics from its members;

(3) Legal advice to its members and the drafting of standard forms of contract;

(4) Joint advertising or joint marketing;

(5) The control of output;

(6) Price policy;

provided the members of the Association preserve their separate identity, and are not financially controlled by the Association.

We propose that when a Trade Association comprises more than 50 per cent. of a trade or industry, or a section of a trade or industry, whether national or local, it may become a recognised or incorporated Association, on the initiative either of the Board of Trade, which shall have a discretionary power to require incorporation, or of the Association itself applying for incorporation.

An incorporated Trade Association shall be subject to the following rules:

(*a*) *Publicity*

The Board of Trade shall be kept informed of the proceedings and decisions of such an Association and of any instructions issued to its members, and shall have a right to send a representative to the meetings of the Association, if it desires to do so. In short, the Association must conduct its business in the eyes of the Board of Trade, which shall have power to publish any information of public interest or importance.

(*b*) *Statistics*

Where the Association is prepared to make itself responsible for the collection of statistics, the Government Statistical Service (see Chapter XI below) should in general obtain its trade statistics through the Association and with its collaboration. In any case, where an Incorporated Association is prepared to make itself responsible for the collection of certain statistics, the Board of Trade may issue an order, at its discretion, to make the supply of these statistics compulsory on all members of the trade, whether within the Association or not.

(c) Power to enforce Association Rules throughout the Industry

We think that cases may arise in which it is in the legitimate interests of a trade or industry that a small minority shall be required to conform to the rules which the majority have decided to impose on themselves. There was a case in point in the recent report of the Committee on Co-operative Marketing in the Coal Industry, where the majority was of the opinion that if, in any district, 75 per cent. of the mines were ready to conform to joint selling arrangements, such arrangements should be enforced on the minority. Whilst the reasonable rights of a minority are often a valuable safeguard and should be carefully protected, we think that there should be some provision, subject to due reserves, for enforcing generally in certain cases, rules set up by a self-governing body within an industry for the general benefit of that industry.

We suggest, therefore, that, where an Incorporated Association can show that 75 per cent. of those affected are in favour of a trade rule or instruction and that there is no difficulty in deciding who would be brought under the rule if it were to be applied generally, the Association shall have the right to apply for powers to issue an order enforcing the rule in question on all members of the trade or industry or of the appropriate section of it, whether within the Association or not. Such enforcements might have either a local or a national application. In granting, withholding, or confirming such an order, the Board of Trade should take account of the public interests, the interests of consumers (including any expression of opinion by associations representing them), and the interests of employees (including any expressions of opinion by their Trade Unions).

In conclusion, we would reiterate the idea which has been running through this and the preceding chapter, namely, that the divorce between responsibility and ownership worked out by the growth and development of Joint Stock Companies, an event which has occurred since the dogmatic ideas of Socialists took shape, together with the prominence of legitimate tendencies towards combinations, cartels, and Trade Associations, provide one of the clues to the future. Private enterprise has been trying during the past fifty years to solve for itself the essential problem, which the Socialists in their day were trying to solve, namely, how to establish an efficient system of production in which management and responsibility are in different hands from those which provide the capital, run the risk, and reap the profit, and where the usual safeguards of unfettered competition are partially ineffective. Private Enterprise has had the great advantage over theoretical Socialism of being able to put forth a considerable range and variety of systems and to try them out in practice.

Private Enterprise by itself has, indeed, far from succeeded in finding an entirely satisfactory solution, but, in combination with the hand of the State (which has slipped in much more often than either theorists or the public have recognised), it has provided us with a fine laboratory and many experiments, the results of which, for good and, sometimes, for evil, we are just beginning to reap. The task of modern statesmanship is to take full advantage of what has been going on, and to discern in the light of these manifold experiments which ideas are profitable and which unprofitable.

CHAPTER IX

THE NATIONAL SAVINGS

IN Book 4 we shall set forth a considerable programme for the development and reconstruction of the national resources. This programme will only be practicable if, *pari passu* with it, we are able to mobilise the national savings. In this chapter we examine the existing machinery for the direction of the flow of the new savings of the country. We consider that it is capable of improvement; and we propose machinery by which the large sums which will come forward annually for capital investment under the general direction of the Treasury may be made available for our Programme of National Development.

1. The Existing Machinery

The best authorities estimate that the aggregate new savings of the country now amount to about £500,000,000 annually. We will preface our proposals with a short account of the auspices under which this flow is now directed into actual capital investment.

(*a*) *Capital Expenditure Authorised or Incurred by Public Authorities*

1. There are, first of all, the capital expenditures directly financed out of funds under the hand of the Treasury. Apart from capital outlays paid for directly out of the Budget, such as the Road Fund, which we have dealt with in detail above, there are the capital resources raised for the Post Office, Telegraphs and Telephones,[1] and those administered through the Local Loans Fund. The latter is a revolving fund vested in the National Debt Commissioners. The resources available for new advances out of this fund are derived partly from issues of Local Loans

[1] Additional capital resources raised for the Telephones in 1926–7 amounted to £11,000,000, out of which capital expenditure amounted to £10,500,000.

Stock and partly from Sinking Fund payments received in respect of previous loans. The amount of Local Loans 3 per cent. Stock outstanding on March 31, 1927, amounted to about £305,000,000. The volume of new advances has been recently as follows:

TABLE 19

LOCAL LOANS FUND—ADVANCES

Year	Advances
1920–1	£31,347,000
1921–2	50,651,000
1922–3	13,689,000
1923–4	6,642,000
1924–5	15,926,000
1925–6	29,231,000
1926–7	37,204,000

Compiled from the Annual Accounts of the Local Loans Fund.

These advances are much larger than what was usual before the War, the annual amounts between 1910 and 1913 averaging about £4,500,000. They are effected through the Public Works Loans Board, which was founded in 1817 and reorganised in 1875, to lend money, at rates fixed by the Treasury, to County, Borough, District, or Parish Councils "for the purpose of works of permanent character and public usefulness." Most of the loans in recent years have been made under the Housing Acts. But many other objects are eligible. Certain Housing Companies and Associations under the Town Planning Act are also entitled to borrow, loans to the former having amounted altogether to £4,715,000 and to the latter to £288,000 (all to Welwyn Garden City). Loans to individuals against property under the Agricultural Credits Act, 1923, have amounted to £4,128,000.

The Local Loans Fund is thus a central fund which can be tapped, through the lending departments, by Local Authorities, and other bodies which are statutorily empowered to borrow in this way. The administration of such loans, decisions about the security which is offered, and so forth, are in the hands of the Lending Departments, subject to statutory regulation. The National Debt Commissioners are merely the custodians of the Local Loans Fund, and cannot refuse to make advances when the Lending Departments produce proper authority. The Fund has been used in the past mainly for social purposes. There are, however, a few exceptions to this, such as certain small advances under the Electric Lighting Acts, the Light Railways Act, and the Tramways Acts, advances which have been for industrial or quasi-industrial purposes. In the case of nearly all these advances, the Treasury makes a charge for its guarantee, exacting a slightly higher rate of interest, generally not more than ¼ per cent., from the Local Authorities than that at which it is itself borrowing.

2. In recent times, under the Trade Facilities Acts, which have now expired, loans have been raised for approved purposes on behalf of private concerns but with the guarantee of the Government. Between 1921 and March 31, 1927, 162 guarantees were given for an aggregate amount of £74,251,780, as follows:

TABLE 20

TRADE FACILITIES ACTS—SUMS GUARANTEED

	No. of Guarantees.	*Amount.*
Ships	47	£20,790,585
Shipyards	4	2,643,345
Electricity—Overseas	11	8,380,000
Electricity—At Home	19	6,874,600
Canals, Docks, and Sewerage	13	1,907,000
Overseas Railways	5	6,230,000
Underground Railways	5	12,583,000
Miscellaneous	50	12,423,250
Sugar Factories	8	2,420,000
	162	£74,251,780

Compiled from "Trade Facilities Acts, 1921–6 *: Quarterly Statements, etc."*

No charge was made by the Government for any of these guarantees.

3. The larger municipalities and County Councils borrow direct and not through the Local Loans Fund. The capital sums they have raised in recent years have been as follows:

TABLE 21

LOCAL AUTHORITIES—NEW CAPITAL ISSUES

1909–13 (yearly average)	£2,063,000
1920	46,571,000
1921	19,004,000
1922	5,555,000
1923	*nil*
1924	10,265,000
1925	21,329,000
1926	41,834,000

4. Loans guaranteed by the British Government, such as (1) and (2) above, and municipal and county loans, such as (3) above, are eligible for investments by trustees under the Trustee Act. In addition, certain other classes of loans are also scheduled under this Act. The prior securities of British railways are here included, subject to certain conditions; also the shares of the Bank of England, but no other obligations of Parliamentary Corporations or of *ad hoc* Public Boards except those of certain Parliamentary Corporations for the supply of water. This last exception is, for obsolete reasons, subject to such conditions that it covers only a small percentage of the Water Boards of the country. For example, the direct obligations of the Metropolitan Water Board are excluded from the privileges of the Act, and the obligations of the Port of London Authority are likewise excluded. Nevertheless, since the Trustee Act covers loans raised by the Government of the Dominions, the Crown Colonies, or India, in which countries many of the services which are provided in Great Britain by Public Boards are provided by the State, it follows that funds raised for various public utilities in Australia, East Africa, or India, for example, are eligible for the privileges of the British Trustee Acts, whilst funds raised for identical purposes in this country are not.

Overseas loans raised under this Act in recent years have been as follows:

TABLE 22

TRUSTEE LOANS TO DOMINIONS, INDIA, AND CROWN COLONIES

(£ *millions*)

	1921.	1922.	1923.	1924.	1925.	1926.
The Dominions, Crown Colonies, and India	75·0	73·2	73·2	69·3	46·2	31·5

Compiled from the Stock Exchange Official Intelligence.

We regard the present provisions of the Trustee Act as highly anomalous and we make proposals for their amendment below.

5. The above headings complete the list of specific outlets for new capital expenditure directly influenced by central and

local authorities. But apart from these outlets, there are large sums annually accruing in the hands of the Treasury or the National Debt Commissioners or other official bodies, available for investment in some shape or form. A part of these funds is in fact employed in the above-named outlets, for example, in financing the Telephones or the Local Loans Fund. The balance is employed in Ways and Means advances to the Treasury or in the purchase of Government securities in the market. The most important of these are:

(*a*) The balance of the Sinking Fund after deducting that part of it which is earmarked for the cancellation of specific securities. The part thus earmarked is a fluctuating amount between £30,000,000 and £40,000,000 per annum, so that with a Sinking Fund of £50,000,000 per annum the unearmarked balance is £10,000,000 to £20,000,000.

(*b*) The annual increments of the Post Office Savings Bank and Trustee Savings Banks. The total deposits in these institutions have amounted in recent years to the following sums:

TABLE 23

SAVINGS BANKS—DEPOSITS

(*£ millions*)

End of Year.	*Post Office Savings Banks.*	*Trustee Savings Banks.*	*Total.*
1919 . . .	266·3	71·9	338·2
1920 . . .	266·5	75·1	341·6
1921 . . .	264·2	73·1	337·3
1922 . . .	268·1	75·8	343·9
1923 . . .	273·1	79·6	352·7
1924 . . .	280·4	82·3	362·7
1925 . . .	285·5	83·4	368·9
1926 . . .	283·7	82·0	365·7

(*Note.*—In the case of the Post Office Savings Bank, these figures include the whole of Ireland up to the end of 1922, and Northern Ireland from 1923 onwards. In the case of Trustee Savings Banks the whole of Ireland is included throughout.)

Compiled from the Statistical Abstract of the U.K.

In addition to these deposits, securities are held for depositors by the Post Office and Trustee Savings Banks, having a value of about £215,000,000.

These figures show that the Post Office Savings Bank is now a dead-alive affair, as compared, for example, with the German Savings Banks, either before the War or since the conclusion of the inflation period.

The failure of the British Savings Bank deposits to show an adequate growth is doubtless due in part to the competition of National Savings Certificates. We should have supposed, nevertheless, that even so the Savings Bank deposits ought to increase by some figure approaching £50,000,000 a year if they were properly encouraged by propaganda, easy facilities, and, we should add, a satisfactory rate of interest. With reference to the last-named consideration, it is not generally known that the Treasury is at present crediting the Budget under miscellaneous receipts with a sum which in 1926–7 amounted to £2,812,000 out of the profits which arise from the fact that Post Office depositors are only paid 2½ per cent. A further sum is used to strengthen the financial position of the Savings Bank, mainly to write off depreciation on securities incurred many years ago before most of the present generation of depositors were concerned. Thus it would seem that the Savings Bank could afford to pay 3½ per cent. to its depositors instead of 2½ per cent. We doubt if this profiteering out of the exiguous interest of the very small investor is a desirable source of revenue.

(*c*) The accumulated assets of the Insurance Funds. Recently, the Unemployment Insurance Fund has been in debt, but in 1920 its surplus amounted to £21,825,600. The totals in recent years of the Health Insurance Fund are given in Table 24.

The extension of its scope under the legislation of 1926 will lead to a much greater accumulation in the course of the next few years. This will include the Equalisation Fund of £9,000,000 a year established under the Widows', etc., Pensions Act.

(*d*) The investments of the Currency Note Account. These are now more or less stationary in amount at a total between £235,000,000 and £245,000,000.

(*e*) Funds in the hands of the High Court, etc.

Thus, Government Departments hold or administer directly or indirectly assets under the above headings (*b*) to (*e*) approaching in the aggregate £1,000,000,000. We do not see why, in future, with proper facilities for small savings, the increment of this aggregate should not reach at least £50,000,000 per annum.

TABLE 24

NATIONAL HEALTH INSURANCE—ACCUMULATED FUNDS

	£
1919	71,882,000
1920	81,443,000
1921	92,231,000
1922	100,437,000
1923	109,439,000
1924	116,559,000
1925	125,089,000*
1926	126,388,500†

* The 1925 total was originally £1,447,500 larger than the figure given above. The reduction is due to the transfer of £1,100,000 to the Exchequer from the Navy, Army, and Air Force Fund under the provisions of the Economy (Miscellaneous Provisions) Act, 1926; to a net reduction of £346,000 consequent on the severance of the National Health Insurance system in the Irish Free State; and, as to the balance, to minor accounting adjustments.

† At the end of 1926 the accumulated funds of the Health Insurance system were held as follows:

	£
Invested with the National Debt Commissioners	69,402,800
Invested by or on behalf of Approved Societies	54,216,200
Cash at Bank	158,800
Cash in hands of Approved Societies and Insurance Companies	2,610,700
	£126,388,500

Compiled from the Statistical Abstract for 1925 (*Cmd.* 2849 *of* 1927), p. 56, *and* (*for* 1925 *and* 1926) *from the Eighth Annual Report of the Ministry of Health,* pp. 272–3, 279–80, *and the Eighth Annual Report of the Scottish Board of Health,* pp. 358–9.

(*b*) *Capital Expenditure organised by Private Enterprise*

We come next to the machinery for investment wholly organised by private enterprise.

1. The most important and the most useful of current methods consists in the building up of the capital assets of joint-stock companies and private traders by the retention of profits within the business. For the year 1924 this type of saving has been estimated on the basis of material in the hands of Inland Revenue (given in evidence to the Colwyn Committee) at no less than £194,000,000. This is, in fact, the main source of new funds for the development of industry and trade.

2. Expenditure upon the building and equipment of houses, etc., out of public funds, the private capital of individuals, and through the agency of those valuable institutions, the Building

Societies, amounts in most years to a very substantial sum. The following table shows the number of dwelling-houses erected in each of the last four years:

TABLE 25

HOUSES BUILT, 1924–7, (ENGLAND AND WALES)

Year ending March 31st.	*State Assisted.*	*Unassisted.*	*Total.*
1924 . . .	18,664	67,546	86,210
1925 . . .	67,669	69,220	136,889
1926 . . .	106,987	66,439	173,426
1927 . . .	153,779	63,850	217,629

Extracted from Eighth Annual Report of Ministry of Health.

This is an average of about 150,000 houses a year, and must represent a capital expenditure of not less than £75,000,000. Part of this total overlaps, of course, with expenditure out of the Local Loans Fund and Municipal Loans.

Other buildings, including shops, hotels, farm buildings, schools, factories, and warehouses, the financing of which partly overlaps with investment under other headings (e.g. 1 above), represent about £30,000,000 in each year. If we make some allowance for improvements to existing buildings and for the furnishing and equipment of new houses, we have a grand total of some £120,000,000 a year.

3. The third chief category of new investment is that made, otherwise than to Public Bodies included under (*a*) above, under the auspices of and by the advice, influence, and solicitation of Insurance Companies, Investment and Financial Trusts, Issue Houses, Underwriters, Stockbrokers, bucket-shops, and (increasingly) newspaper publicity. Savings invested in this way flow on a substantial scale (say, £70,000,000 per annum), into loans to Governments and Public Utility Undertakings abroad (including Overseas loans under the Trustee Acts), a smaller but probably more lucrative proportion (say, £25,000,000 to £30,000,000 per annum) into more speculative foreign undertakings in Rubber, Oil, Mines, and the like, and the balance (say, £60,000,000 to £70,000,000 per annum) into miscellaneous British industries. By no means the whole, however, of the last item represents new

capital over and above those items already given. A great deal of it represents the sale to the investor of businesses of which the capital has been already accumulated by one of the other methods catalogued above.

If we are to risk a rough guess at the proportionate importance of the different channels through which new savings are invested, then, taking £500,000,000 as their total amount, we should say that the figures are roughly as follows:

(i) Under the influence of the Government (Central and Local), including repayment of Government external debt, the Road Fund, Telephones, and Local Loans Fund, and capital expenditure by Local Authorities	£90,000,000 [1]
(ii) Through the accumulation of reserves by the retention of profits within existing businesses	£195,000,000
(iii) Dwelling-houses and their equipment, otherwise than by Public Authorities or under other headings	£65,000,000
(iv) Through increased Bank loans and advances, etc. (net)	£25,000,000
(v) Through the New Issue Market for new capital expenditure at home not covered by previous headings and excluding exchanges of existing capital through the machinery of the New Issue Market .	£25,000,000
(vi) Through the New Issue Market and the Stock Exchange for investment abroad (net)	£100,000,000

Each of these items may be subject to considerable fluctuation from one year to another. But this table will serve to give a good general idea of the channels through which the savings of the country are distributed. The reader will understand that this is not a classification of the *sources* of savings, but of their *outlets*; though in the case of (ii) the outlet is closely associated with the source.

[1] In 1926 this figure probably exceeded £100,000,000, whilst the total under (ii) must have been less on account of reduced profit through the strikes.

For the fruitful direction of savings under the headings (ii), (iii), and (iv) we have no criticisms. We are not so well satisfied as to the machinery for New Capital Issues under (v) and (vi). Two possible grounds for criticism arise. First, as regards the interests of the investor himself. Whilst there are undoubtedly opportunities for the financial shark, quantitatively the volume of undesirable new issues is relatively small. On this count, therefore, we do not wish to make any concrete suggestions except that there should be some legal limitations on the amount which may be expended in commissions, brokerage, and advertisement in the flotation of a new issue, so as to limit the amount which can be expended on pushing second-rate wares on the public; and that, if possible, some check should be put on the activities through the post of outside brokers who are not members of any recognised Stock Exchange.

Secondly, there is the question of the right distribution of savings in the national interest between investment abroad and investment at home. So far as industrial, agricultural, and mining overseas enterprises are concerned, we think that the freedom of foreign investment has in the past greatly increased the national wealth and is increasing it now. We see no reason to do anything but encourage the trading, business, and pioneering private enterprise of British citizens abroad. We also think that in the Railway Age, the development of foreign and colonial railway systems abroad out of British capital, when British materials, British savings, and British engineering enterprise were opening up the world for the supply of food and raw materials, was greatly in the interest of this country as well as of the world. But we are more doubtful whether, at the present time, the existing machinery for investment necessarily preserves the correct balance between expenditure on Public Utilities at home and loans for similar purposes abroad to Government, Provinces, Municipalities, and other public bodies in foreign countries and in the Dominions. Our constructive proposals below will be based on the assumption that the development and expansion of transport facilities, public utilities, industries, housing, and agricultural equipment *at home* should be a first charge on the national savings, and that only the surplus, after the satisfaction of all reasonable domestic requirements under these headings, should be made available to public bodies abroad. We think it possible

—we cannot say more until the whole matter has been explored in detail from the practical point of view—that it might be to the advantage of the country if (say) £50,000,000 less were lent each year to public bodies abroad and £50,000,000 more were devoted to the development of the national resources and equipment at home. We think that such a reduction of lending on our part would no longer exercise the same harmful effect, now that the United States is in the field as an alternative, and indeed an eager, international lender, as it might have done in days when a loan which London would not float might not be floated at all.

2. A Proposed Board of National Investment

We think that, even apart from the programme of development proposed above, the national efficiency would be increased if we were to take stock of the position annually and consider as a whole the capital expenditure which is being currently incurred under some form or another of public authority. We think that the funds available for such purposes should be pooled and that no desirable development should be postponed so long as a margin of savings exists to finance it. We suggest, therefore, that there should be prepared annually a Budget of Capital Expenditure, on some such lines as have been followed for many years past by, for example, the Government of India, setting forth on the one side the developments to be financed during the year, and on the other side the sources from which funds will be available.

With this object in view, we propose that there be established a Board of National Investment. This Board should take over the functions of the National Debt Commissioners and of the Public Works Loans Board and also certain additional duties to be outlined below. It should be a subordinate department of the Treasury subject to the authority of the Chancellor of the Exchequer, who should make periodic statements to Parliament and give opportunities for discussion.

All capital resources accruing in the hands of Government Departments should be pooled in the hands of this Board, including, *inter alia,* the assets of the Post Office Savings Bank and of the Insurance Funds, and the repayment by way of amortisation of funds previously advanced. In addition the Board should be authorised to issue, when necessary, either for cash subscription or in substitution for existing Dead-weight Debt, National Investment Bonds (as they might be called) having a Government guarantee.

Out of this pool there should be financed new capital expenditure by all central, local, or *ad hoc* official bodies, by means of advances precisely on the lines of those now made from the Local Loans Fund. That is to say, the scope of the Local Loans Fund should, in effect, be extended so as to cover the Post Office, the Road Board, all Local Authorities, instead of some only, and also *ad hoc* Public Boards.

Repayment, as in the case of the Local Loans Fund, would take the form of annuities, to include interest and sinking fund, spread over an appropriate number of years having regard to the character of the expenditure; the rate of interest charged being calculated slightly above the rate which the Board of National Investment must itself pay, the excess varying—again, as in the case of the Local Loans Fund at present—within moderate limits according to the status of the borrower and being placed to reserve to meet possible defaults. There would, of course, be many other technical details which it is not necessary to enter into here.

Such advances would have to be approved in accordance with a programme, on the advice, where necessary, of the appropriate Department, as, for example, the Treasury or the Ministry of Health.

The Board would have regard in drawing up this programme to the amount of the resources automatically flowing into the pool, to the state of the investment market and the demand for National Investment Bonds, to the urgency and importance of the demands upon it for advances, and to the state of employment. The methods and aims of such a Board would necessarily be a matter of gradual evolution. We think that the Board should pay special attention to the provision of Bonds of a type suitable to the small investor, and that in this connection the Post Office Savings Bank should be reorganised on terms more favourable to the depositor; for we believe the Post Office Savings System is capable of great expansion if the terms are improved and popularised.

We should not necessarily limit the advances to be made by the Board of National Investment to the above categories. The Board should also be authorised to advance funds for new capital improvements to railways or other Parliamentary companies on terms to be mutually agreed, and also, exceptionally where special arguments of national advantage could be adduced, to any other Public Company, on the lines of the Trade Facilities Acts. In particular, we should welcome advances on approved terms to Building Societies and Co-operative Societies, to Garden City Companies and to Agricultural Credit Corporations and Land Banks. This would not, of course, preclude these bodies from also borrowing in the ordinary way.

In the case of loans to the Dominions, India, and the Crown Colonies, which are, at present, admitted as Trustee securities in very large volume, we think that in future new loans of this kind should not be given the privilege of admission to the Trustee list unless they are issued with the approval of the Board of National Investment.

We are, further, of the opinion that the Board of National Investment, acting in conjunction with the Bank of England, should be given some power of emergency control over the public issue in Great Britain of loans to Government and other public bodies overseas, such as are already exercised informally by the Bank of England, and in the United States by the Treasury. These powers should only be used in emergencies or when the currency position demands some measure of regulation of overseas issues. Overseas loans to Governments and other public bodies should at such times be made only with the permission of the Board of National Investment. Unless the loan is for the purpose of war or armaments or the borrower is in actual default in respect of previous loans, such permission should not be given or withheld on any ground except the availability of surplus national savings, and it should not imply any opinion as to the security or desirability of the loan as an investment.

We believe that, without any encroachment on the legitimate field of private enterprise, the Board of National Investment would in time become a factor of the utmost importance in the development of the national resources, in particular because it would be able to direct investment into profitable fields of enterprise at home at present uncared for and incompletely explored, in which the national savings can be employed to the fullest economic and social advantage. For we see no reason to anticipate any shortage of savings. Our task is, rather, to ensure that no profitable and nationally desirable outlet for them is overlooked through deficient organisation, particularly in the important fields of development which now tend to be neglected through falling somewhere between public enterprises and purely private enterprise.

If, in accordance with the recommendation of the Colwyn Committee, the Sinking Fund is increased to £100,000,000 per annum, it would be possible to substitute National Investment Bonds for Dead-weight Debt up to this amount without adding to the aggregate volume of British Government loans; which, with funds coming in from other sources, might raise the resources of the Board to the neighbourhood of £150,000,000 per annum altogether. In course of time the annual instalments of repayment for loans previously made would double this sum. We have here, with the least possible disturbance, an instrument of great power for the development of the national wealth and the provision of employment. An era of rapid progress in equipping the country with all the material adjuncts of modern civilisation might be inaugurated, which would rival the great Railway Age of the nineteenth century.

These arrangements would not interfere in any way with the normal operation of the Sinking Fund for the reduction and eventual extinction of the Dead-weight Debt—just as this is not now affected by the financing of the Telephones or the issue of Local Loans stock. The Dead-weight Debt would continue to be reduced each year by the amount of the Sinking Fund, and the Budget would be progressively relieved of interest charges by a corresponding amount.

It might, however, be advisable, with a view to avoiding unnecessary expenses, to adopt a technical method, which has been long practised by the Government of India. If the Board of National Investment needs to borrow funds against the issue of National Investment Bonds at a time when the Sinking Fund has assets available to purchase Dead-weight Debt for cancellation (apart from debt to which specific Sinking Funds are attached), the double purpose can be served by a transfer of cash from the Sinking Fund to the investment account of the Board of National Investment in return for the Board taking over for the future the service of a corresponding amount of existing debt. The point is purely one of detail. But we feel that the existing practice by which the National Debt Commissioners may be buying up Government stock at a time when some other Government department, e.g. the Local Loans Commissioners, is selling new stock in the market may be uneconomical.

We attach importance to its being clearly understood that the work of the Board of National Investment would leave unaffected the normal operation of the Sinking Fund, because there is too often a confusion between capital outlay for productive purposes and the current expenditure which is properly paid for by taxation. We shall never succeed in getting economy where it is needed, if we encourage the muddle-headed attitude which regards capital developments to improve the national health, resources, and equipment as suitable objects for "economy" just as much as expenditure on armaments or administrative waste.

As regards the effect of capital developments on the rate of interest, it may be true that if we were to stop building houses and roads and power stations the Treasury, finding fewer competitors in the market (apart from overseas borrowers), might be able to borrow a little more cheaply. But a project of lowering the rate of interest by suspending so far as possible new capital improvements—in fact, by stopping up the outlets and main purposes of our savings—would surely be desperately misguided. Put directly perhaps, no one would uphold such a policy. Nevertheless, it lurks unrecognised behind much opposition to schemes of national development.

CHAPTER X

AN ECONOMIC GENERAL STAFF

THE problems of modern Government have become more numerous and more technical. Parliamentary time, to an increasing degree, is occupied by questions which are primarily economic rather than political in the older sense of that word. Government Departments have been subdivided and new administrative bodies have been brought into existence, not because of any bias towards bureaucracy, but by the sheer pressure of evolution in an industrialised nation. No matter how firm the determination of any government to avoid interference with industry, it finds itself called upon to remove difficulties from its path or to assist it. In any case, it is driven to recognise that in modern conditions its policies necessarily affect industry.

1. Policy and Preparedness

Nevertheless, the Cabinet has no body of skilled advice on which to depend. The result is that troubles ahead are not anticipated, and, when they arrive, solutions to meet them are hurriedly improvised. Or, if competent Commissions are appointed to study them, their reports come too late. Ministers and Departments of State are necessarily concerned in the main with daily events and with the task of carrying on. The big problems of economic policy are only theirs when they are becoming ripe to be the subject of actual administration or legislation. It is, therefore, a vital need for a modern State to create a thinking department within the Administration, at the elbow of the inner ring of the Cabinet, which shall warn Ministers of what is ahead and advise them on all the broad questions of economic policy.

As the problems of government become more technical, expert knowledge on them must be at the disposal of the Government. It is not the duty of experts to decide matters of policy. But it is the duty of those who are responsible for important decisions to make the fullest use of expert analysis and of expert statements as to the results which may reasonably be anticipated from this line of action or from that. It becomes more and more clear to the student of affairs, and indeed to the public, that many of the mistakes and blunders made by Governments are due, not to ill-will or prejudice, but to sheer unpreparedness and ignorance. A list of the major problems which Governments holding office since the War have had to face illustrates the need of systematic thought in advance of executive decisions. There have been problems of a new kind as well as of unforeseen magnitude. The cause and effects of currency crashes abroad; the policy of returning to the gold standard; tariffs and policies of national self-sufficiency; the condition and prospects of agriculture; the condition and prospects of the staple export trades; the effects of foreign loans; the development of the national resources; the housing problem; unemployment,—none of these issues have been handled with wisdom or foresight or adequate co-ordination of plans. In all of them, primary economic issues have been involved.

Many of them are inter-departmental; and it has not been clear whose duty it is to exercise initiative or foresight. What is clearly required is that the Cabinet should have at its disposal the best advice based on the fullest knowledge, and that the country as a whole should know that economic tendencies are not merely being recognised when some crisis occurs, but that they are being constantly watched and studied, so that the Government of the day may have a chance of averting difficulties and of meeting them with adequate measures.

2. A Proposed Economic General Staff

(1) *Its Duties.*—We propose, therefore, as an essential instrument of better and wiser government, the creation of what, following Sir William Beveridge, we may call an Economic General Staff, with duties in general terms as follows:

(i) To engage in continuous study of current economic problems affecting national policy and the development of industry and commerce.

(ii) To co-ordinate and, where necessary, to complete statistical and other information required by the Government and by Parliament.

(iii) To act on its own initiative in calling the attention of the Cabinet (or the Committee of Economic Policy suggested below) to important tendencies and changes at home or abroad.

(iv) To suggest to the Government plans for solving fundamental economic difficulties, such, for instance, as measures for stabilising trade conditions, avoiding unemployment, and developing national resources.

(2) *Its Importance.*—A body of this kind will be useless unless it is clothed with great prestige and placed at the centre of the administration. In the daily tasks of Government it is with the executive and administrative officers that actual power inevitably tends to lie. An advisory department is always in danger of being frozen out, and being handed all the problems to the examination of which it is politic to give some measure of lip-service but which do not really matter. The administrative chief will always endeavour to keep the living problems in his own hands, even if he has no time to do them justice. Moreover, politicians are generally unwilling to listen to matters which are not yet burning topics in Parliament or the Press. There is no Government and no Party which will not be prepared to support this idea of an Economic General Staff as soon as the notion has caught on as a word and a phrase. The difference will lie between the type of Government which will be ready to make it a reality and the type which will not. Those who believe in an Economic General Staff as a reality of high importance will have their work cut out to prevent it from becoming an academic body drafting endless memoranda, probably excellent memoranda, which nobody reads. The Chief of the Economic General Staff must be given a position of such power and importance that he can take up the handling of any question he chooses with the assurance that the Prime Minister and the Cabinet will, whether or not they do what he asks, at least listen seriously to what he says. His position in time of peace must be comparable to the position in time of war of the First Sea Lord or the Chief of the Imperial General Staff. That is to say, he must be a considerable officer of the State. He should hold office for five years at a time and not beyond fifteen years in all.

(3) *Its Constitution.*—The Economic General Staff should be

closely associated with the Prime Minister and the Cabinet; and also, at the same time, with the principal Economic Departments of State. We recommend, therefore, that the Economic General Staff itself should consist of the Chief and the Deputy Chief of the Staff, the Permanent Secretary of the Treasury, and the permanent heads (or their deputies) of the Board of Trade and the Ministries of Labour,[1] Health, and Agriculture. The higher personnel of the Secretariat of the Economic General Staff should be very few in number, the best experts available, and well remunerated on Civil Service standards.

3. A Committee of Economic Policy

The existence of the Economic General Staff would facilitate a further reform, desirable for its own sake, namely, the establishment of a Committee of Economic Policy, which should be constituted as a Standing Committee of the Cabinet under the chairmanship of the Prime Minister, consisting of the following:

The Prime Minister,
The Chancellor of the Exchequer,
The President of the Board of Trade,
The Minister of Labour,
The Minister of Health,
The Minister of Agriculture.

All questions of economic and financial policy should be referred to this Committee in the first instance.

The Chief of the Economic General Staff should act as Secretary to this Committee. Other members of the Cabinet and high officials, including the other members of the Economic General Staff, and, for example, the Financial Controller of the Treasury, the Chairman of the Board of Inland Revenue, the Governor of the Bank of England, the Chairman of the Development Committee, etc., would, of course, attend the Committee from time to time for special purposes.

We think that much of the work now done by Royal Commissions and Departmental Committees—excellently, in many cases, but too late, too slowly, and with indifferent co-ordination—might well be initiated and organised by the Economic General Staff, which should have power, with the assent of the Prime

[1] See Chapter XVII for our proposals on the future of the Ministry of Labour.

Minister, to set up Committees, on which outside experts and representatives would sit, to report, sometimes for publication and sometimes for the private information of the Government, on particular problems and projects. The Economic General Staff should also have power, with the assent of the Departmental Minister concerned, to request any appropriate Department to supply it with information or to conduct for it any needful enquiry; and it should command an adequate fund to finance special enquiries at home or abroad, by individuals outside the Civil Service.

With the Committee of Economic Policy and the Economic General Staff, aided by the development of the Government Statistical Service proposed in the next chapter, the Government of the day, of whatever political complexion, would be far better equipped for handling and foreseeing the complex economic problems of modern administration.

CHAPTER XI

BUSINESS STATISTICS

AT all times, accurate and quantitative information about the facts of production and consumption is necessary to economic efficiency, and the avoidance of loss and waste. But three conditions, particularly characteristic of to-day, make it more needful than ever: (*a*) the tendency to overproduction in particular directions, and the difficulty, when markets and sources of supply are international and the time-interval between the beginning of the productive process and the date of actual consumption is considerable, of accurately adjusting demand and supply; (*b*) the ignorance of the investor, who supplies a large part of the capital, about the actual profitableness and future prospects of different branches of business, and the consequent risk that new savings may be directed into wrong channels; and (*c*) the difficulty of proving or disproving the suspicions of Trade Unionists that capital is earning an excessive rate of profit, sometimes leading to trade disputes which may be founded on a misapprehension of the facts.

1. The Bane of Secrecy

The improvement of economic information is necessary for wise intervention or guidance by the State. But it is not less necessary for the efficient functioning of individual enterprise. It is impossible for individual businesses to pursue a correct policy if they do not know in a general way what other businesses are doing. We believe that secrecy in business is one of the greatest factors of inefficiency in British economic life to-day, particularly in comparison with the United States. We think that the Government should take the most drastic and uncompromising measures against it, yielding nothing to prejudice and custom. Secrecy and the withholding of facts may sometimes benefit an individual; but they can never benefit the community as a whole.

The improvement of business statistics may sound a dull proposal which no one could make interesting. But is this really so? The nationalising of knowledge is the one case for nationalisation which is overwhelmingly right. It goes to the root of the chief political and social evils of the day. It is the lack of it which lies behind much class suspicion, breeding industrial strife and malicious idleness. It is the lack of it which makes possible the acquisition of those great fortunes which are due, not to any real contribution to the common pot, but to the private possession and cunning withholding of particular facts which ought to be within the knowledge of all concerned. It is the lack of it which breeds the risk, uncertainty, and precariousness of business, from which spring, on the one hand, unemployment, bankruptcies, and waste, and on the other hand, those great fortunes which fall to the not specially deserving individuals who are lucky in the lottery.

2. Official Statistics—their Present Inadequacy

Part of our proposals for curing these abuses has been given above in the section on Publicity of Accounts in Chapter VII. That part which deals with general and collective facts rather than with those relating to particular businesses is in place here.

Fifty years ago, in the early days of official statistics, the British Board of Trade, largely owing to the influence of Sir Robert Giffen, was a pioneer. Now, under the influence of misplaced economy, we have fallen far behind, especially in comparison with the United States. This is not due to any lack of skill or competence on the part of the officials in charge. The Board of Trade, the Ministry of Labour, and the Board of Inland Revenue—to take three outstanding examples—have done wonders with the resources at their disposal, with their meagre staffs, their curtailed printing bill, and their lack of compulsory powers. Nevertheless, the deficiency of vital information and the ineffective publication of the information which we have are —as those who have conducted this Enquiry have learnt to their cost—scandalous and disgraceful. How can capital flow into the right channels if no one knows the rate of profit in the different branches of trade? How can Labour be trustful if we do not know the real earnings of Capital in any industry? How can business men arrange their programmes of production with prudence and success if they do not know the stocks in hand, the rates of consumption and of production, and the current output of their industry as a whole? How can the State frame a policy or deal in a rational and scientific manner with the problem, for example, of unemployment, if we do not know the rates of growth and of decay in different directions and the actual trend of the industrial system? How can economic science become a true science, capable, perhaps, of benefiting the human lot as much as all the other sciences put together, so long as the economist, unlike other scientists, has to grope for and guess at the relevant data of experience?

This is an instance where the wastes of economy have been extreme. There is a certain very vocal type of publicist who greets every proposal to increase economic knowledge with the cry of Government extravagance, of the futile growth of bureaucracy, and of the ruin of business men by the filling up of unnecessary forms. It is time that these people were told plainly that they are enemies of the light and of science and honest truth, missionaries of secrecy and suspicion. The task of economic illumination is a suitable one for the Liberal tradition.

It is not necessary or appropriate that we should set forth in detail in this place a programme of development for the official statistical departments which will be required. But, speaking broadly, the measures to be taken can be classified in two classes.

3. The Full Use of Existing Knowledge

There are, first of all, those improvements of which nothing stands in the way, except the provision of increased resources of money and of staff—for example, the more rapid and up-to-date publication of data which are already collected. It is notorious that many official figures are available too late to be of practical use; the prompt issue of the monthly details of imports and exports is a signal, but almost unique, example to the contrary, which shows what it is possible to do. Nothing but lack of funds and of staff has delayed until now the publication of the details of the Census of Production of 1924. Much other information is collected but not used owing to lack of staff for its convenient classification. The figures of unemployment are capable of fuller analysis at more frequent intervals. The evidence of Mr. W. H. Coates, formerly Chief of the Statistical

Department of the Inland Revenue, before the Colwyn Committee on National Debt and Taxation, gave a glimpse of the wealth of material in the hands of Somerset House, the fruits of which are not at present available. In giving some figures for the rates of profit on turnover at different dates and for different trades, he mentioned that some 250,000 different businesses are now voluntarily supplying the authorities with full particulars of their turnover, etc. A strong statistical department working on the material in the hands of the Inland Revenue and gradually improving the quality of the material collected might soon work wonders in the illumination of obscure corners of the economic field. Other information, again, is collected at unduly long intervals. We suggest, for example, that the Census of Production, instead of being taken at long intervals, should be in operation continuously and that the figures collected should be made rapidly available. Some published indices should be under continuous revision, instead of being modified at long intervals, as, for example, the index number of the cost of living. In other cases, estimates which are at present little better than guess-work should be put on a sound basis of statistical knowledge, as, for example, the several items of the international balance sheet, and much of our agricultural statistics.

Under this same heading falls the publication of available material at a low price and in a convenient form. We think that the Stationery Office should revert to the previous practice of selling official publications at prime cost.

4. The Further Knowledge Required

In the second place, there are a number of new developments to be made in the collection of statistics which lie at present outside the scope of any particular department. For example, stocks of commodities, the state of the order books in leading industries, the volume of trade, the volume of goods transported, index numbers of wage-rates and of hours actually worked, indexes of the quantity of electrical power in use, and a large mass of banking and monetary statistics which are at present veiled in deep mystery and gloom.

We think that the Economic General Staff should keep an eye on the completeness and co-ordination of the information collected and on the prevention of overlapping. But we do not propose the creation of a separate statistical Department. The detailed work of collecting, arranging, and expounding statistical and other information will be better left to the existing Departments, which are also concerned administratively with the subject-matter of the different categories to be handled. But it may also prove advantageous to make as much use as possible of the assistance of Trade Associations (as suggested above) and of Auditors and Accountants acting through their Institute.

The State can also do a great deal for industry by educative means. Even if all our suggestions for improving the state of business knowledge were carried out in full, much would remain to be done before this knowledge would be properly used by business men. The use of statistics and other information and the application of progressive methods to production and marketing depends to a large extent on business tradition. It is true that the right business tradition cannot be created by the State, but nevertheless it is possible for the State to help in making it.

CHAPTER XII

BUSINESS EFFICIENCY

IN the foregoing chapters we have made various proposals for the reform of the structure of our business organisation. Such reforms cannot, of course, supply the mainspring of business efficiency. This can only be supplied by business men themselves.

1. British Industrial Leadership

The most vital factor in our industrial efficiency is the human factor: the quality of the manual workers and the quality of those who direct their work. We necessarily depend on the capacity, alertness, enterprise, and good judgment of those who manage our businesses; and in the last analysis the influence of public policy is necessarily very limited.

The efficiency of our business management is often arraigned in a sweeping and wholesale way. The average British business man is portrayed as much less efficient than his opposite number abroad; and it is sometimes suggested that our industrial difficulties are mainly attributable to this cause. We do not think that such general charges can be sustained. The leading place we have won in the development of some of the newer industries—artificial silk, electrical engineering, and even motor-cars—despite the great handicaps imposed (relatively to America) by the interruption of the war period, shows that we still possess some of the most efficient and enterprising industrial leaders in the world; while in some of the industries which have suffered severely in post-war years there are many individual British concerns of which the organisation and equipment compare favourably with that of any other country in the world.

Speaking generally, indeed, the fact that British industry affords a materially higher standard of life to its workers than any continental country, and still holds its own in world-markets as well as it does, confutes any general assertion that British industry as a whole is less efficient than that of our European rivals.

2. Remediable Inefficiency

None the less, it is true, we think, that there is much remediable inefficiency in British industry; and that particularly in the long-established industries there is too often a wrong tradition—individualism instead of co-operation, secretiveness instead of publicity, neglect of marketing, indifference and often hostility to research. Let us attempt to indicate where, in our opinion, the most serious charges of this sort are justified.

Experience shows conclusively that in an undertaking of moderate size, everything depends on the man at the top. He controls policy, selects and promotes the higher staff, and sets the whole tone of the business. A change in the directing personality of a concern very quickly affects the whole organisation for good or ill from top to bottom. The success of any concern depends on getting the right man to the top, and giving him the right incentive and the necessary power. The amazing material progress of the Victorian era was due to the combination of industrial expansion and private enterprise. The incentive was profit; competition ensured that success and power depended upon ability; and gross incompetence was generally eliminated by bankruptcy. When industrial conditions are not over-complex, competitive industry on these lines has been proved all over the world to be the most efficient machinery for cheapening product that has yet been discovered. It is particularly good in discovering and giving opportunities to talent. The weakness of the system is its lack of any principle for securing the perpetuation of the most efficient leadership, once a business is established. The family business passes by inheritance to sons or relatives who by no means necessarily inherit the required managerial capacity. This tendency is doubly destructive. There is the direct loss due to the exercise of administrative powers and functions by those unfitted to sustain them. There is the far greater indirect loss due to the fact that the promotion of able administrators is hampered by the necessity of finding jobs for representatives of family or financial interests. Commissions in the industrial army are too frequently awarded by purchase. The career open to talent is restricted, and, as the scale of industry grows, the alternative of independent venturing presents fewer opportunities.

Under modern conditions, where industrial problems have become much more complex and difficult than in the Victorian era, the efficiency even of the individual firm often suffers because the varied powers and trained abilities required by the directors of both small and large busineses are often lacking. The prospect of professional advancement in accordance with fitness and free from favouritism of any kind is the strongest single instrument at the disposal of industry for securing an adequate supply of trained administrators of the right type. Any obstacle to the free working of this process is not only undemocratic; it has a widespread effect on efficiency by discouraging just those able men of all classes who, given opportunity and incentive, would develop into the leaders of the next generation. The traditions of Victorian individualism have persisted in an age whose needs have outgrown them.

3. The Organisation of Industries as a Whole

It is not, however, in the affairs of the individual business that criticisms of inefficiency have most weight, but rather in the general problems of the industry as a whole, which are not the formal responsibility of anyone engaged in it, and which are therefore apt to suffer from the neglect which is too often extended to what is "everyone's business." In no country is an obstinate prejudice to what is called "rationalisation" stronger than in Britain. We propose to illustrate the importance of rationalisation in industry by three examples.

Our first is that of the coal industry, which has become notorious in recent years. Our collieries are not at present working at full capacity. The difference between the best and the worst collieries in the cost of producing a ton of coal is something like 6*s*. to 8*s*. If the worst collieries could be shut down and the remainder worked full time, there would be a double saving, firstly, a saving owing to the elimination of these collieries, and secondly, a further saving by working the remaining collieries at full or about full capacity. With the coal problem as a whole we deal elsewhere; we recognise that there are difficulties; but there is no difference of opinion in any informed section of the community that enormous economies could be made. It is the most crying need for rationalisation in the country.

Our second illustration is from the steel industry. This industry is in deep depression owing to lack of demand, and most of the concerns are losing money heavily. There is one great reform that could be made. The cost of rolling steel depends on the quantity of any given section that can be rolled. If an agreement could be made to distribute the orders among the different works in such a way that each would have the most continuous possible work on the smallest varieties of sections, there would be a substantial saving. It simply means organising the industry for mass production. It is understood that proposals of this sort have been before the industry for ten years, and that everyone agrees in principle that this should be done and that great economies would result. No steps, however, seem likely to be taken.

Our third illustration is from the fairly prosperous industry of flour-milling. Here we have an over-production estimated at about 30 per cent., with big mills in the various ports sending their flour to all parts of the country with serious overlapping, and therefore with heavy unnecessary charges for salesmen and for transit. In this case most of the mills are highly efficient, and only slight economies would be practicable. But big economies are certainly possible if the worst situated and equipped mills were closed down and the production concentrated on the best. Here again it is agreed by everybody in the industry that big savings could be effected in this way, but in no other way, yet nothing is done.

We have, then, three industries in each of which large savings could be made merely by rational conduct of the industry as a whole. Every reader who is connected with industry will be able to supply other illustrations. The lack of scientific management of industries, as industries, goes right through our economic system. An immense amount of time, of thought and ability is devoted to increasing the efficiency of the individual concern—very little to the rationalisation of industry. It is not only questions of structure, organisation, and marketing where rationalisation is required. It is also the whole question of technical development and the exchange of information—largely developed in the United States, but hardly begun here, except under the direction of the Ministry of Munitions during the War. There are questions of standard costing systems, and of adequate statistics, to which we referred in the last chapter. There is the whole question of standardisation and simplification of types, where far-reaching economies are certainly possible in many industries.

Why has not more been done? There are, of course, technical difficulties. Although it is in some cases easy to see broadly on what lines reforms should proceed, it is always difficult to work out a practical detailed scheme. But the main difficulties are personal—jealousy and mistrust among people at the top of various concerns, vested interests of all kinds, the carrying on of things as they are, apathy and lack of imagination to realise the importance of reform. Clearly, this is a matter for industry itself.

4. Education for Management and Direction

The increasing need for reform makes necessary the introduction into industry of men with the training and education which fits them to wrestle successfully with its problems. The prejudice against University men in business is giving way to a growing recognition of their value. In the United States there are far more University graduates turned out every year per thousand of the population than in this country, and they are eagerly taken into industry. The principal administrative positions in most industries, both in Germany and America, are filled by University men, and there is no doubt that a University education, whatever its merits or defects in other directions, does give a wider outlook and a power of understanding the bigger problems. The present tendency towards the creation of large industrial units is a particular reason for industry to select administrators with the broadest and most highly educated outlook. The excellent work done by University Appointments Boards has already done a good deal to accelerate the flow of University men into business appointments. But there are still far too many obstacles. The improvement and extension of the educational devices for bringing the best brains of all classes to the Universities must be followed up by express arrangements for an avenue from the Universities into the higher walks of business, such as has long existed, to the great advantage of the State, into the Civil Service. This is particularly important in the case of Public Concerns, railways, banks, insurance offices, and the great industrial Trusts of the present day. But all large businesses of diffused ownership should do their utmost to replace the bad system of hereditary and family influence in the higher direction by employing the best brains and abilities of the country thrown up from all classes by the educational system.

Other aspects of the question demand particular attention from industry itself. The science of dealing with personnel is for the most part still in a primitive condition. In discussing the Public Concern we have suggested that those who administer large undertakings of this type will require a high degree of adaptability. At the present time there are but few of the larger industrial establishments in which there is any definite and organised system of promotion, and there are too many enterprises in which the transfer of any member of the executive staff is regarded as a disloyal act to be hampered or prevented by long-term agreements, limiting the freedom of the officer concerned in seeking any kind of alternative employment. The structure of industry is, in fact, evolving more rapidly than the minds of those who are responsible for its direction. Technical evolution does not wait upon the slow teaching of experience. Methods which were good enough for one-man businesses may be wholly inadequate in concerns employing thousands or tens of thousands of workpeople increasingly conscious of their needs and rights, and of their ultimate dependence on scientific management, control, and direction. Not only is it true that the education of the workers cannot be regarded as finished at fourteen; it is true also that the higher direction demands the wider outlook that a University education gives, and that refusal to regard education as finished with the taking of a degree, which is the final proof of a University education being worth while.

Though the task of reform, towards the accomplishment of which developments such as those in the last paragraph can help, is one primarily for business, the State can help. We recommend later the formation of a new Ministry of Industry, with a bigger conception of its duties in stimulating and encouraging the efficiency of industry. A remarkable example of what can be done in this direction is furnished by the very substantial results obtained under Mr. Hoover's energetic and wise guidance in America in the direction of standardisation and simplification. No less remarkable, though on a smaller scale, is the work done in this country by the National Institute of Industrial Psychology for industrial and commercial firms.

The work of the National Institute is naturally limited by the resources it commands. Were its methods more widely applied and the range of its labour extended, they might appreciably increase the efficiency of business.

In our opinion, the State can assist to increase industrial efficiency by helping to found and forwarding the work of an Institute of Management, the functions of which would not be so much the promotion of pure research as the discussion of problems of organisation, and a policy of fostering the application of the results of research throughout the whole of industry. We recommend that such an institute should be founded by Industrialists, Labour Organisations, and the State working together, and that the State should take whatever steps are necessary towards its foundation.

In addition both to helping in the foundation of an Institute of Management and to carrying out reforms, the State should undertake the following functions:

(i) It should extend the range of work now done by it in a manner comparable to the work already being done in this country for one great industry by the British Engineering Standards Association, and over a wider field in America by the Bureau of Standards.

(ii) It should undertake or at least initiate enquiries—which might be undertaken by business groups—into various problems of distribution. Here again the American example serves.

(iii) It should develop and press vigorously all possible forms of simplification.

(iv) It should co-ordinate and strengthen the work of technical and managerial education, of vocational selection and training, and of the various new developments of factory technique towards which the National Institute of Industrial Psychology has already made a most valuable contribution.

5. Marketing

So far we have spoken of rationalisation from the point of view of those processes which we commonly think of when we speak of "production." There is, however, a field of at least equal importance in those later stages which are equally parts of the process of production—marketing, transport, distribution, retail selling, etc. Corn stored on the prairie in Canada is useless for satisfying the wants of consumers in Britain. It acquires value as the result of transport, sale, and distribution. Economic progress has been achieved at least as much by developments in marketing, etc., as by changes in the factory or on the farm. These later processes to-day employ as many persons as the so-called production processes; the proportion so employed will tend to increase in the progress of civilisation; and their efficient organisation is of an importance at least equal to that of any other part of the industrial problem.

Unfortunately, marketing is the heading under which there is perhaps most reason to doubt the efficiency of our existing organisation—a doubt which applies particularly to our methods of selling goods abroad, and more especially to the traditional methods of some of our old-established industries, which are now finding it difficult to hold their own. The machinery for marketing British goods abroad grew up and took firm root in days when the conditions were very different from those which now obtain. On the one hand, British goods were everywhere in great demand, and it was not so necessary as it is now to spend time and thought in attracting customers. On the other hand, foreign trade was attended by various risks and difficulties which have now diminished. Under these conditions a class of specialised merchants grew up, who acted as intermediaries between manufacturers in this country and the markets for which the goods were ultimately destined. The great merchant houses became the chief directing agency of manufacture for foreign markets, and have played a larger part in the development of British exports than has the corresponding class in any other country.

There is reason, however, to doubt whether this merchanting system is in all cases best adapted to the altered conditions of international competition in the modern age. In the keen competition from Germany and the United States which developed towards the end of the last century our rivals did not rely, to the extent to which we are still accustomed to do, on the general merchant. American and German manufacturers sent their agents everywhere. They pushed their sales directly, and were not content with merchants either at home or in the countries where they desired to sell their goods. And the new methods, although expensive, seem on the whole to have been more efficacious than the old.

It is not, we believe, without significance that those industries which are now finding it most difficult to hold their own are the old-established industries in which the merchanting system has struck its deepest roots. In the new industries which have grown up in recent years it has been comparatively simple to adopt modern marketing arrangements. But where an elaborate merchanting system is already in existence, it may prove, by its very virtue, an obstacle to the development of new methods. The Manchester Royal Exchange represents the most perfect expression of our traditional marketing arrangement. But it is far from clear that it represents the methods which are really best adapted to enable the Lancashire cotton industry to recapture its lost trade.

Anyone who proposed to abolish the Manchester Exchange would quickly discover how deep-rooted are our traditional methods and the difficulty and complexity of the problem of altering them. But the importance of efficient marketing arrangements, both for the home and for the foreign markets—from the standpoint of the manufacturer and the consumer alike—can hardly be exaggerated. Marketing efficiency is of commensurate importance with productive efficiency. Yet while manufacturers generally are keenly on the look-out for improved machinery and will scrap obsolete plant without hesitation, marketing arrangements are far less sharply scrutinised. The problem of introducing better marketing methods is in many cases more difficult than that of productive efficiency, because it involves in a greater degree the organisation of the industry as a whole as distinct from that of the individual firm.

The question of marketing acquires a special importance in any industry where demand is tending to decline and the problem of "surplus capacity" presents itself. Where such conditions obtain, as is notably the case to-day in coal and cotton, unrestricted competition among a large number of businesses marketing their products independently of one another forces prices down to unremunerative levels in an aimless, haphazard manner, which impairs the financial strength of the industry and ultimately its efficiency, without contributing effectively to the recapture of lost markets. Under such conditions, accordingly, the need becomes manifest for "organised marketing," i.e. for a system which will enable the industry, in the words of the Lewis Committee on Co-operative Selling in the Coal-mining Industry, "to choose a policy, and to carry that policy out."

There is urgent need, we believe, in many of our leading industries, struggling as they now are with adversities which seem beyond their control, for some organisation of the industry as a whole which will enable it to steer a deliberate course, adapted to the conditions which it has to meet, instead of drifting helplessly before them. The particular system of organisation which circumstances render most appropriate and most feasible will vary from industry to industry; and we shall, therefore, not attempt to go further into detail. But it is vital that the need should be clearly recognised. Just as a nation may be able to rub along more or less satisfactorily in times of peace with very little Government and with a loosely organised social structure, but will assuredly succumb in time of war unless it is capable of a high degree of collective discipline and corporate action, so, for an industry which can do well enough in ordinary times as an unintegrated mass of independent atoms, a prolonged period of severe adversity brings the same need for closer organisation, for common purpose, for discipline, and above all for deliberate policy.

BOOK 3

INDUSTRIAL RELATIONS

(*a*) SURVEY

(*b*) PROPOSALS FOR REFORM

ARGUMENT OF BOOK 3

The existence of discontent in the field of industry is displayed in trade disputes and restrictive practices. The workers' grievance arises from a sense of the inadequacy of their reward, of their insecurity of livelihood and tenure, and of their lack of information as to the financial results of their work. The resulting unrest is largely responsible for the growth and consolidation of Trade Unions, faced by a corresponding array of Employers' Associations. This situation has been mitigated by special arrangement in certain industries, by the operations of the Industrial Court, and by the intervention of the State. State action for the regulation of industry has been mainly confined to legislation respecting hours and conditions of work, and the fixing of minimum wages by Trade Boards. The State has also fostered industrial self-government by the establishment of Whitley Councils and of the Railway National Wages Board. Voluntary arbitration has been encouraged by the Ministry of Labour. No system of compulsory arbitration is recommended.

A wise wage-policy should aim at the highest practicable wage-levels. These, however, are dependent upon the maintenance and increase of efficiency uninterrupted by industrial warfare; and efficiency is in turn dependent upon the effective removal of the workers' sense of injustice. A just wage should recognise (a) the minimum requirements of the worker and his dependents, (b) his effort and capacity, and (c) his interest in the common enterprise. For (a), the minimum wage should be fixed for each industry by an extended use of the methods adopted by Trade Boards; the introduction of Family Allowances may be found desirable by industries to which they are suited. For (b), the best possible negotiating machinery is desirable for the fixing of standard wages, due regard being had to the existing inequalities between "sheltered" and "unsheltered" industries. For (c), a variable addition to wages should represent the pros-

perity of the concern; profit-sharing schemes should confer a legal right to the proportions distributed, provide for full financial information, and secure trade-union rates as the minimum remuneration in all cases.

Industry should be assisted towards a system of self-government and co-operation. This may be achieved by the extension of Trade Boards to all industries which require them; by the addition of neutral members to Whitley Councils and the conferment, under proper safeguards, of compulsory powers; by the creation of joint bodies for consultation upon general industrial policy in industries where no such bodies exist; by providing in the case of specified "essential" industries a system of negotiation, delay, and conditions of employment which will reduce the risk of stoppages to a minimum, while safeguarding the ultimate right to strike. These developments should be assisted by improved publicity and information as to the facts of industry and by the establishment of a Ministry of Industry, to take over the work of the Ministries of Labour and Mines as well as the industrial work of the Home Office.

For the improvement of industrial relations at which we aim, it is essential that, associated with the Ministry, there should be a small Council of Industry charged with the continuous review of industrial problems, of the work of Trade Associations, and of all applications by joint bodies for compulsory powers.

The worker's relations with his employer should be improved and defined by the compulsory establishment of Works Councils in all industrial or distributive undertakings employing more than fifty persons. These councils should have power to agree factory rules and the right to receive information as to trading facts and prospects, as well as to be consulted upon factory organisation and proposed changes therein.

The worker's status should be improved by the provision of safeguards against dismissal. Assurances should be provided against arbitrary dismissal: (a) for disciplinary or other offences; (b) for alleged inefficiency; (c) on account of shortage of work or other economic grounds. Every worker should be provided with a plain statement of his terms of employment and rights in the event of dismissal.

The present ownership of industry is unduly concentrated and should be diffused as widely as possible among industrial wage-

earners. Such diffusion, tending towards the popular ownership of industry, may be effected partly by progressive taxation and restrictions upon the inheritance of large fortunes, but more directly by the stimulation of employee-ownership under schemes of profit-sharing and investment by employees, by the encouragement of popular banking and investment, and by the creation and development of investment trusts. All these processes should be encouraged and, where necessary, regulated by the State.

CHAPTER XIII

INDUSTRIAL DISCONTENT AND ITS CAUSES

THE existence of widespread discontent among a large proportion of our working population, and the constant friction which results from it, are among the most serious obstacles to efficiency in a production, and therefore to trade revival. Unless we can find the means of removing these discontents, we cannot hope for that co-operative national effort which is necessary if we are to overcome our difficulties and turn them into opportunities of progress. It is useless to deny the legitimacy of the grievances from which unrest springs, or to assume that they are the consequence of economic forces beyond our control; men are happily so constituted that they will not permanently accept what they believe to be unjust because they are told it is inevitable. The way to approach the problem is to analyse the extent and character of the unrest; to examine sympathetically its causes; and to work out patiently the means whereby these causes may be removed. These are the aims of the present section of this Report.

1. Industrial Disputes

The most obvious and striking evidence of industrial unrest is to be found in the frequency and duration of industrial stoppages. It is perturbing to discover that during the last generation there has been a marked increase in the number of stoppages, and a still more marked increase in the amount of working time, and therefore of earnings, lost as a result of these disputes. This is brought out by a comparison between three periods, each of eight years—the period since the War, the period immediately before the War, and the period before that again.

TABLE 26

LABOUR DISPUTES

Period.	No. of Disputes.	No. of Workers Involved.	Average per Annum.	No. of Days Lost.	Average per Annum.
1898–1905 . .	4,371	1,345,000	168,000	34,500,000	4,300,000
1906–1913 . .	5,561	4,546,000	568,000	89,300,000	11,100,000
1919–1926 . .	6,553	11,084,000	1,385,000	357,000,000	44,300,000

Compiled from Ministry of Labour Gazette.

Assuming an average wage of 10*s.* a day, this means that in the first period the loss of wages due to industrial disputes, calculated at present money values, was about £2,000,000 a year, in the second period £5,500,000 a year, and in the third period £22,000,000 a year. What these disputes cost the community in dislocation of trade, in loss of markets, and in other indirect ways there is no means of calculating.

Preponderance in Mining and Transport

But a closer analysis of the figures is necessary before we can appreciate their full significance. The first noteworthy fact is that the burden and loss have been due mainly to a few industries, and in a peculiar degree to the mining industry. Of the 186,000,000 working days lost during the twenty-one years before the War, 104,000,000, or 56 per cent., were lost in the mining and quarrying industries—nearly all in coal-mining. Of the 357,000,000 working days lost during the eight years since the War, 253,000,000, or 62 per cent., were lost in these industries. In other words, industrial strife has been more serious and more costly in the mining industry than in all the rest put together.

Next to mining, the transport industries have suffered most from industrial disputes. Mining and transport occupy about 13½ per cent. of the working population; they account for perhaps 75 per cent. of the loss due to industrial disputes. If the loss of working time due to disputes in these industries were deducted from the total, the average loss from trade disputes spread over the rest would be small. There are great industries—such as iron and steel, or boots and shoes—in which serious stoppages have been unknown for a generation; and in the manufacturing industries as a whole, as distinct from mining and transport, the loss of time and of productive power due to this cause is almost negligible. Even including mining and transport, the average loss of working time through industrial disputes, spread over the whole working population, was in the first of our three periods only one-quarter of a working day per head in a year, in the second period less than half a day, and in the third period about two and a quarter days. In other words, if stoppages in the mining and transport industries could be kept down to the scale normal in manufacturing industries, the time lost through industrial disputes would be negligible.

Comparison with Losses from Sickness, etc.

Although the prevalence of strikes and lock-outs is a cause of grave national loss, the waste of working time and of productive power due to this cause must not be exaggerated. It is far less than the waste caused by sickness and unemployment. In 1924—a year of relatively few disputes—sickness caused the loss of 26,000,000 weeks' work, unemployment of 58,000,000 weeks, and industrial disputes of less than 1,500,000 weeks. Even in 1921, a year which saw a long-drawn dispute in the coal trade, sickness and unemployment caused more than eight times as much unproductive idleness as industrial disputes. If we consider only the avoidance of wasted time, a sound health policy and a constructive unemployment policy would do more than even a total cessation of strikes and lock-outs to maintain and improve the productivity of the nation.

2. Other Effects of Discontent

But the significance of industrial disputes lies not so much in the actual loss they cause, great though that is, as in the evidence they give of friction and dislocation.

We are producing substantially less wealth than we could produce with our available supplies of capital and labour. This is, no doubt, partly because we cannot find markets for our maximum output. But it is also because we are not utilising either our capital or our labour as efficiently as we might. The blame for this lies partly with the employers, partly with the employees. In the first place, there is often deliberate restriction of output. Some employers, when they are in a position to do so, sometimes restrict their output not merely because the market is restricted, but because they prefer a small output at a high price to a large output at a lower price. The policy may be good for the individual employer, but it is not always good for the community. For it limits employment and fails to supply the public with the goods in question at the lowest price compatible with good labour conditions.

Restrictive Practices

On the other hand, the organised workers in many industries have adhered to certain practices which involve restriction of output, thus discouraging men from putting forth the maximum effort of which they are capable without undue strain, have put obstacles in the way of the adoption of labour-saving devices and of methods of payment calculated to stimulate energy, and in some cases have done everything in their power to limit the entry of new workers even into trades in which there is a great demand for them. In general, the workers, whether as organised bodies or as individuals, have not felt any responsibility for the increase of efficiency in production in their industries. That, they have felt, is the business of the employer, and they have often criticised the employer, with reason, for a failure of efficiency on his side while they were hampering him on theirs. The employer, in general, accepts the view that the responsibility for efficiency rests exclusively with himself; in most cases it has not even occurred to him that it can or ought to be shared with his workers. If this point of view is to persist on both sides, the co-operative pursuit of efficiency will never be achieved.

The prevalence of these restrictive practices has varied very widely from trade to trade. Some trades have been almost free from them. Rarely have they been carried so far as in the building trades, wherein, since foreign competition is impossible, it has seemed practicable to impose the whole cost upon the community. Entry into these trades has been narrowly restricted; and the amount of work which the craftsman may do in a day has been reduced so low that in his estimates for the Housing Act of 1924 Mr. Wheatley had to assume an average rate of bricklaying far below what the average bricklayer can easily achieve. The results have been that building costs have been greatly increased, the community has had to submit to a cruel shortage of housing accommodation; and the amount of employment available has been reduced. The building trades are exceptional; but corresponding practices have existed in some degree in many trades. They have had the effect of restricting the mobility of labour, and therefore of increasing the difficulty of finding work for the unemployed. They have also increased the cost of production, and consequently reduced sales, and therefore contributed to increased unemployment. In so far as they have prevailed they have gravely impaired the efficiency of British industry.

Reasons for Restrictive Practices

But it is not enough to say this without recognising that there have been reasons for these restrictive usages. Some of them are measures of protection against over-pressure. Some of them spring from the natural jealousies of crafts which see their province being invaded by mechanism, or from the rivalries of different Unions. Many of them are influenced by the haunting fear of unemployment, which leads men to make their jobs last as long as possible. The restrictions upon entry into a trade are a natural safeguard against a competition which might beat down wages. The objection to methods of payment by results springs from a fear of over-pressure, and has been strengthened by the folly of many employers who have reduced rates for no better reason than that their employees were earning big wages. Yet, when all is said, these usages would not have been so prevalent and persistent if there were a general belief that labour would get its full share of any increased production which might result from improved efficiency. Behind restrictive usages, as behind industrial conflict, lies a deep suspicion that the worker does not get a "fair deal," that the industrial system is in many respects unjust, and that there is an ineluctable conflict of interests between capital and labour.

3. The Causes of Discontent

What, then, are the causes of this discontent which finds expression in wasteful strife or in still more wasteful restriction of effort and output? The thinking workman makes five main complaints against the existing industrial system:

(1) For all his toil, it does not supply him, in many cases, with an income sufficient to give a comfortable livelihood for himself and his dependents, together with a margin for rational enjoyment and for saving.

(2) It has failed to give him security of livelihood, however willing and eager to work he may be; accident, a spell of sickness, or a shortage of work due to no fault of his own, may at any moment throw him out of employment, use up his savings, and inflict hardship and humiliation on his children. Of all these menaces, unemployment is the most serious, and it inspires the belief that there must be something wrong with a social order in which, amidst flaunting luxury, such insecurity haunts the life of the worker.

(3) The existing industrial order denies him the status which seems proper for a free citizen. He may be dismissed at a week's or a day's notice, and thus deprived of his livelihood without redress or appeal, perhaps for no better reason than that he has offended an autocratic foreman. While, as a citizen, he has an equal share in determining the most momentous issues, about which he may know very little, in regard to his own work, on which he *has* knowledge, his opinion is seldom asked or considered, and he has practically no voice in determining the conditions of his daily life, except in so far as trade-union action has secured it. Indeed, where management is inefficient and autocratic he is frequently compelled to watch waste and mistakes of which he is perfectly well aware without any right of intervention whatever. And this, despite the fact that when these errors issue in diminished business for the firm concerned, he, and not the management, will be the first to suffer by short time working or complete loss of employment.

(4) Knowledge of the financial results of industry, and of the division of its proceeds, is denied to the worker, and of this he is becoming increasingly resentful. He has little means of judging to what extent he is in fact participating in the fruits of his own labours, or whether or no he is getting

a " square deal "; and his dissatisfaction with the existing order is proportionately intensified.

(5) He believes that the products of industry are unfairly divided between Capital and Labour; that under the capitalist system society is divided into two classes—a small class of masters who own the means of production and live luxuriously by owning, and a huge class of workers who receive in return for their work only what they can force the owners to pay. He believes that under such a system there can be for his children no true equality of opportunity with the children of the more fortunate classes.

4. Legitimate Complaints

All these grounds of complaint are felt, in an educated generation, by an ever-growing number of workpeople. They are legitimate discontents, inspired by legitimate aspirations; they are, in Tennyson's phrase, " liberal discontents," which, if rightly guided, should lead to progress. In actual fact, we have, during the last hundred years, advanced a long way towards meeting them. The real wages of the workpeople have been multiplied fourfold. The system of social insurance has erected genuine barriers against the worst consequences of insecurity—old-age pensions, workmen's compensations, sickness insurance, health insurance, widows' and orphans' pensions. The emancipation of the Trade Unions has given to the workers a powerful voice in determining the conditions of their work. The creation of a national system of education has at least begun the advance towards equality of opportunity. And it is legitimate to point out that all these advances have been mainly due to Liberal policy.

But it is natural that men who have to bear the brunt of our social imperfections should forget the achievements of the past, and should be more alive to the distance we have still to travel than to the steep and toilsome track we have already traversed.

It is not surprising that there should be industrial unrest. It is not surprising that this unrest should have become doubly acute in the post-war period, on which we entered with such high hopes of social advance. It is patently one of the main factors which prevent us from facing our difficulties as a united nation, with all our strength. But it will continue until the legitimate complaints and the legitimate aspirations of the mass of the workpeople are recognised as valid, and until the industrial system is reorganised in such a way as to make it plain that, with patience and effort, the complaints can be met and the aspirations satisfied.

The root of the matter is that the relation of master and servant, upon which the organisation of industry has rested during so many centuries, has become untenable in a democratic era. We have to find our way to a new system of relations, based upon partnership, in which the position of the worker will not be out of accord with his standing as an equal citizen in a democratic State. This is one of the most inspiring tasks of our generation. There are those who hold that what is loosely called the "capitalist system" is fundamentally wrong, and that the necessary change can only be achieved by destroying the existing "system" and erecting in its place a new system, conceived upon a different plan. This seems to us to be a mistaken view, because it overlooks the fact that the existing "system" is not a fixed or static thing, that it has always been changing, and that it is changing to-day more rapidly than ever. The process of evolution has, indeed, been in the direction which we have indicated as necessary.

In the following chapters, therefore, we shall first describe the process of collective bargaining and the part which the State has played in it, with a view to discovering what are the factors that offer most promise for the future; and we shall then consider what changes or modifications are best calculated to meet the complaints or to satisfy the aspirations which we have analysed.

CHAPTER XIV

COLLECTIVE BARGAINING

OVER the greater part of the range of British industry, the wages, hours, and conditions of labour are determined by the process known as "collective bargaining," between Trade Unions on the one hand and Associations of Employers on the other. It is by this process of bargaining—by an eternal tug-of-war between highly organised rival forces, often hostile to, or at least suspicious of, one another—that the vitally important social functions of dividing the product of industry between the various factors that combine to produce it, and of determining their respective rights, are normally carried on.

Those industries in which the great majority of workmen and of employers are members of their respective organisations and accept the decisions of their representatives, and in which, consequently, these decisions are in practice observed throughout the country, are known as "organised" industries and include all the major industries and services except agriculture and domestic service, as well as a large number of minor industries. There are, indeed, few even of the "organised" industries in which some of the employers and workpeople do not remain outside their respective organisations; but, so long as these are too few to be able to stand out against the agreements of the majority, their existence does not affect the "organised" character of an industry. There are, however, still many "unorganised" industries, mostly small, in which representative organisations of employers and workpeople are either non-existent or so weak as to be unable to bind the whole body. But on the whole, "collective bargaining" between highly organised negotiating bodies has become so much the established usage that we take it for granted as if it were part of the order of nature.

1. Development of Collective Bargaining

It is not generally realised how recently this state of things was established. Until the middle of the nineteenth century the Trade Unions were mostly small local bodies, scarcely able to deal on equal terms with the employers. Even when great Unions on a national scale came into existence—beginning with the Amalgamated Society of Engineers in 1851—they were confined to the skilled crafts, and they carried on their negotiations not with representative bodies of employers, which scarcely then existed, but with individual firms or small local groups. It was not until the last decade of the nineteenth century, after the London Dock Strike of 1889, that Unions of unskilled or semi-skilled workers began to be formed. Their appearance changed the trend of British Trade Unionism. The Unions of skilled craftsmen, being able to levy substantial contributions from their members, had developed elaborate systems of mutual benefits; and as they were reluctant to imperil these funds by big controversies on a national scale, they preferred to localise their disputes as far as possible. The Unions of unskilled or semi-skilled workers, unable to levy large contributions or to offer substantial benefits, tended to use their strength in struggles to raise wage-levels by strike action on a wide scale. In the big industrial conflicts of 1911–14 the policy of striving for the fixation of wages and conditions on a national scale was widely adopted and has become increasingly common since that date. The rapidity of the change may be illustrated by the fact that while in 1913 the Railway Companies were still refusing to negotiate with or to recognise the Railway Unions, in 1921 these Unions were actually recognised by statute as the authoritative representatives of the men in the constitution of a National Railway Wages Board.

But this could not have happened if there had not been, concurrently with the growth of the Trade Unions, an equally marked growth of collective organisation among employers. Long inhibited by the keenness of competition among rival firms, this process was primarily stimulated by the necessity of common action in dealing with the Trade Unions; but it was also encouraged by the tendency to combine for the fixation of prices and for other purposes. Combination on both sides, on a great scale, was in fact part of the movement towards consolidation which has been a feature of industrial development during the twentieth century. It was stimulated and accelerated by the War; and the formation of immense consolidations both of Capital and of Labour has been among the most distinctive features of the post-war period. It may be taken for granted that the tendency to consolidation, which is at work in every industrial country, will certainly continue. It is a factor of primary importance.

2. The Strength of Trade Unionism

The rapidity of the change can best be illustrated by the growth of trade-union membership. We have no figures of total membership before 1892, but we have the figures of the membership represented in the Trades Union Congress, which has, since 1892 and probably earlier, amounted to something like two-thirds or three-fourths of the total. In 1866, when the Congress started, it represented 110,000 members. In 1873, after Trade Unionism had been legalised by the Act of 1871, the membership leaped to 500,000. It remained round about that figure until the nineties, when the rapid development of unskilled Unions brought another sudden leap to over 1,000,000. A steady growth followed, until, with the acute industrial strife of the years immediately preceding the War, the 2,000,000 mark was passed in 1912. During the War and the following years, advance was yet more rapid: 3,000,000 in 1917, 4,500,000 in 1918, 5,250,000 in 1919, 6,500,000 in 1920. The trade-slump which followed led to a decline, and the figure fell to 4,300,000 in 1924; the disasters of 1926 have probably caused a further decline; but there has been no relapse to the pre-war scale. These figures are echoed by the total membership of all Trade Unions, which we possess only since 1892. From 1,500,000 in that year they rose to 3,000,000 in 1911, reached the maximum of 8,300,000 in 1920, and declined to 5,500,000 in 1924.

It is important to realise the extent to which the wage-earning population is covered by the Trade Unions. The total "occupied population" amounted in 1924 to nearly 20,000,000. Of this total, the Trade Unions included about two-fifths at their highest point of expansion in 1920, and not much above one-fourth in 1924. But the "occupied population" includes the whole of the employing and managing classes; the professional classes (about 300,000); a host of small shopkeepers and independent tradesmen; a million children under sixteen, not to speak of young people between sixteen and eighteen, few of whom are members of Trade Unions; 1,300,000 agricultural workers, of whom only 61,000 were Trade Unionists in 1924; the whole class of domestic servants; and all the military and police forces, who are of course excluded from trade-union membership. When all these deductions are made, it would appear that the Trade Unions must include about one-third of the wage-earning industrial population.

3. Trade-Union Organisation

Consolidation.—Alongside of the increase in trade-union membership has gone a steady process of consolidation, through the amalgamation of small Unions, or their federation under a more or less centralised control. Some of these Federations are loosely organised, but others, such as those of the cotton weavers and the iron and steel workers, are almost as effectively centralised as if they were single Unions. The result is that, in spite of the formation of many new Unions in unorganised trades, the number of Trade Unions has declined from 1,358 in 1896 (when the total membership was 1,600,000) to 1,155 in 1924 (when the total membership was 5,500,000). Even these figures do not adequately represent the change, because the official returns reckon separately all the federated Unions, and credit (for example) the miners with 105. There are still a good many single-branch Unions, of a primitive type, with a mere handful of members. But, broadly speaking, the Trade Unions of to-day are bodies of national scope, immensely bigger and more consolidated than their predecessors of thirty years ago. They have become incomparably more powerful factors in the industrial, social, and political life of the nation. This is, in the main, a new phenomenon of the post-war period, and it profoundly affects the whole problem of industrial organisation and industrial relations.

Of the 1,155 Unions of 1924, with their total membership of 5,500,000, only 484 were registered with the Chief Registrar of Friendly Societies, and were therefore entitled to the full privileges of the Trade Union Acts. These 484 had a membership of

4,500,000, and a gross revenue of £11,200,000. But no less than 4,000,000 of the membership and £10,000,000 of the funds belonged to the hundred largest Unions. And there are ten gigantic organisations (either huge single Unions or closely-knit Federations) which include almost half of all the Trade Unionists of Great Britain, each having a membership of over 100,000. These giant bodies largely dominate the trade-union movement, and their officials are the magnates of the Labour world. They include the miners, the railwaymen, the transport workers, the engineers, the weavers, the iron and steel workers, and two huge combinations of unskilled men. The older Craft Unions, once the aristocrats of the Labour world, now count for little in the framing of general Labour policy at Trades Union Congresses, in comparison with these giants.

Three Types of Union.—Three main types of Trade Unions ought to be distinguished; they differ sharply in their organisation and methods, and approximately one industrial dispute in seven is occasioned by friction between them. *The Craft Unions,* which in general are the oldest, aim at combining men who pursue the same skilled trade, whatever industry may employ them. They are confronted to-day by a number of problems arising from the invasion of their crafts by semi-skilled labour and from uncertainty as to the precise scope of the part which the different crafts should play in modern industry. The *Industrial Unions* are a modern development, inspired by the idea of enabling all the workers in an industry, whatever crafts they may pursue, to present a united front against the employers. The solidarity of labour within the industry, rather than pride of craftsmanship, is their inspiring motive. The *General Labour Unions* aim at the inclusion of semi-skilled and unskilled workers in many industries. Their growth has been rapid during the last thirty years—a reflection of the fact that, as machinery develops in complexity, the importance of specialised skill and training is proportionately diminished. Obviously, the organisation of unions on such different principles is bound to involve a great deal of overlapping and uncertainty; and the process of "collective bargaining" is greatly complicated by the existence of their conflicting claims.

Methods of Organisation.—Practically the whole country

is systematically covered by the elaborate organisation which the greater Unions have wrought out. In every case the unit is the local branch or lodge, with whose members, in theory, ultimate authority rests. These local lodges are seldom composed of the workmen in any particular factory. Perhaps for this reason the mass of ordinary members do not always take their lodge meetings very seriously. The lodges are usually grouped into districts, served by a paid official; and at the head of all is a national executive with a few permanent officials who take the predominant part in fixing the policy of the whole organisation, and who wield in practice an immense power. There is, however, a wide difference between different Unions in the degree of autonomy they leave to their local organisations. As a rule, the maintenance of a large staff of paid local organisers is involved, and it is upon these men that the main burden rests of carrying on detailed day-to-day negotiations with employers.

4. Trade-Union Method and Outlook

On the whole, the trade-union organisation materially contributes to the smooth working of industry. But in some industries the whole organisation is driven by a desire to weaken or undermine "the existing system"; and in nearly all industries it may be said that, while compromises and agreements are fairly and honourably interpreted, the trade-union official seldom feels any responsibility for the maintenance of efficiency. That is not the angle from which he looks at his work; he is apt rather to regard his task as that of being a watchdog against the employer. A change in the angle of vision adopted by the trade-union organisation—a more general recognition that efficiency in output is quite as much the interest of the workman as of the employer—would, without any sacrifice of the workers' interests, bring about a great and beneficial change in industry. The greatest need of British industry to-day is, not (as some foolishly suppose) to weaken the power of the Trade Unions, but to foster in the minds of Trade Unionists the already dawning recognition that efficiency in production is of the first importance to them. It can only be brought about by a recognition of, and an honest attack upon, the causes of industrial discontent.

Upon the maintenance of this elaborate organisation the

Trade Unions naturally spend a large proportion of their funds —nearly two-fifths of their members' total subscriptions. The proportion is less than two-fifths in the case of those Unions which have large subscriptions and big benefit schemes; but it is much more in the case of the unskilled Unions. The superficial criticism is often made that the cost of management is unduly high. But this complaint overlooks the fact that the upkeep of such an organisation is the primary purpose for which the Unions exist.

At the same time it should be remembered that the network of officials serve not only to carry on negotiations, but also to work political propaganda, and to maintain disciplinary control over the rank and file of members. The disciplinary powers of the Unions are indeed formidable. They can make the life of a recalcitrant member exceedingly unpleasant. More than that, they can, by expelling him from membership, practically forbid him in many cases to earn his livelihood by his trade, and at the same time deprive him of the benefits for which he has paid substantial contributions, extending it may be over many years. It is the strict discipline of the Trade Unions, exercised through their widely distributed staff of paid officers, which constitutes their main strength in dealing with the employers, and enables them both to make and, as a rule, to keep their bargains. But it sometimes has its cruel side. The only effective protection against abuse of these powers lies with the body of Trade Unionists themselves. In any case, the sanctions of Trade Union authority are so formidable that if there should come a clash between a Trade Unionist's obligations to his Union and his duty to the State, his choice will often be a very hard one.

5. Employers' Associations

So much for the one side in the process of collective bargaining. Of the other side there is less to be said, partly because the organisation of the Employers' Associations is far simpler, since they are concerned with a much smaller number of units; partly because the facts about them are much less known, no analytical returns being published such as the Registrar of Friendly Societies issues in the case of the Trade Unions. We do not know how their funds are raised, or in what amount, or how they are spent. The Ministry of Labour informs us that there were 2,403 Employers' Associations in 1924—more than double the number of Trade Unions; but this enumeration includes a multitude of small local or sectional organisations which are in practice embodied or federated for the purposes of negotiation. We do not know just how many national negotiating bodies there are on the employers' side. In many cases the same firm will be represented on several negotiating associations for different parts of its work. But, in general, negotiations are, and probably must be, carried on between a single Employers' Association on the one side and a group of Unions, sometimes in a condition of friction with one another, on the other side. Taken as a whole, the Employers' Associations wield as great a power over the life of the nation as the Trade Unions; and it is a strange thing that we know so little about them. They ought to be registered, and the facts about them ought to be made as fully public as the facts about the Trade Unions.

6. The Third Party in Industry

Between the Operatives' Unions and the Employers' Associations stand the technical and managerial staffs. Their special position is a matter of recent development, and is as yet not sufficiently recognised. The modern tendency is towards a steady increase in the numbers of those in industry whose duties are of a technical or managerial character, but whose relationship to the owners or directors is that of salaried employees, in some ways not dissimilar to that of the workers. The boundaries of this large group are difficult to define with precision. At one end of the scale are executive officers who exercise a high degree of responsibility; at the other end come the foremen, clerks, and other subordinates, who have some small degree of authority in the industrial structure. Between these extremes are many grades of salesmen, technicians, and others. Attempts on the part of these intermediate grades to organise themselves on trade-union lines are apt to be regarded as "disloyal" to the employer, and sometimes those who have taken a lead in such organisation have found themselves penalised in consequence. At the same time the workers are apt to be suspicious of "black-coated" unions, as they are sometimes called. Thus in 1926 the Trade

Union Congress declared that "there was no third party in industry"—a declaration clearly at odds with the observed facts. In our view, however, the tendency of the managerial and technical staffs to form organisations of their own, with a view to the formulation and pursuit of their common aims and the expression of their common point of view, is a healthy development, and employers and Trade Unions alike would do well to encourage it.

7. The Attitude of the Law

The law of the land is very indefinite in regard to combinations both of workers and of employers. Both are included under the term "Trade Unions," and the terms of the Trade Union Acts in theory apply equally to them. Both enjoy certain privileges conferred by statute, but for which their position in the eyes of the law would be prejudiced by the fact that they are, in the majority of cases, combinations "in restraint of trade," and as such not recognised by the courts.[1] When such combinations are "in restraint of trade," as a lawyer understands the term, agreements between an employers' combination and a workmen's combination, or between either and its own members, cannot be enforced at law, at any rate directly; thus, a member of a Trade Union cannot bring an action against the Union to recover benefits towards which he has contributed, nor can an Employers' Association bring an action against one of its members for violation of an agreement which is "in restraint of trade." Yet in actual fact these powerful organisations, whatever view the law may take of them, have become essential organs for the common regulation of industry and trade, and vital forces in the life of the nation. This being so, it would seem to be high time that they were in some way worked into the recognised framework of our social system, and given responsibilities corresponding with their power. The statutes by which Trade Unions are regulated, which range from the Trade Union Act, 1871, to the Trade Disputes and Trade Unions Act, 1927, need

[1] For a full explanation of the position see the Legal Appendix to Ramsay Muir's *Trade Unionism and the Trade Union Bill,* published for the Inquiry in 1927.

to be reconsidered and codified; and we suggest that a Commission, on which representatives of employers' and workers' organisations should be invited to serve, should be appointed to inquire into the whole problem.

8. Results of Collective Bargaining

The comparatively recent growth of these powerful organisations on both sides may be a force for good or ill according to the way in which they are used. At first sight it must appear ominous that Capital and Labour should thus stand facing one another in disciplined armies, as suspicious and as ready to take advantage of one another as the armed nations of Europe before the War and before the creation of the League of Nations; and still more perturbing that they should, like rival factions of barons in the Middle Ages, claim the right of private war, and wage their conflict over the prostrate and lacerated body of the community, which is impotent to stop their strife.

On the other hand, it is a sound and wholesome thing that the necessary co-operative factors in production should be so organised that they can deal with one another on equal terms; a good thing that labour should be able to make good its claim to a share in the regulation of the conditions of work; a good thing that the rates of wages and the conditions of work should be broadly regulated on a national scale for industries as a whole. No doubt it is unfortunate that this process of regulation should be carried on by means of trials of strength between highly organised rival forces in an atmosphere of mutual distrust, and often by open and wasteful warfare. But it is permissible to hope that this is only a painful stage in a healthy process of development, that conflict may be replaced by co-operation, and that "collective bargaining," which too often means a blind tug-of-war, may develop into "joint ascertainment," in the light of ample knowledge, of the wage-levels and other conditions which are best for the prosperity of all. To explore the possibilities of this development is the primary purpose of this part of our inquiry.

9. Progress towards Peaceful Settlement

Already, indeed, real advance has been made in several directions towards this end. To begin with, some of the major industries have succeeded in almost banishing strikes and lock-outs by the establishment of efficient systems of conciliation and arbitration, set up by agreement.

(*a*) In the *Iron and Steel* trades—a highly organised industry with a powerful industrial union—there has been no serious dispute for about fifty years. This is due to two facts: first, that both sides have agreed to revise wage-rates periodically according to the selling-price of the product, an arrangement which provides an agreed principle for the settlement of wage-questions, accepted beforehand: and, secondly, that a very complete system of arbitration and conciliation has been set up throughout the industry, under which every grievance is dealt with first at the works, and then in district bodies with a neutral chairman as umpire, whose decision is accepted as final.

(*b*) In the *Cotton* trade—a highly organised trade with a number of Craft Unions—the "Brooklands Agreement," reached after a strike in 1893, set up local and central joint committees to which all disputes were to be referred, and both sides pledged themselves not to cause a stoppage until this machinery had been fully used; though the Brooklands Agreement was terminated in 1913, it was replaced by other agreements of a similar kind. It was stated in 1923 that of 600 or 700 disputes which would normally take place in an average year, not more than twenty would get as far as the central committee, and not more than two or three would lead to temporary stoppages in individual mills.

(*c*) *The Boot and Shoe Trade.*—This is an outstanding example of what can be done by collective bargaining, and we deal with it here at some length in view of the special interest attaching to its provisions. After the lock-out in 1895 the terms of a settlement were agreed between the Employers' Federation and the National Union of Boot and Shoe Operatives, in which it was categorically stated that "No strike or lock-out shall be entered into," and £1,000 was deposited by each side with trustees to guarantee the due carrying out of the provisions of the agreement.

One interesting feature of the agreement is that the first three clauses dealt with piece-work statements, and provided for the setting-up of Local Boards of Arbitration and Conciliation, consisting of equal numbers representing the management and the workers respectively, to prepare such statements and keep them up to date. These statements are very elaborate, fixing rates for hundreds of operations for different classes of workers and necessitating constant meetings. For instance, the Kettering Board meets regularly once a month; once or twice a year they find a difficulty in agreeing and call in a local umpire. There is now a National Joint Standing Committee to whom, if necessary, an appeal can be made.

This habit of constant consultation has led to an attitude of mutual confidence, and so to discussion and agreement on a great variety of matters. The original 1895 agreement still stands; but its terms have been absorbed in the "National Agreement" which is arranged periodically at a National Conference presided over by an independent Chairman. The present Agreement, known as "The National Conference (September 1926) Agreement," runs till 1928. The 1895 agreement, which is regarded as the Charter of the Trade, is reprinted in full as an appendix to the National Agreement. The latter contains twenty-six new clauses dealing with many matters, of which we may mention three as of special interest:

1. A scheme for compulsory contributions from employer and worker to provide for annual holidays.

2. A clause which provides that there shall be no restriction of output. "It is understood that operatives use their trade skill and productive ability to the best advantage and to the fullest capacity provided they are paid a full rate of wages for all output."

3. A clause which stipulates that if any strike or lock-out shall last more than three days a claim may be made on the fund—

   (i) by way of fine or penalty;
   (ii) by way of damages or compensation for loss sustained.

Another important and suggestive factor is the belief of all parties in the industry that its welfare is best served by collective bargaining between two strong and fully representative organisations. This is emphatically set forth in the following resolution, passed originally in 1913, and reprinted with the Conference Agreement of 1926:

"For the more effective enforcement of any agreements, awards, or decisions, as well as for the general advantage of the industry, the Federation and the National Union equally recognise the importance of their respective organisations being as numerically strong and as fully representative as possible of employers and operatives in all centres of the shoe trade, and is of opinion that the best interests of the trade will be observed, if all manufacturers can be encouraged to join the Boot and Shoe Manufacturers' Federation and all operatives encouraged to join the National Union of Boot and Shoe Operatives."

This resolution is largely due to the fact that the employers' organisation only covers about 90 per cent. of the trade; it is said that 10 per cent., who remain outside, pay a lower wage and give worse conditions, and in this way cause very serious competition. Failing complete organisation, the industry is anxious to have compulsory powers to force these employers to observe the agreed conditions. On several occasions the industry has passed the following resolution:

"This National Conference again urges upon the Government the desirability of giving to national agreements voluntarily entered into and approved by Joint Industrial Councils the same validity as awards under the Trade Boards Act, with the object of ensuring the observance of fair conditions of labour, by all engaged in the industry, and requests the Government to give facilities for putting into law the Industrial Council Bill read a second time on 29th May, 1924."

Detailed procedure is laid down for dealing with disputes, which as a last resort are considered by the Local Board of Arbitration and Conciliation or, failing settlement there, by an Arbitrator or Umpire. The penalties imposed upon the Employers' Federation or the Operatives' Union are claimed before and assessed by an Umpire appointed for that purpose.

The success of the scheme may be judged from the fact recorded by the Balfour Committee that in the first twenty-five years fines were inflicted totalling only £838.

Practically speaking, there have been no strikes or lock-outs in the thirty-two years since the agreement was made, and it is clear that there has been a steady increase of co-operation between the two sides throughout the whole of this period, in spite of the extraordinary difficulties caused by war conditions. This is all the more important and reassuring in view of the fact that the boot and shoe trade is a highly competitive industry, subject to the full blasts of foreign competition.

(*d*) *The Railway Experiment.*—One other experiment calls for notice. In one of the most vital of all industries—the railways—a very complete system of consultation and discussion closely akin to the Whitley Scheme has been established under the Railways Act of 1921, and by agreement between the Companies and the Railways Unions. Conciliation machinery had been established in 1907, but as recently as 1913 the Railway Companies were refusing to have any dealings with the Unions. The change of outlook represented by this new system is therefore remarkable indeed. All questions of pay, hours, and conditions of labour are negotiated between district committees representing the two sides; national questions are negotiated by a committee on which both sides are represented. In the event of disagreement, the question at issue is referred to a Central Wages Board, consisting of an equal number of representatives from each side. From this body an appeal lies to the National Wages Board, in which six representatives from each side are joined by four representatives of the users of the railways under a neutral chairman appointed by the Ministry of Labour; and it is agreed that there shall be no stoppage until the National Wages Board has given its report, which must be within twenty-eight days.

All who have experience of the working of the National Wages Board agree that the presence of the five neutral members has been of real value in settling obstinate differences. This is a point of considerable importance, because most of the other major industries have hitherto strenuously resisted calling in a neutral element in this way. This rather elaborate conciliation machinery has the wholehearted support of the management and of the unions, and has on the whole worked exceedingly well.

Even more interesting has been the development of a complete system of co-operative discussion at every stage. Joint Local Departmental Committees representing groups of grades at every important centre discuss the convenient arrangement of working hours, holiday arrangements, rules, improvements in organisation, and obstacles to efficiency, and the best ways of handling traffic. Above these are Sectional Railway Councils, not more than five on each of the four big systems, which discuss the local application of national agreements, suggestions as to operation, methods of securing more business and greater efficiency or economy, the modes of recruitment to the staff, and the general well-being of the staff. Above these is a Railway Council for each system, consisting of ten representatives from each side. At present all these arrangements apply only to operating staffs; but similar machinery has lately been agreed for the workshop staffs and will shortly be in operation. Here is a complete system, not merely of "conciliation" when disputes arrive, but of co-operation which, if it works well, will utilise the hitherto wasted abilities of the staff, and give to the man of ability every opportunity of making his mark, not by creating trouble but by using his brains. Surely this system, made by agreement in one of the public services which has hitherto been much disturbed, affords evidence of the direction towards which our industrial system is tending.

10. A Habit of Consultation

The four examples we have given are encouraging evidence that in some parts of the industrial field there has been a strong and successful movement towards the organisation of peaceful modes of settlement. A settled habit of constant consultation between the management and the workers has grown up. They are learning to know and trust one another, and their negotiations, even when acute differences arise, are carried out in a friendly spirit, and with a background of mutual confidence.

It is only necessary to turn one's thoughts to the mining industry to realise how utterly collective bargaining has failed to achieve this result in certain cases. The industrial friction and strife which result are ruinously wasteful; they concern not only the two parties directly involved. The nation, represented by the State, forms a third party whose interests cannot be disregarded. No effort must be spared by the State in endeavouring to establish throughout industry the high standards which some industries have already succeeded in attaining for themselves. Accordingly we must next consider what part the State has taken, and is taking, in the promotion of industrial peace.

CHAPTER XV

THE STATE AND INDUSTRY

THERE are still many people who hold that the State ought not to "meddle with industry," or to intervene in any way in the conflicts between capital and labour, but should confine itself to holding the ring while the disputants fight out their differences. This is an untenable doctrine, which is quite out of relation with the facts. The State cannot look on indifferently while civil war rages between organised bodies of its citizens, for its primary function is to substitute the rule of reason and law for that of force. It exists to maintain peace, justice, and liberty for all its citizens, and this obligation does not cease in the sphere of industry. Accordingly, whatever statesmen might believe in theory, they have been forced by the pressure of events to intervene more and more actively in industrial matters. They have often acted reluctantly, taking out of the hands of industry the settlement of many important questions, simply because industry had no satisfactory machinery for settling them justly itself. This process has been going on for nearly a hundred years, and both of the older political parties have had a hand in it, though the Liberals have been incomparably the more active.

1. Legislative Intervention

At one point or another the State now deals directly in numerous instances with conditions of employment, with the hours of labour, with the determination of wage-rates, with the classification and selection of workpeople, with the training of recruits for industrial work, and with the maintenance of unemployed workers.

Conditions of Employment

State regulation of the conditions of labour has been mainly embodied in the long series of Factory Acts and Mines Acts.

The first of these to be effective was the Act of 1833, carried in the first year of the first Liberal Government. Its main provisions were taken over from Tory philanthropists who had failed to carry it in Tory Parliaments; but there was added a new provision creating a staff of factory inspectors, and this was what made the Act effective. Not only did the inspectors see that the Act was carried out; their reports showed the need for further provisions, and the Factory Code was in the main due to their suggestions. As the Factory Code expands and becomes more complex—and this must happen as mechanism develops—it is surely desirable that bodies of men possessing expert knowledge of the questions involved, from the point of view both of employers and of workpeople, should have some part (though not the final decisive voice) in framing these regulations. The factory legislation of the future, specialised to meet the special needs of different industries, must draw its ultimate sanction from Parliament, and be not only administered but often suggested by bureaucratic experience. But much of the work of adjusting it to the practical needs of industry ought to be entrusted to competent bodies representative of managers and workpeople.

Hours

State regulation of the hours of labour was begun in the early Factory and Mines Acts, primarily in regard to the labour of women and children, but the limitation of their hours brought with it also a limitation of the hours worked by men. In the main the regulation of hours has been determined by collective bargaining. But the pre-war Liberal Government legislated directly on the hours of labour in two industries—retail distribution in the Shops (Hours) Act, and mining in the Eight Hours Act. The State took action in the first instance because the workers concerned were unorganised, in the second instance because the feeling between employers and workers was so much embittered that no settlement by agreement was possible. Since the War the eight-hours day, or the forty-eight hours week, has been secured by means of collective bargaining practically throughout the range of British industry.

An attempt has been made in the Washington Hours Convention to extend this standard internationally, so as to prevent competition in working hours prejudicial to the worker. Great Britain has not yet ratified the Hours Convention, though some other countries have done so. The grounds given for our non-ratification are that the terms of the Convention, as drafted, are not sufficiently elastic, and do not allow for special conditions which exist in particular industries. In particular, (1) the method of regulating overtime prescribed by the Convention is less suitable to British conditions than that which in practice exists; (2) the provisions of the Convention are in contravention of those embodied in the Railways Act of 1921, though these latter equally secure the end in view; (3) the terms of the Convention would not, without adjustment, permit of the institution of a weekly half-holiday, practically universal throughout British industry. The whole system has been under continuous discussion for the last six years, in connection with which the admirable work of the International Labour Office is deserving of the highest praise, and agreement between Great Britain and other industrial powers upon the terms of a revised Convention ought not to be difficult. Such agreement ought to be strenuously pressed forward, as it is highly desirable that the principle of the 48-hour week should be safely established by the law of the land. Such a law would make the new standard safe against infringement. It would be an instance of what we conceive to be the right procedure under a rational system of industrial self-government. A standard is established by agreement after discussion, and it is then ratified and made legally enforceable by the sovereign authority of Parliament; but the detailed application of the principle to the conditions of particular industries should be left to their representative regulating bodies.

Wages

The determination of wage-rates is pre-eminently a subject for collective bargaining, and constant readjustment is needed as the conditions change through the introduction of new processes, the expansion and contraction of markets, and the rise and fall of prices or of the cost of living. But there are many minor trades so ill-organised that collective bargaining cannot take place. Here the unqualified dictatorship of the employer still survived, and the result was sweating. In 1909 the pre-war Liberal

Government introduced the Trade Boards Act to deal with this problem. The Act constituted a very striking new development of State action. In effect, the State set up machinery for the fixing of minimum wage-rates where lack of organisation deprived the worker of adequate protection, and for enforcing these rates by process of law: it was to be made an offence to pay less than the defined minimum. Collective bargaining has never been able to use such formidable sanctions for the enforcement of its decisions.

2. The Trade-Board System

The duty of fixing minimum wage-rates was entrusted to bodies in which the conditions of collective bargaining were as nearly as possible reproduced through the presence of equal numbers of employees and workpeople. But these representatives were nominated by the Government—at first by the Board of Trade, later by the Ministry of Labour. Where any organisation on either side existed in the trade, it was naturally invited to propose names; but the representatives were actually appointed by the Government, not by their trade organisation. Moreover, there were added a neutral chairman and other neutral members, nominated by the Government; and experience has shown, not only that the final decision has often rested with them, but that their presence has made the other elements more reasonable, both sides being anxious to win the neutral members to their side. The rates fixed by these Boards have to be approved by the Ministry of Labour, and a full opportunity is given to the trade to lodge objections. But once an order is issued, the rates become legally enforceable as if they had been laid down by statute. The employer who does not pay them may be prosecuted and fined; he may also be sued for arrears by the aggrieved workman. A staff of inspectors is maintained to see that the rates thus fixed are observed, and to initiate prosecutions where necessary.

It is essential that all parts of the industry, and not merely those represented by any organisations which may exist, should be represented; otherwise, for example, those elements in the trade which were situated in large towns would be able to fix rates unfavourable to competitors in country districts. This is why the Ministry keeps the ultimate appointments in its own hands. The presence of a neutral element also helps to secure justice, as between these competing interests, besides helping the two sides to come to an agreement. It is further necessary that the range to be covered by the decisions of a Board should be clearly defined. This task of demarcation presents many difficulties; but they have been successfully overcome by the staff of the Ministry.

In the first instance this striking new procedure was limited to trades in which wage-rates were "exceptionally low," and by 1914 only seven trades, covering 500,000 workers, had been brought under its scope. It was also restricted to the fixing of minimum rates, on the ground that Government interference was only justified by the social necessity of preventing sweating. From the first the system worked extremely well. It not only protected the workers, it protected the good employers against the bad; and instead of ruining the trades concerned, the enforced increase of their wages led to an improvement in efficiency both because the workers were more fit to work, and because the employer was forced to study the methods of production more closely in order to cover his costs. In 1918 the scope of the system was greatly extended. It was made applicable to any "unorganised" trade, and in two years no less than 28 Trade Boards, covering 1,000,000 workers, were established. Moreover, the Boards began to fix not only minimum rates, but standard rates throughout the industries affected; and it now became possible that a failure to pay not merely a subsistence wage, but a high rate, might be punished in the courts as a criminal offence—a thing which has never been possible in the most highly organised trades. In a modified form the system has also been applied to agriculture.

But with this exception, owing to a change in the attitude of the Government, no addition has been made to the number of Trade Boards since 1921. There are now Trade Boards in thirty-seven industries [1] covering 1,500,000 workers.

[1] Trade Boards are at present in existence in the following industries (date of establishment in brackets):

Aerated Water (1920)
Boot and Floor Polish (1921)
Boot and Shoe Repairing (1919)
Brush and Broom (1919)
Button Making (1920)
Chair (1910)
Coffin Furniture and Cerement Making (1919)
Corset (1919)
Cotton-waste Reclamation (1920)

Having regard to the immense difficulty of wage regulation since the War, we consider the Trade Board Acts to have been surprisingly successful and to be among the most beneficent measures of social reform ever introduced.

3. Fostering Industrial Self-Government

The State, then, has undertaken the task of industrial regulation in a great many spheres, instead of leaving it to industry itself. These interventions have been socially beneficial. But, in fact, the enlargement of the industrial functions of the State has been undertaken at every stage with reluctance; and while it has been taking place there has also been a steady movement of opinion towards the view that the voluntary organisation of industries for self-regulation offered the true line of advance.

It is instructive to trace the stages in the formulation, at first vague and dim, of this new conception of the organisation of industry. In 1891 a Royal Commission on Industrial Relations reported that voluntary action on the part of Capital and Labour in the creation of machinery for the settlement of disputes was the best line of advance, and that Government ought to assist this development by setting up a department to watch industrial issues, and to offer mediation when possible. The result was the passage of the Conciliation Act in 1896, which empowered the Board of Trade to undertake mediation work—a function transferred in 1917 to the Ministry of Labour, and performed with steadfast patience and a good deal of success.

Footnote (*continued*).

Dressmaking and Women's Light Clothing (1919)
Flax and Hemp (1920)
Fur (1919)
General Waste Reclamation (1920)
Hair, Bass, and Fibre (1920)
Hat, Cap, and Millinery (1920)
Hollow-ware (1914)
Jute (1919)
Lace (1910)
Laundry (1919)
Linen and Cotton Handkerchiefs, etc. (1920)
Made-up Textiles (1920)
Mantle and Costume (1919)
Milk Distributive (1920)
Ostrich Feathers, etc. (1921)
Paper Bag (1919)
Paper Box (1910)
Perambulators, etc. (1920)
Pin, Hook, and Eye (1920)
Rope, Twine, and Net (1919)
Sack and Bag (1921)
Shirtmaking (1914)
Stamped or Pressed Metals (1920)
Sugar Confectionery (1914)
Tailoring (1909 and 1919)
Tin Box (1914)
Tobacco (1919)
Toy (1920)

Whitleyism

In 1916, half-way through the War, when men were beginning to think of the work of reconstruction which awaited them when peace came, Mr. Asquith (then Prime Minister) appointed a Committee on Industrial Relations under the chairmanship of a Liberal member, Mr. J. H. Whitley (now Speaker). Its instructions marked a new conception of the industrial problem. It was instructed not merely to recommend methods of conciliating disputes, but "means for securing that industrial conditions . . . shall be *systematically reviewed by those concerned*." In accord with these instructions the Committee presented a report which gave the first clear outline of a reconstructed industrial system, based upon the co-operation of organised Labour and organised Capital.

A New Ideal of Industrial Organisation

It proposed the establishment, in every organised industry, of standing Joint Industrial Councils, composed of equal numbers from both sides, for "the regular consideration of matters affecting the progress and well-being of the trade, from the point of view of all those engaged in it." These Councils were to exist primarily not for the purpose of conciliation, but for the purpose of regular consultation and co-operation; and the kind of subjects they were to discuss were broadly indicated. They were to include:

(1) the better utilisation of the practical knowledge of the workpeople;
(2) the means of securing to workpeople a greater responsibility for determining the conditions of their work;
(3) the settlement of the general principles governing the conditions of employment;
(4) the establishment of regular methods of negotiation;
(5) methods of fixing and adjusting earnings, and of securing to the workpeople a share in increased prosperity;
(6) technical education and industrial research;
(7) the provision of facilities for inventions and improvements designed by workpeople;
(8) improvements of processes, machinery, and organisation;
(9) proposed legislation affecting the industry.

This embodied a new and more generous conception of the part which joint bodies might play in the regulation of their industries; and it was also recommended that a full system of district committees and works councils should be set up, all to be organised upon a half-and-half basis, though the precise relations between these various bodies were not clearly indicated.

In illustration of what the Committee had in mind, a short description may be given of one of the Councils which have been most successful in interpreting the ideas of the Whitley Committee.

The Printing Trades Joint Industrial Council

The Joint Industrial Council for the Printing and Allied Trades was set up in 1919 and consists of 70 members, 35 representing the two Employers' Associations, and 35 representing the seventeen Trade Unions concerned. The objects, as stated in the Constitution, are very similar to those suggested by the Whitley Committee, and set forth in detail above.

A great deal of the work of the Central Council is done through committees, of which there are nine, all of them joint with an equal representation of both sides.

The subjects with which these committees are concerned are as follows: General Purposes, Finance, Organisation, Conciliation, Health, Unemployment, Costing, Apprenticeship, and Betterment.

The *Organisation Committee* is responsible for the setting up of joint District Committees; a District Committee has now been organised in practically all large centres. The *Conciliation Committee* deals with all disputes referred to it by a District Committee or by the national negotiating bodies. Its findings do not bind the parties to a dispute, but they have only been disregarded in two cases out of forty dealt with in eight years. The *Costing Committee* has approved a costing system which is now generally in operation. The *Apprenticeship Committee* has prepared an agreed apprenticeship scheme, which has also received the Council's approval. The *Betterment Committee* aims at enlisting the co-operation of the workers in the sphere of production; it has under discussion such problems as piece-work payment, the reduction of costs, and the possibilities of profit-sharing.

The Whitley scheme represented an ideal for the better order which we all hoped was about to begin after the War. At first it was welcomed with great ardour, and travelling officers of the new Ministry of Labour went about the country stimulating the formation of Joint Industrial Councils. Before the end of 1921, seventy-four Industrial Councils had been set on foot. In some industries, notably printing, pottery, quarrying, and the electrical trades, the new system has worked well; there has been valuable discussion on many of the constructive issues suggested, which has genuinely increased mutual understanding and strengthened the sense of a common interest in the success of the industry. But, on the whole, the system has not justified the glowing hopes of its founders. Twenty-seven of the original seventy-four Councils have broken down altogether, and some of the others are in a comatose condition. It would be gravely misleading, however, to say—as is sometimes said—that the Whitley scheme has failed. In those industries in which the conditions were favourable, it has not only worked well, but has given birth to a new conception of what the co-operative regulation of industry may be.

The Successes and Failures of Whitleyism

It is important to understand the causes of the limited degree of success which has attended the Whitley scheme; for when these causes are understood, it becomes apparent that what has happened offers far more ground for hope than for discouragement.

(i) The experiment was launched at what was probably the most difficult possible moment—just at the end of the War, when everybody was cherishing fantastic and unrealisable expectations. Everywhere men were being captivated by the rosy haze of the Socialist mirage, whose insubstantiality had not yet been demonstrated; and the modest promises of Whitleyism seemed trivial in comparison. The new system had to establish itself during years of the fiercest industrial strife that this country has ever known; and it is fair to say that the Whitley industries were less affected by this strife than others. The surprising thing is, perhaps, that so many as forty-seven councils should have survived this ordeal.

(ii) The new system needed, during the years of its establishment, careful help and guidance by some central body representative of industry, especially to help it in overcoming the difficulty of demarcation between industries, and in adjusting the general scheme to the varying needs of different trades. During the first years the Ministry of Labour tried to perform this function, and a staff of local officers were active in stimulating the organisation of Councils. But this help was suddenly cut off when the Geddes Economy Committee applied its axe to the great departments.

(iii) The Councils were not endowed with any definite powers. So far as wage-agreements were concerned, they had neither more nor less than the old powers of collective bargaining: their conclusions depended for their validity upon the prospect of their being enforced by strike or lock-out, and there were no other means of enforcement. In regard to the new constructive themes which they were asked to discuss, this lack of power robbed them of much of their appeal to busy and practical men.

(iv) Finally, they lacked precise knowledge about the actual financial facts of the industries whose prospects they were called upon to consider. One or two of them tried to remedy this defect by calling upon firms in the industry to supply facts, which were collated by the secretary, and presented to the Councils in a generalised form. One has only to glance at the returns laid before the Council of the Wire Industry—showing the total capital invested in the industry, the total return upon it, the total cost of materials, the total outlay on wages, and so on—to realise that with such a body of material before it, the deliberations of an Industrial Council must assume quite a different character, more realist, more practical, more understanding. But few attempted this method, which cost a good deal of trouble; and in any case, there was no power to compel member-firms to make the necessary returns, which would be useless unless they were complete.

It is not surprising that, having to face all these difficulties, the Whitley Council experiment did not at once achieve complete success. The surprising thing is that it should have done as well as it has actually done.

4. Prevention and Settlement of Disputes

Besides encouraging industrial self-government, the State has set up central machinery for dealing with industrial disputes. The first successful step in this direction was the Conciliation Act of 1896. This marked a real advance in the two directions. It set up arbitration machinery which was purely voluntary; nobody was compelled to have recourse to it or bound to accept its decisions except as a matter of honour. In other words, Government machinery was set up which depended for its success upon goodwill, and from that date the system of arbitration has steadily gained public confidence, and has been able to render useful service.

Secondly, responsibility for dealing with certain Labour questions was laid upon the Board of Trade, who had to allocate the duties connected therewith to a suitable staff. In Sir William Mackenzie's words, "In retrospect we see that the important consequence of the Act was that under it a corner of a Government Department became concerned with industrial disputes as a matter of official duty, and what I may call the art of conciliation and arbitration began to develop. It became someone's 'job' to take a hand, from an imperial standpoint, and with the authority of the Government behind him, in a dispute, which was involving loss and public inconvenience." The department of the Board of Trade concerned reached, specially under Lord Askwith, a position of great importance and influence; the Act must certainly be accounted a success, though comparatively few cases were submitted to arbitration under it, the greatest number in any year being 99 in 1913.

The Ministry of Labour

The dual system of conciliation and of arbitration has continued. In 1917 the duties of the Board of Trade in this matter were handed over to the newly created Ministry of Labour.

The Ministry [1] performs four main functions:

(1) It administers the Unemployment Insurance Scheme, and the network of Labour Exchanges which cover the country.

[1] For our constructive proposals regarding the Ministry, see pp. 220 ff.

(2) It administers the Trade Boards Acts, sets up Trade Boards as required, provides them with secretarial aid, and issues Orders fixing wage-rates.

(3) Through the *Labour Gazette* and in other ways it provides statistical and other information bearing upon labour questions; but the main body of statistical material bearing upon the industry falls outside its scope.

(4) It maintains an Industrial Relations Section, which has officers stationed in the principal industrial centres of the country, whose duty it is to keep in touch with industry, to prevent disputes occurring, and to endeavour to compose them when they do occur. At the appropriate moment they may suggest reference to arbitration, though it is an accepted principle that this should not be done until the parties have found it impossible to agree otherwise, for voluntary agreement is always better than arbitration. Until 1921 this section was active in stimulating the formation of Joint Industrial Councils. Since then this has been impossible on account of the reductions of staff forced by the Geddes Economy Campaign.

The Industrial Court

One of the important results of the work of the Whitley Committee was the setting-up, under the Industrial Courts Act, 1919, of the Industrial Court. This is the first Permanent Arbitration Court set up in this country. It is presided over by a whole-time professional expert of high standing, who is assisted by a panel of chairmen, at present numbering three, and a panel of members, of whom at present there are nine. The chairmen and members (following the recommendation of the Whitley Committee) are "persons who have practical experience and knowledge of the industry, and who are acquainted with the respective standpoints of employers and workpeople." Cases may be heard before a single arbitrator, but normally the Court consists of the President (or one of the chairmen) sitting with two other members.

The wages system of the country is of the utmost complexity, and every change has reactions which can only be foreseen by experts. The most brilliant amateur, casually called in to deal with some technical wage problem, cannot possibly act with the wisdom of a permanent tribunal which is dealing every day with disputes covering an immense variety of trades.

The Court has dealt with over 1,000 cases, and its decisions have almost invariably been accepted by both sides. It must be remembered that recourse to it is purely voluntary, and that it can only continue to function so long as it gives satisfaction.

The suggestion has sometimes been made that such a Court might in course of time work out a body of principles in accordance with which disputes and differences can be decided, and so, in the phrase of Mr. Justice Higgins, add a "New Province to Law and Order." Sir William Mackenzie, for five years President of the Industrial Court, has put this possibility in the following words:

"We see in the Industrial Court something akin to the old Courts of Common Law. Their early decisions are decisions on particular facts rather than on principles of law, for the principles of law had hardly begun to be ascertained. Gradually settled principles emerge which to-day appear commonplace. The Common Law has had a slow and gradual growth, but it had a beginning; the authority for early decisions must have been nothing more than some principle springing from the general social conscience. It is a recognition of this fact which has led the Industrial Court to move considerably in advance of previous arbitration practice in this country. Its decisions are in the main reasoned decisions, sufficiently explicit to show by what considerations the Court has been moved. *In short, it has made a beginning in the task of laying down our corpus of industrial law.*"

Such a development, whatever its future, has not proceeded far as yet. A Court is, however, in a position to formulate in precise terms the custom of an industry and to crystallise agreement as it is reached. Moreover, the mere process of argument before a Court tends to strengthen the influence of reason and lessen the influence of mere force in industrial settlements.

If for any reason the parties to a dispute prefer it, they may, instead of going to the Industrial Court, go before a single arbitrator or before a special board of arbitrators appointed for the occasion. The Minister also has power to set up a special Court of Inquiry, with or without the assent of the parties, not to give a judgment, but to lay before the nation a full and unbiased statement of the whole case. It is, however, felt by those who share the views of Sir William Mackenzie that a temporary Court of this sort, set up under a Judge who does not know the conditions prevailing in the different industries, is apt to give decisions which will have unforeseen and undesirable repercussions on other industries.

5. Compulsory Arbitration

Encouraged by the success of the Industrial Court, some have urged that the State might proceed to establish a system of compulsory arbitration whereby all disputes not settled in the process of collective bargaining should be referred for judicial decision to a tribunal clothed with the State's authority, and empowered to enforce its decisions by pains and penalties. Important and valuable experiments in this direction have been made in Australia, New Zealand, and Germany. We have carefully studied these experiments, and have been forced to the conclusion that they cannot with advantage be imitated in this country, for the following reasons:

(1) Compulsory arbitration would not be an extension, but in some sense a reversal, of the policy which has been set up by the Industrial Court; for the essence of this policy is that resort to the Court must be voluntary, and it lays the utmost emphasis upon the importance of agreement between the two sides.

(2) No judicial system can work with general assent unless it administers a set of known and established rules, based upon generally accepted principles. We have already shown that no such principles can be defined as regards wage-levels in different industries. In these circumstances the decision of a Court could not be the application of an accepted rule; it would rather be an attempt to reach a workable compromise—that is to say, it would be conciliatory rather than judicial.

(3) It would often be difficult if not impossible to enforce an unacceptable decision upon powerful organisations covering whole industries. Neither side is yet willing to contemplate the complete abandonment of the right to strike

or to lock out which is implied in compulsory arbitration. Australian experience supports this conclusion. But if the system cannot be made fully compulsory, it is better to recognise this from the outset.

(4) An attempt to enforce arbitration might actually have the effect of diminishing the anxiety of the parties to come to an agreement, since they would know that in the last resort there would be a reference to the Court; and each side, convinced that it was right, would hope for a favourable decision. A further disadvantage of an Arbitration Court is that it is usually held in public, with the Press present, and that the advocates on both sides are therefore tempted to overstate their case, so as to make their supporters feel what a good fight they have made. This leads to the presentation of two extreme claims and makes the task of the arbitrator, in trying to arrive at the best result, much more difficult than that, for instance, of the chairman of a Trade Board, who can talk confidentially to the two sides in private. The general use of arbitration would tend therefore to weaken the sense of responsibility of the two sides, and retard the growth of industrial self-government by discussion and agreement.

For these reasons we conclude that it would be a mistake to resort to compulsory arbitration. We believe that the Industrial Court as it exists to-day is well adapted for the purpose both of a Court of Reference and perhaps of gradually building up a practical set of principles for the settlement of industrial disputes. But it cannot, by itself, provide a solution of the industrial problem. It is not by conciliation after disputes have arisen, but by the practice of discussion, the gradual formulation of principles, and the growing recognition of common interests, that health will be found. When the Court of last resort is constantly called into play, friction and disunity must be deep-seated; and it will be the best omen of industrial well-being when the Court is scarcely needed at all.

CHAPTER XVI

THE REMUNERATION OF THE WORKER

THE huge and complex machinery of collective bargaining which we described in the last two chapters is mainly used for fixing wages; and the friction and misunderstanding between management and labour, which so gravely restrict our productive power, mainly arise from differences about wages. Hence the primary purpose of any improved system of industrial relations must be to make agreement about wages easier. For that reason, before describing the reforms which we suggest, it is necessary to discuss, in some detail, the principles which ought to govern wage-adjustment. We do not propose to enter upon any elaborate analysis of the theory of wages, which is a highly technical branch of economic science, but to discuss, as broadly and clearly as possible, the practical considerations which ought to govern the process of wage-fixing, and which therefore ought to influence the structure and working of the bodies that carry on this process.

A. General Considerations

The Importance of High Wages.—It is a primary interest of the whole community, and not merely of the wage-earners themselves, that the general level of wages should be as high as possible; and the chief reasons for desiring industrial progress is that higher wages should be made possible in order that the general standard of life may be raised. Industry is not an end in itself; it exists in order to provide livelihood for the whole community, and livelihood is expressed, for the vast majority, in terms of wages or salaries. The claims of capital and labour, therefore, stand on quite a different footing. The social justification for giving an adequate return to capital is that unless this is done people will not save, there will not be a sufficient supply of new capital to meet the needs of industry, and therefore the livelihood (i.e. in the main, the wages) of the nation will suffer. The social justification for paying high wages is not merely that this will lead to better production, though it often does so; high real wages are an end in themselves, because high wages mean general well-being. Capital is a means to an end, and the end is the provision of livelihood. It is the best test of a sound industrial system that it should bring about a steadily rising level of wages while yielding a sufficient but not extravagant return to capital.

1. Mistaken Notions

On both sides in the argument mistaken notions are very prevalent, and it is the clash of these conflicting errors that is the chief cause of friction. Let us consider first the mistaken notions that are prevalent among employers, and then the mistaken notions that are prevalent among workpeople and their leaders.

The Employers' Fallacy.—It is often assumed by employers to be obvious that their interest must be for prices to be as high as possible and wages as low as possible. If that were so, their interest would be in direct conflict with that of the community as a whole, and with that of the workers in particular; these must both desire that prices should be low and wages high. When the matter is viewed from the standpoint of one employer alone and at a particular time, no doubt there is such a conflict; if prices were suddenly to rise or wages to fall he would profit, and if the opposite were to occur he would lose. But from the standpoint of the employing class as a whole, and over a long period of time, the case is different. Since the wage-earning classes form the great majority of the purchasing public in the home market, the higher the general level of their wages and the more they have to spend, the better it is for trade, and therefore for the employers. And the lower prices can be kept, while still returning a profit, the wider, again, will be the manufacturer's market, both at home and abroad. The true interest of the employer, therefore, is to combine a policy of high wages with one of low costs, and this can only be achieved by securing the efficiency of his own organisation and by fostering the efficiency of labour. The immense prosperity of American industry is largely due to the fact that, in many fields, it has succeeded in reconciling these two factors which appear to be incompatible: it has raised wages and lowered prices simultaneously.

When British employers set themselves, as a matter of deliberate policy, to keep wages at the highest practicable level, and when they are able to prove to their workers (as they will have every motive for doing) that they are really pursuing this aim not for philanthropic but for business reasons, one of the chief obstacles in the way of mutual understanding and co-operation will have been removed. For both sides will be striving after the same thing—high wages.

The Workers' Fallacy.—The mistaken notion which is most prevalent on the side of labour is that labour can only improve its position at the expense of capital, and that all the advances which it has been able to secure have in actual fact been won by means of the belligerent action of the Trade Unions. Behind this idea lurks the half-defined theory that there is only a permanently fixed amount of wealth to divide, and that there must always be a tug-of-war between labour and capital to decide which is to get the better share of it; whereas it is nearer the truth to say that the amount available depends upon how much can be drawn out of the well, so that if, instead of pulling against one another, all hands were pulling on the rope together, the amount available might be almost indefinitely increased. The notion that labour can only advance at the expense of capital is very widely held, not by workpeople only. But it is quite incorrect, and is contradicted in the most striking way by the facts of history. It is worth while to dwell briefly upon these facts, because they are very illuminating.

2. Why Wages Have Risen

Sir Josiah Stamp has shown that during the nineteenth century the real wages of the workers were on the average quadrupled—their money-wages being roughly doubled, while the purchasing power of the pound was also doubled. This is a generally accepted fact: Mr. William Graham, for example, who is one of the ablest economists of the Labour Party, accepts it as established in his book on wages. But it was not only wages that rose. All incomes rose, in roughly the same proportion. Therefore the increase in wages cannot have been at the expense of other sections of the community.

Nobody, of course, can doubt that the steady pressure of the Trade Unions has very greatly contributed to improve the position of the workers, and to secure for them, not only in better wages, but in greater leisure and in better provision against insecurity, an ampler share in the growing wealth of the nation. But the improved wages have not been primarily, or even mainly, due to the work of the Trade Unions. They could have achieved very little if the wealth of the nation had not been increasing; and the primary cause of the rise of wages has been an increase of efficiency in the production of wealth.

This conclusion is forcibly borne out by the history of wage-movements during the last hundred years. It is unnecessary to trace the story in detail. But broadly it may be said that real wages, measured by their purchasing power, advanced steadily and rapidly during the greater part of the nineteenth century; and that, in the last years of that century and during the year preceding the War, the rate of advance slowed down until it became almost stationary. In the first of these periods Trade Unionism was weak: it was not legalised until 1871, and at that date did not count more than 400,000 members. On the other hand, the productive capacity of British industry was growing very rapidly during that period, and its markets were expanding. In the second period, when the advance of wages was slowing down, Trade Unionism was growing very rapidly, and was pursuing a belligerent policy: its membership exceeded 2,000,000 on the eve of the War. On the other hand, during this period British industry was faced by intense foreign competition, and was in many fields showing less alertness and efficiency than some of its rivals, one reason for this being, perhaps, that labour and capital, instead of pulling together, were pulling against one another. In other words, the rate at which wages increase has been found to depend in prime degree upon the standard of our efficiency in producing wealth, and only in the second degree upon the strength or weakness of Trade Unionism.

During the War conditions were so abnormal that no inferences as to normal development can be drawn from it. The War undoubtedly brought about a great increase in our productive capacity in many important industries; and this might have been expected to lead to a substantial improvement in the level of wages. What has actually happened? The hours of labour have been greatly reduced, and in some "sheltered" trades and many unskilled occupations real wages have been substantially increased. On the other hand, real wages have fallen definitely below pre-war levels in some of the biggest industries, and for seven consecutive years we have had at least a million unemployed, as well as a vast deal of short time. On the average, real wages appear to be slightly better than before the War; but the movement has been very unequal in various trades. Trade Unionism has been far more powerful and far more belligerent than in any previous period of its history; yet all its efforts have failed to achieve for labour an improvement of wage-rates equivalent to our increased capacity for producing wealth. The reason is that we have been faced by exceptional difficulties in foreign trade, and that these difficulties have been gravely increased by the waste due to industrial friction at home.

3. High Wages Dependent on Efficiency

The moral of this story stands out very clearly. It is that the level of wages depends upon (*a*) our efficiency in production, and (*b*) our ability to find markets for what we produce. When our productive power was increasing rapidly and our markets were expanding, wages rose rapidly, even though Trade Unionism was weak. When our progress in efficiency slowed down or our markets were restricted, wages rose slowly or remained stationary, however strong and active Trade Unionism might be; and one of the causes of inefficiency and of loss of markets has been industrial strife. In so far as the Trade Unions can make sure of an increase in our productive efficiency—and they can certainly help in this—they can also make sure of advancing wages; otherwise, not.

From these broad facts some may be tempted to draw two quite illegitimate conclusions. They may think these facts go to prove that Trade Unionism has failed; and they may think that, in practice, capital does not obtain more than its fair share. Neither of these conclusions follows.

4. Trade Unions and Efficiency

Trade Unionism is indispensable as a means of ensuring that the workers are fairly treated. It is, as we have seen, invaluable for the smooth working of big-scale industry. But, more than that, it has contributed very greatly, and it can contribute even more, to the forwarding of efficiency in production, which is the source of rising wages. It is a good thing for industry that there should be a steady pressure for increased wages, because this stimulates management to improve its efficiency. The pressure of the Trade Unions has in England played the part which in America has been played by the shortage of labour and the high price which it is therefore able to command; it has forced employers to seek for means of cheapening production and avoiding waste, when, if they had been free to do so, they might have taken the easier but retrograde method of keeping down wages. It is to be hoped, not merely for the sake of the workers but for the sake of industry, that this pressure for higher wages will never cease, though it may well take more constructive forms. It is more needed now than ever, because big combinations have diminished the fierceness of competition, which used to be the main stimulus to efficiency.

But the Trade Unions can make an even more direct contribution than this; and some Unions, especially in America, have found an extremely effective way of doing it. Thus the Amalgamated Clothing Workers of America demand very high wages, but, recognising that these can only be paid with a high rate of output, they undertake to ensure this rate. They deliberately accept a share of responsibility for productive efficiency. If an employer says he cannot pay the rates demanded, they reply that they will show him how it can be done; and they maintain experts for the purpose. In this way they have immensely improved the wages of their members in the only possible way—through increased efficiency; and they have at the same time greatly increased their own influence and power.

5. The Share of Capital

A second invalid inference which might be drawn from the facts we have stated is that capital does not in fact receive more than its necessary return. No such statement can legitimately be made, because nobody can define, in general terms, what is the "necessary" return on capital. Capital will not be forthcoming for any enterprise unless it can expect (*a*) a normal rate of interest such as is paid on Government securities, and (*b*) in addition to that a "risk-rate" corresponding to the chance of loss in the particular business; and this risk-rate must vary according to the conditions of every industry and of every concern. There is a great deal to be said for the proposition that, when capital has received a fair return, corresponding with its risks, the balance of the product of their industry should belong to those who have been actively engaged in creating it. The structure of many industrial companies, in which preference shares are held by investors whilst the ordinary shares are retained by those running the business, has been an unconscious preparation for such an arrangement. On the other hand, the tendency of the moment to issue to investors deferred shares of nominal value, which are, in fact, counters with which they may gamble on the effort of others, is wholly vicious, and will, if it continues unchecked, make the task of the reformer difficult indeed. In any event, no rational adjustment of return between investor, manager, and worker can be made until we know whether, over the whole field of industry, capital receives more than is necessary to attract it; and the facts are not available. We know that in some trades, and in some businesses, capital gets a good or even a rich return; that in others it often gets little or nothing; and that in many cases it is totally lost. We know that to-day, in the industries where wages are lowest, the return on capital is so low that it is obviously out of the question to increase wages at the expense of the return on capital.

It is essential that we should have ampler knowledge of the return which capital receives, over industries as a whole. If this knowledge, which neither employers nor workers possess, was available, the process of wage-adjustment would often be far simpler. It would be possible to tell whether a proposed increase of wages could be taken out of profits, or whether it would involve an increase of prices with the consequence of a decrease of sales and a growth of unemployment; and the two parties would then be more ready to consider whether the desired end might not be met by an increase of efficiency, to which both of them could contribute. For this reason we attach very great importance to the proposals for securing greater publicity about the facts, which we make in other parts of this Report (see pp. 218 and 235). Until this knowledge is available, labour will continue to believe that capital on the average gets more than its "fair share," i.e. more than is sufficient to attract it into industry.

It is right that the spokesmen of labour should be anxious to prevent capital from taking more than its "fair share" (whatever that may be). But even if this happens, the gain that labour can make by depriving capital of its surplus is far less than the gain to be made from increased efficiency. For in many industries the total profits are so small in comparison with the total wage-bill that if excessive profits were divided among the whole body of workers, they would spread very thin.

We return, then, to the conclusion that high wages are dependent first and foremost upon productive efficiency, to which both employers and workers can and ought to contribute. But full efficiency is itself dependent upon justice. It is impossible to get whole-hearted effort from men unless they are satisfied that they are getting a "square deal"; and they will never be so satisfied unless they are consulted, and acquainted as fully as possible with the facts. It is not even enough that the wage-system should be just in itself; it must be visibly and demonstrably just. And this conception ought to inspire the whole system of wage-negotiation.

B. The Elements of a Sound Wage-System

If a wage-system is to give full satisfaction to the desire for justice, it ought to include three elements:

(i) A recognition of the human need of the worker, by providing that no worker shall be paid less than will suffice to maintain himself and his dependants in decency and comfort.

(ii) A recognition of the worker's effort and capacity, by providing that the wage, above the minimum, shall be graded according to the effort and skill required, and shall, so far as possible, enable extra effort to earn extra reward.

(iii) A recognition of the worker's interest in the concern

for which he works, by providing that he shall receive a share of its prosperity, to which he can, in his degree, materially contribute.

We shall discuss these three elements in turn, under the titles of the Minimum Wage, the Standard Wage, and Profit-sharing.

1. The Minimum Wage

It is now an established principle of public policy that no worker ought to be paid less than a "living wage," though a "living wage" is not easily defined. If industry cannot itself achieve this, the State takes up the task; and the Trade Board system which has been already described (p. 169 above), was set up for this purpose. The minimum defined by a Trade Board is enforceable by law, and any employer who cannot pay it must go out of business. In actual fact the industries concerned have succeeded in adjusting themselves to the new wage-scales by making themselves more efficient.

There are many who hold that we ought to define by law a national minimum below which no man's wage shall be allowed to fall. The Independent Labour Party has taken up this idea as a means of attaining "Socialism in Our Time." It proposes that every industry should be required to pay a minimum wage which its popular propaganda fixes at £4 a week, and that every concern failing to do so should be taken over by the State. There are two main reasons why this proposal is utterly impracticable. In the first place, if every member of the occupied population received £4 a week at the present value of money, more than the whole national income would be swallowed up. In the second place, the State would have to take over at once all the least prosperous and worst-run concerns, and, even if this sudden change did not lead to any decrease of efficiency, there would be a colossal budget deficit, which would have to be met by the other industries, through taxation. Thus burdened, they would, of course, be unable to carry on and would soon fall below the line, and be in their turn taken over by the State. In a very short time each industry would be run at a loss, which would have to be met by the other industries—also running at a loss! It would be very desirable so to improve the national production and distribution that even the worst-paid workers might receive £4 per week; nor is such a figure beyond the bounds of hope for the future. But obviously the improvement must come first. It is an imposture to pretend that the procedure can be reversed.

Such proposals need not be taken seriously, but they help to illustrate the difficulty of the universal minimum wage. If such a wage was fixed too high, it would ruin many industries; if too low, it would have no effect. It is unfortunately very difficult to attain a minimum of even 30*s.* or 32*s.* in agriculture. But what would be the use of a minimum at that level in London? On the other hand, a minimum that would represent any real improvement in London would throw almost the whole agricultural population out of work, and turn most of the land into prairie.

The only satisfactory way of dealing with the problem of the minimum is the way which has already been adopted—that of tackling it industry by industry, having regard to what is practicable in each case, but stimulating a steady upward pressure. The Trade Boards, however, which alone have the necessary powers, do not cover the ground. We therefore recommend elsewhere (p. 211) that the Trade Board system should be extended as may be necessary; and we also recommend (p. 212) that in every industry the negotiating bodies should be expected to define minimum rates below which no one should be employed, and should be empowered, under proper safeguards, to obtain legal enforcement for these decisions.

Family Allowances

When we face squarely the problem of the minimum or living wage (which is based upon the "human needs" of the worker and his dependents) we come up against the difficulty of determining how many dependents the minimum wage ought to be expected to provide for. It is usually assumed that the wage should be sufficient for the needs of a "normal family," consisting of a man, his wife, and three children. Only a small fraction of workers, however, have precisely four people dependent upon them, and there are a good many who have more. The minimum wage which would be adequate for the few "normal families" would be more than adequate for smaller families, and less than adequate for larger families. When a Labour Government in Australia proposed to establish a national minimum on the assumption that every worker had a normal family (it was calculated, on the basis of Australian standards and costs, at £5 16*s.* 6*d.* a week), the Government statistician reported that this would require more than the total national income. Miss Eleanor Rathbone has shown that the same result would follow in England; and Mr. Paul Douglas has shown that even the superior wealth of America would be insufficient.

To get over this difficulty it has been suggested (and the proposal has been successfully tried in several continental countries) that employers, after the payment of a basic wage to all employees, should pay a fixed sum weekly for every employee into a pool, which should then be divided out among those employees with dependents according to the number of dependents for whom they are responsible. In effect this would mean that employees, at a time when they have no family responsibilities, would make some sacrifice of wage in order to help to support the children of their married comrades. Even those who accept the doctrine "from each according to his ability, to each according to his need," might hesitate about this practical application of their creed. Nevertheless it presents the most feasible way of providing for family needs, while still leaving a margin for the reward of special ability and effort. From another angle the proposal means that the loss of wages which the employee without dependents suffers is a compulsory saving or postponement of wages against the time when he has a family and needs a supplement to his standard wages. Alternative modes of meeting the need might be found (*a*) in an adaptation of social insurance for this purpose, and (*b*) in a system of direct State grants to children. The latter method is excluded, as things now are, by the enormous burden it would throw upon the Exchequer; while the former would involve an inopportune increase in the contributions payable by employers and employees. If the need of family maintenance, which is the heart of the living-wage problem, is to be met, it can probably only be by a system of pools including whole industries. The Coal Commission recommended this method to the attention of the coal industry. We think that it might be tried in selected industries as one way of raising wages when prosperity is increasing, so that no actual reduction of wage would be involved; and we recommend that the negotiating bodies in the various industries should be asked to study the proposal in the light of their own conditions.[1]

2. Standard Wages

In fixing minimum wage-rates, the governing consideration must be the human needs of the worker and of those dependent upon him. But in fixing wages above the minimum a different principle comes into play, and the primary consideration is the amount of skill and intelligent effort demanded from the worker. Accordingly, in all industries, wages are elaborately graded, and it is universally assumed that a man's wage ought to correspond with the skill which his job demands; this is equally true whether the payment is measured by the amount of time occupied or by the amount of work done. But in the application of this principle there are necessarily great difficulties, especially when the methods of production are constantly changing; and here lies the whole complexity of wage-negotiation. The difficulties are of two kinds: first, the adjustment of the wages as between man and man (or job and job) in the same industry; and secondly, the maintenance of a reasonable parity between jobs demanding comparable skill in different industries.

One of the most obvious difficulties arises from the incessant improvement of processes and introduction of labour-saving machinery, which is essential to advance in efficiency. The prime object of all such improvements is to reduce the cost of production so that the goods may be sold at a lower price, and the market for them be enlarged. If this does not happen—that is to say, if the main benefit of the change does not accrue to the consumer directly or indirectly—the net result must be a diminution of the amount of labour employed. On the other hand, the immediate result must usually be, not only that less labour is required, but that the degree of skill demanded from

[1] The case for family maintenance is forcibly presented in *The Disinherited Family*, by Miss E. F. Rathbone, and in the literature of the Family Endowment Society. *Family Allowance in Practice*, by H. H. R. Vibart, is a study of continental schemes in operation. Professor Gray's *Family Endowment : a Critical Analysis*, and an article by Professor Macgregor on Family Allowances in the *Economic Journal* for March 1926, should also be consulted.

the worker is reduced; and on this ground he may be pressed down to a lower wage-rate. This being so, it is not surprising that organised labour is slow to encourage improvements of this kind, and often puts obstacles in their way. Plainly, the constant adjustments of wage-rates thus rendered necessary ought not to be made with a high hand, but should result from reasonable discussion, and the conduct of these discussions is among the essential services which the Trade Unions can render. The only basis upon which such discussions can lead to good results is that it should be assumed on both sides: (1) that the main result to be aimed at is to keep down the price to the consumer, in order that an enlarged market may bring about the re-employment of displaced labour; and (2) that the workers actually employed should have, as a result of the change, a fair chance of increasing their earnings, or, at the least, of avoiding a reduction which they might otherwise have to face. Only on such an assumption can it be expected that there will be effective co-operation in the pursuit of efficiency.

Time-rates and Piece-rates

The majority of workers are paid at flat time-rates; and this must necessarily be the case wherever work is intermittent in character or not repetitive, or where output is not measurable or depends mainly upon factors outside the worker's control. Time-rate payment has this drawback, that the abler or quicker worker cannot get any advantage from his superior skill or energy; and that, both for this reason and also because he does not want to "show up" his slower comrade, he is tempted to reduce his rate of working. This tendency is, of course, adverse to efficient output, which demands rather that the slower worker should be encouraged to emulate his quicker comrade, so far as this can be done without strain.

The readiest way of meeting this difficulty is by some form of payment on results, of which the most direct is piece-work payment. In some great industries, such as cotton, boots and shoes, iron and steel, and coal-hewing, the piece-work system is thoroughly established, and neither employers nor workers would willingly abandon it; though even in these industries there are many workers on time-rates, and sometimes the piece-worker has assistants whom he himself pays at time-rates, not always too generously. These, however, are industries in which not only is the amount of work done by each man easily measurable, but the methods of work are so uniform that it is possible to fix piece-work lists by negotiation for whole districts, or even for the whole industry. Where such conditions exist, and the trade is well enough organised to be able to enforce the agreed rates, the objections to piece-work disappear.

But there are other industries in which general or district piece-rates cannot be adopted, though piece-work can be applied in the individual shops. The outstanding example is engineering, where designs differ in every shop, and lists common to a number of shops are impossible. In these cases the rates have been fixed by the employer, and varied by him at his discretion. Too often where the employer has thought that the men were earning too much, the rates have been arbitrarily cut. It is not surprising that the workers should have come to regard piece-work as a method of speeding up work without adequate remuneration, and that many of the Trade Unions should have set their faces against the system. Latterly the majority of employers have begun to recognise the folly and injustice of such practices. They have learnt that success in a piece-work system depends upon winning the confidence of the men, that if they earn a large wage they will be allowed to keep it, and that the rates will not be revised without very good reason and only after full and open consultation with their representatives. Processes are constantly being improved and better plant installed, and for these reasons it is essential that there should be means of revising rates; but it is equally essential that this should be done in consultation, with all the facts and the time-study figures on the table. When these conditions are observed, individual piece-work may work as well as piece-work settled on district-rates; and in actual fact there has recently been a great increase in piece-work in the engineering trade, where the objections have hitherto been very strong. We are, however, still far behind America in the extent to which piece-work is employed. There seems to be no reason why there should not be an extension of the system also in other trades; the one essential condition is that there should be an accepted and trustworthy system of negotiation, frankly and honestly worked. Upon this depends the possibility of any large expansion not only of piece-work but of other methods of payment by results; efficiency depends upon co-operation.

The unfair use made of the system by many employers is not, however, the only reason for the hostility to it which the workers have hitherto displayed in many industries. They feel that it may lead to scamped work, and there are cases in which this fear is justified. They fear that harder work may lead to a reduction of the amount of available employment; the argument is economically unsound, but it is natural, and it is inspired by good motives. Above all, perhaps, there is a feeling that piece-work introduces the wrong kind of appeal, stimulating, not team-work, but jealousy and rivalry between man and man; and this is a feeling which deserves respect, especially from those who recognise that one of the highest tasks of good management is the encouragement of the team-spirit.

In the hope of meeting these difficulties, some fruitful experiments have been made in the way of what may be called "collective piece-work," whereby a group of workers, whose jobs are closely related to one another, are guaranteed their regular time-rates but are promised, over and above these, an agreed share of the costs they may save by producing a given amount of work in a shorter time than that normally allowed to it. This system, which is known as the "fellowship bonus" system, involves very careful calculations, in all of which the men must be fully consulted and satisfied. But it has the merit that it evokes the team-spirit; the workers stimulate one another while co-operating with one another, and feel that they are gaining not at their comrades' expense but by their comrades' aid. To achieve such an end is worth an infinity of trouble. Here, again, intimate and open consultation is the only way to success. This method has the further advantage that it can be applied in many cases where "straight" piece-work is wholly or partially impracticable.

Increases in individual output and higher efficiency throughout an enterprise are, however, by no means necessarily dependent upon the immediate weekly incentive of a system of direct payment by results. Indeed, where there are strong social or economic objections to it on the part of the workers—even if these objections are not wholly sound—insistence upon it may actually lower the level of efficiency. Many other motives besides the thought of the week's pay impel workers to do their best—pride of craftsmanship and the desire for recognition as good workmen being among them. It is the function of good management to mobilise these motives; and when this is done, and every improvement in output is promptly and generously recognised by advances in time-rates, the results obtained will in many cases be fully commensurate with those obtained under a direct piece-rate incentive. But here again, success must depend upon the creation of mutual confidence, and the establishment of a conviction that the workers are regarded and treated not as tools but as partners; and this can only be done by means of accepted machinery of co-operation, such as we shall describe in later chapters.

Wages in Different Industries

So far we have been considering wages within single industries; and the conclusion is justified that by a proper grading of jobs according to their difficulty, and by the application, in frank consultation, of methods of payment which will make reward correspond with effort, it should be possible, though not easy, to arrive at a just wage-system. Indeed, in the majority of organised industries, there is already an approximation to such a system.

But when we come to consider the level of wages between one industry and another, we find a very different state of affairs. Whereas in pre-war days there was some approximation to a standard level of wages for a job requiring a given amount of skill, that is no longer the case. Since the boom in 1920, the sheltered trades have retained their high wages, whereas wages in the staple export trades have been forced down by competition, until we have a condition of affairs which is chaotic and indefensible. It is only necessary to consider the wages in the engineering and building trades respectively. In order to eliminate any question of skill, let us take the case of the labourer. The same man, working in the same engineering works, may one week be carrying bricks for a bricklayer, in which case he gets £3 a week, and the next week be carrying iron for a fitter, for which the wage is £2 a week. Bitter complaints are made that the skilled engineer, who, with a wage of 57*s*. for a 47-hour week, is struggling to maintain our export trade in machinery against the German engineer with wages of £2 for a 52-hour week, is hampered in the struggle by high local rates and high railway freights, owing partly to the high wages of the sheltered trades, railways, and municipal services. The situation is a serious one; if it lasts long enough some of our greatest industries will lose many of the skilled men upon whom their hopes of recovery must depend.

The level of wages in each industry is determined mainly by the price at which it can sell its goods; engineering, for instance, is keenly competitive with engineering in Germany, where a fitter is only paid £2 a week. Although, as we have already said, such differences are indefensible on any principle of a "fair or just" wage, there seems at the present time to be no remedy. Any attempt to increase the engineer's wages up to the level of those of a bricklayer would certainly result in enormous unemployment for engineers and in complete disaster to the trade. Any attempt to reduce the wages of the bricklayer would meet with the full resistance of the building Trade Unions, nor would public opinion be in favour of any such reduction. We must therefore face the fact that at the present time any "just" level of wages in the sense that a job of a given difficulty should be paid a given wage is out of the question. All that is possible is to work gradually towards it.

In the unsheltered trades, management and labour, forgetting their mutual suspicions, must explore every means of getting rid of obstacles to efficiency, in order that they may regain as much as possible of their trade, and raise their wage-levels; they are already doing so, for example, in shipbuilding. On the other hand, the sheltered trades must recognise that if any trade cannot render its service or supply its goods at prices which correspond with the current purchasing power of the community, it will sooner or later suffer, either because the demand will shrink or because alternative methods will come into existence. This is already happening in some degree in the case of the railways and in the case of the building trade. The only way of averting this danger is that the sheltered trades should use every effort so to increase their efficiency that the services they render or the goods they supply shall be at least as cheap as they used to be, relatively to the purchasing power of the community.

So far as practicable, we think that the Government should constantly use its influence towards the maintenance of a reasonable parity between the wages for occupations of comparable skill. For this reason we recommend in another chapter that the Council of Industry, a body representative of industry as a whole, shall keep this problem under continuous review, and make reports thereon for the consideration of the negotiating bodies in the various industries.

3. Profit-sharing

The third element in a sound system of remuneration for the worker ought to be a variable element, dependent upon the prosperity of the concern in which he is employed. It should be an addition to, and in no degree a substitution for, his agreed standard wages; and should consist of a share of residual profits after capital has received a fair return, proportionate to the risks it has to run. "Profit-sharing" is the accepted term for this element in remuneration. The term is sometimes loosely used. We confine it here to cases in which employees receive, as contributors of labour and not of capital, a share of profits fixed in advance, and based upon their labour contribution.

This element in remuneration has hitherto been little used, though much discussed. In the last year for which full figures are available (1925), only 252 firms in this country had profit-sharing schemes in operation, and the number of workpeople benefiting was only 161,000, or about 1 per cent. of the working population. In our view it is of the highest importance that the system should be made general throughout the field of industry. We believe that this would constitute a contribution of great value to the solution of our industrial problems.

This belief is not based upon any assertion of abstract right, which is always inconclusive. Thus the statement that capital has a "right" to the whole product of industry after labour has received its agreed wages seems to us as unconvincing as the counter-claim that the workers have a "right" to the whole product of their labour. The only sound criterion is social utility. Social utility demands that capital should obtain a reward proportionate to its risks and sufficient to attract an adequate supply of new capital for the needs of industry. But social utility seems to us equally to demand that, when capital has received an adequate return, the worker should enjoy a share of any surplus profits in order that he may have a personal interest in the concern for which he works, and feel that he is treated as a partner and not merely as a tool.

The Purposes of Profit-sharing

It is important to be clear as to the purposes which a sound system of profit-sharing ought to be expected to serve, for misconceptions on this head have often led to unreasonable disappointment and to the abandonment of promising schemes. In the first place, it ought not to be the sole aim of a profit-sharing scheme to bring about increased output on the part of each individual worker, though it should undoubtedly tend to have this effect. But a yearly or half-yearly bonus or dividend, often small in amount, is too remote and precarious to be a constant and direct inducement to effort, which is better achieved by some system of payment by results that will immediately show itself in the weekly wage. Nor should profit-sharing be expected to provide a large addition to the worker's income. The existing schemes in this country yielded, in 1924, an average annual return of £9 13*s.* 4*d.* per head, which was equivalent to 5 per cent. on the wages of the beneficiaries; and although an annual bonus of nearly £10 is not a negligible thing for a working man, it is a small matter in comparison with his main wage. From the point of view of income, the worker will always, and rightly, prefer a rise of wages to a share of profits if these are regarded as alternatives.

The real purpose of profit-sharing, in conjunction with the system of organised consultation which is described in the following chapters, is to show that the worker is treated as a partner, and that the division of the proceeds of industry is not a mystery concealed from him, but is based upon known and established rules to which he is a party. If this end is to be secured, it is obviously essential (1) that the amount of the bonus should not depend upon the will of the employer, but should be determined by a scheme settled beforehand and clearly understood; and (2) that the workmen entitled to benefit under the scheme should be given access to such financial data as will show that it has been carried out. When this is done, the primary purpose of a true profit-sharing scheme will be fulfilled even if there are no profits to divide.

We have been impressed by the testimony on this point of a large employer who shared in our deliberations. When there was a good bonus, he said, the workers were apt to be content, without further inquiry—like shareholders in a similar case. But when there were no profits to divide, they were eager to know the reason why, and listened with keen and critical attention to the statement on the financial condition of the business which he always felt it his duty to put before them. In other words, they felt that the prosperity of the business was their concern, and not merely the employer's concern; and the effect of this feeling in improving relations and making real co-operation possible was marked. Moreover, when the divisible profits are small or non-existent, it becomes obvious that not much can be gained for labour by reducing the remuneration of capital, but that the true path to a better return for both sides is to be found in an increase of efficiency; and this makes it easier to organise a co-operative attack upon waste of time or materials, or to introduce mechanical improvements, with general agreement. Improved efficiency may make a rise of wages possible, and may therefore lead to no increase in the distribution of profits; nevertheless the profit-sharing system will have created the conditions which make this advance possible.

It is essential for the success of profit-sharing that it should be generally realised that its primary object is not to bring about an increase of output per head, nor to increase directly the worker's remuneration (though both of these aims may be incidentally attained), but to improve industrial relations by making it clear that the product of industry is divided on known and established principles, and thus to facilitate co-operation in the pursuit of efficiency.

Failures and Successes

It is because many employers have not grasped this essential principle that the schemes they have designed have often failed. They have looked for results which profit-sharing cannot reasonably be expected to yield; indeed some profit-sharing schemes have been started for quite illegitimate reasons, such as a desire to undermine the loyalty of the workers to their Trade Unions, or to persuade them to rest content with relatively low wages. The fact that these motives are sometimes present, and are suspected even where they do not exist, explains the general hostility of Trade Unions to the system of profit-sharing.

Unsound aims and unreasonable expectations on the part of some employers who have experimented with profit-sharing, together with the suspicions which they have engendered in the Trade Unions, have been among the main reasons for the slow development of the system, and for the widespread impression that it is a failure. This impression is encouraged by the form in which the official Government reports on the subject are issued. They divide all schemes into two categories only—"abandoned" and "continuing," and they show a rather larger number of schemes "abandoned" than "continuing," leaving it to be assumed that abandonment means failure. We have had access to the results of an elaborate investigation into this question, carried out on behalf of a well-known firm which was contemplating the adoption of a scheme. This investigation shows that, on the testimony of the employers concerned, only 36 per cent. of the abandoned schemes were regarded as failures, and even in these cases often because they had been started with wrong motives. Schemes are, in fact, often abandoned for quite other reasons than failure. After a scheme has worked successfully for twenty or thirty years, the employer dies, and his business (and with it the scheme) is wound up; or the business is turned into a limited company, or incorporated with some other concern, and the new controllers fail to appreciate the value of the scheme. Or a good scheme may be wrecked by a departure from sound principle which will destroy the confidence of the beneficiaries; for example, money divisible under the scheme may have been put to reserve, and then divided among the shareholders alone.

The Conditions of Success

If they are to avoid these dangers, it is essential that profit-sharing schemes should fulfil the following conditions:

(i) The financial basis of the scheme, including the rate of interest to be first paid to capital, provision for reserves, etc., must be fixed by an enforceable agreement between the parties, so that the workers (once the agreement is made) shall have a legal right to their share, so long as the scheme is in existence. There must be no room for manipulation by the setting aside of reserves not provided for in the scheme, or by unduly increasing the reward of direction, or otherwise; and the figure taken for capital must be a fair one, not inflated for the purpose.

(ii) The participants must have adequate means of satisfying themselves as to the accuracy of the accounts, and there must be a full annual statement showing how the profits have been distributed.

(iii) It should be laid down that wages shall not be below trade-union (or other agreed) rates; employees must be left free to join a trade union; there must be no unreasonable provisions aimed at the freedom or mobility of labour; and authorised strikes must not be penalised under the scheme.

If these conditions are satisfied, and if the basis of division between capital and labour is in itself fair, a profit-sharing scheme should have every chance of achieving its legitimate ends; and trade-union opposition is not likely to impede it.

Types of Schemes

There can be no one "best" scheme of profit-sharing; on the contrary, there ought to be a wide variation of method, according to the nature of the industry, the size and age of the business, the ratio between the amount of capital engaged and the number of employees. In general, it is a sound principle that the division of surplus profits should in some definite way relate the volume of wages paid to the aggregate interest paid on capital. In some cases the amount of capital is small in proportion to the number of employees. In these cases the surplus profits will be apt to yield small individual dividends, and it may be best to place the whole share of labour in a single fund to be administered for the common good in such ways as holiday funds, provision for recreation, and the like.

There are two main forms of profit-sharing. In the first, which may be called profit-sharing proper, the dividend is distributed in cash to the beneficiaries; in the second, which is usually known as co-partnership, the divisible surplus is reinvested in the business, and credited to the beneficiaries in the form of shares. Many schemes have features borrowed from both types. Each type has its merits. We should especially desire to see an extension of the second type, in all suitable cases, because it helps to bring about a wider diffusion of ownership; we shall return to this point in a later chapter (below, p. 249).

Encouragement of Profit-sharing

But whichever type is preferred (and this ought to depend upon the preference of the employees as well as of the employers), we think it of great importance that the system of profit-sharing should be extended as widely and rapidly as possible, and we have given much thought to the possibilities of bringing pressure to bear for this purpose.

It has been proposed that profit-sharing should be generally enforced by law. We believe this to be impracticable, in view of the wide variety of method necessitated by the varying conditions of different concerns. Again, it has been proposed that every business should be required, before a given date, to submit a profit-sharing scheme to the Board of Trade. We believe that this would lead to the production of many bad schemes which would do harm rather than good; and, for the reasons already given, it would be impracticable to confer upon the Board of Trade, or any other central authority, the power of revising and amending schemes.

In a limited number of very big concerns of widely diffused ownership, however, we believe that compulsion can be successfully applied; and we accordingly recommend (see above, p. 95) that all concerns falling under the proposed new category of public corporations should be required to adopt profit-sharing schemes.

While compulsion is impracticable in the infinite diversity of smaller concerns, it is highly desirable that both guidance and pressure should be brought to bear from the centre. We therefore suggest that the Council of Industry which we propose should be attached to the Ministry of Industry (see below, p. 222) should be definitely commissioned to promote the extension of profit-sharing. As a first step, it should be required to define the principles that ought generally to be followed in drafting schemes;

to draw up model schemes of various types; to supply full information regarding the working of existing schemes in this and other countries. It should also urge Joint Industrial Councils and other negotiating bodies to work out the types of schemes most appropriate for their industries; and, where there is sufficient agreement, these bodies should be encouraged to apply for power to enforce the adoption of suitable schemes by all concerns under their jurisdiction.

In this chapter we have set forth the principles of what seems to us to be a sound, just, and practicable system of labour-remuneration. Each element in this system depends, for its satisfactory working, upon the existence of workmanlike and trusted negotiating or consultative bodies, both in industries as a whole and in particular concerns. In the following chapters we turn to consider what changes or developments are necessary in this regard.

CHAPTER XVII

A PROGRAMME OF INDUSTRIAL CO-OPERATION

THE facts set forth in the preceding chapters show that we are already advancing towards a new industrial order, though its outlines are still cloudy. This new order may be described as a system of industrial self-government under the regulation and encouragement of the State. It is the business of statesmanship to perceive the direction of this movement, and to guide and assist it. The function of the statesman is not that of an architect, who draws the plans of an entirely new house to be erected on the ruins of the old; it is that of a gardener, who waters and prunes a growing plant, but cannot change its essential form. The new order which is gradually coming into being will be—and, indeed, already is—quite unlike the harsh individualism and the employer-autocracy of the nineteenth century, which Socialist preachers mostly have in mind when they denounce "Capitalism." But it will also be quite unlike either the scheme of rigid State control or the scheme of trade-union dictatorship, between which the vague dreams of popular Socialism waver.

1. General Outline

Those aspects of the coming system of organised co-operation which relate to the individual factory, where the relations of employer and workman must be most intimate, are dealt with in the next chapter. In this chapter we are concerned with the common regulation of industries as a whole. We conceive that the aim which should govern our policy is that the common affairs of each industry, and the rules to which every concern within it must conform, should be regulated either by the law of the land or by joint bodies representative of management and labour, to whom should be added, for some purposes, representatives of the consumer. These bodies should make their regulations in the light of an ample knowledge of the facts, such as is not now available, with a view always to the twofold end of efficiency in production and justice in distribution. They should by no means limit themselves to the fixation of wage-rates or the settlement of disputes, but should consider such matters as the conditions of entry into an industry, and the methods of training its recruits; the best ways of stimulating inventions and improvements, and of opening careers to talent; the methods of giving to various groups of workers an appropriate share of responsibility, and of diffusing as widely as possible a share of ownership, and the sense that the industry in some degree belongs to all who are engaged in it.

This scheme of industrial self-government has long been accepted by Liberalism; it was, in broad outline, embodied in the resolutions adopted by the National Liberal Federation at Nottingham in 1921, and since then it has been the accepted policy of the Party. But it is obvious that no rigidly uniform scheme of organisation can be imposed upon all industries, both because of their infinite diversity, and because of the difficulty of clearly marking off one industry from another. The conception set forth in the last paragraph must be regarded not as a cut-and-dried scheme which can be established by a single Act of Parliament, but as an ideal by which legislative and administrative policy can be guided; and there must be the utmost elasticity in its application. The industrial world is, in fact, already developing in this direction; but there is necessarily great variety in the methods adopted by various industries, and there are still many gaps to be filled.

Before this ideal of a new structure of industry can be translated into reality, there are three main needs which must be satisfied. The first is the development of better organisation, with more adequate powers, in the industries themselves. The second is the equipment of the negotiating bodies in all industries with adequate knowledge of the financial facts, which at present they lack. The third is the provision of stimulus and leadership at the centre. We shall discuss these three topics in the order given. But for the sake of clarity it is necessary to anticipate two important recommendations which we shall make under the third head. We shall propose that the functions of the Ministry of Labour shall be enlarged, and that its new scope shall be expressed in a new title—the Ministry of Industry. And we shall propose the constitution, in close relation with the Ministry, of a representative Council of Industry. Throughout the following pages we shall assume the existence of the reconstructed Ministry and of the representative Council.

2. Negotiating Bodies

Our first task, then, must be to consider how the existing machinery of negotiation or regulation can be improved so as to accord with the aims defined above. There already exists a great variety of negotiating bodies, of widely different types. The *Trade Boards* are under a high degree of Government control. The *Joint Industrial Councils,* set up under the Whitley scheme, are self-governing bodies whose functions are not limited to wage-settlements, but include the consideration of the general needs of their industries; but they have no power to enforce their decisions, and in many cases they are imperfectly representative of the industries with which they deal. Besides these, there are many *other negotiating bodies,* some of which are, within their range, highly effective—as in the cotton trade or the iron and steel trade. But in effect they limit themselves to wage-problems and do not deal with the general problems of their industries; in other cases these bodies are very loosely organised and inadequately representative. We shall discuss these different types in turn, with a view to discovering what developments they need and can usefully undertake. We shall also discuss separately the special category of the *essential public services,* which need special treatment because of the dependence of all industry upon their smooth working.

There are, however, certain problems affecting the negotiating bodies in all industries which must first be considered. If these bodies are to have power to make regulations binding upon their industries as a whole, the limits within which these regulations apply must be clearly defined, and the regulating body must be fairly representative of all sections of the industry. In the most highly organised industries these difficulties do not seriously arise; just because they are fully organised, there is seldom any difficulty in determining who is covered by an agreement. In the least organised industries the difficulty has been overcome by the authoritative definition of the Ministry of Labour, which prescribes the range to be covered by the decisions of a Trade Board, and secures by nomination that the whole industry is fairly represented. But there are many intermediate industries in which clear demarcation, and a fuller assurance that all sections of the industry are represented, are needed before agreements can be satisfactory, especially if they are to be legally enforceable.

We strongly hold that it is better for industries to solve for themselves, if they can, the problems of demarcation and representation, than to leave them to be solved by a Government Department, though its aid ought to be available. Where difficulties arise as to the scope or limits of a negotiating body, we suggest that the question should be referred to the representative Council of Industry, which will be in many ways the pivot of our scheme of reform.

We have been much impressed by the value of neutral members, not only in Trade Boards but in the Railway Wages Board and other negotiating bodies, in facilitating mutual agreement and understanding between the two sides, and we should like to see a neutral element introduced into all negotiating or regulating bodies. In some cases this has already been voluntarily done. We do not suggest that such members should be forced upon these bodies. But we hold that a negotiating body ought not to obtain legal sanction for its decisions unless neutral members, representing the consumer and the community, have taken part in the discussion. We do not suggest that these members should be nominated by the Ministry, or that they should hold the balance in all decisions: it is essential to industrial self-government and co-operation that the decisions arrived at should result from an agreement between the parties. But we think that this agreement would often be facilitated if neutral members were present and shared in the discussions. We therefore recommend that the Council of Industry should bring all reasonable pressure to bear upon negotiating bodies to invite such members, with the right to vote only on proposals for which it is intended to ask for legal sanction. In order to facilitate this, the Council should maintain a panel of suitable persons willing to serve in this capacity, or, alternatively, should approve persons nominated by the negotiating bodies themselves.

In many industries—especially those in which the scale of

the productive process is increasing—the salaried managerial and technical staffs play a part of growing importance. We have already noted that, because it is unorganised, this element has played no part in the work of collective bargaining. Indeed, it could not properly take part in the determination of wage-questions, which must normally be settled between the parties concerned—those who pay the wages and those who work for them. But on all questions of general industrial policy and methods, which will, we hope, form a growing part of the work of these bodies, managers, salesmen, and technicians can make contributions of the highest value, and we think it desirable that they should be represented in such discussions. We do not suggest that any negotiating body should be compelled to admit this element; but we strongly urge upon Joint Industrial Councils and similar bodies the desirability of inviting representatives of these important groups, under such conditions as each Council may define, to serve either upon the Councils themselves or upon their committees.

The introduction of a neutral element, and of representatives of managerial and technical staffs, would involve a departure from the principle of a balanced representation of two rival interests which has hitherto governed the contribution of these bodies. This would be a departure of real importance, and for that reason we recognise that the bodies concerned ought to decide for themselves whether they are prepared to make this departure or not. But we strongly feel that, while a balance is necessary, and will continue to be necessary, for the conduct of bargaining about wages, it is neither necessary nor helpful for the conduct of those searching discussions of the problems of industry which we earnestly desire to see these bodies undertaking. It is worth noting that in the boot and shoe trade, which has been so successful in avoiding strife, it has been thought desirable to keep wage-bargaining apart from the general discussions carried on by the Joint Industrial Council.

We now proceed to consider in turn the various types of negotiating bodies.

(*i*) *Trade Boards*

We have already (p. 169) described the Trade Board system. It now covers thirty-seven industries which are more or less unorganised, and which in the past paid the lowest wages. In these industries, so long as they remain unorganised, collective bargaining is impossible, and without State intervention there would be no means of securing a reasonable standard of living for the worker. The Trade Board system has proved, in practice, an effective substitute for collective bargaining. The Whitley Committee on Industrial Relations, while urging an extension of the system, held that as the organisation of these industries improved, they ought to advance to the stage of fixing their rates by agreement. This has not yet happened in any instance, nor is it likely to happen so long as the change would involve a loss of the power of making wage-rates enforceable at law. The difficulty would be diminished if, as we propose, voluntary negotiating bodies were enabled, under proper safeguards, to obtain legal sanction for their agreements. We think that industries under Trade Boards should develop towards a type of machinery which, while retaining compulsory powers and the advantage of a neutral element, would cover the wider field now dealt with by Joint Industrial Councils, and would represent organisations on both sides.

No new Trade Boards have been established since 1921. But there are undoubtedly other industries or crafts whose organisation is inadequate and whose wages are unduly low, which would benefit from being brought under the Trade Board system. The system should be extended to all trades or industries which are not sufficiently organised to be able to make and keep satisfactory agreements about wage-rates and other conditions. But as industries impinge upon one another, it is desirable that before any trade or industry is either taken out of or put into the Trade Board group, a body representative of industry as a whole should be consulted. We propose that this function should be performed by the Council of Industry.

Since the War many of the Trade Boards, instead of confining themselves to fixing wages for the lowest-paid workers, have fixed wage-rates for all classes of labour throughout the industry, and have enforced them in the same way as minimum rates, by making the employer who fails to pay them liable to a criminal prosecution as well as to a civil action by the aggrieved worker. It is desirable that the fixing of *general* wage-rates by Trade Boards should continue. But a distinction should be drawn between a living minimum wage and other rates. It is right that failure to pay the minimum should be liable to criminal prosecution, and that the neutral members (who represent the community) should have a voice in fixing them, because the reason for fixing minimum rates is the social necessity of preventing sweating. But higher rates are on a different footing. They should be fixed by agreement between the two sides, the neutral members sharing in the discussion, but not voting; and they should be enforceable only by civil action. To make this distinction would encourage organisation on both sides, which is on every ground desirable. In the same way not only wage-rates but working conditions should be defined by agreement between the two sides, the neutral members not voting except where the fixing of socially desirable minima is involved, though they might well take part in the discussion.

In short, we recommend that the Trade Board system, which has been the means of a great social advance, should be extended to every industry in which it can be shown to be needed, and that its functions should be enlarged beyond the narrow limits originally conceived; but that it should be regarded as only a stage on the way towards a more complete system of co-operative regulation.

(ii) *Joint Industrial Councils*

We have elsewhere described (p. 172) the origin and the early development of the Whitley scheme of industrial organisation which led to the establishment of Joint Councils in many industries; and we have shown that some of these Councils have been successful in introducing a new and active spirit of co-operation into their industries, but that the system has by no means extended over as large an area as was at one time hoped. Their greatest weakness has been that they have been unable to enforce their decisions. They share this lack of legal powers of enforcement with the highly organised staple industries, such as cotton or iron and steel. But the latter are strong enough to enforce their own decisions, while less highly organised industries are not. The system of Joint Industrial Councils will not make much progress unless such powers are obtainable. The Association of Joint Industrial Councils feels this so strongly that it has long demanded the grant to the Councils of compulsory powers like those of the Trade Boards; and in 1924 a Bill for this purpose, introduced by Mr. Frank Murrell, a Liberal member, received a second reading in the House of Commons. We agree that the Joint Industrial Councils ought to be endowed with compulsory powers; but it is clear that some safeguards are necessary.

(1) Any agreement for which legal sanction is sought should have been accepted by majorities of both the employers' and the workers' representatives; and neutral members should have been present with power to take part in the discussion and to vote.

(2) Reasonable adjustments should be made, where necessary, to ensure that the regulations proposed will not unfairly affect particular sections of the industry or parts of the country.

(3) Where the Joint Industrial Council is not fully representative of the industry, spokesmen of the unrepresented elements should be given an opportunity of laying their views before the Council.

(4) The Council ought to be able to prove the necessity for enforcing its rates by law by showing that in some sections of the industry rates are being paid, or hours and conditions are being maintained, which are undesirable and below the levels usual for occupations of comparable skill; and that the rates, hours, or conditions proposed to be enforced are fair in themselves and not materially above or below the standards observed in occupations of comparable skill. It ought not to be possible for industries which are able to pass on all their costs to the community to obtain legal enforceability for rates which are altogether out of relation to those paid in occupations requiring similar skill.

Subject to these safeguards, we believe that the possibility of obtaining legal enforceability for their decisions would add greatly to the effectiveness of the Joint Industrial Councils, would lead to their becoming more genuinely representative of their industries, and would tend to a steady improvement of standards and of efficiency. In particular, we consider that every industry, whether represented by a Trade Board or not, should regard it as part of its duty to fix minimum wage-rates below which no worker in the industry should be allowed to fall; and these minimum rates should be made legally enforceable in the same way as Trade Board rates.

The procedure to be followed in giving legal force to the decisions of a Joint Industrial Council should be similar to that followed in the case of a Trade Board. The Council of Industry would first satisfy itself that the conditions defined above have been fulfilled, and would advise the Ministry of Industry to that effect. The Ministry would then give due notice to the trade concerned, in order that objections might be lodged, which would be referred to the Council of Industry for report. The final decision would rest with the Ministry, as responsible to Parliament; if, after considering the report of the Council of Industry, the Minister was satisfied that legal sanction ought to be given to the proposed regulation, he would issue an Order, which, after lying on the table in Parliament for a period, would be enforceable in the courts of law by civil action.

(iii) *Other Negotiating Bodies*

We turn to the considerable group of industries in which neither Trade Boards nor Joint Industrial Councils have as yet been established. Some of these are among the most highly organised industries in the country, such as cotton, iron and steel, shipbuilding, and engineering. They have worked out for themselves elaborate and efficient machinery for settling wage-rates and for avoiding disputes on these subjects; and, recognising their high value, we have elsewhere (p. 161) described some of these schemes. But in general the highly organised industries, satisfied with their existing machinery, have not tried to work out methods of discussion and co-operation on the general problems of the industries, such as the Joint Industrial Councils have provided. There are also many imperfectly organised industries in which no adequate machinery exists even for wage-negotiation, beyond occasional *ad hoc* conferences when subjects of controversy arise. In some of these cases Joint Industrial Councils have nominally been created, but are inoperative.

In the case of the highly organised industries, we are far from desiring to interfere with their existing systems of wage-negotiation, which are in some cases models of efficiency; nor do we wish to impose upon them any rigid uniformity of structure. But in most of these industries the employers have hitherto been unwilling to take the representatives of the workers into consultation on many questions affecting the well-being of the industry which lie beyond the wage-bargain. We believe that they would gain much by setting up machinery for the regular discussion of such questions, either in connection with wage-negotiations or (as may be preferable) apart from them. We believe also that it would be advantageous to them to obtain compulsory powers under the conditions we have already described; for while these industries are so well organised that the majority is usually able to impose its will upon the minority, this is by no means always the case, and beneficial common action is sometimes prevented by a recalcitrant minority. There are many questions upon which it is important that an industry should pursue a common policy, arrived at after discussion between the parties concerned. For example, a common system of costing would be of great value in many industries; and it is important that in devising such a system the workers should be taken into consultation, if they are to accept the results as a basis for wage-negotiations. Again, consultation is necessary in working out the best methods of recruitment for the industry, the scale on which it should be done, and the system of apprenticeship or other training. Yet again, the whole problem of unemployment, the possibility of mitigating it by distribution of work, and the best ways of dealing with it—by short time or otherwise—when it comes, affect both sides equally and should be discussed by both. These are only examples of the way in which efficiency and goodwill can be improved by organised consultation. Each industry ought to be free to work out its own system; but we hope that the Council of Industry will steadily exercise all the influence it can wield to extend the practice of regular consultation and co-operation on the lines we have defined.

As for the industries in which negotiating machinery is inchoate or rudimentary, we feel that the strongest pressure should be continuously used to equip them with the means of consultation. In some cases, as we have already suggested, Trade Boards should be established by the authority of the Ministry of Industry. Wherever organisation is more highly developed, the Council and the Ministry should give stimulus and assistance in the formation and working of Joint Industrial Councils, as was done in the first years after the Whitley system was devised. We believe that the possibility of obtaining compulsory powers would afford a real stimulus.

When in every industry an organised body, commanding the confidence of employers and employed, is engaged not merely in discussing differences as they arise, but in dealing with all matters of common interest, with the knowledge that in suitable cases their decisions can be given the force of law, we shall be within sight not merely of industrial peace, but of effective co-operation to achieve efficiency in production and justice in distribution.

(*iv*) *Special Provisions in Essential Public Services*

The interdependence of industries is in no respect so clearly illustrated as in the group of industries which may be described as the essential public services. These include the public health services, the supply of water, gas, and electricity, and the main transport services, especially the railways. Any interruption of these services may entirely dislocate the rest of industry, and inflict upon the public loss and suffering out of all proportion greater than that resulting from a stoppage in the manufacturing industries.

It is not possible even in these industries to abrogate the ultimate right to strike or lock out, since this is the foundation of negotiating power. No absolute guarantee against interruption is therefore possible. But, short of this, we can take steps to ensure full deliberation before a stoppage takes place, and to make it as unlikely as it can be made. In the first place we can ensure the creation of complete machinery for negotiation, and in the second place we can devise means of bringing great pressure to ensure that this machinery shall be fully used before any stoppage can take place.

The general type of organisation which we should like to see in these trades would be similar to that which we have already sketched; negotiations over any dispute would begin in the district and would ultimately come before the Joint Industrial Council or the main negotiating body of the trade. But in these cases the system should go further than is necessary in ordinary industries. In the case of the railways, as we have seen (p. 164), an elaborate system of negotiation has been worked out, culminating in a National Wages Board which includes neutral members. In some respects this system might be taken as a model for all the essential services. But, though it has worked well, it has defects. In the first place, it only provides for a delay of twenty-eight days after a question in dispute has been submitted to the National Wages Board, at the end of which a stoppage may take place without further discussion. In a case where national interests are so deeply involved there should be a further delay—such as was provided for by the Canadian "Lemieux" Act[1]—to allow of a public inquiry by such a body as the Court of Inquiry which the Ministry of Labour is empowered to set up. In some industries which have succeeded in banishing strikes and lock-outs (iron and steel, boots and shoes) there is a provision for ultimate reference to arbitration; no such provision exists in the railway scheme. Finally, there are no guarantees that the negotiating machinery shall be fully used, such as the forfeitable deposits which were voluntarily arranged by the boot and shoe trade: although there was an agreement on the railways that neither side would stop work until the whole process of inquiry had been exhausted, this was broken in the general strike of 1926. While, therefore, the railway system marks a real advance, it would seem that it is not a perfect model, and that the community has a right to claim more adequate safeguards against an interruption of the services upon which its very life depends.

What guarantee is it possible to secure that the machinery of negotiation, whatever form it may assume, should be fully used?

In the first place the workers in these essential services might be organised on an establishment basis, as are the Police, the Civil Service, and the "conciliation grades" on the railways, with special pension, holiday, and other privileges which would lapse on a breach of service. This would clearly be a considerable incentive to maintain peace and obtain any demands by negotiation wherever possible.

Secondly, all contracts of employment in these services might be made for a longer period than usual, say a month or three months, so that neither employer nor worker could bring about

[1] The Industrial Disputes Investigation Act.

a stoppage with less notice than this; and the provision of the Act of 1875,[1] which imposes special penalties for breach of contract of service in certain cases, might be extended to all essential services.

A third method might be a voluntary agreement by the Trade Unions and the employers' organisations to deposit substantial sums which would be forfeited in the event of a breach. This has been done effectively in the case of the boot and shoe trade; the deposits would, however, have to be very large to be effective.

A fourth method might be to enact that, in the case of the essential services, the privileges of the Trade Disputes Act of 1906 would not apply unless the machinery of negotiation had been fully employed. This is a matter which would naturally be investigated by the Commission on Trade Union Law we suggest elsewhere (p. 160). The main privilege conferred upon Trade Unions by this Act was immunity from actions of tort (i.e. wrongful acts other than breach of contract). The result of the proposed provision would be that if either the employers or the Trade Unions caused a stoppage before the negotiating machinery had been fully employed, they would be liable to actions for all damages suffered by anybody as a consequence of the stoppage.[2] This liability is so difficult to define and may be so heavy that few employers or Trade Unions would risk the responsibility for a stoppage with such a threat hanging over them. It would, of course, be necessary to protect Trade Unions against being penalised for unauthorised strikes; their immunity from action would not be interfered with unless the Union had taken an active part in promoting the stoppage. The privileges of 1906 would not be withdrawn; but they would be limited to stoppages which took place *after* the whole process of conciliation had been gone through. This

[1] The Conspiracy and Protection of Property Act, 1875, § 5.

[2] The safeguard here proposed is quite different from that which the Trade Disputes and Trade Unions Act, 1927, seeks to provide. Under the provisions of the latter Act, the immunities conferred by the Trade Disputes Act, 1906, are not applicable in the case of "illegal" strikes and lock-outs. But the strikes and lock-outs which that Act renders illegal are defined as strikes and lock-outs which, in addition to threatening the community, extend to more than one trade or industry. Hence the Act of 1927 does not affect the present position regarding the Essential Public Services unless a stoppage in one of those services is complicated by a "sympathetic" element; while the Act goes much further in other respects than we are here recommending.

would probably prove to be by far the most powerful and effective way of ensuring the full use of the negotiating machinery before a stoppage took place.

We do not attempt to put forward a single uniform scheme to cover all essential industries, because we hold that, whenever possible, such a scheme should rest upon agreements made within the industry itself, and should be adapted to its special circumstances. But we do propose that a special responsibility should rest upon the Council of Industry in these cases. It should (1) schedule the "essential public services"; (2) request all industries falling within the schedule to submit a scheme for a complete system of conciliation machinery, with adequate guarantees for its full utilisation; and (3) in cases where no proposals, or inadequate proposals, were submitted, it should itself frame a scheme, and submit it to Parliament for legislation.

3. Publicity of the Facts about Industry

When the representatives of employers and workers meet to consider a proposed adjustment of wages or any other industrial problem, they cannot arrive at a sound decision without full knowledge of the facts. At present such knowledge as they possess is mainly provided by the employers. But the employers' statements are apt to be regarded with suspicion by the other side, and in any case each employer is bound to interpret the facts by his own limited experience. Both sides need, and neither has access to, a trustworthy body of statistical knowledge; and this must somehow be provided before the results of collective bargaining can be made satisfactory. What is needed is not knowledge about the financial condition of individual firms, but generalised knowledge about the industry as a whole, and about various sections of it—its output, the prices obtained in home and foreign markets, the cost of raw materials, the amount of capital involved and the average rate of interest paid on it, the number of employees, and the total cost of wages in the industry. If these and other facts, for the industry as a whole, were before the negotiators, the effect upon their discussions would be very great. For example, if a rise of wages is demanded, the facts ought to show whether the additional charge can be taken out of profits wholly or in part, and whether an increase of prices would involve a loss of markets and therefore cause unemployment. In a discussion thus based upon facts, the negotiators are likely to go on to consider whether there is any way in which the efficiency of the industry can be so increased as to enable it to yield a greater return. This is the most solid path to better conditions, and both sides can help to build it.

How is this necessary knowledge to be made available? Some Joint Industrial Councils, recognising the need, have tried to meet it by asking all firms in the industry to make confidential returns to the secretary, or to an accountant appointed for the purpose, who works out the totals for the whole industry. Something can, no doubt, be done in this way. But it is unlikely that sufficiently complete returns will be made. In another part of this Report we recommend that a higher degree of publicity of accounts should be required from trading companies of a certain size. A great deal of knowledge can also be put together from the records of various Government departments. It is, indeed, mainly by using the resources of the public departments that negotiating bodies can be supplied with the knowledge they need. To collect and co-ordinate this material and to make it available in a convenient form is one of the services which can be rendered by an adequate organisation at the centre. It is not only knowledge about their own industries which negotiating bodies need; they need also knowledge of the conditions existing in other industries upon which they are dependent for necessary goods and services, and knowledge of the effects likely to be produced upon other industries by any rise in the cost of their own products. For industries are not carried on in water-tight departments; they are all mutually dependent, and all more or less directly affected by one another's decisions. It would be one of the duties of the Economic General Staff, whose functions we describe elsewhere, to survey generally and make recommendations as to the statistical equipment of the nation. The need of information by the bodies we are describing is one of the purposes for which our statistical machinery must make provision.

4. Central Guidance

The main subject of this section of our Report is the substitution of an organised system of co-operation for the existing system of conflict. At every point in our survey it has been apparent that this cannot be achieved merely by an Act of Parliament, though legislation on a good many points may be and is necessary. The greatest need is that of steady and wise guidance continued through a long period. This guidance ought to be of two kinds. In the first place, continuous administrative action is necessary, through a properly organised department of State. In the second place, it would seem to be essential that there should be some organ representative of industry as a whole, to afford leadership and stimulus in the development of the machinery of co-operation, to keep continuously in mind the interaction of industries one upon another, and to ensure that the direction of industrial policy in this field shall not be merely political or bureaucratic in character. To work out a system which will satisfy both of these needs, and to ensure easily workable relations between the two parts of it, is perhaps the most important practical step that can be immediately taken towards the improvement of industrial relations.

A Ministry of Industry

It was only in 1917, when the Ministry of Labour was instituted by the Coalition Government, that the need of a special department of State to deal with these problems was recognised. We have already described (p. 176 above) the very important functions which are performed by this Ministry. They include the administration of the Unemployment Insurance Acts, the Employment Exchanges, and the Trade Boards, and the conduct of the governmental system of industrial conciliation. In spite of the great importance of these functions, the Ministry of Labour has never ranked among the leading offices. Yet the function of helping British industry to find its way to peace and to efficiency —the two things are mutually dependent—ought surely to be recognised as one of the highest and most exacting tasks of statesmanship. Part of the reason for this is that the functions of the Ministry are too narrowly conceived. They are limited to problems of labour, which cannot be separated from other industrial problems. Even in this sphere they are incomplete: the administration of the Factory Acts, for example, is retained by the Home Office, for purely historical reasons.

We recommend that the functions of the Ministry of Labour should be greatly enlarged, and that its new scope should be recognised by giving it the title Ministry of Industry or (if the phrase be preferred) of Industry and Labour. It should take over the functions now performed by the Home Office under the Factory Acts, the Shop Acts, and the Workmen's Compensation Acts. It should also take over the administration of the Mines Acts, now entrusted to a semi-detached Mines Department subordinate to the Board of Trade. It should be responsible for the administration of the rules relating to incorporated Trade Associations proposed in Chapter VIII above (p. 98). Finally, it should be required to provide a far fuller and more varied statistical service than is now the case, being made responsible for the provision of all the information needed by the negotiating bodies in industry. In short, it should be responsible for the whole system of State regulation of the conditions under which industry is carried on, and for all those activities in which the State finds itself brought into relations with the great organisations of employers and workpeople whereby industrial conditions are regulated. These functions are all so closely inter-related that they cannot usefully be separated; and the functions which the State has to perform in regard to industry cannot be well performed until they are properly co-ordinated. Thus reconstructed, the Ministry would become one of the greatest offices of State, as it ought to be.

The functions of such a Ministry ought not, however, to be limited merely to the administration of existing laws about industry. This is too generally supposed to be the sole function of a public department, and it is, of course, its primary function. But there is also a function of leadership and stimulus which a public department can give within the sphere which it covers. This kind of work is already done in regard to Local Authorities, for example by the Board of Education and the Ministry of Health, though in these cases guidance of this kind is closely related to the exercise of authority under statutes. In the sphere of industry the function of leadership is a much more delicate and difficult one, since here it is concerned with powerful voluntary bodies, Trade Unions and Employers' Associations, which are not subject to central authority save in a very minor degree. Yet the history of the American Ministry of Commerce, under

Mr. Hoover, has shown how well this kind of work can be done by a public department which has scarcely any definite administrative powers. By common consent Mr. Hoover has made contributions of extraordinary value to the development of industrial efficiency in the United States. He has done this mainly by constant conference with the leaders of industry, by stimulating them to take common action, and not by issuing authoritative edicts. We hold that work of this kind is even more necessary in England than in America, and that it should be regarded as one of the primary duties of a Minister of Industry to assist and forward industrial efficiency, not by overriding or disregarding the organised bodies of employers and workpeople, but by bringing them together and working with them. In short, the Ministry should be made responsible for the State's part in that work of developing industrial efficiency which is described in Chapter XII of Book 2 of our Report (p. 131 above).

A Council of Industry

It would, however, be undesirable to leave the function of guiding and stimulating industry into new courses wholly to a public department, however well organised. Industry itself must provide leadership. Industrial policy must be safeguarded against those sudden reversals which are apt to follow changes of Government, and against any risk of a too rigid bureaucratic method. For these reasons we recommend that the new Ministry of Industry should from the first work in association with a statutory Council of Industry, which should be so constituted as to represent, and to command the confidence of, the industrial world. It should be a body of workable size, capable of meeting frequently; and the statute establishing it should provide for its meeting at regular and frequent intervals. We suggest that it should consist of nine representative employers and of nine representatives of organised Labour, selected by the Government from a panel nominated by representative bodies of employers and wage-earners; and that there should also be six other members directly appointed by the Minister. In order to ensure continuity of policy, and at the same time the infusion of fresh blood, three employers, three Trade Unionists, and two appointed members should be chosen in each year.

We attach very great importance to the creation and active working of the Council of Industry, as affording the means both of giving leadership to industry from within itself, and of keeping the Ministry and the Government in touch with the best industrial opinion on both sides.

One very important function for which we suggest the Council of Industry should be made responsible would be in connection with the sanctioning of Compulsory Orders, as regards wages and other matters, asked for by Trade Boards or Joint Industrial Councils. The ultimate responsibility for such sanctions must rest with the Minister of Industry, who is directly responsible to Parliament. But we consider it important that the Minister should be advised in this matter by the Council of Industry, which will be in close touch with industry and can be relied on to look at the matter from a purely industrial point of view. The Council would be in a position to give authoritative advice to the Minister as to whether there were any objections to a proposed Compulsory Order, whether the issuing of the Order would tend to industrial peace, and whether it was consistent with the general reasonable level of wages throughout comparable industries. We believe that the Industrial Council in this way would have a slow but steady influence towards the elimination of the extreme differences which now exist between the wages paid for comparable jobs in different industries, and so attain a fairer adjustment of wages throughout industry. Apart from this the main functions of the Council would be as follows:

(1) To keep under continuous review the machinery in various industries which deals with industrial relations, and to make suggestions for its improvement and enlargement. In its recommendations it should have special regard to the need of increasing the efficiency of industry by steps which commend themselves to all concerned.

(2) To make reports to the Minister regarding the establishment or reconstruction of Trade Boards, applications for compulsory powers from Joint Industrial Councils and other negotiating bodies, schemes for avoiding interruption in essential public services, and the like.

(3) To keep under continuous review the movement of wages and all substantial changes in hours and conditions,

and to direct attention to any undesirable disparities between one industry and another.

(4) To keep under continuous review the work of Trade Associations in regard to price-fixing, the regulation of output, joint marketing, and the like, and to direct the attention of the Board of Trade to any instances in which the policy adopted seems to be dangerous to the public.

(5) To submit to the Ministry, for publication, an annual report on these subjects, together with special reports on other subjects affecting the progress of co-operation and efficiency in industry.

(6) To give preliminary consideration to measures affecting industry proposed to be introduced in Parliament.

(7) In general to advise the Minister on all subjects affecting the work of his department which he may refer to them, and to make representations on any subject affecting the organisation and well-being of industry.

The institution of a permanent body, of high status, to perform these functions would, we are convinced, produce results of the highest value. It would help to ensure that both legislation and administration were carried on with due regard to the needs and opinions of the industrial world, and would itself be a very material contribution to the development of industrial self-government.

A National Industrial Council

For these purposes the formation of a large National Industrial Council, representative of the whole of industry, has often been urged, and was definitely recommended by the Industrial Conference held in 1919. We have very fully considered this proposal, to which some of our own number are strongly attached. It has much to recommend it. But it is necessary to consider the possibility that in the present stage of industrial development a large body of this character might become an arena for sterile and perhaps acrimonious debate, leading to no very definite conclusions; and while some of us hold that it would be worth while to run this risk for the sake of the good results which might flow from such exchanges of view, we are agreed that a smaller and more workmanlike Council, such as we have defined, working in intimate relations with a reorganised Ministry, would be able to perform many of the most useful functions of the larger body, as well as some others which would be beyond its reach.

These proposals, however, should in no way impede the establishment of a National Industrial Council on the amplest scale when industry is more fully organised and when the practice of co-operation is more widely established.

In the meanwhile, the urgent thing is to provide a nucleus round which instructed opinion in the industrial world can form itself, and to give driving force to the movement towards a better industrial order. That is the aim of these proposals.

CHAPTER XVIII

THE STATUS OF THE WORKER

IN our pre-occupation with collective bargaining on a national scale, and with the development of co-operation between the national organisations of employers and workpeople, we are a little apt to overlook the fact that, after all, industry is carried on in individual workshops, factories, and mines. It is here that the actual worker comes into daily contact with the actual process of production; it is here that his capacity, his interest, and his loyalty are either utilised or allowed to run to waste.

1. THE FACTORY AS THE UNIT

It is a remarkable fact that Trade Unionism in this country has never used the factory as its unit of organisation, except in the printing trade, where the "chapel" is a very living force. The smallest trade-union unit is the local lodge, which consists of men of the same occupation who happen to reside in the same district, but who are commonly employed by a number of different concerns. Perhaps this is why lodge meetings are not usually well attended: they do not deal with the things upon which their members' minds have been mainly occupied during the day—the problems and difficulties of work in a particular factory, under particular managers and foremen. The relations of the factory with the Trade Union are limited to dealings with the local official, who takes up serious grievances, or complaints that a national agreement or an accepted usage has been disregarded. On the whole, this work is well done, but it comes as an interference from outside, and therefore leads more easily to friction than if it had resulted from a discussion within the works. The trade-union movement itself has been aware of this weakness. The shop-steward movement, which reached such magnitude during the War, was essentially an attempt to base the struggle for better conditions upon the natural unit of the factory. It was in the main an irreconcilable extremist movement, but it was also a protest against trade-union bureaucracy, and a demand for a more adequate recognition of the factory unit.

Since the War some of the Unions have somewhat modified their policy. The Amalgamated Engineering Union, in particular, has now secured from the employers the recognition of shop stewards, and its District Committees have a voice in their appointment. All this indicates that there is a tendency towards the recognition of the factory unit, and a feeling that the workers in the factory ought to have some organised means of dealing directly with their employers; but even in the case of engineering there is still no means of common action or discussion for the whole body of workers in a factory, but only for those who happen to belong to a particular Union. We strongly feel that, from the point of view of labour, this need will have to be generally met, as it is met already in well-managed concerns in this country; and that the whole body of workers in a factory ought to have adequate means of ensuring (to take two instances only) that the rules under which they have to work are fairly conceived and fairly administered, and that men are safeguarded against arbitrary dismissal.

From the point of view of the employer, also, a development of this sort is needed. One large element in successful management is the evoking of a team-spirit. This can best be got by consultation. The manager who is unable or unwilling to see that co-operative working is more effective than autocracy, though more difficult to direct, confesses his incompetence as a manager. Alike from the point of view of the employer and the workman, alike from the point of view of efficiency, of justice, and of good-feeling, some effective machinery to enable the employee to have a real voice in determining the conditions in which he spends most of his working hours, a real protection against unfair dealing, and a real chance of making his contribution, ought to exist in every factory.

2. Consultation not Control

There have been many different plans for recognising the claim of the worker to an effective voice in those aspects of the business which concern him. The value of any plan must in the end be tested by its effect in increasing or impairing the efficiency of the business. We are often told that in the Socialist State, or at any rate in the Guild Socialist State, "workers' control" will be so complete that managers and foremen will be elected by the men who have to work under them. This would ensure complete failure. Mr. Sidney Webb, writing on this point, has said: "No self-governing workshops, no trade union, no professional association, no co-operative society . . . has yet made its administration successful on the lines of letting the subordinate employees elect or dismiss the executive officers or managers. . . . The relationship set up between a foreman or manager, who has throughout the working day to give orders to his staff, and the members of that staff who, assembled in general meeting, criticise his action or give him directions, with the power of dismissing him if he fails to conform to their desires, has always been found to be an impossible one." It is, indeed, the first condition of successful business that the responsibility of management, which is a highly complex and skilled kind of work, must not be impaired. Consultation with a body of workers will improve and strengthen it; anything that can accurately be described as "workers' control" will destroy it.

3. Workers and the Directorate

It has often been suggested that the claim of the workers to a share of control might be met by giving them one or two seats on Boards of Directors. This method seems to us of questionable value. Boards of Directors as at present constituted very seldom deal with the aspects of management which especially concern the workers; they leave these to the managerial staff. They are mainly concerned with complex questions of finance and broad issues of policy: the terms on which new capital shall be raised, the best way of meeting the shock of bad trade, the possibility and probable effects of expansion, the problem of marketing, the prices of material, the conclusion of working agreements with other concerns, and the like—questions upon which the workman, *qua* workman, has no special knowledge and no contribution of value to make, unless he happens to be the sort of man who ought to be in a managerial position. During discussions on such points, a workman-director would be apt to sit dumb and dubious, only half understanding what was going on. If he tries to insist upon the discussion of Labour questions, he will only confuse the business of the Board; if he does not, his constituents may think he is betraying their interests and becoming "a tool of the capitalist." The position of a workman-director is, in short, likely to be anomalous, uncomfortable, and thankless. The work of looking after workpeople's interests, and the work of controlling the finance and general policy of a big concern, are so different that they cannot easily be combined.

In one case only would the appointment of workman-directors be advantageous. If the workpeople of a concern, either individually or collectively, have an established right to a share of residual profits, they might fairly be asked to appoint a director whose business it would be to see that the concern was conducted in such a way as to yield a return to those whom he represented; but this would introduce an entirely new ground for representation on the Board. We conclude that the appointment of workmen as directors, though it sounds well, is really an illusory device, more likely to cause trouble than to do any good to anybody; but that this objection disappears if and when the body of workpeople obtain a definite share of ownership in the business. For example, the experiment of workmen directors in an industry in which co-partnership schemes have been peculiarly successful—the gas industry—is said to have worked well. The South Metropolitan Gas Company, for example, has long had representatives of its workers on its Board, and has greatly profited by their co-operation.

These objections, however, would not apply in such force if the plan described in Chapter VII (p. 91) were adopted, under which, in companies of diffused ownership, a Supervisory Council would be appointed, leaving the more detailed work to be carried out by an Administrative Board. There would be a strong case for the representation of workers as well as shareholders on a Supervisory Council, which would be consulted on broad questions of policy, but would have nothing to do with the detailed control of business.

4. Works Councils

Experience in this and other countries has shown that the best way of making real consultation possible is the establishment of a Works Council in every factory or workshop, at whose periodical meetings management and workpeople can take counsel together about their common interests. In Germany and in Sweden the establishment of a Works Council in every concern of more than a certain size has been made compulsory by law. We sent investigators to Germany to report upon the working of the scheme there; they reported that the workpeople regarded it as of real value, and would not willingly part with it; and that while some employers made little of it many spoke warmly in its favour. It is held by many in this country that to make such a system compulsory would be unwise, since its effectiveness must depend upon the readiness of the management to use it, and an indifferent management can reduce it to futility. Those who take this view believe that the application of compulsion may retard rather than assist the practice of consultation. We recognise that there is some force in this contention. There are two purposes for which a Works Council can be used: the first is the ventilation of grievances, and the assurance of an opportunity of expressing the workpeople's view with regard to the rules under which they have to work; the second is the pooling of ideas, and the enlisting of the workpeople's help in securing efficiency. The latter can be made of no avail by a hostile or indifferent management, but the former can certainly be secured if regular meetings are bound to take place. We conclude, therefore—and our opinion is fortified by German experience—that the advantages of a compulsory establishment of Works Councils outweigh any defects which may attend it.

Three different forms of Works Councils are possible. (1) The Council may be organised purely as a representation of wage-earning workers, who will discuss their complaints or proposals together and then submit them corporately to the management. This is the type of Council which has been established in Germany. Its drawback is that the Council has not sufficient material before it when forming its conclusion, and is apt to meet the management in an attitude of hostility. This method emphasises the separation rather than the community of interests.

(2) In the second type of Council, management and workers are represented in equal numbers. This was the type of Council recommended by the Whitley Committee of 1916, on the analogy of the Joint Industrial Councils which they recommended for whole industries. We have already seen ground to question the soundness of the method even in Joint Industrial Councils, which are often engaged in negotiation on wages and the like; we think it still more unsuitable for Works Councils, whose primary business is not negotiation, but consultation. Even when points of definite negotiation and agreement arise, it is obvious that the management's assent must be obtained before there can be agreement. Nothing, therefore, is gained by an exact parity of numbers. At the same time it is essential, from the worker's point of view, that the management should be effectively represented, though not necessarily on a fifty-fifty principle.

(3) We therefore prefer the third method, which does not count heads, but endeavours to secure that every important group of workers, whether by brain or by hand, from the heads of the concern downwards, shall be represented, and shall be enabled to take part in discussion on the problems and prospects of the concern as a whole, as well as on the grievances or suggestions of particular sections. This is not, of course, incompatible with the holding of separate meetings of workers to discuss particular questions before they are raised at joint meetings. Such meetings should not only be allowed but encouraged; and in a well-organised big concern the General Works Council would be only the apex of a system of committees in various departments. Such an organisation has been worked out in many successful concerns; its structure must necessarily vary according to the size and character of the concern, and would naturally be a subject upon which the General Works Council should be consulted. But we do not think that legislative compulsion should be applied in such a matter, in which the utmost elasticity should be maintained. The essential thing is to set up in every factory a General Works Council, representative of all elements engaged in the work of the factory. We therefore recommend that this should be made a statutory obligation upon every concern employing more than (say) fifty persons, or, alternatively, upon every concern coming under Factories and Workshops Acts. We think that the obligation

should be extended to distributive firms employing more than fifty persons, such as the big shops. The Act should require the free nomination in writing and election by ballot of representatives of every important section of employees. It should also make it clear that these Councils are not intended to take the place, or to undermine the authority, of national negotiating bodies. Their deliberations should all be limited and governed by national agreements, in regard to which the functions of Trade Unions and their officials would remain as before.

5. Agreement on Rules

In the main the functions of the Works Councils would be deliberative and consultative. But they ought to have certain definite rights secured to them by Statute, with a view to the protection of the employees against unfair treatment, and especially against arbitrary dismissal. In particular, the working rules of the factory should be defined in agreement with the Works Council, and a copy should be made available for every employee. We attach great importance to the existence in every factory of a Schedule of known Rules, not liable to arbitrary alteration. This is, of course, the practice of all good firms, but it is not universal. Consultation and agreement upon working rules would, in our judgment, do much to create a healthy spirit in the works, and to destroy the idea that the employer was an irresponsible autocrat. "That community is free," said William Penn, "in which the laws rule, and in which the people are a party to these rules." Agreement on this head is so important that if the Works Council cannot agree with the management on a Schedule of Rules, we recommend that the points in dispute should, wherever possible, be referred to a local negotiating body; and that in the last resort they should be referred to the Ministry of Industry, which should be empowered to apply by statutory order an appropriate set of rules, not inconsistent with national or district agreements applicable to the factory concerned. We do not think that the Ministry would often be troubled, but this power of ultimate reference would insure effective consultation upon a vital matter which lies at the root of good relations in the factory.

The general character and scope of the rules thus to be defined should be laid down in a Schedule to the Act creating the Works Councils, and we print in an appendix[1] the heads which, in our judgment, ought to be covered: they are based upon the practice of a number of well-managed concerns in this country whose rules we have studied. But we recommend that certain provisions bearing upon dismissal, which rarely find a place in such rules, should be included. The fear of arbitrary dismissal, and the ill-feeling aroused when such dismissals take place or are supposed to have taken place, are among the most fruitful causes of friction. Nothing rankles more in the mind of the workman, nothing gives him a greater sense of insecurity and of the injustice of the industrial order, than the knowledge that he may at a week's notice be deprived of his means of livelihood—a terrible penalty—possibly for no better reason than that he has incurred the displeasure of a foreman. Too many employers or managers leave these matters to foremen; and always support the action of the foreman on the ground that "discipline must be maintained." Of course discipline must be maintained; but the right way to maintain it is to give guarantees that it will always be justly used, and that no man will be submitted to the terrible penalty of deprivation of livelihood and perhaps also loss of his good name without being heard. Every man who is unjustly discharged is a fomenter of resentment and unrest; and every man who is arbitrarily discharged will find it easy to convince his friends that he has been unjustly used.

6. Dismissal

There are three possible reasons for discharge: a serious moral or disciplinary offence; inefficiency as a workman; and shortage of work. There should be definite legal protection secured by the rules against unfair treatment in any of these three cases. In the case of a moral offence (such as stealing) or a gross breach of rules (e.g. of safety rules), every man should have a right to appeal from the foreman or other officer who dismisses him either to a defined superior officer or preferably to a discipline Committee, including some workmen, before whom he should be able to state his case and produce evidence. In the case of dismissal for inefficiency, it should be

[1] See Appendix I, p. 238.

provided that no man who has been in the employ of a firm for (say) six months should be discharged on this ground until some body or person representing the workers has had an opportunity of considering the case and making representations on it to the management. As for the third reason, shortage of work, all employees know, unhappily, that the necessity of dismissals on this ground may at any time arise; but they fear that favouritism may have a hand in the choice of men to be dropped; and whether the fear is just or not, it is a source of unrest. The safeguard here is that when discharges have to be made, they should be discussed beforehand with a representative or representatives of workers, perhaps shop stewards, perhaps a Committee of the Works Council; and although these men are unlikely to take the invidious responsibility of choice, the mere fact that they have been consulted will be felt to be a safeguard against injustice. In the same way short-time arrangements should always be a matter for consultation. We recommend, therefore, that it should be provided by law that the Schedule of Rules should contain a statement of the safeguards against unfair usage in each of these cases.

7. Terms of Employment

We also recommend that every firm should be required by law to give to every man taken into its service a printed or written statement of the terms on which he is engaged, including a statement of the grounds upon which, and the way in which, he may be discharged. We print in an appendix [1] an indication of the points which should be dealt with in these terms of appointments. The effect of their provision by law would be that if any man was discharged without being allowed the safeguards provided for, he would have a ground of action in the courts against the firm which discharged him. Probably few men would be ready to incur the cost and publicity of such an action on their own account; but it is likely that the Trade Unions would take up cases often enough to make it certain that the provisions of the law would be generally observed. In Germany a whole system of local Labour Courts has been set up to deal with cases of this character, and the existence of these tribunals,

[1] See Appendix II, p. 239.

which are very freely used for the settlement of individual disputes that might otherwise lead to serious friction, has had the effect of giving a real sense of security, and of conjuring away the feeling that the workman is always at a disadvantage in dealing with the employer and must swallow injustices as best he can.

We shall probably be told that in these proposals we are descending to minutiæ, and that at the same time we are threatening to undermine the proper authority of management, which is indispensable for efficiency. Provisions which safeguard men against injustices that may strike at the very foundations of their lives—injustices, moreover, which have been very prevalent, not through malice but through carelessness—can never be trivial; and we are satisfied that these provisions will do more than will at first sight be recognised to give to the workman a feeling that he is really being fairly treated, and that the talk about improving his status is not insincere. Nor will these provisions undermine any legitimate power of management. These provisions only secure to the workman in his daily life an assurance of the rudimentary justice of being heard before he is condemned and sentenced to a very serious penalty.

8. Information

Participation in the framing of factory rules and protection against arbitrary dismissal are the chief definite new rights which would be secured to the employees by the legal establishment of Works Councils. But beyond this there are many points upon which the Works Councils should be entitled to information or consultation. First among these we should put the right to be kept informed regarding the trading prospects of the concern and its financial results. Many hands will be held up in horror at the idea of introducing workpeople to a knowledge of these arcana. But why not? Their livelihood is involved. And such knowledge is the very foundation of useful co-operation. This information will have more effect, and appear more practical, if the workpeople possess a right to a share of profits, or are part owners of the concern either corporately or individually, as it is desirable that they should be.

But we are not here concerned with profit-sharing, which has been discussed elsewhere. The kind of information which we think ought to be laid before Works Councils is equally important whether a profit-sharing scheme exists or not. We recommend that it should be a statutory obligation upon every employer to lay before the Works Council at regular intervals, say every three months, a statement as to trading conditions, and to explain and discuss it with the Council; while once a year he should be required to lay before them the concern's balance-sheet, and to explain it to them. A balance-sheet may be a very uninforming document; and we should be inclined to require also a trading-account, were it not that in some cases this might involve the publication of facts which the management may be quite justifiably unwilling to reveal, lest they should be made use of by trading rivals. But in any case the explanation should be as full and candid as possible. One great concern whose methods we have studied submits all the details of its accounts, with full explanation, to a small sub-committee of its Works Council, and makes a statement in more general terms to the Council as a whole. In any case, we think it is time to establish the principle that the workers in a concern, whose livelihood depends upon its prosperity, have a right to be kept informed of its financial situation and prospects, and of the trading problems with which it has to deal. This is the very foundation of an effectual co-operation.

9. Workshop Practice and Promotion

Next, the Works Council should have a statutory right to be consulted about the organisation and arrangements of the factory, to be informed of the reasons for changes in this regard, and to be given opportunities of discussing ways in which work can be more conveniently arranged or greater efficiency secured. This is a sphere in which workpeople, once their interest is aroused, can make contributions of very great value. The Baltimore and Ohio Railway some years ago introduced the practice of consultation and discussion of this sort in its engine workshops. The immediate result was a quite remarkable economy and increase of efficiency as the result of a multitude of small changes suggested by the men, who showed a new keenness when they found they were in a large measure controlling their own working arrangements. This sort of co-operation is stimulated by, but is not dependent upon, a just system of profit-sharing. To the same category belongs the function of suggesting methods of encouraging and rewarding inventive power among the work-people, which could obviously be stimulated by a Works Council; and this would help to stop the waste of good brain-power which goes on among our people, and to prevent the unfair exploitation which it sometimes has to suffer. Again, it would be reasonable to require that the Works Council should have an opportunity of discussing, not particular appointments, but the principles of promotion in the concern. It would itself help to clear the way for the promotion of able men, who could reveal themselves through the working of this system in a way not now open to them. British industry is suffering from its failure to open careers to talent; and although this responsibility must always rest primarily upon the management, a system of Works Councils, working in the right spirit, would make a great difference.

10. Welfare Work

What is commonly called "welfare work" forms another sphere of activity peculiarly appropriate for Works Committees. All the questions affecting safety at work, provisions for cleanliness and the brightening of factory environment, arrangements for holidays and organised recreation, and all those activities which naturally spring into existence among any body of men and women who feel themselves to be a community, would naturally be discussed by the Works Council, and perhaps wholly or mainly placed under its charge. "Welfare work" has an unpleasantly paternalist and patronising sound. It loses that character when it is mainly carried on by the people themselves; it becomes a stimulator of team-work, and of the community spirit; a teacher of mutual responsibility. It is a grim and saddening reflection that in the majority of British factories the workers tramp in in the morning, and after their allotted tale of work hasten out in the evening to find their real life elsewhere, never for a moment feeling that they are members of an organised community brought together for the purpose of rendering a common service and all mutually interdependent.

11. Joint Ownership Schemes

It is needless to labour in detail the subjects which might properly be discussed by a Works Council, as the common organ of a large body of people banded together by a common task and united by common interests.

There is, however, one specific function which ought, in our judgment, to be included among the essential duties of all Works Councils. That is the duty of consulting with, and if possible agreeing upon, the best way of giving to the employees a share of ownership in the concern, established by agreement and not merely as a revocable and insecure concession. We do not here discuss the methods of achieving this end, because the subject will be dealt with more fully later (p. 249 below). But we regard it as of real importance.

If the status of the worker in industry is to be made satisfactory, if he is to be given real ground for feeling that he is treated as a partner and not as a mere tool, if he is to be justified in showing "loyalty," not to a master (which is the virtue of a slave) but to a disciplined co-operative society of which he is a member (which is the virtue of a free man), he should be given in the first place the sense that he is genuinely and fully consulted, that he has a share in determining the conditions of his own work, and that he is a member of a really free society because it is one in which "the laws rule, and the people are a party to these rules." This is vital, and it is the main theme of this chapter.

But more than this is desirable. He should be given a share in the ownership of the concern for which he works, or at least some chance of acquiring such a share, and to this we pass in the next chapter.

APPENDIX I

Works Councils: Scope of Agreed Rules

The schedule to the Act setting up statutory Works Councils should prescribe under what heads rules are to be formulated between Works Councils and management. These heads are as follows:

(i) Hours of beginning and ending work.

(ii) Arrangements in regard to overtime.

(iii) Period of notice of dismissal which must be given on either side.

(iv) Methods of calculating wages (reference being made to whatever national or district agreements, Trade Board orders, etc., apply to the concern in question).

(v) Arrangements for paying wages.

(vi) Arrangements in regard to holidays.

(vii) Absence from sickness or other cause.

(viii) Dismissal for any moral or disciplinary offence: arrangements which will enable an aggrieved individual to state his case to some responsible person or body.

(ix) Dismissal for inefficiency or other industrial reason: arrangements for enabling the Works Council or some other representative body to discuss the circumstances with the management.

(x) Dismissal on the ground of shortage of work: arrangements for the discussion of the personnel selected for discharge by the Works Council or some body representing it.

(xi) Short time: arrangements for discussion of methods of short time working, and of personnel "laid off," etc., with the Works Council or some other representative body.

APPENDIX II

Engagement of Labour: Scope of Agreed Terms

Points which should be dealt with in the printed or written document to be given to every worker on engagement:

(i) Hours of beginning and ending work.

(ii) Arrangements in regard to overtime.

(iii) Period of notice of dismissal which must be given on either side.

(iv) Methods of calculating wages (reference being made to whatever national or district agreements, Trade Board orders, etc., apply to the concern in question).

(v) Arrangements for paying wages.
(vi) Arrangements in regard to holidays.
(vii) Absence from sickness or other cause.
(viii) The following provisions regarding dismissal:

The conditions upon which the above Firm offers you employment are as follows:

The Firm undertakes to give . . . days' notice of dismissal, and you may not leave your employment without giving . . . days' notice.

You will not be dismissed for misconduct or breach of rules without full inquiry, in the course of which you will be entitled to state your case to . . . . . .

If you are dismissed, the reason for your dismissal will be notified to you by . . . . .

If you have been in the employment of the Firm for not less than . . . months you will not be dismissed for inefficiency or other industrial reason without warning, notice of which shall also be given to (the Works Council or some body or person deputed by them).

You will not be dismissed on the ground of shortage of work until the selection of the persons for discharge has been discussed between representatives of the Firm and (some individual or body representing your work-fellows).

The document might also embody such other relevant information as can appropriately be presented in this form. Such items as the following could be given if desired:

Capacity in which the employee is engaged.
To whom responsible.
Punctuality.
Payment of wages to a deputy.
Passing-out authorisations.
Cleaning machinery, etc.
Loss or damage of property.
Accidents.
Transfer from department to department.
Safety devices.
Protective clothing.
Use of tools, etc. (e.g. measuring instruments), which are the property of the firm.

Deductions from wages.
National Insurance.
Cycles, etc.
Smoking.
Rest intervals.
Continuation classes.
Works Committees.
Profit-sharing Committees, etc., etc.

The document should embody the decisions arrived at in the formulation of the statutory Works Rules.

CHAPTER XIX

THE DIFFUSION OF OWNERSHIP

IT is a formidable charge against the existing economic order that it has divided society into a small class of owners who live by owning, and a very large class of workers whose labours enrich these owners. When all the necessary qualifications have been made, it remains true that the means of production—land, buildings, machinery, railways, working capital—belong to a small section of the population, which derives from this property a very large revenue; while the mass of the population is, in the main, rightly described as a "propertyless proletariat," living by the sale of its labour.

1. Present Distribution of Property

It is difficult to obtain trustworthy statistics about the actual distribution of ownership, though the broad facts are unquestionable. The best analysis is that recently made by Professor Henry Clay,[1] on the basis of the death-duty figures for 1920–21. The following table summarises Professor Clay's conclusions:

TABLE 27

OWNERSHIP OF PROPERTY. CALCULATED FROM ESTATE DUTY STATISTICS, 1920–21.

Range.	*Number of Owners.*	*Percentage of Property Owners Included.*	*Percentage of Property Owned.*
		Per cent.	*Per cent.*
Under £100	13,360,000	75	7½
£100–£5,000	4,048,000	23	28½
£5,000–£25,000	244,700	1½	26
Over £25,000	48,800	⅛	38

Compiled by Professor Clay from the Annual Report of the Commissioners of Inland Revenue 1920–21.

[1] Manchester Statistical Society, 1925.

These figures show that nine-tenths of the nation's capital is owned by less than one-quarter of the 17.7 million persons included in the above total; and that nearly two-fifths of it belongs to a tiny group, less than the population of one of our smaller towns. Professor Clay has also shown that the distribution of property appears to be more uneven than in any other country for which we can make a reliable estimate of its distribution.

That property always has been unevenly divided is notorious. It may be that inequality of division is a condition of economic progress. But the fact to be faced is that the discrepancies now in this country are so glaring, and consciousness of them so acute, that the resulting discontent endangers the continuance of economic progress itself.

We regard it as essential, therefore, that industry should aim deliberately and consistently at getting the ownership of its capital into many hands, not into few, and particularly into the hands of industrial wage-earners. The ways and means of accomplishing this aim require longer discussion, but its justice is as plain as is the expediency of breaking down the antagonism of Capital and Labour by identifying the antagonists.

2. Popular Ownership, not Public Ownership

The point at which uneven distribution becomes mal-distribution must be largely a matter of opinion. We agree with the Socialists in thinking that a distribution so uneven as is at present found is mal-distribution. But with the methods proposed by the Socialists for correcting that mal-distribution we disagree profoundly. The remedy, in our view, is not concentration in the hands of the State, but the diffusion of ownership throughout the community. We stand, not for public ownership, but for popular ownership. The aim must be not to destroy the owner class, but to enlarge it. To put the ownership of capital into the hands of individuals is essential if the supply of savings for industrial development is to be secured; to put it into the hands of the largest possible number of individuals is equally essential if the condition of the wage-earning classes is to be substantially and permanently improved. Some 62 per cent. of the nation's income [1] now goes to wages and salaries. Wage-earners and salary-earners should have a growing share in that other 38 per cent. of the national income which now goes to rent, interest, management, and profits. Liberalism has stood consistently for private property as an institution. We believe that "to have a bit of property" safeguards personal liberty, buttresses self-respect, and teaches responsibility. But for that very reason the enjoyment of private property should not be limited to the few. On the contrary, it is the liberty of the many which ought to be safeguarded, and the incentives created by the possession of private property ought to extend to every member of the community.

A policy for diffusing ownership more widely must therefore make its main attack on existing evils at two points. On the one hand, it will aim at checking the process by which great accumulations are built up, while safeguarding the reward of exceptional enterprise and ability, and will search for means of breaking up big fortunes which pass by inheritance. On the other hand, bearing in mind that large fortunes have hitherto been the main source of the supply of new capital, it will do everything possible to encourage popular saving and to facilitate the acquisition of property by the classes which are now for the most part propertyless.

3. The Redistribution of Existing Capital

The measures we have recommended in Chapters VI – VIII of Book 2 of this Report will do much to prevent the accumulation of "plunder fortunes" without in any way discouraging enterprise. But they will not by themselves put ownership within the reach of men who now have no share in it. What more ought to be done, and—an even more important question in relation to policy—what more can be done, by any means within the disposal

[1] In 1924, according to Bowley and Stamp, *The National Income*, the social income of the nation (i.e. aggregate income less National Debt interest and pensions) was £3,800 millions. Of this total, some £1,600 millions went in wages and £740 millions in salaries. Of the remainder, it is impossible to say precisely how much is "earned"; roughly, some £520 millions can be brought under this heading. This leaves about £940 millions of "unearned" income, or, if National Debt interest is included, some £1,200 millions in all. For an elaborate analysis of the national income, considered from different points of view, the reader is referred to the work cited.

of the community? To answer the first question, with constant deference to the test imposed by the second, is the purpose of this chapter.

(i) *Progressive Taxation*

First must be considered the use of taxation for this purpose. During the last thirty years we have developed a steeply graduated system of taxation by income-tax, super-tax, and death-duties, which has taken from the very rich nearly half of their incomes, and up to 40 per cent. of their capital at death. These burdens have been imposed partly to meet war-charges, but largely to defray the growing cost of the social services, expenditure on which has risen from £22,600,000 in 1891 to £338,500,000 in 1925, including war pensions.[1] This expenditure has been paid out of taxation raised mainly from the rich, and has been spent on social services mainly for the benefit of the working classes. Professor Clay has estimated it as equivalent to 12½ per cent. on the total wages paid, or, including employers' contributions under Insurance Acts, 14.7 per cent.; its effect has therefore been to cause a substantial redistribution of the national income. The social benefits of this redistribution are beyond dispute, but it has had little effect on the redistribution of ownership.

None the less, progressive taxation has had certain indirect effects on the supply of capital and the distribution of ownership, which must be brought out.

[1] The distribution of the totals is as follows:

	£ millions. 1891.	1925.
1. Expenditure under the Education Acts	11·5	89·4
2. ,, ,, Acts relating to the Relief of the Poor	9·1	40·4
3. ,, ,, the Housing Acts	·2	18·4
4. ,, ,, the Public Health Acts	·5	9·1
5. ,, ,, the Lunacy and Mental Deficiency Acts	·9	4·8
6. ,, ,, the National Health Insurance Acts	nil	32·5
7. ,, ,, the Unemployment Insurance Acts	nil	50·6
8. ,, ,, the War Pensions Acts	nil	66·5
9. ,, ,, the Old-age Pensions Acts	nil	25·8
10. Other expenditure	·4	1·0
Total £ millions	22·6	338·5

The above figures are compiled from H.C. 135 of 1926.

(*a*) In conjunction with the rise in the lower levels of wages and the decrease in the size of families, it has helped to increase the margin for saving among the working classes, and has probably also stimulated thrift by affording a foundation upon which to build.

There has been unquestionably a remarkable increase in working-class saving and investment during the last fifteen or twenty years. There are no figures showing working-class savings as such. But, as Mr. Runciman has shown, all the institutions which most definitely attract working-class savings, e.g. Building, Friendly, and Co-operative Societies, Savings Certificates, etc., have shown an immense increase in their funds. The increase, however, has not been on such a scale as materially to modify the distribution of ownership, and it has scarcely affected the ownership of industry. The standard of comfort is rising, but the instinct to save is still strong, and grows stronger as hope and security increase. The inference seems to be justified that if the process of investment were made easier and its reward more alluring, a substantial expansion might be expected even in present conditions, and a very great expansion when prosperity returns.

(*b*) On the other hand, the pressure of taxation has reduced the savings of the rich and of the "well-to-do" far more than it has increased the savings of wage-earners, so that the amount annually available for investment has decreased by something like £150,000,000 or £200,000,000. A second inference seems here to be justified, namely, that if we are to find the fresh capital needed for the development of our home resources and the replenishment of our foreign investments, we must develop new outlets of investment for small savings.

(*ii*) *Inheritance*

Another way of dealing with the gross disparities which exist in the ownership of property is to restrict the inheritance of huge masses of unearned wealth. The problem of inheritance has been marked out as a task for Liberalism since the time of John Stuart Mill. In the death-duties we have already found a means of taking a very large part of big estates at death, for the purposes of the State, and thereby diminishing the amount of inherited estates; in some cases, especially those of the big landed estates, the result has been a breaking-up of great accumulations.

It is the policy of the Liberal Party to increase death-duties still further, so far as this can be done without interfering unduly with saving, and without causing excessive evasions [1]; much thought has been given by Liberals to the best methods of achieving this end.[2]

We do not propose here to examine this question in detail, since it does not strictly belong to industrial policy; but we regard the wise and firm handling of inheritance as essential for the satisfaction of the sense of justice, and for the democratising of ownership.

4. The Creation of New Ownerships

It is not, however, so much to the redistribution of existing capital as to the distribution of new capital that we must look for the wider diffusion of ownership among those strata of society who at present own either no capital at all or very little. If it be thought that this involves a very slow advance, let it be remembered at how rapid a rate new capital is created and old capital replaced. Even in these bad times something like £500,000,000 of new capital is created every year, apart from replacements; and the total capital wealth of the nation would, at this rate, be more than doubled in the course of forty years.

Let us consider, from the point of view of the possibility

[1] Cf. the following passage from a resolution passed by the N.L.F. at Birmingham in 1919:

> "This Council believes that the national income is far too unevenly distributed, and that a nearer approach to economic equality must be the foundation of all social progress, and it therefore advocates that both income and super-tax should be more steeply graduated and more fairly adjusted; that death duties should be materially increased; and that there should be no taxation on the necessaries of life.

[2] For a detailed treatment of the problem of inheritance the reader is referred to three pamphlets by members of the Liberal Summer Schools: *Property and Inheritance*, by Henry Clay; *Inheritance and Inequality*, by H. D. Henderson; and *The Inheritance of Riches*, by E. D. Simon. The first two of these were published in the "New Way" Series.

of wider distribution, the two main sources from which new capital comes:

(i) The creation of reserves by industrial undertakings themselves; and

(ii) The investment of private savings—

(*a*) by the rich out of their ample margins, and

(*b*) by the small investor by systematic thrift.

Under (i) we have to ask whether it is either necessary or socially desirable that the whole of the reserves for expansion should go to the owners of the existing ordinary shares, and whether it would not be to the advantage of industry and of the community that ownership in these reserves should be shared by those whose labour (of brain or of hand) helps to create them. Under (ii) we have to ask whether the reduction in the amount saved annually by very rich cannot be balanced by an increase in the new capital forthcoming from the small investor—especially if he can be enabled to share some of the advantages in investment hitherto enjoyed mainly by the rich. It is along these two lines that we can best hope to make progress towards a real diffusion of ownership. The elastic and adaptable system of the limited liability company opens a variety of means whereby this end can be attained.

Something like three-fourths of the new capital invested in industry is set aside out of profits. It is this immense fund to which we give the name of "expansion-reserves." Before any funds can be available for expansion-reserves, a business must have met a variety of charges. It must have paid to management its agreed salaries, and to labour its agreed wage-rates. It must have made reasonable provision against depreciation. It must have provided standard interest on fixed-rate capital, and a reasonable return on ordinary stock; and, where the ordinary stock-holder has foregone a fair return in order to build up the business, it ought to have made provision for a return for this abstention. It ought also to have provided a stability-reserve, to keep the business going in periods of pressure.

But after all these needs have been met, it would seem to be both equitable and socially desirable that any new capital created out of the surplus should be shared with those who have helped to create it, and should not be exclusively credited to the owners of the ordinary capital, who may have contributed nothing at all to the exceptional prosperity of the concern, and who have, *ex hypothesi,* already received a fair return on their investment.

5. Ownership Sharing

We have elsewhere urged the desirability of sharing the surplus with the workers by brain and by hand (see the section on profit-sharing, above, p. 198), basing the argument not upon abstract right, but upon social utility, and the argument need not be repeated. Here we are concerned only with that form of profit-sharing which consists in assigning to the workers a share of new capital created out of profits, as distinct from the distribution of cash bonuses. If the argument from social utility was strong in the case of ordinary profit-sharing, it is stronger still in the case of share-distribution out of profits. For this method has two definite advantages which ordinary profit-sharing lacks. In the first place, it facilitates the creation of new capital, while ordinary profit-sharing may actually discourage it, by distributing in small sums, likely to be promptly spent, funds which might otherwise have been reinvested. In the second place, it directly contributes to the solution of the vital problem of bringing about a wider diffusion of ownership.

We do not suggest that the whole of the surplus assigned to the workers should invariably and necessarily be thus reinvested. The business might not be in a position usefully to employ all the funds thus available in a very prosperous year; and in some cases the sums available for individual workers might be too small to be worth treating in this way. But we do strongly urge that all profit-sharing schemes should at the least preserve the possibility of using the divisible surplus for investment rather than for distribution. It is eminently desirable that the capital required by industry should to the largest possible extent be drawn from profits, and that as large a share of these reinvested profits as the fair claims of capital permit should be assigned to the brain and hand workers.

It is sometimes said that it is not fair to the worker to insist that his money should be invested in the concern for which he works, since this involves the risk that bad trade may deprive him of his employment and of his dividend on his investment at the same moment. This argument, which is valid against any pressure upon the employee to invest his personal savings with his employer, does not seem to us to have any weight when the investment is made, not out of personal savings, but out of the profits earned in the business.

One stipulation, however, ought to be made in regard to this method of treating the employee's share of a surplus. If it is in any true sense to create new ownerships, it must give to the employee a marketable security. He should receive shares like those of any other shareholder, which he can sell if he so desires. If it is felt that the proprietary interest thus given to him ought not to be given up so long as he remains in the business, at least it should be secured that on leaving his employ he shall receive a marketable security in return for the rights which he is compelled to abandon.

The creation of employee-ownerships out of profits may assume many different forms, appropriate to concerns of different types. These may best be illustrated by four examples. The first two are English, the third American, and the fourth from New Zealand, a land of social experiment. All have their features of value, which are deserving of imitation in suitable cases.

6. Typical Schemes of Ownership Sharing

(a) *The Taylor Scheme*

The co-partnership scheme inaugurated by Messrs. J., T. & J. Taylor, woollen manufacturers, of Batley, has been in existence for some thirty-five years. Any profits made by the concern, after payment of 5 per cent. on capital, is apportioned between capital and labour in an agreed ratio. The bonus credited to each worker is given in the form of fully-paid shares in the company. The amount which each wage-earner receives depends on the amount of his wages; double bonus is credited to workers who have been not less than five years with the concern. The bonus shares do not carry votes—in this sense the scheme is not a true co-partnership; but there is a strong co-partnership committee which consults with the management in regard to questions affecting the workers. The results of the Taylor scheme have been very remarkable. By 1920 £600,000 had been paid to the workers in bonus and in dividends on their shares: they then owned over half the capital of the concern and received three-quarters of the profits.

(*b*) *The Brush Electric Co.*

The scheme adopted by the Brush Electric Co. in 1926 is a good example of profit-sharing developing into ownership sharing, in which rights of ownership are secured to the employees both as a corporate body and individually. It is embodied in a formal contract, signed by representatives of the directors and shareholders on the one hand, and of four classes of employees on the other. A schedule defines the procedure to be adopted in distributing profits, and the method of ascertaining the amounts to be allotted for replacement, reserves, etc. It provides that after the ordinary shareholders have received 10 per cent., all further profits are to be divided between them and the employees, in proportion to the total dividend on ordinary shares and the total wages and bonuses. A Council, composed of six members elected by the employees and two by the directors, is set up to administer the proceeds of the scheme, which can be used either for the common good of the employees or for distribution to individuals in proportion to their wages, the payment to be, at the choice of the recipient, either in cash or in ordinary shares, which the company undertakes to issue for this purpose at par, though the market price of the £1 share was (at the date of the scheme) 25*s*. or 26*s*. This is a binding contract, enforceable at law. It constitutes the whole body of employees as corporate part-owners of the concern, with a right to a large proportion of residual profits; it also enables individual employees, without outlay on their part, to become ordinary shareholders with full voting rights, able to sell their shares if they so desire. A scheme such as this must in time lead to a real diffusion of ownership, if the concern prospers; and the scheme itself will contribute to its prosperity. In any case, it constitutes a valuable recognition of ownership-rights.

(*c*) *The Dennison Scheme*[1]

The most striking and successful method of employee ownership is the Dennison scheme, under which the original

[1] A fuller analysis of this scheme is given in *America the Golden*, by J. Ramsay Muir (Williams & Norgate, 2*s*.).

shareholders are turned into preference shareholders, without voting rights, which are reserved for persons actively engaged in the business. All profits after payment of dividends are reinvested in the company; and the new capital thus created is divided among all the employees, from the president downwards —two-thirds, with voting-rights, going to the managerial class in proportion to their salaries, one-third, without voting-rights, to the operatives in proportion to length of service. The disappearance of even a semblance of control on the part of "functionless" shareholders, and the fact that the directors have to satisfy active workers and not mere dividend-receivers, are the main features of this scheme, which is probably the most complete and satisfactory device for restoring the connection between work, ownership, and responsibility that has anywhere been made. It is not, however, adaptable to every type of business.

(*d*) *The Valder Scheme*

A rather different illustration may be derived from New Zealand, where in 1924 the Legislature passed an Act empowering trading companies to adopt a scheme of labour-ownership known as the Valder scheme. This is perhaps the most interesting and practical scheme yet devised with the object of capitalising the labour contribution of the worker. Under this scheme the company issues labour shares of no par value, and without payment, which are distributed to all employees from the general manager downwards, roughly in proportion to their pay. These shares take all profits after the ordinary shares have received (*a*) interest and (*b*) a "risk-rate," which varies with the industry, and is pre-determined. Holders of labour shares have voting rights equally with ordinary shareholders. A possible variant of this scheme would be the issue of a block of no-par-value shares to be held by a trust on behalf of the employees as a whole, or various groups of them, the dividends to be distributed as the beneficiaries thought best. Since, under this system, the employees would constitute a specific financial interest, they might well be represented, in that capacity, on the board of directors, where their business would be to see that a dividend was earned for the interests they represented.

These schemes (selected to illustrate both general resemblance and individual variation) are alike in this, that they use what we have called "expansion-reserves" as a means of diffusing ownership-rights among those engaged in a concern, that they thus stimulate the creation of new capital, and that they base the new ownerships thus created upon a legally enforceable right, not upon the mere goodwill of an employer. They are essentially "ownership-sharing," not profit-sharing.

We have already recommended (Chapter VIII, p. 95) that the duty of initiating schemes of employee-shareholding should in certain cases be assumed by public corporations. The schemes illustrated represent the kind of experiment that we would wish to see undertaken.

7. Popular Investment

If we mean to reduce the proportion of the nation's capital which is owned by the very rich, and to increase the proportion owned by the million, it is not enough (1) to mulct the rich by differential taxation of income and capital, or (2) to encourage the break-up of their estates by bequest, or (3) to ensure that the active workers in industry shall henceforth share with the existing owners of capital the monopoly which the latter have hitherto enjoyed in surplus profits reinvested in industry. All these methods, right and necessary as they are, will tend to diminish the reservoirs of wealth now available for investment; and we must discover new sources of supply, and indeed increase the supply. The small savings of the million must take the place of the unspent super-abundance of the 0.28 per cent. of property owners who now own 38.5 per cent. of the nation's capital.

Present Volume of Popular Savings

Is this possible? There are good reasons for supposing that it is. The success of the Savings Certificates, in spite of a period of bad trade, shows how readily investment is undertaken when the procedure is made easy. By 1926 £376,000,000 had been thus invested, and the accrued interest amounted to about £100,000,000. This growth was not made at the expense of other forms of popular saving. In view of the low rate of interest allowed, it is significant that Post Office Savings Bank deposits rose from £169,000,000 in 1910 to £285,000,000 in 1926. Deposits in Trustee Savings Banks in 1926 amounted to £83,000,000, and the two types of Savings Banks held £215,000,000 of Government securities for the credit of depositors. The Co-operative Societies increased their membership from 3,000,000 in 1912 to 4,600,000 in 1924, and their capital—all subscribed by their members—from £42,000,000 in 1912 to £99,000,000 in 1924. The Friendly and Benevolent Societies increased their funds from £49,000,000 in 1910 to nearly £80,000,000 in 1923, while the Collecting Friendly Societies rose in the same period from £9,000,000 to £25,000,000, and the Industrial and Provident Societies doubled their membership, and increased their assets from £67,000,000 to £202,000,000. The Building Societies increased their membership from 600,000 in 1911 to 1,130,000 in 1925, their share capital from £44,000,000 to £128,000,000, and their advances on mortgage from under £9,000,000 to nearly £50,000,000.

All this shows that the habit of saving is growing, not dwindling, and that favourable opportunities for investment are used. As yet this development of popular saving does not seem much to have affected industry. But the experience of the Lancashire cotton industry shows that wherever the machinery of industrial investment is made easy to work, widespread popular use of it follows. An investigation, the results of which were published by the *Economist* in December 1926, suggests, indeed, that the small investor has begun to buy certain classes of industrial shares. This investigation showed, not merely that the average holding in big industrial concerns is small—that is due to the fact that the investor has learnt to spread his risks very widely—but that in an important group of big concerns (such as Brunner Mond's, Courtauld's, and the Cunard Co.) more than one-third of the holdings were of less than £100.

Difficulties of the Small Investor

The advance in small investment would be more rapid, beyond a doubt, but for the difficulties which stand in the way of the small investor. It is so important to stimulate small investments so that they may supply the deficiency in large investments, that every means should be taken to overcome these obstacles. What are they?

(i) Nothing encourages saving more than the possession of a banking account. Until recently British banks despised small accounts. They have changed their attitude, but the small account is severely discouraged by the *2d.* duty on cheques, which is the most short-sighted of taxes. If this duty were abolished or greatly reduced the convenient habit of paying wages by cheque would rapidly spread, and there would be a great and desirable increase in the number of banking accounts. The recent attempt of the Midland Bank to issue unstamped quasi-cheques for sums of less than £2, and the warmth with which it was welcomed, are significant. But more than this is needed. The duty on cheques, if it cannot be abolished, should be cut down to ½*d.*, at least on cheques for small sums. The total yield of this duty in 1925–6 was £3,422,000.

(ii) The machinery of investment is too mysterious for the small investor. If he has a few pounds to invest, he does not think of going to a stockbroker. He therefore lacks sound guidance in the choice of his investments; and he either has to fall back upon modes of investment which yield him a very poor return, or become the easy prey of sharks and bucket-shops.

(iii) The man with a bank account can often pay for his investments by instalments. The weekly wage-earner, who seldom has a bank account, and probably would not get advances for such a purpose if he had, cannot purchase shares by instalments. He needs facilities of this kind. The astounding recent development of small investment in America is mainly due to the application of the instalment system in this field, to which it is peculiarly appropriate, and in which it is easily safeguarded.

(iv) The small investor is at a disadvantage as compared with the large investor, not only in his inability to get good advice, but still more in the difficulty of distributing his risks wisely when he has only a small capital to invest. A man with £10,000 will often distribute it over 100 concerns, under the best advice, so as to get security against serious loss, an average good return, and some chance of capital appreciation. The small man has usually to be content with security and a small return with no chance of capital appreciation.

8. Means of Encouraging Industrial Investment

How can the small investor's difficulties be overcome? So far as possible protection should be given to his savings, and he should be guarded against exploitation. There are dangers in each of the methods which we set forth below, and it seems necessary that some supervision or regulation should be exercised.

i. Employee Share Purchase

There has been an immense development in America, especially since 1923, of systematic sales of stock to employees, under carefully drawn plans which offer substantial advantages to employee-purchasers. Almost invariably the stock is paid for by instalments deducted from wages at an agreed rate. The employee is often given at par stocks which are quoted at a premium, and in some cases a special bonus is paid to the employee shareholder so long as he holds his share. It is estimated that the value of the shares purchased by employees under these schemes amounts to considerably over $700,000,000. The system is beginning to be extended to this country: Hazell, Watson & Viney, Ld., have long had a scheme, which is linked up with their profit-sharing scheme, and the L.M.S. Railway is also trying an experiment. But the system of purchase of shares by instalments—which is valuable because of the stimulus it gives to saving—has not yet taken root in Great Britain.

This method has some marked advantages. It encourages almost automatic saving. It gives real advantages to the employee as compared with the outside investor. It provides him, as a rule, with a marketable security which he can realise if need be. But it also has dangers. There is a danger that the employee who does not purchase may find himself at a disadvantage. Again, it is generally undesirable that the employee's personal savings should be in the concern which employs him, for if things go wrong he will lose his savings and his wages at the same time. This danger is not serious when the shares purchased are preferential securities in concerns of good standing.

Subject to proper safeguards, we see no reason why this method of diffusing ownership should not be encouraged in this country: there is much that is attractive in the close association of saving and investment with work and wages, and the machinery is simple and easily worked. But we suggest that no organised scheme for the sale of stock to employees should be lawful unless it had been approved by the Ministry of Industry (see p. 220), whose business it would be to ensure (1) that the class of stock proposed to be sold was suitable for the purpose, (2) that no illegitimate pressure was brought to bear upon the employees, and (3) that the terms of purchase (or of cancellation when purchase was uncompleted) were fairly adjusted. For a scheme thus authorised, we suggest that a company might be authorised to deal in its own stock.

ii. Customer Share-Purchase

During the last few years America has adopted the method of direct sale of stock to customers even more widely than that of sale to employees. This method is mainly used by the public utility companies—telephone and telegraph, light and power, tramways, etc. The relations between such concerns and their customers are so close that it is easy to organise direct sales of stock, thus cutting out the complexities of the stock-market. In some cases a commission is given to employees on sales of stock of this character. The purchasers under this head are drawn from every class, and they mostly acquire only one or two shares at a time. Small investments of this type have expanded in America at a very remarkable rate—far more rapidly than employee share-purchases.

There is much to be said in favour of this method of raising funds for the public utilities, whose preferential securities are often very suitable for the small investor. Thus new sources of capital supply are tapped and thrift encouraged. But, as in the case of sales to employees, safeguards are necessary. We think that public utility concerns should be empowered to sell their shares direct to their customers only when the Board of Trade has approved the conditions of the proposed sale.

iii. Sale of Government Securities

We have elsewhere recommended (p. 111) that a Board of National Investment should be established in the Treasury, to administer all the capital funds which are available for purposes of national development. The extent of these funds will depend largely upon the volume of savings which the nation can be stimulated to supply. Already something is done, through the Post Office Savings Bank, to facilitate the purchase of Government securities by the small investor; and the National Savings Certificates scheme has provided another avenue. We believe that much more can be done in this direction; and we recommend that the Board of National Investment should devise means for facilitating the continuous, direct sale of National Bonds of low denomination, through the Banks and the Post Offices. The remarkable American "drive" for the sale of Liberty Bonds during the War affords a model which is capable of adaptation.

iv. Investment Corporations

The best form of investment for the small investor is in a soundly managed investment trust, which enables him to distribute the risks on his small savings over a wide variety of concerns, so as to get a better return than in trustee securities or savings banks. He may also hope for some capital appreciation, owing to the wise buying and selling of securities by the directors. In short, through an investment trust the small investor is to some extent put on a level with the big investor. There has for these reasons been a rapid growth of investment trust companies in recent years. But these companies are for the most part as inaccessible to the very small investor as other companies—he does not know how to buy their shares, which are sometimes issued in denominations too large for his convenience. Moreover, the very rapidity of their growth suggests the need for regulation.

We recommend that a new type of popular investment corporation should be authorised by law, of a type suitable for the most modest investor, and under special safeguards. These corporations should be empowered to finance share-purchases for their members, accepting payments by instalments and charging at the lowest possible rate for the accommodation thus afforded. In the case of these corporations, income-tax should not be deducted at the source, their investors being presumably below the exemption limit in many cases, and covered by the allowances in others. In order to ensure, so far as possible, that they were of this character, the amount of stock capable of being held by an individual should be limited. Popular investment corporations should be authorised to open branches, by agreement with employers, in factories or other places of business, to form investment clubs like the Savings Associations, and to receive subscriptions through Savings Banks and in other ways. No popular investment corporation should be allowed to start business with a smaller capital than (say) £50,000 or to issue capital beyond a maximum of (say) £5,000,000. The character of their investments should be defined with some particularity: it might be provided, for example, that one-third of their capital should be invested in Government stocks, one-third in debenture or preference securities of a high class, and the rest at the discretion of the directors. Every investment corporation of this type should be subject to license by the Board of Trade, and should be subject to a public audit. We submit that the development of a series of institutions of this type, under proper regulations, would have an immediate effect in stimulating saving and investment on a large scale.

The objection may be raised that by framing regulations of this kind, and consequently giving a special cachet to concerns which conformed with them, the State would be regarded as having guaranteed them, and would therefore be held responsible if anything went wrong. Some of us think that this objection is valid; the majority hold that it has little weight, and that it ought not in any case to stand in the way of the proper regulation of a movement which is already assuming large proportions and which may have great social value. The State already regulates Banks, Insurance Companies, and Friendly Societies; if anything went wrong with any of these institutions, nobody would dream of holding the State responsible. But up to the present they have very seldom gone wrong, because the regulations are wisely conceived. We think it right that the small investor should be given the opportunity of distributing his risks which a sound investment trust affords, and that he should be safeguarded by a proper system of regulation. Unregulated, the popular investment trust may offer many dangers, and a rapid expansion of the system might lead to results which would give a serious setback to popular saving. Rightly regulated, it should be an invaluable means of stimulating the flow of small savings both into national development and into general industrial activities.

9. Conclusions

Our conclusions, then, are:

(i) That the existing distribution of ownership is socially undesirable.

(ii) That it has been and can still be considerably influenced by progressive taxation and by bold handling of inheritance, but that care must be exercised in further developing these methods so as to avoid unduly reducing savings or encouraging evasion.

(iii) That rights of ownership should be given, whenever possible, to those actively engaged in industry; and that the duty of stimulating this change should be imposed upon the proposed Council of Industry.

(iv) That a very great expansion of popular saving and investment is necessary in the national interest; that this involves a wider diffusion of the banking habit and the encouragement of popular investment:

(*a*) by employee-share-purchase under proper safeguards;

(*b*) by customer-share-purchase in public utilities;

(*c*) by the encouragement of investment trusts.

(v) That all these developments need to be supervised and regulated for the protection of the investor; and that this duty should be imposed upon the Board of Trade or the proposed Ministry of Industry. These departments, in putting forward constructive proposals, should seek to secure the fullest co-operation of the Board of National Investment.

If all the methods which we have discussed in this chapter are systematically pursued, there seems to be no reason why a very substantial annual investment of new capital should not be anticipated. The investors would be drawn, of course, not only from among weekly wage-earners, but from among shopkeepers, clerks, teachers, small professional men, and others, all of whom need encouragement to save and help in making the best use of their savings. In strengthening their own position they will also be strengthening the position of the nation, and helping to make possible the forward movement which we have advocated in this book. The result of an intelligent system for encouraging and helping the small investor, added to the results of a policy of distributing a reasonable share of industry-created capital among the workers, should be a steady and even rapid change in the distribution of ownership, and a real advance towards that goal of Liberalism in which everybody will be a capitalist, and everybody a worker, as everybody is a citizen.

BOOK 4

NATIONAL DEVELOPMENT

ARGUMENT OF BOOK 4

Unemployment due to normal trade fluctuations can best be dealt with by a calculated regulation of credit and timing of public expenditure. But special measures are required for the exceptional unemployment of the post-war period and the Unemployment Insurance system should be relieved of uninsurable risks. In this way the present insurance scheme could be fairly revised and its conditions with regard to alternative employment reconsidered.

A vigorous policy of national reconstruction and development, directed by a Committee of National Development, would increase Britain's capital resources while serving to reduce unemployment. Advantage should be taken of the opportunity presented by unemployment to carry through a long-range programme of road construction, housing, and slum clearance. This national programme should be financed by organised savings through the Board of National Investment, by the restoration of the Road Fund to its legitimate purpose, by a betterment tax and a tax on improved site-values, supplemented if necessary by a Road Reconstruction Loan raised on the revenues of the Road Fund. Slum clearance should be an organic part of a scheme for securing a healthier distribution of the population, through the improvement of transport and the establishment of garden cities. Electrical development and the improvement of docks, harbours, and canals should also be regarded as part of a continuous and comprehensive plan.

Agriculture must be revived by security of tenure, the provision of credit facilities by the financing of organisations for agricultural credit, and by the improvement of marketing by organised distribution under a Central Marketing Authority. Land reclamation, drainage, and afforestation should play a dual part in adding to the national resources and relieving unemployment, while rural industries should be systematically developed.

The mining industry must be reorganised. Nationalisation is open to practical objections; but the State should co-operate with miners and owners in reorganising the industry. The State should acquire the mining royalties and give a national Coal Commission power to promote the development of new mines in replacement of those that are obsolete, and to facilitate desirable amalgamations by utilising the landlord's power of leasing all mining properties. Open consultation in the industry should be secured by the establishment of Pit Committees, District Boards, and a National Mining Council. Distribution and marketing should be improved by the development of selling agencies and the sale of coal by local authorities. Research and the more complete and economic utilisation of coal should be stimulated. The surplus of labour in the industry should be reduced by the limitation of recruitment, the facilitation of transfer to other industries, and the pensioning of older mine-workers.

Imperial development is of importance to British industry, since Empire markets account for approximately one-third of Britain's overseas trade. But it does not follow that Imperial policy necessitates a system of Preference, the objections to which are insuperable. Imperial development must be forwarded by other means: in the case of the Dominions, by improved communications, organised assistance to emigrants substantially aided by the Dominions themselves, and the wise direction of capital for overseas development; in the case of India, by political security, practical education, and a system of popular banking; in the case of the Crown Colonies, by the facilitation of loans, the prosecution of social and economic research, the effective training of administrators, and a liberal native policy.

The inter-related problems of education and juvenile employment must be treated as one. Hours of work of all juveniles should be definitely limited, and related to continued education and technical training. An increase in the number of secondary-school places in all areas is imperative. Local Education Authorities should be required to give all young persons an effective choice between whole-time education up to fifteen and part-time day continuation schooling up to sixteen years of age, as the next step in educational advance. Training should be provided for all juveniles unemployed up to the age of eighteen, and the placing and advising of young workers should be in the hands of the Local Education Authorities, advised for this purpose by the Ministry of Labour.

CHAPTER XX

THE PROBLEM OF UNEMPLOYMENT

1. A Symptom of Economic Disease

UNEMPLOYMENT is the gravest of the social maladies of the day—a disease incalculably harmful in itself, and symptomatic not only of the deep-seated *malaise* from which British industry is suffering, but of fundamental defects in our economic organisation. Its economic and its social consequences are alike deplorable. Its economic effects include the handicap which the necessity of providing for the unemployed imposes upon industry; the slackening of effort on the part of wage-earners due to the belief that—whatever economists may say—there is only a limited amount of work, and to go workless is to go hungry; and the contraction of the demand for goods in the home market which inevitably follows a shrinkage of wage-earners' incomes. Not less serious are the social consequences of unemployment and of the fear of its occurrence. The possibility of falling out of work is a standing threat to the security of domestic life, and is largely responsible for the friction which exists between capital and labour in so many of our industries. And the effects of unemployment itself, when it occurs on the scale to which we have become accustomed, can only be compared with the ravages of war and of disease. Both the physique and the *moral* of the nation's manhood and womanhood will deteriorate, rapidly and often irreparably, to an extent which cannot be measured in terms of money, but which constitutes an element of social waste, the magnitude of which is not less appalling than the complacency with which it is tolerated.

Unemployment before the War

Unemployment is not, indeed, a new problem. It has been a recurrent feature of our economic organisation since the Industrial Revolution. It seems to be a price which we have had to pay for the great material developments that have taken place under the system of private enterprise, bank-credit, and the specialisation of labour. Whether it was an inevitable price was exercising the thought of statesmen and economists to an increasing extent in the decade immediately preceding the War. The labours of the Poor Law Commission of 1905–9 were largely concerned with an examination of the problem, while a prominent place in the legislation of the day must be accorded to two remedial measures carried out by successive Liberal Governments, the Labour Exchanges Act of 1909 and the National Insurance Act of 1911, Part II of which put Unemployment Insurance experimentally into force. This legislation is itself some evidence of the gravity of the pre-war problem. On the other hand, it is true, as we shall show, that the unemployment problem since the War has changed somewhat in character; new and disturbing elements have entered into it, which must be considered in relation to, but separately from, those elements of which it has always been composed.

Unemployment Abroad

The presence of a post-war unemployment problem unprecedented in extent has not been confined to this country alone. No mere unemployment statistics—even if they existed—could give in cold print any real measure of the human suffering involved in the economic upheaval in Russia. But leaving this extreme case out of account, the records show that at times the percentage of unemployment in various countries has been even higher than in this country. Thus in Germany the proportion of wage-earners known to be unemployed has exceeded 20 per cent., and on more occasions than one over 2,000,000 persons have been known to be seeking work. For the United States of America no comprehensive statistics exist, but it was estimated that during the crisis of 1921 over 5,000,000 workers were unemployed in that country. Over 32 per cent. of registered workers were unemployed in Denmark at the end of 1926, and almost as high a proportion in Norway. None of these figures is strictly comparable with ours, but they serve to indicate how acutely some other communities have suffered under the stress of post-war industrial dislocation.

Such figures have been the natural corollary of the dislocation and loss of markets, the collapse of credit, the social upheavals, the monetary chaos, the loss of capital, the foolish and extreme measures of protection with which many nations, from a mistaken sense of their national interests, obstructed international trade, and many other consequences of the War which have affected many nations in varying degree.

But the disturbing feature of the British situation is that in spite of comparative immunity from actual physical destruction during the War or from the worst forms of monetary collapse or social upheaval after it, our unemployment figure has remained at a high level for so many years. It is true that the great share which we have in the world's international trade and commerce renders us peculiarly vulnerable to disturbances in other countries, and an unending series of troubles, some at home, some abroad, has seemed to nip in the bud every promising revival. At the same time, the persistence of high unemployment cannot be dismissed as the result merely of a series of consecutive misfortunes. The account already given of the state of British industry shows that deep-seated causes are also at work.

Whereas in the countries mentioned, as in most other industrial countries, periods of good and bad employment have alternated one with another much as they did before the War, in this country we have had, for a period now extending over seven years, an abnormal degree of unemployment to contend with. Never, since the spring of 1921, when the rapid industrial slump which followed the price-boom of 1919–20 culminated in a stoppage of work in the mining industry, has the number of wage-earners known to be seeking work fallen substantially below the level of a million. Year in and year out British industry and trade have had to carry this unprecedented burden. It is the seeming impossibility of discovering any short way out of this economic impasse that gives a distinctive character to the problem now before us.

2. Extent and Course of Unemployment

Facing the following page two charts are given showing (*a*) the annual fluctuations of employment among members of certain

Trade Unions since 1850; (*b*) the monthly fluctuations of unemployment among trade unionists since 1900 and among insured workpeople since 1921. The charts clearly bring out the following points:

First, that there was a marked and fairly regular swing in employment before the War, corresponding to the ups and downs of trade; secondly, the pre-war fluctuations were comparatively small compared with the great post-war movement; thirdly, that since the first recovery from the post-war crisis the level has remained far above the pre-war level—indeed almost at the worst figures reached during pre-war depressions; fourthly, that the level has remained high far longer than in any pre-war period of bad trade; and finally, that, as in pre-war days, the effect of industrial stoppages and other violent distortions of the curve do not affect permanently the normal trend, which appears to resume a normal movement after the crisis is over.

The figures of the last few years are not at all satisfactory. The recovery was clearly checked in 1923 before employment had become normal in Great Britain. From the middle of 1924 to the middle of 1925 in fact we actually lost ground again, due to a number of causes, including a general recession in international trade, the cessation of the special stimulus to British industry of the Ruhr occupation, and the prospects and effects of the British return to gold in April 1925. In June 1925 the numbers unemployed were some 250,000 more than a year previously. It was only in April 1926 that the number first fell below the million level, and to-day (December 1927), after having during one or two weeks been just below a million, the total is now slightly above that figure. Therefore, after three years we are substantially where we were so far as numbers of unemployed are concerned. From the point of view of employment we are rather better, because we have been able at any rate to absorb the numbers of young persons becoming available for employment during that period. As far as percentages are concerned, therefore, the figures of 8.7 per cent. for May 1927 (being calculated on a larger total of insured persons) is the lowest recorded since the slump of 1921, the previous lowest figures being 9.1 per cent. in April 1926 and 9.4 per cent. in June 1924. Subsequent figures show an increase to 10 per cent.

It should be added here that the Unemployment Insurance

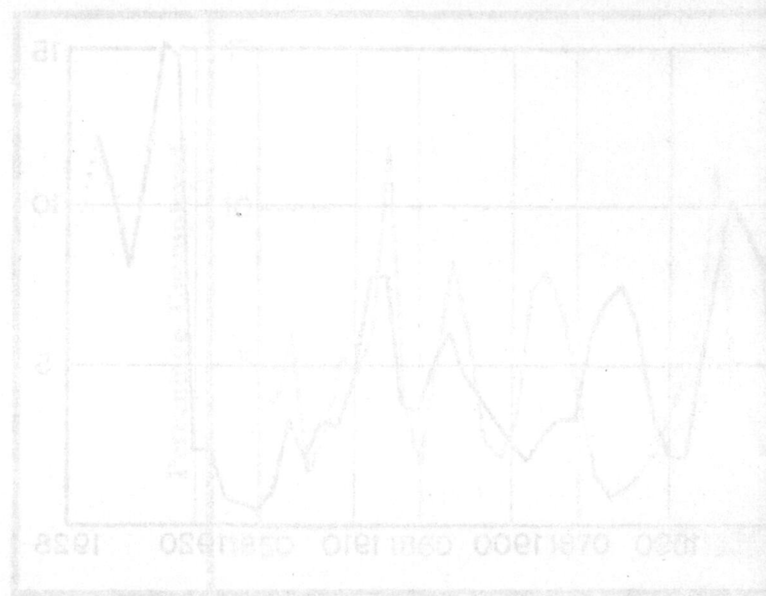

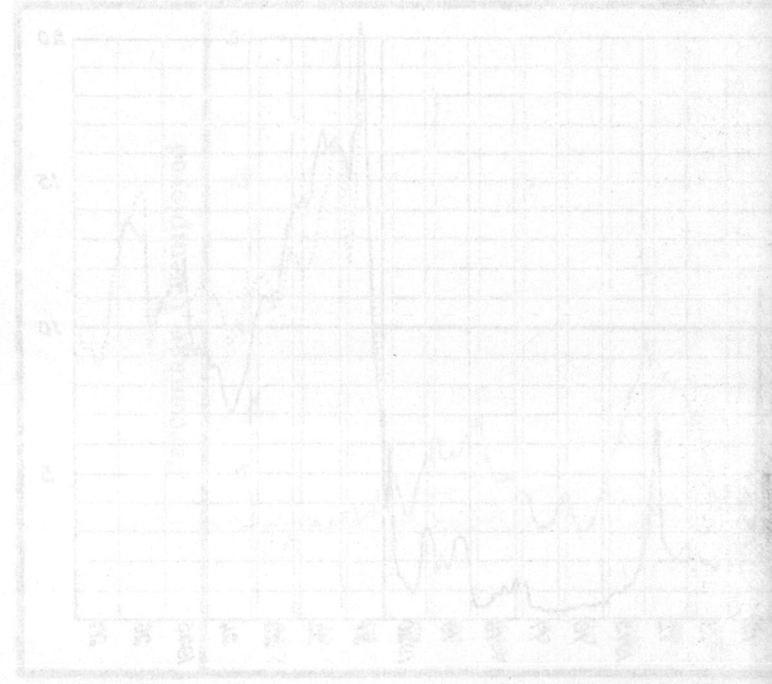

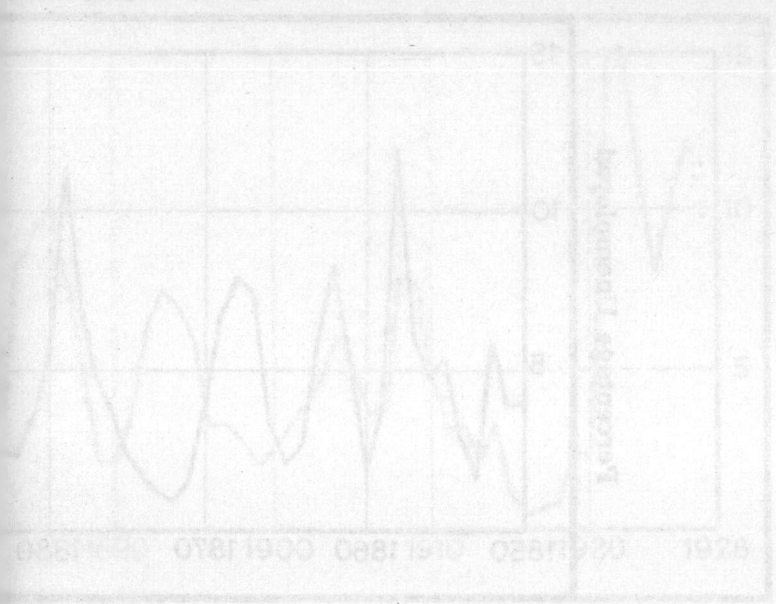

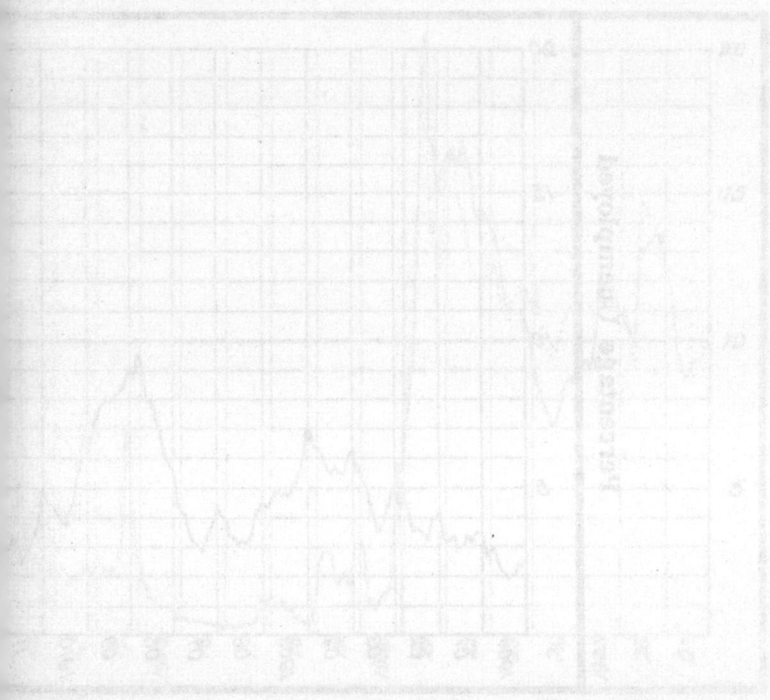

statistics published by the Ministry of Labour do not give the full total of unemployed, as they exclude unemployed persons belonging to several classes, e.g. a certain number of able-bodied persons in receipt of out-relief from the guardians; clerks and other middle-class workers over the £250-income limit; men not on the permanent strength of railway companies; and persons engaged in agriculture, domestic service, and other trades outside the scope of the Unemployment Insurance Acts. It is not possible to estimate, even roughly, the number of unemployed persons who do not figure in the official returns, although we know that many thousands have been transferred to the care of the guardians through the tightening up of the conditions for the receipt of unemployment benefit.

3. The Classification of Unemployment

With these charts in front of us we are in a position to analyse our problem with reference to its causes. The number of men and women who are seeking work and who cannot obtain it has never, in recent years—save for a brief period during the War—fallen even in times of good trade below 200,000, and in pre-war times when trade was neither particularly good nor particularly bad was in the neighbourhood of 500,000. In the last seven years it has never, except for one short period of six weeks, fallen below the level of 1,000,000. To what causes is the existence of this army of workers for whom work cannot be found—in a community which is far from oversupplied with the necessities and amenities of life—to be attributed?

There would seem to be five main types of unemployment:

(1) *Normal periodical unemployment,* such as occurred before the War, due to cyclical fluctuations of trade.

(2) *Seasonal unemployment.*

(3) *Unemployment incidental to industrial change and growth.*

(4) *Unemployability.*

(5) *Abnormal unemployment* resulting from war and post-war conditions and centred primarily in the export trades.

All of these types have to be taken fully into account, and

particular attention at the present time has to be directed to the fifth.

Periodical Unemployment

As regards the first four of these categories, we are on familiar ground, and have nothing novel or decisive to suggest. With the trade cycle and its possible mitigation by the regulation of credit we deal further in Chapter XXVIII. Two points only need be made here. The first is that whatever the relative importance of the causes of cyclical changes may be—and on this there is room for great difference of opinion—it is agreed that little can be done to mitigate the violence of these movements, either by conscious action in the sphere of monetary policy, or by moderating the psychological influences that may be at work, unless we have a much more complete knowledge of production, trade, stocks, and other essential economic information.

The second point is that if fluctuations cannot themselves be eliminated altogether, their effects can to some extent be counteracted by the action of the State and local authorities in adjusting their expenditure and concentrating it in those periods when private orders are slack. This proposal, which dates from pre-war days, and has ample support from many quarters but has never seriously been put into practice, is the counterpart on a small scale of the more comprehensive programme which we set out in the next chapter.

Seasonal and Incidental Unemployment

Secondly, there is always some unemployment arising out of the temporary maladjustment of industry. This group of causes covers a number of separate phenomena which may here be briefly summarised:

(*a*) Certain industries are wholly seasonal in character, and most industries exhibit some seasonal variation, corresponding either to fluctuations in the supply of their raw materials, or to the special character of the demand for their products, or to necessary adjustments to the conditions under which they are carried on.

(*b*) A certain number of industries again are dependent, as things stand, upon the existence of a reserve of labour upon which they can draw in times of stress. Of these casual labour industries the lading and unlading of ships affords the most conspicuous example. It goes without saying that the co-operation of all concerned in the decasualisation of unskilled labour at the docks and elsewhere is, as it has long been, an urgent need.

(*c*) A third factor is the ebb and flow of demand for finished goods in accordance with changing tastes and fashions. Employment in Nottingham, for example, depends largely upon the maintenance of a demand for lace; Northampton enjoyed a temporary burst of prosperity two years ago when there was a sudden widespread demand for Russian boots.

(*d*) Finally, there are always changes of a more deep-seated character going forward in the organisation of industry itself. The introduction of labour-saving machinery may at one blow deprive whole classes of workers of their means of livelihood; changes may take place in the location of an industry which, while they ease the problem of employment in some areas, create a new problem in others.

All these causes are in greater or less degree continually present. They must be considered as an element—but as no more serious an element than they were before the War—in the present situation.

The most that can be done towards the solution of these problems is to reduce them to the smallest practicable proportions by greater foresight and more intelligent planning on the part of employers and business men; and secondly, to provide against their harmful effects by adequate provision of Unemployment Insurance benefits for those individuals who, through no fault of their own and in the interests of the community, are condemned to involuntary unemployment as the price of progress.

The Unemployable

Unemployability is not an unemployment problem, though it of course verges upon it. Unemployment is the failure to obtain work by a worker able and willing to work. Unemployability is the condition of a worker who is not able or not willing to work. The treatment will depend upon the cause of the unemployability;

that is to say, whether it arises out of sickness, invalidity, old age, lack of training or education or character. The first serious attempt (outside the Poor Law) to deal with these questions was made by Liberal Governments before the War. They are to be found in the establishment and development of old-age pensions, sickness and invalidity insurance, and in provision for the training and direction of juvenile labour. Since that time they have been extended and developed, and whilst at the present time they are by no means complete, yet they represent a very great advance on the position of twenty years ago.

Abnormal Unemployment

There remains the question of abnormal unemployment, the causes of which have already been dealt with in Book I. The special facts upon which emphasis must be laid are, firstly, that the incidence of post-war unemployment has been mainly upon certain industries and certain areas, with the effect of intensifying the burden of high rates in just those areas which can least afford to bear it; secondly, that a high proportion of the abnormal unemployment now in evidence is in one industry—coal; and thirdly, that an abnormal proportion of young men are found in the ranks of the unemployed.

In July of the present year approximately 1,000,000 insured wage-earners were out of employment. Of these approximately half the total were to be found in some half-dozen industries; and of these again approximately half were in the mining industry. The other industries showing a high degree of unemployment were: engineering, shipbuilding (with ship-repairing), transport services (canals, docks, harbours, etc.), and iron and steel. To these should be added cotton, in which industry, as far as percentage figures go, unemployment does not appear to be high, but in which organised short time is being worked on a considerable scale.

In all these industries the position, since the slump of 1920–21, has been one of relative stagnation. The particular circumstances of each industry have already been dealt with in some detail in Book I of our Report. The measures which it is suggested should be taken to counteract these influences are presented, not in this chapter, but in our Report taken as a whole.

4. Relief of Unemployment

The proper way of dealing with unemployment is, as in the case of any other disease, to remove its causes, and we endeavour in the following pages to outline the measures which, in our opinion, should be undertaken to achieve this purpose. At the same time it is also the function of the doctor to relieve pain. The Liberal Government were the first to take measures for alleviating the distress arising from unemployment. They laid the foundations of the present system of Unemployment Insurance in 1911, when an experimental scheme, limited to certain selected trades and covering about 2¼ million workpeople, was introduced and formed part of the great National Insurance Act. During the War the scheme was extended to cover a further 1½ million persons engaged in munition and allied trades. The general extension of the scheme, however, took place in 1920, when nearly all manual workers and a large number of non-manual workers (totalling about 11¾ million persons, almost the entire industrial population) came under the scope of Unemployment Insurance. It was fortunate that this country, after the War, had in existence the machinery of Unemployment Insurance; it has, without question, enabled us to pass through these seven lean years without the health of the mass of the working population being impaired or the standard of living lowered. A glance at the categories of unemployment mentioned above, however, shows at once that this machinery has been strained to deal with a much bigger task than that for which it was designed. Unemployment Insurance was meant to cover the fairly easily calculable risk of recurring periods of unemployment due to trade depression, seasonal unemployment, or exceptional unemployment. The fund was never intended to support people permanently out of work for many years together. Moreover, the regulation of Unemployment Insurance was framed on the assumption that sooner or later workpeople would find employment again in their previous occupations. No provision was made for what would happen if the occupation of large masses was definitely gone for good.

That unemployment of this character should fall on the Insurance Fund is not a satisfactory arrangement. The essential principle of insurance is that the persons insured are all subject to certain common risks, more or less uniform in their incidence, so that there is a rough correspondence between the premiums which the insured must pay and the risks against which they are protected. So long as the principal causes of unemployment were temporary fluctuations in the demand for labour, seasonal, cyclical, etc., a general system of Unemployment Insurance with uniform rates of benefit and contribution was sufficiently in accordance with this principle for practical purposes. But now that the relief of unemployment means, in a very large degree, the maintenance of a large surplus of labour, attached to a certain group of industries, the arrangement is far less conformable to the principle of insurance, and its equity and expediency are both open to question. It is certainly not insurance to throw the maintenance of the surplus of miners on the contributions of employers and workers in the great mass of occupations where the risk of unemployment is probably not greater than it was in pre-war days. It means, in effect, maintaining the miners by a peculiar sort of tax, which is partly a poll-tax on insured workers and partly a tax on employment.

This is not an arrangement which can be defended on its merits, though it is less objectionable than the only alternative which is available at present, namely, to fall back on outdoor poor-relief, financed out of local rates. Already the local rates in the depressed areas have to shoulder too large a part of the burden of relieving unemployment; and this constitutes, as we argue in Chapter XXXI, a most serious obstacle to the recovery of our hardest-hit industries. It is undesirable, in our view, to attempt to exclude any genuinely unemployed men from insurance benefit so long as the effect of this must be to transfer the burden to the rates. For this reason we regard as a most retrograde step the "30 contribution clause" in the Government's Unemployment Insurance Act (1927).

In Chapter XXXI, however, we recommend, among other proposals for relieving rates, that the whole business of able-bodied poor-relief should be taken over by the State. When the relief of unemployment, outside the Insurance system, has thus been made a national function and a national charge, it will become possible and desirable to relieve the Insurance system of a burden which it ought not to carry, and to reduce the contributions of employers and workers to a proper actuarial basis.

The Unemployment Insurance system is often criticised as an obstacle to the free movement of labour into new channels. It would be a great mistake to attribute the present lack of mobility to this cause alone. The mobility of labour has been much more definitely impeded by causes altogether apart from Unemployment Insurance, notably the widespread shortage of houses and the consequent difficulty experienced by a man with a family who wishes to change his place of residence. Nevertheless, it seems to be true that the system has to some extent checked that mobility of labour which must be secured if changes and fluctuations in industry are not to result in serious local unemployment.

This criticism arises from the extension of the method of insurance to purposes which it was never intended to serve. It does not imply any doubt as to the rightness and efficacy of the method within its own sphere. It was intended to prevent destitution resulting from normal unemployment. The principle that the risk of normal unemployment should be insured against stands unshaken. The unemployed cannot be allowed to fall into destitution or to have no resources but the Poor Law. To speak of Unemployment Benefit as "the dole" is to misrepresent the facts and to disregard the principle involved. Of the total paid in benefit between November 1920 and December 1926, namely, £291 millions, the workers contributed £92 millions, and the employers £102 millions; the State's contribution was £69 millions; Service Departments provided £4 millions, and the balance (£24 millions) was borrowed from the Treasury to make good the deficiency due to the abnormal volume of Unemployment. In our view, the rate of benefit at present paid to adults is not too high; nor are the contributions either of employers or employed too low. The debt existing on the scheme, due, it must be repeated, to its use for purposes for which it was not designed, is, if not a war charge, at any rate a charge peculiar to the post-war period.

None the less, we recognise the necessity of adapting the scheme to present conditions. It has long been evident that the definition of "suitable employment" needs reconsideration, with a view to increasing, rather than restricting, fluidity of labour as between different occupations and areas.

The new German Unemployment Insurance Act provides that an unemployed person may refuse work (1) in a situation vacant on account of a trade dispute, (2) under conditions less favourable than those to which he accustomed, or (3) when the work may endanger his physical or moral health, or prevent him from supplying adequately the needs of his family. For the first nine weeks of unemployment he may also refuse work on the grounds that it does not correspond to his occupational training. In several respects the German law is much more severe than ours, e.g. an unemployed person refusing to undergo a re-education or vocational guidance course is deprived of his allowance for four weeks; the receipt of their allowance by unemployed persons under twenty-one years may be made conditional upon their performing some work in the public interest.

The present position in Great Britain is different. An insured contributor eligible for "standard" benefit may, to all intents and purposes, refuse an offer of employment in occupations other than his own, since it is unlikely that work under conditions comparable to those he enjoys will be available for him in alternative occupations.[1] Claimants to "extended" benefit may, however, be asked to accept employment in other occupations, and in so far as the Minister of Labour has exercised, in respect of such claimants, the discretionary power which he possesses, mobility has been in some small degree facilitated.

The position, which is clearly unsatisfactory, has been altered by the Unemployment Insurance Act, 1927, which comes into force in April 1928. This Act abolishes the distinction between "standard" benefit and "extended" benefit, and with it the discretionary power of the Minister to which reference has just

[1] Under the provisions of the Unemployment Insurance Act, 1920, as subsequently amended, an insured contributor who otherwise fulfils the statutory conditions for benefit may decline:

"(*a*) An offer of employment in a situation vacant in consequence of a stoppage of work due to a trade dispute; or

"(*b*) An offer of employment [in his usual occupation] in the district where he was last ordinarily employed at a rate of wage lower, or on conditions less favourable, than those which he might reasonably have expected to obtain having regard to those which he habitually obtained in his usual *employment* [occupation] in that district, or would have obtained had he continued to be so employed; or

"(*c*) An offer of employment [in his usual occupation] in any other district at a rate of wage lower, or on conditions less favourable, than those generally observed in that district by agreement between associations of employers and employees, or, failing any such agreement, than those generally recognised in that district by good employers."

(The words in square brackets were added by the Unemployment Insurance Act, 1927.)

been made. A provision has therefore been inserted in the Act (section 5 (2) (ii)) by which claimants to benefit may be asked to accept work in occupations other than their own, under approved conditions. We recognise that some such provision is necessary; administered under rules which will properly safeguard legitimate trade-union rights, it should go far to meet the difficulty to which we have drawn attention. Experience alone can show, however, whether the wording of the new Act is sufficient to secure the ends in view; its working will need to be carefully watched in the light of the considerations we have emphasised.

It is clear that a workman should not for an indefinite time be entitled to refuse work merely because it is not in his usual occupation. Every effort should be made to find him work in his own craft. If he fails within a reasonable limit of time and it appears that there is no early prospect of his obtaining that work, we think he should be required to take other work within his physical capacity and skill. These problems would, however, all be much easier of solution if the heavy load of abnormal unemployment could be lifted, and it is to this that we turn our attention in the following chapters.

CHAPTER XXI

A PROGRAMME OF NATIONAL DEVELOPMENT

1. Need for a General Programme

THERE are two important fields of action in which we can work for the restoration of a vigorous and healthy economic life. On the one hand, we must use all possible means to regain old markets, to open up new ones, and to encourage world trade on the basis of international division of labour; and on the other, we must endeavour to awaken in British industry a spirit of joint endeavour, based upon frankness and fair treatment, and of striving after efficiency that will keep us in the forefront of material progress. Our detailed proposals in the second of these two fields form the substance of the second and third Books of this Report. The energetic pursuit of these two policies should in the long run ensure a substantial improvement in the employment situation. At the same time these results are likely to be slow, and if we are right in our conclusion that we are faced at the present time with a certain amount of abnormal unemployment of a quasi-permanent character, then it is not sufficient to rely solely on the gradual improvement of productive efficiency. Definite and energetic steps must be taken in other directions to restore the balance of our national economic life. We need an enlightened, energetic, and statesmanlike policy of development and reconstruction in other fields, proceeding side by side with the improvement in our industrial efficiency; and in this and the following chapters we outline such a policy.

Since the slump of 1921 there has been a prevailing tendency, occasionally interrupted but invariably resumed before there has been time for a real recovery, towards parsimony and restriction. This has been the result partly of monetary deflation, but also of a muddle-headed confusion about the meaning of economy—namely, the idea that every form of avoidance of expenditure, quite indifferently of whether it consists of really wasteful expenditure or of a capital investment in developing the nation's productive resources, is alike "economy." The cumulative effects on unemployment of an official policy of discouraging new capital developments can scarcely be exaggerated. A nation's labour force is by far the most important part of its daily accruing resources, and an inability continued over several years to direct some 10 per cent. of it or more to any useful purpose not only involves a disastrous impoverishment of the nation, but is in itself a demonstration that the machinery for directing the available labour into appropriate fields of enterprise has broken down. We cannot acquit the timid, unimaginative, unenterprising policy of the present Government of a major responsibility for damming up in the stagnant pool of unemployment so much of the available forces of willing labour, which might be employed—if only the stimulus, the encouragement, the central direction, were there to give it the lead—to make the soil more fruitful, the roads more serviceable, the housing more sufficient, and the environment of life ampler and more decent.

We put, therefore, in the forefront of our proposals a vigorous policy of national reconstruction embracing within its scope, *inter alia,* the rehabilitation of agriculture, still the largest of our national industries; an extensive programme of highway development; afforestation, reclamation, and drainage; electrification, slum clearance and town planning, and the development of canals, docks, and harbours.

The policy which we advocate must have two sides to it—a programme of useful and remunerative developments and a scheme for the provision of financial resources. In the succeeding sections of this Book we set forth the former in its broad outlines. Our proposals for the concentration and mobilisation, through a Board of National Investment, of that portion of the national savings which is at present dealt with piecemeal by the Government or by local authorities have been already set out in Chapter IX. Since that chapter is mainly concerned with methods and machinery, we had better state here the broad foundations of our conviction that we need not hold back through the fear of the inadequacy of our prospective capital resources, and that the timidity, which inspires opposition to whatever is conceived in a spirit of hopefulness and breadth, is groundless.

2. Development of Capital Resources

During the nineteenth century the normal growth of capital and the technical improvements in methods of production would have sufficed for an even greater raising of the standard of life than actually occurred (which was in fact unprecedented in rapidity and scale) if it had not been for the concurrent necessity of equipping and housing a prodigious growth of population and for the dissipation of wealth in wars and preparations for war.

Before the Great War we were spending every year £10 per family on armaments plus £3 in interest on debt incurred as the result of previous wars. This is about equivalent to £20 per family in terms of post-war money. During the War the British Government spent a sum of money equal to the whole pre-war capital of the country, including the value of land, houses, furniture, railways, mines, quarries, factories of all kinds, and trading capital.[1] To-day we are paying £13½ per family for our present armaments, £7 for war pensions, and £37 as interest on the cost of the War—a total of £57½ per family per annum for past or future wars.

As regards the growth of population, we are now in a position to foresee that, unless there is some unlikely change in the trend of the existing birth and death rates, the increase in numbers in Great Britain by 1941 will not exceed 5 to 8 per cent. of the present total at the outside.

As regards war and armaments it is unhappily less possible to predict with confidence. But here also there is far more hope than there was a generation ago for pacific policies in Europe and the drastic reduction of armaments. If this hope is doomed to disappointment, we admit that our ideas may need to be revised. But this is only one more reason, if one were needed, for a readiness on the part of this country to lead the way in abandoning preparations for war.

Meanwhile the growth of wealth is again proceeding, after the interval of the War, with cumulative strength. In the U.S.A. savings are being made at a prodigious and unprecedented rate, which is certainly considerably in excess of £2,000 millions a year. Even in this country, despite unemployment and other

[1] Sir Josiah Stamp (*British Incomes and Property*, pp. 404–5) has estimated the capital (including all the items above named) of the U.K. in 1914 at £14,300,000,000.

handicaps, the national savings in 1924 were estimated at £500 millions, which was about 2 per cent. of the existing national wealth. At this rate the national wealth will have increased by 50 per cent. within twenty years from now. The supply of capital throughout the world is bound to benefit from these vast accretions.

The same is true of the improvement in the technical methods of production. The 1925 Census of Manufactures for the United States shows that on the average of all the factories in the country output per head was no less than 40 per cent. greater than in 1919; whilst the primary horse-power employed in factories was 22 per cent. larger than in 1919 and 60 per cent. larger than in 1914. We see no reason why a considerable proportion of this improvement should not be realised in this country also. The preliminary results of our Census of Production for 1924 seem to indicate that the net output per hour per person employed is about 15 per cent. higher than in 1907. The calculations of Sir Josiah Stamp and Professor Bowley as to the amount of the national income lead to much the same conclusion, though the effects of this are obscured by the wastes of unemployment and short-time working of machinery, plant, and organisation.

Accordingly we look forward to the possibility of an ample supply of capital and an ever-growing volume of output. Our problem is to translate these potentialities into fact. In the earlier part of this Report we have set forth some of the depressing facts of the recent past, and have endeavoured to indicate the weaknesses of our competitive position and the nature of the struggle which we have been conducting so far not too successfully. We are justified here in exhibiting the other side of the shield—our opportunities, the chance we have to lift the level of life of the whole community, if only we can learn to use the powers which lie at hand, to grow, to expand, and to live.

We should like to emphasise here not only the sufficiencies of our resources to enable us to meet the situation, but, on the other hand, the wastefulness of not meeting it. Our greatest asset is the daily supply of our labour available for useful work. Our daily-continued failure to make use of the services of more than 1,000,000 workers (who must be maintained whether they are working or not) is a supreme example of national power running to waste. This is the more deplorable when there are existing conditions which constitute a drag upon the economic life of the nation which could be improved by the utilisation of the available labour.

3. The Present an Opportunity

Unemployment means suffering and waste, and this is generally recognised. What is, however, equally true and equally important, but does not seem to be recognised in any appreciable measure, is that a condition of unemployment provides a great opportunity to improve our productive resources. It is a well-recognised fact that it is during the depression period of business that the most vigorous and effective steps are taken to improve the efficiency of the individual business enterprise. During a phase of prosperity the level of efficiency is apt to fall. Machines run at full output and repairs are postponed. The large demand for labour leads to a certain relaxation of effort. Orders are freely obtainable and profits abundant, and management grows slack. In all sorts of ways wasteful and second-best methods are allowed to develop. A kind of fatty degeneration sets in. Then, under the sudden stress of depression, strong efforts are made to raise the whole level of the productive efficiency of the business. The majority of businesses succeed in doing so, and those which fail drop out.

In the same way in agriculture the time for the repair and overhaul of the farm is not when harvest is at its height, but at the slack periods of the year when time and labour are available. It is then that the farmer surveys his land, repairs his hedges and his ditches, and considers where permanent improvements can be introduced.

Just in the same way the nation should recognise that a time like the present offers it a special opportunity to survey its resources and to carry out repairs, improvements, and developments which in times of greater prosperity would not be possible because of absence of the necessary time and labour. We have a great reservoir of unemployed labour, we have the necessary financial resources, there are all sorts of directions in which these resources can be utilised in such a way as to raise the whole level of our national efficiency in its widest sense. Is it not the height of folly to neglect such an opportunity?

4. The Foreign Example

Finally, many foreign countries have set us an example of what might be done in this kind of way. In a report which Sir Leo Chiozza Money made to us on the recent rapid developments in Italy, it was pointed out that the enormous strides made in the industrialisation of Northern Italy have been largely due to the schemes of electrification, which have been undertaken under the direct supervision of the State. Indeed, the progress of electrification in most of the countries of Europe has had direct State encouragement, e.g. in Sweden, Switzerland, and Austria. The French electrical system has been developed principally by State-aided private enterprise, the water-power stations of the Alps and Pyrenees being connected with the coal generating stations of Central France to form to some extent a co-ordinate system. The Federal and State Governments and local authorities in Germany have all played an important part in an extensive policy of power development. The loss of coal-producing areas after the War has been made up by the exploitation of lignite and the unification of the electrical supply; these have been accomplished by the active assistance of the Federal Government. In most countries the State has intervened in these post-war years to enable industry to overcome difficulties due to a very abnormal state of affairs. German industry has been re-organised with direct State assistance. Closer association has been maintained between the State and industry by the former actively participating in certain industries through holding large blocks of shares in important concerns, by direct subventions to large manufacturing firms, by special tariffs for railway transport, by the guarantee of export credits to the chief industries, and by increasing participation in the control of public activities. French post-war economic policy has aimed at securing the maximum national production in every branch of industry capable of development on French soil or in the French colonies. The State has directly supported the reconstruction and re-equipment of factories, mines, transport, and power stations in the devastated areas. The outcome of this policy has been the creation of a new manufacturing complex, equipped with the most modern appliances and resulting in a remarkable expansion of output. The French Government has also supported the efforts of industrialists to establish themselves in strategical centres in Europe, carried out elaborate railway electrification schemes, and reduced railway charges, financed foreign powers, and directly advanced the interest of French industrialists abroad. In England alone we have confined ourselves to the modest efforts of the Trade Facilities Acts and export credits to enable industry to keep on its legs.

5. A Committee of National Development

It will be obvious that the programme of national development outlined in this chapter covers a wider field than the activities of any one Government Department. It involves co-ordinated action by the Ministry of Agriculture, the Ministry of Labour, the Ministry of Transport, the Mines Department of the Board of Trade, the Central Electricity Board, the Forestry Commissioners, the Development Commissioners, and the Rural Industries Bureau, and necessitates the sympathetic and active assistance of the Treasury. We propose, therefore, that the direction of National Development should be placed in the hands of a Committee of the Privy Council, which might be called the Committee of National Development. This Committee would be directly responsible to the Prime Minister. Its duty would be to formulate a consistent and comprehensive policy for the development of national resources, and to co-ordinate the work of the Departments on which the executive duties would fall. It is obviously desirable that this Committee of National Development should take over the work now being performed by the Development Commission, whose work must, it is now evident, be backed by larger resources and carried through with the utmost energy on the greater scale envisaged in this book.

CHAPTER XXII

ROADS AND HOUSING

THE extension and improvement of our road system must stand in the forefront of any present-day policy of National Development. The petrol-engine is to this century what the steam-engine was to the last. But steam contributed to the undue concentration of population in the towns, whereas petrol creates possibilities, only now beginning to be recognised, of spreading the population more evenly over the land.

The progress of civilisation has always been dependent in large measure on transport. Roads were the arteries of the Roman system. The growth of inland and overland trading of the Middle Ages was made possible by the growth of roads. The large-scale manufacture which followed the Industrial Revolution only became possible when MacAdam and Telford gave us roads, Brindley canals, and Stephenson railways. Transport is more than ever essential to the modern industrial community. Without adequate transport facilities modern large-scale production and trading must be strangled. *Per contra,* really adequate transport facilities must give it a definite and important stimulus.

1. The Growth of Road Transport

What will be the respective importance of rail, road, and air transport in the future we need not stay to discuss. The rapid increase in the number of motor vehicles in the last few years indicates how heavy is the demand now being made on existing roads. In 1919–20 we had in this country 550,000 motor vehicles, and in 1925–6 1,651,000, an increase of 200 per cent. in six years. Nor can we count on any important slackening of this rate of increase for some time to come. Only road strangulation can falsify Lord Montagu of Beaulieu's prophecy that in a few years' time the present total will have doubled. If, indeed, the rate of growth experienced through our greatest period of trade depression should continue, we should have over 3,000,000 motor vehicles by 1930–31, or nearly twenty vehicles per mile of road. We have at present one motor vehicle to every twenty-six persons as compared with one to six in the U.S.A. and one to eleven in Canada. It is not necessary to assume that in this country we shall attain the motor density of the United States. It is reasonable, however, to suggest that we are yet very far from saturation point.

Moreover, the mere increase in numbers of vehicles is no adequate index of the demand upon our road facilities. The increase in numbers of persons and in weight of goods transported is much greater, as is also the increase in mileage per vehicle. A recent Traffic Census showed that the weight of traffic on all Liverpool roads had increased tenfold in ten years, and on some of the roads twenty-fold. On the Carlisle–Edinburgh main road traffic increased from 1,979 tons per day in 1922 to 4,392 tons per day in 1925. On the London–Worthing road the increase in the same period was from 2,278 tons to 5,213.

To show the increase over a longer period, traffic on the Gloucester–Bristol road was 1,891 tons per week in June 1913 and 28,267 tons in August 1926, an increase of practically 1,400 per cent. Roads in the industrial areas naturally showed the higher rates of increase. But the larger burden to be borne by the roads is distributed over the whole country: in 1925, for example, the Redruth–Bodmin road showed an increase of 144 per cent. and Class I roads in Cornwall generally of 261 per cent. over 1913.

2. Road Facilities To-day

What steps, then, have we taken as a nation to meet this renaissance of the roads—this new Transport Revolution? Though it has been so rapid, it was not unforeseen. As early as 1909 steps were taken by the Liberal Government to meet the situation which they foresaw would develop. A Road Board was established and funds placed at its disposal in the form of special taxation of motor vehicles. The machinery was therefore established for adapting British roads to the demands of the new traffic by improving the surface, widening where too narrow, and constructing new roads where the old roads were unequal to the requirements of the new traffic, and a means was provided by which resources for road development would grow automatically with the growth in motor transport. What is, then, the position to-day?

It is often said that we have the finest roads in the world, and in a sense that is true. For historical and geographical reasons we had at the commencement of the motor era the most highly developed road system in the world, and we have to-day undoubtedly the finest roads for pleasure motoring. But our roads are quite inadequate for our present industrial, commercial, agricultural, and social requirements, while they are entirely failing to keep pace with the rapidly increasing demands upon them.

The 152,736 miles of roads[1] in England and Wales are divided as follows:

TABLE 28

ROADS OF ENGLAND AND WALES. MILEAGE AND CLASSIFICATION.

	Miles
County Main Roads	29,439
District Roads	110,254
Roads in County Boroughs	10,853
Metropolitan Boroughs and L.C.C.	2,190
	152,736

Compiled from the Report on the Administration of the Road Fund for 1923–4.

Of this mileage only 12.3 per cent. is in Class I, and 7.4 per cent. in Class II. Over 80 per cent. of our roads, therefore, are unclassified. The County Councils Association, in a recent Memorandum, have thrown a startling light upon the facts. In sixteen typical counties approximately only 48 per cent. of the existing classified main roads are, according to these figures, fit to carry modern traffic; and, of the remainder, 38 per cent. require reconstruction at an estimated cost of nearly £25,000,000, and 27 per cent. require, in addition, widening or diverting at an estimated cost of nearly £44.5 million. These figures, be it noted, refer only to the small proportion of the roads which are classified. As regards unclassified main roads, figures put forward by the Association relating to ten typical counties show that only 7 per cent. are equal to

[1] The Report on the Administration of the Road Fund for 1927–8 gives the total mileage as now being 153,616, of which 30,702 is of County Main Roads: Class I are now 12·6 per cent. and Class II 7·8 per cent. of the total.

the burden of traffic upon them; and of the remainder, 89 per cent. require reconstruction at an estimated cost of over £4.5 million, and 48 per cent. require widening or diverting at an estimated cost of nearly £5.75 million. These figures of cost relate, it will be seen, only to these selected counties and not to the country as a whole. The proportion of district roads unfit to carry the traffic with which they are now called upon to deal is, in their view, probably greater than in the case of county main roads. Moreover, many bridges are entirely unsuitable for modern traffic. The latest Report of the Administration of the Road Fund calls attention to this subject and adds: "From many parts of the country urgent representations have been made to the Minister by manufacturers, traders, Chambers of Commerce, road-hauliers, etc., that grave disabilities are imposed upon trade by the weakness of these bridges. . . . The inconvenience is naturally most acutely felt in the busiest industrial areas where the intersections of roads with railways and canals are most frequent." County Council Association figures for seventeen counties show 740 county bridges requiring reconstruction at a cost of nearly £4.5 million.

Many of the County Surveyors lay special stress on the necessity for extensive road widening. The Lancashire County Surveyor says:

> "The need for extensive widening of existing main roads in this county is most urgent and pressing. The growth of mechanically propelled traffic during the past few years has been so great that most of our principal roads have become positively dangerous owing to their limited width. The average increase in weight passing over the whole of those roads has been multiplied by six between 1911 and 1925."

Expenditure on roads has increased, but to nothing like the extent which the situation demands, while many authorities, in spite of the limited assistance they have received from the Road Fund, have for some time been compelled to ration expenditure on their roads; that is to say, to spend less than they need for adequate maintenance. In other words, the ratepayers' capacity is reaching, or has reached, its limit. Without a change in policy not only will essential development not take place, but a good deal of the value of the work already accomplished will be lost.

3. The Wastefulness of Inadequate Roads

It is impossible to estimate accurately the actual money-cost of congestion of traffic. But every business firm whose vehicles have to work through crowded town streets knows how greatly its running costs are increased by traffic blocks and delays. The Railway Companies, for example, estimated to a Departmental Committee in 1920 that they suffered a loss of £50,000 a year simply from the "unnecessary detention" of their vans at Billingsgate Market, this detention being due partly to the inadequacy of space within the market, and partly to the congestion in the roads around the market. The London General Omnibus Company, according to a statement made in November 1927 by Mr. Frank Pick, "lost in actual out-of-pocket expenses a million pounds a year" by reason of delay in congestion on the streets. A traffic expert (the late Chief Constable A. E. Bassom) gave the Institute of Transport, in November 1924, detailed figures of traffic and delays at certain points in London, and he showed that the delays at twelve only of the busiest points cost the business community as much as £1,000 a day. Traffic blocks occur at hundreds of points in Greater London. The General Secretary of the Commercial Motor Users' Association put the cost of traffic congestion in Greater London as high as £25,000,000 per annum. If we take into account also the cost of congestion in other towns, and particularly in the great urban agglomerations of the industrial North, it will be seen that our tolerance of cramped and congested streets is a heavy handicap to our competitive capacity as an industrial nation, and that the amount of employment available for our people is thereby reduced.

To this direct cost of congestion must be added the cost of using smaller vehicles, or carrying smaller loads than are economic, because of narrowness or inadequacy of roads and bridges. We are in agreement, therefore, with the United States Department of Agriculture when it says:

> "Improved roads are not a luxury to be enjoyed if we have the means and put aside if we have not. The fact is that we lose more by not improving them than it costs to improve them; so that we may say that *we pay for improved*

roads whether we have them or not, and we pay less if we have them than if we have not." [1]

The first essential is to ensure that the main roads of the country are adequate. In this connection we have in mind the improvement of the roads primarily from the point of view of industrial and trade needs, and not from that of pleasure motoring. We urge the need for highways, not speedways. The main roads must be broadened and strengthened to take the heavy commercial traffic of the present and future. We have mentioned that in seventeen counties alone some 740 bridges are inadequate for traffic needs. This involves a direct handicap to the economic life of the country. The competitive struggle is now so keen that a very slight margin may make all the difference between a British contract gained or lost. For shorter distances, and particularly for perishable or breakable commodities, the ability to transport readily, directly, and quickly from factory or farm to warehouse or dock by road transport may represent that difference. To-day coal and cattle, cotton and wool, meat and dairy produce are transported by road, and a substantial increase in home trade awaits the improvement of our road facilities, particularly in the neighbourhood of the towns.

But while the main roads represent the most obvious direction in which road improvement is called for, they are not the only direction, nor necessarily the most important. As we shall show shortly, one of the factors absolutely essential to a revival of agriculture is the development of a great nation-wide organisation for the marketing of agricultural produce. If this is to be done, use must be made of a system of collection of loads from individual farms by mechanical lorries; and for this purpose the district rural roads must be wide enough and strong enough to take this traffic, and must be kept in such a condition that perishable goods will not be damaged by undue road shocks. That they are not so at present is indicated by the Memorandum of the County Councils Association to which we have referred above, in which it is specifically stated that in ten typical counties only 7 per cent. of the unclassified roads are equal to the burden of traffic upon them, and that in their opinion the proportion of district roads unfit to carry the traffic with which they are called

[1] U.S. Dept. of Agriculture, brochure on *Highways and Highway Transportation*, 1924. The italics are ours.

upon to deal is probably greater than in the case of county main roads. The growing of sugar beet in this country has already thrown a new problem of road maintenance on a number of rural district authorities. It is essential to a policy of agricultural revival and development that there should be a complete overhaul and improvement of rural roads, both as a means of transport of produce from the farms to market and of materials to the farm. The idea that road transport can be developed only or mainly at the cost of railway traffic seems to us fundamentally false. There should be a linking together of these two main forms of land transport, and we would like to see a Parliamentary Committee set up to examine the whole question and in particular the extent to which the railway companies are restricted in running motor-vehicles on the roads.

4. Financing Road Development

This brings us to the question of finance. How is all this development to be reconciled with the obvious need for national economy, and how is it all to be paid for?

We have already dealt by implication, in an earlier chapter, with the former question. Economy is not synonymous with the restriction of expenditure. Economy means wise and productive expenditure. In its original use the word was concerned with the wise expenditure of the housewife. Wise household management consists not in an arbitrary cutting down of expenditure in every direction, but in seeing that every shilling is so expended as to secure the best return. In the same way we believe that a wise expenditure, even of very large sums, in road development will be economical even in the narrowest sense.

As to where the money is to come from, we have to our hand two immediate and large sources of supply. The first is that of the Road Fund established by the Liberal Government in 1909. The receipts credited to the Road Fund in 1920–21 were £9.4 millions. In 1926–7 they were £21.6 millions, more than double. In every year that the present rate of duties continues we may confidently expect a steady growth in the revenue. Furthermore, we need not regard ourselves as restricted to this current revenue. In another chapter (Chapter XXXI) we propose a transfer to the Road Fund of the greater part of the outlay upon the upkeep of roads at present imposed upon the rates. But even if this is done, it will still be possible, by raising a loan on the security of the rapidly increasing income of the Road Fund, to undertake a very large programme of road construction without any additional charge to the taxpayer or ratepayer. This would be in every way wise and justifiable finance. The policy of road development should be consistent and continuous, but, if any variation at all is to be made in the amount to be expended, it should be in the direction of increasing, and not reducing, the amount of expenditure in times of depression. If the Road Fund is to be at the mercy of Budget exigencies, it will be just at the time of depression when it is likely to be raided, whereas it is just at this time that the whole of its resources should be concentrated on a large-scale policy of road development as a contribution to the unemployment problem and a counterpoise to the falling off of purchasing power in other directions; all this being quite apart from the value of the work itself from the point of view we have been considering, of wise development of our national resources. The policy of road development out of loans is justifiable on all grounds. In the United States the Federal Government provides funds for this purpose, not with a view to relieving unemployment, but because of the importance which is attached to the improvement of the road system. The several States, moreover, are spending money freely to the same end. During the last ten years approximately 40,000 miles of road have been constructed annually, at a total cost of some £200,000,000.

5. Betterment Taxes

The second great source of revenue available for the financing of arterial roads, and in particular those avenues through and from the cities to which we have referred, lies in the appropriation of part of that increase in site values of the land adjoining these roads, which follows automatically from their development. As the Annual Report of the Chief Factory Inspector has recently pointed out, the marked growth of industry in the south of England is "taking place especially along the routes of the new roads." The expenditure of millions of pounds on roads, coupled with the development of electricity schemes, the rehabilitation of our agriculture, and the better distribution of population made possible by a far-sighted and comprehensive housing and town-planning policy, will enhance the value of great areas of land. The recent extension of London's underground railway system to Edgware on the one hand, and to Merton and Morden on the other, has drawn the attention of railway directors to the inequities of the present system under which the land values created by works of public improvement go, not to persons or corporations undertaking the expenditure, but to persons who happen to own the land directly or indirectly affected by the improvement. The Underground extensions were financed under the Trade Facilities Act, the Government guaranteeing the principal and interest of a loan of £6½ million. Sir Robert Perks, at a general meeting of the Southern Railway in February 1927, called attention to the sale at an average of £3,000 an acre of land at Golders Green which "before the expansion of the Tube" was to be sold from £200 to £300 per acre. Lord Ashfield, at the annual meeting of the Underground Railway group in the same month, said that the Edgware extension of the London Electric Railway had continued to develop its traffic, though "at a slower rate than was anticipated," and went on to suggest that the explanation of this retardation in growth might be that land speculation at the Edgware terminal had forced up prices to a level which restricted purchases. He continued: "This is an evil which besets all railway enterprise," and suggested as a remedy "some means by which the increment in the value of the land could be appropriated to pay some share of the enormous cost attending the construction of Underground Railways in Greater London." Lord Ashfield's suggestion applies not only to London and not only to railway undertakings. It applies to all major transport undertakings and public improvements in every part of the country. The increase in land values might in some cases pay the whole cost of the development and in all cases a large part of it.

Again, the rise in land values along the arterial roads constructed since the War is extreme. The new arterial road, for example, from London through Essex to Southend has forced up land prices so that, to give one example, a farm at Rochford rented at £80 12*s.* 0*d.* gross per annum was sold at auction in 1925 for £6,600. Land abutting on a new arterial road constructed in a suburb of Manchester has recently been sold at £900 an acre. We give these instances merely to illustrate the argument that land values created by public improvements, carried out at the public cost, should contribute very substantially to the costs incurred, and that in site-value taxation and in betterment charges (the principle of which is already recognised by Parliament) lie a copious source of revenue, scarcely tapped as yet, for financing the reconstruction of the road system which the country so urgently needs.

6. Roads and Unemployment

What we have said so far in this chapter on transport is based on the twofold principle of the action which should be taken to cope with the evil of unemployment. The first, that the nation must be fully equipped at every point for industrial efficiency if its world markets are to be maintained and regained; the second, that a large-scale and far-sighted policy of road improvement, reconstruction, and development would provide immediate and direct productive employment for a large number of men. Furthermore, this employment would not be concentrated in one area or a limited number of areas, but would be very generally distributed. Housing difficulties and other problems of immobility of labour would therefore be avoided. Road-making, moreover, involves a relatively small expenditure on plant and a correspondingly high proportion of expenditure in wages. Finally, it is work which, while by no means capable of being undertaken by all classes of labour, yet demands no great degree of skill or training in the rank and file. It is, therefore, work peculiarly suited to our present unemployment situation. The measure of the contribution which a policy of road development can afford is indicated by an estimate that the raid on the Road Fund by the Chancellor of the Exchequer is tantamount to depriving 130,000 men of a year's steady work. From the point of view alone of its possible contribution to the immediate problem of unemployment it deserves primary attention. But it is at least equally important from the broader point of view of national development.

Building, and the building of houses in particular, is a peculiarly useful contribution to the unemployment problem for various reasons. In the first place, so large a proportion of the total cost is represented by labour. Then the great bulk of the materials used are produced in our own country. Furthermore, we have to have regard not only to the number of builders actually employed directly, but those producing the raw materials, the bricks, the castings, and so on, and those transporting them, and then to those people engaged in the making of furniture and other house furnishings and fittings. Thus apart from the direct reduction in unemployment resulting from the road programme, the indirect reduction occurring as a by-product of it would also be very material indeed. Not only would unemployment be directly reduced in this way, but the better housing would at one and the same time make for the greater health and contentment of the worker and develop his sense of citizenship and so increase his economic value, and, on the other hand, would materially contribute towards that mobility of labour which is so important a factor in the solution of the unemployment problem at a time of transition like the present.

7. Roads and Housing

But our road policy has a more important bearing on the life of the nation, for it is directly related to the whole problem of Housing, the inadequacy of which is responsible for city congestion and the continued existence of slums. Congestion and slums will never be permanently cured by mere rebuilding. Clean cuts must be made through and from the congested areas before this inflammation will disappear from our cities. When we say this, we have not in mind merely a little widening here and a straightening there, but the cutting of broad avenues from the city centre to the open country outside and the provision on these avenues of rapid and cheap transport.

There has been a great movement of the well-to-do to the country outside our cities, and this has gradually extended down through the middle classes to include a large proportion of the clerical and similar workers. But the general mass of the town workers have yet to share in this movement.

The alternative is to-day presented to large numbers of our workers either of living in over-crowded and unhealthy conditions or of wasting time, money, and energy on dilatory and uncomfortable travelling. Under present conditions of traffic congestion it may take the worker an hour to travel ten miles or indeed even five. Improved transport side by side with effective land reform offers the key to the situation in two ways. The cutting of broad avenues from the city centre to the open country outside will, on the one hand, reduce the time and the cost of travelling from the surrounding districts into the city, and on the other make possible the decentralisation of industrial activity and the removal of the factories, etc., into self-contained satellite towns in which the worker would be within walking or cycling distance of his work.

8. The Toll of the Slums

This leads us to the consideration of the second great section of our development programme. It requires no argument to emphasise the social and economic importance of good and sufficient housing for the people. The housing conditions in the centres of too many of our towns to-day are a disgrace. Room to live and room to play are the rights of every deserving citizen, and if these rights are ignored the price must be paid in ill-health and ill-will, in poor physique and poor production.

It has long been common knowledge that the death-rate of urban areas, where free access to light and air is lacking, is higher than that of the countryside. Before the War, the former was something like 50 per cent. above the level of the latter. Since then, with the continued improvement that has taken place in urban sanitation, the gap between the two has narrowed. But the expectation of life is still greater in the country than in the town. And the more congested the conditions under which the town-dweller lives, the less that expectation of life becomes.

Figures of infantile mortality are particularly significant. Infantile mortality depends upon many factors, but overcrowding is undoubtedly one of them. In 1925, deaths of children under one year in England and Wales averaged 87 per thousand in all county boroughs; 72 per thousand in other urban districts; 64 per thousand in all rural districts. And this in spite of the low wages and wretched housing conditions which too often obtain in the countryside, and of the continued drift into industrial occupations of the strongest and healthiest of its sons.

A much more startling contrast is revealed when we make comparisons between well-to-do and poor areas of the towns. For example, in the triennium 1923–5 the corrected death-rate of Shoreditch was 13.3 per thousand, and of Bermondsey 12.8, as compared with 10.9 for Hampstead and 10.3 for Lewisham. Infantile mortality-rates for the same triennium were: Shoreditch 85 (per thousand births), Bermondsey 76, Poplar 69, as compared with 52 for Hampstead and 31 for Lewisham.

The death-rate from tuberculosis may similarly be cited. Tuberculosis is typically a disease of darkness and congestion, and its incidence in overcrowded areas illustrates strikingly the waste of life and vigour for which our slums are responsible. Despite all that has been done successfully to combat the disease, for the years 1923–4 the tuberculosis death-rate of Bermondsey was 1.20 per 1,000; of Shoreditch, 1.28; of Southwark, 1.35; whereas for Hampstead it was .62 per thousand and for Lewisham .74. In the notorious Tabard Street area in Southwark, before the slum clearance scheme only now being completed was begun, the phthisis rate was no less than 3.88 per 1,000 persons living, as against the then figure of 2.09 for the borough in which the Tabard Street area is situated, and of 1.44 for London as a whole. An inquiry recently made in Glasgow, comparing in detail the vital statistics of Langside and Cathcart on the one hand, and Mile End and Gorbals on the other, points the moral even more clearly. The figures may be set out in tabular form:

TABLE 29

DENSITY OF POPULATION AND DEATH-RATES (GLASGOW)

	Mile End.	*Gorbals.*	*Langside.*	*Cathcart.*
Density: persons per acre . . .	136	207	45	22
Birth-rate per 1,000 persons living .	31·0	27·3	12·4	10·2
Death-rate per 1,000 persons living .	17·6	17·2	9·2	8·7
Infant mortality rate: in first year per 1,000 births	163	128	44	52
Phthisis: death-rate per 1,000 persons living	1·04	1·03	·38	·18
Respiratory diseases: death-rate per 1,000 persons living . . .	3·66	3·84	1·08	·76

Extracted from the Résumé of Work of the Public Health Department, Corporation of Glasgow, 1926–7.

So appalling a wastage of life, under preventible conditions, is a stain upon our industrial civilisation.

9. A Policy for Slum Clearance

A continuous and comprehensive policy for the abolition of slums is an essential part of the programme of National Development.

Attention necessarily and properly has been given to the need for building new houses since the War; the elements peculiar to the slum problem as such are even to-day not generally recognised. The million houses built since the War have, to a large extent, met the increase of demand created in the last ten years. But the arrears of new construction which accumulated during the War have not yet been caught up; much less has any serious impression been made on the accumulated arrears of slum clearances.

Slums are a resultant of poverty, overcrowding, bad planning, and dilapidation. They began to be a problem of magnitude when the houses built in the towns during the period of most rapid urban expansion began to reach the end of their natural lives. Experience shows that the average life of the brick cottages erected in the towns in the last century is about a hundred years, and the slum clearances which were undertaken between 1890 and 1914 were predominantly schemes for demolishing little congeries of the houses built a hundred years previously. The slum problem is more acute now than it was before the War, not only because practically no clearances have been carried through since 1914, but because with each decade of this century larger areas reach the stage of dilapidation. Slum clearances which ought to be undertaken now in London, or which will have to be undertaken in the near future, will involve areas not of 3 or 4 acres, but of 20 or 30 acres, or more. Slum clearances undertaken on this scale must include large measures of replanning and rebuilding, and any undertaking of this size must be carried out in accordance with some definite plan for distributing the population with reference to the places of work and the other factors which affect the structure of our towns. The development of the slum problem is more obvious in London than elsewhere, but all great centres of population will have to face in the next few decades the necessity of clearing away unhealthy areas on a scale which hitherto they have scarcely contemplated.

When the main factor in the slum condition is bad planning, bad building, or dilapidation, re-conditioning is sometimes an effective, if temporary, remedy. But in so far as slumminess is caused largely by the overcrowding of houses on the land and by the overcrowding of families in those houses, it is evident that the population to be dishoused cannot be rehoused on the same site. There must be some displacement of population, and this displacement should be carried out as part of the wider policy of placing new factories and other places of work in those areas which, because of their physical character or of the transport facilities available, are best suited for the purpose.

The million houses built since the War have, on the whole, been sited in a haphazard manner without co-ordination of effort and without regard to any general plan for increasing the efficiency and health of our towns. Towns to-day, in actual fact, very often do not correspond to existing Local Government boundaries. To use London again as the outstanding illustration, the area administered by the London County Council is only a part of what is London for the ordinary purposes of business and residence. A large proportion of the slums which ought to be cleared are situated in the older central areas where no sites for rehousing are available. Many of the work-places in Central London are, under modern conditions, retained there only because their workers still live in the neighbourhood; and the paradoxical situation is arising that factories which have found it possible to remove to the outskirts still, to a large extent, draw their workpeople from the areas from which they have removed. A plan for the development of London as a region would enable housing, transport, and the siting of work-places to be co-ordinated, and we call attention here to the proposals for Regional Authorities set out in *Towns and the Land*.[1] Under the policy there set out, Regional Authorities would be created in the main urban areas of the country, and it would be the duty of these authorities to provide, or arrange for the provision of, adequate housing accommodation wherever a housing need arises in the region which cannot be met in the areas of the separate Local Authorities.

The policy for slum clearance, then, must be regarded as part

[1] *Towns and the Land:* The Urban Report of the Liberal Land Committee, 1923–5. (Hodder & Stoughton, 1s.)

of the whole plan of urban reconstruction, and we suggest that the Board of National Development should be given special power to aid Regional Authorities, especially before they can collect revenue to be drawn by them from betterment taxes and rates on site values created by the improvements.

10. Garden Cities

Great Britain has been the pioneer in creating those new towns, planned from the start as whole units and for health and efficiency, which have become known as garden cities. Although neither Letchworth nor Welwyn is yet complete, their experience already proves two things: first, that new towns of this type have a special contribution to make to social contentment and to the ultimate efficiency of British industry; and secondly, that after the lapse of a few years a good and thoroughly well-secured dividend may be expected on the capital expended on their establishment and development, thanks to the fact that the building of a city converts agricultural land values into urban values, and these, after repaying the cost of construction, are available for the corporate use of the city. Letchworth and Welwyn owe their existence to the private enterprise of a few public-spirited individuals, notably Sir Ebenezer Howard. If they are to be not merely achievements in themselves but the forerunners of a new type of town, larger forces of direction and encouragement must be put behind the movement. So much industrial unrest and inefficiency is due to the cramped space allowed both to factories and homes by the congestion of the old industrial towns that the desirability of establishing factories in new centres wherever possible is self-evident. The argument for garden cities is to-day almost universally admitted, and Parliament has so far given it the stamp of its approval as to insert a clause in the Housing Act of 1921 making special provision for giving financial assistance to garden-city schemes. Up to the present, however, the actual work of creating garden cities has been left to the pioneers of the movement. The time has come when it should be taken up with greater vigour and determination as an integral part of our national housing policy.

Modern conditions, and road transport in particular, have brought new factors into play in determining the location of industry. Where there are open sites, adequately served by power-supply and transport and economically situated in relation to supplies of raw material and to markets, new factory areas could be developed in conjunction with housing schemes to much greater advantage than if the new buildings were squeezed into the centre of existing industrial areas or even tacked on to their outskirts—in other words, new towns can be deliberately created to redress the ill-balanced development of the old.

At the beginning of any such enterprise there is in the nature of the undertaking a period during which current revenue cannot cover the interest on capital expended. The period of fructification, as it is called, is, as in the case of railways, a somewhat prolonged period. Subsequently revenues and profits can be safely expected to make good the arrears of interest as the towns develop and land values are created. We suggest, therefore, that the Board of National Investment should be empowered to guarantee in proper cases the interest on the bonds issued by Associations authorised to build Garden Cities, subject to arrangements for the ultimate relief of the guarantees when financial stability is reached.

The location of new towns of this type in different parts of the country would be in accordance with regional plans, based largely on considerations of the transport facilities available. The plan of each new town should in all cases provide for the scheduling, as agricultural land and as open space, of a belt of considerable width around the area which is to be covered by its factories, houses, shops, and other buildings.

II. Preserving the Countryside

While we are urging the necessity of planning for the wider and wiser distribution of the industrial population, it is important to make clear that the real threat to the English countryside is contained not in planned development, but in the sporadic, unplanned development that is now going on. We wish, therefore, to call attention at this point to the necessity of taking decisive action to preserve the downs, moors, lakes, woods, hills, and commons of the countryside, and we suggest that the time has come for national action to conserve their beauties and their amenities for future generations. We owe a great deal to private munificence and to such bodies as the National Trust and the Commons and Footpaths Preservation Society. But as the population increases, and as it is spread more evenly over the land, as a result of better roads, motor-transport, electrical power supply, and that decentralisation of industry and of population which we hope to promote, the preservation of Britain's open country passes outside the power of private persons or of societies interested in public welfare. What is required is an extension of the principle of town-planning so as to preserve permanently from sporadic building and other forms of ill-considered exploitation all those areas of the country whose fullest contribution to national welfare lies in their preservation as open spaces. We suggest, therefore, that the Ministry of Health should have power to schedule as national open spaces areas as many of the Surrey commons, the South Downs, Salisbury Plain, Dartmoor, Exmoor, and parts of the Peak and Lake Districts; that it should be commissioned at once to schedule such areas; that any action involving a material change in the outward aspect of such areas should require express permission; and that there should be power either now or at any future time to take over them or any part of them into public ownership on the payment of reasonable compensation assessed on the principles accepted in the present Town-planning Acts. The expense would not be great; the benefit to the nation would be immeasurable.

12. Distributing the Population

The proposals made in the immediately preceding paragraphs recognise the rightness of protests made against the desecration of the countryside, and, we think, provide a means of making those protests effective. Open spaces must be preserved. But the countryside as a whole must thrive. The wholesomeness of national life to a very large extent depends on the interaction of town and country, and on breaking down the social and economic barriers between agriculture and other industries. To all this transport is the key.

The effect of transport on the distribution of population is well illustrated in Belgium, where, as Mr. Seebohm Rowntree ascertained in 1900, 56 per cent. of the population lived in country districts, although only about 23 per cent. depended on agriculture for their main livelihood. The distribution of Belgian population is, we understand, still much as it was found to be twenty-seven years ago. Residents in the Belgian countryside for the most part cultivate some land. The division between the urban and the rural worker is thus, to a large extent, broken down. An industrial worker, if he loses his employment, generally occupies himself on his own land or gets a job with a farmer. In this way he keeps a footing in the country, and often, when he grows older and his chances of getting regular work lessen, he depends more and more upon his land until ultimately he relies upon it altogether, gradually adding to his holding until it is sufficiently large to make him self-supporting. This interconnection of urban industry and rural life is made possible only by facilities for rapid and cheap transport and, in particular, by the " vicinal railways." The development of these railways has been a constant object of national solicitude. They not only link town to town and town to outlying village, but they bring countryside and town together in organic relationship.

13. National Overhead Charges

To cleanse our towns of squalor is more than a programme of " social betterment " in the narrowest sense of that phrase. Social organisation is the complement of industrial organisation. What the factory produces is affected by the home conditions of the workers who produce it, by the air and light which they enjoy, the means of transport at their disposal, and their opportunities for education and recreation. Only now, at the end of a long period in which towns have been allowed to grow up anyhow (and have consequently grown up badly), is the only durable conception of towns coming to be recognised, namely, that they are in part social organisms and in part industrial plants. The conception of towns as social organisms means bringing all their several parts to work in harmony and planning them not as aggregations but as units. The conception of towns as industrial plants means paying collective attention to those overhead charges which fall on the manufacturer as a result of social conditions. The ill-health that comes from homes unfit for human habitation, the discontent that properly voices the demand for better physical conditions and wider opportunities, congestion of traffic in the streets, darkness in the factory itself—all these are actual handicaps on our competitive efficiency. Every nerve must be strained to provide work for the unemployed. But the work which is undertaken should be part of a plan for the physical improvement and the economic betterment of towns and of the country as a whole. As a result of such work the nation should emerge from the present period of unemployment not with impaired assets but rehabilitated. Unemployment should leave as its mark, not shabby homes and flabby muscles, but new roads, new bridges, new houses, new schools, new towns, cleared watercourses, drained fields, newly afforested hillsides, land reclaimed from marsh or won back from the sea, new power lines, an altogether more efficient economic equipment, and a population not daunted and demoralised, but braced by work which, however unaccustomed, will be in the future a source of pride.

CHAPTER XXIII

ELECTRICITY, WATERWAYS, AND DOCKS

1. Electricity

ANOTHER great field of enterprise in which national development wisely directed can contribute to the solution of the unemployment problem is that of electrical supply. A detailed treatment of the subject, which has been dealt with in *Coal and Power,*[1] is not here required, but we must call attention to the amount of direct employment involved in increasing the electrical plant and equipment of the nation, and to the increase in our national competitive power which would result from a wider use of electrical energy for manufacturing purposes.

It is true that there has been a rapid increase in this country of electrical output—an output of 1,600 million units in 1913–14 had by 1925 grown to 8,125 million units. But such development must be considered comparatively. In a list of the main industrial States of Europe, together with the U.S.A. and Canada, arranged according to the output of electricity per head of population, Great Britain stands fourth from the bottom. The position is shown in Table 30.

Although the output per head of population in Great Britain is just ahead of that in France, from every other point of view the table indicates how vast the room for expansion must be in this country. Even though the three countries at the top of the list might be expected to be ahead of us, because of the high cost of labour in the United States and Canada, and of the exceptional supply of water power in Switzerland, yet the gap is so large that there is clearly immense scope for development in this country.

[1] *Coal and Power.* (Hodder & Stoughton, 1924, 1s.)

TABLE 30

PRODUCTION OF ELECTRICITY IN NINE INDUSTRIAL COUNTRIES, 1925

Country.	*Total Output of Electricity from All Sources.*	*Proportion taken by Industry.*	*Output per Head of Population.*
	Million Units.	*Per cent.*	*Units.*
Canada	10,110	95	1,150
Switzerland	3,900	—	1,000
U.S.A.	81,801	69	710
Germany	20,328	83	318
Belgium	2,274	—	291
Great Britain	11,814	69	282
France	10,000	90	250
Italy	7,600	95	195
Poland	1,800	over 80	63
Total	149,628	—	430

Compiled from official sources and supplied by Mr. Hugh Quigley, of the Economic and Statistical Department of the British Electrical and Allied Manufacturers' Association.

Until recently arrangements for both the manufacture and distribution of electricity have admittedly been most unsatisfactory. Our engineers have designed and built some super-power stations which are equal in efficiency to the best in the world, but for the most part the country is covered with small and inefficient stations, and between them proper intercommunication does not exist. The Electricity (Supply) Act of 1926 which set up the Central Electricity Board is a big step in the right direction; although it does not give the Board the full powers asked for in *Coal and Power,* yet it goes a considerable distance in the right direction. But immediate and revolutionary results must not be looked for; to produce out of the present chaos a wise and far-sighted scheme reconciling all the antagonistic interests that have grown up is a very difficult task.

The 1926 Act gives to the Electricity Commissioners the duty of preparing a number of schemes which will eventually cover the whole country. The area to be brought within each scheme has to be determined after very careful inquiry into the geographical and industrial sources of energy and after consideration of the best system of linking up the different parts of the area, the possibility of future interconnection with other areas, and the efficiency and situation of existing generating stations. The scheme in draft form has then to be sent to the Central Electricity Board, who finally decide the form in which it shall be put into force. It has then to be published, and any or all of the numerous undertakings or persons affected may within one month claim to be heard. A right of appeal against the decision of the Central Electricity Board is given in certain cases, and altogether it is possible to have a period of several months between the inception of the scheme and the commencement of work within an area.

All experience of administration of local affairs by local men proves that it is necessary to provide for local opinion being heard and then given full consideration in regard to any proposals which interfere with the control of the public utility services, otherwise there would be strong opposition to the scheme, however good it might be.

The first scheme under the 1926 Act (that for the Central Scottish area) was received by the Central Electricity Board some months ago, after which they met informally the representatives of all those undertakings within the area who desired to be heard, with the satisfactory result that not a single undertaking exercised its right of appeal, and the scheme is now so far advanced that orders have been placed for the major portion of the plant. The second scheme (that for the South-east of England, which includes the London area) has now been sent to the Central Electricity Board, and is being dealt with. The preparatory work in another area is well advanced, so that the national scheme is proceeding at a faster rate than anyone anticipated, in marked contrast to previous experience in regard to electricity supply development.

As the schemes for the different areas will be prepared one by one, and issued at intervals, it is obvious that under the most favourable circumstances they will be spread over a considerable period of time, and that any immediate placing of immense orders for machinery is impracticable. It is also undesirable, as it would flood the market, prices would be put up against the Board, and export trade would probably be lost. The right policy is undoubtedly to use the orders which are to be given out by the Central Electricity Board as a balance to secure constant work for the British factories, at something like full output, over a period of years. This means a reduction in the manufacturer's overhead charges, and will therefore tend to put the British manufacturer into an improved position to compete in overseas markets against his foreign competitors.

From the point of view of preventing unemployment in the electrical trades, of encouraging the export trade, and of providing a satisfactory scheme of power production which will stand the test of time, gradual development would seem undoubtedly to be the right policy. The Board will require the constant and steady backing of the Government if time is not to be wasted, and although the Act of 1926 marks a distinct step forward as regard powers, yet experience has already shown that further powers are required. If electricity is to be taken into the rural districts, the transmission lines must be cheap. A low-tension overhead line in its simplest form must not cost more than a maximum of £200 a mile. In many continental countries such lines are built at a cost as low as £100 a mile. In this country, owing, it is said, to unnecessarily high standards, and to the opposition of vested interests in granting wayleaves, such lines are in many cases costing £500 a mile and more. Under such conditions a satisfactory and complete scheme of electrical power distribution is impossible. We are of opinion that there should be an immediate inquiry into this matter.

There is little doubt that in other ways experience will show that further powers are required. A fairly satisfactory beginning has been made, but steady and constant pressure is required from the Government if we are to have, in a reasonable time, a complete and first-class scheme for the production of electrical power. The danger is that the policy of electrical development may be crippled by parsimony as road development has already been crippled. As with roads, so with electricity, we have a peculiar opportunity of raising our economic life to a higher power at the very time when we have a surplus of labour which must be maintained. Public opinion, realising the evils of unemployment, should insist on that opportunity being grasped, so that part of our surplus labour may be employed in bringing the electrical equipment of the country at least to the level of that already reached by our competitors.

2. Inland Waterways

The neglected condition of our inland waterways, in striking contrast to the efficiency of the continental system, has long been the subject of criticism. Since the advent of railways, little has been done to render our canals fit for modern traffic requirements; instead of improving, enlarging, and equipping them with mechanical means of haulage and loading, and with better wharves and warehouses, many have been allowed to deteriorate. When the Liberal Government was in power in 1906, it appointed a Royal Commission to inquire into the condition of the canals and inland navigations of the country, and to report on, *inter alia,* "facilities, improvements, and extensions desirable in order to complete a system of through communication by water between centres of commercial, industrial, or agricultural importance, and between such centres and the sea," and on "the prospect of benefit to the trade of the country compatible with a reasonable return on the probable cost." The Commission recommended the unification of the waterways and the transfer of their administration to a Central "Waterway Board." It was suggested that the functions of this body should include the improvement of four main routes (viz. Birmingham and Leicester to London; Leicester, Burton, and Nottingham to the Humber; Wolverhampton and Birmingham to the Mersey; and Wolverhampton and Birmingham to the Severn), and that subsequent action should be taken to acquire and unify any further waterways as branches or feeders of the main routes or as new schemes.

The Commission stated that they—

> "realised more and more, as their inquiry proceeded, how hopeless it would be to expect anything from the waterway system of England and Wales in the future, for the benefit of trade and industry, if the waterways were left in the present disunited and unimproved condition. With a few notable exceptions, the canals at least would become less and less efficient and useful; and many would swell the list, as years went on, of disused or derelict canals. Thus a system of transport which in foreign countries has become of great value to trade, as a result of measures of unification and improvement, would in this country be practically lost."

The Report was published in 1909, and before public opinion could be sufficiently aroused to take any action on it, the War had begun. A Departmental Committee, under the chairmanship of Mr. Neville Chamberlain, was appointed in 1920 to review the whole question of the future development of waterways. The policy recommended almost unanimously by this Committee can be put briefly as the gradual grouping of the principal inland waterways into seven systems which, it was suggested, should be owned and operated by a series of public trusts, composed principally of local authorities, representatives of canal companies, users of waterways, and others. Apart from valuable improvements of the River Trent, little other action was taken. Mr. Neville Chamberlain, as recently as 1922, advocated the linking of Birmingham with the Bristol Channel ports—a scheme which had the support of the Birmingham Chamber of Commerce and prominent local representatives. Here, again, nothing has materialised, owing, it is said, "to the difficulty of adjusting the financial responsibility of the undertaking." Had the State interested itself in the project, this difficulty could doubtless have been overcome. While our Government has adopted a purely passive attitude and our canals have deteriorated, France, Germany, and other continental countries have been overhauling their already admirable and extensive system of waterways so as to equip them for the new conditions of trade and industry.

France

The important part played by the canal system in the economic life of France is too well known to require emphasis. It has been invaluable for the transport of heavy goods in the industrial regions of the north and the north-east. Since the War a comprehensive national programme for the development of inland waterways was drawn up by the Minister of Public Works. Although financial stringency has resulted in slow progress, nevertheless three of the schemes have been on such a scale and of so great importance as to attract international attention, viz. those of the Rhône, the Grand Canal of Alsace, and of the Marseilles–Rhône Waterway. Apart from their value in facilitating transport and creating industrial development, some of the schemes, e.g., the Rhône scheme, will also serve as a means of generating electricity and irrigating adjacent lands. The State has been making increased grants both for ordinary upkeep and repair and for new construction and improvements; over 100 million francs was voted in the 1926 Budget. The growth in traffic since the War has been considerable; the canals carried 18 million tons in 1925 as against 14 million in 1921.

Germany

During the War Germany realised the great value of her canals as a means of supplementing road and rail transport, and a stimulus was given to the construction of inland waterways. This stimulus has continued even after the War, and to-day we find that the Reich in its budget for 1927–8 voted 91.5 million marks for waterway construction, a considerable increase on previous years. The States concerned also contribute large amounts for works passing through their territories. The schemes at present in progress include, *inter alia,* the Rhine–Maine–Danube works, the so-called Mittelland Canal, and the canalisation of the Neckar. An interesting feature of the present programme is the proposal to extend, at a cost of nearly £10,000,000, the Hansa Canal to link Hamburg with Bremen and the Westphalian industrial districts; the canal will take ships up to 1,000 tons. Traffic returns have in consequence shown an increase on previous years, and in Western Germany the traffic is even greater than in 1913. Steps are being taken to increase efficiency and promote facilities by the combination of inland waterways companies by the Reich's scheme for greater unification by creating 12 administrative centres and by reducing the number of local inland waterway authorities by one-quarter. Even under existing conditions it is significant that whereas in Germany the tonnage of canal and river traffic is equivalent to one-fifth or one-sixth of rail-borne traffic, in Britain the canals carry less than one-twentieth of the tonnage of goods hauled by rail.

Belgium

Similar developments have taken place in Belgium, where canals have for years been an important feature of the country. Credits sought for river and canal work in 1926 amounted to 82½ million francs. Among the chief schemes in progress is the

Brussels–Charleroi Canal, which will afford direct communication between Antwerp and the coalfields and the industrial areas of Charleroi and Mons, and further, with the French canal system. Other works include a waterway linking Antwerp with the Campine coal basin and the important industrial districts of Liège.

While we have marked time, other countries have gone forward. Our chief need at present is a bold and comprehensive scheme of canal development on the lines of the recommendation of the Royal Commission as modified by the changed economic conditions of the country. Unity of administration under State control would effect economies and enable the much-needed extensions and improvements to be undertaken. It must not, however, be thought that we advocate the resuscitation of inland waterways as competitors with rail and motor transport, but as a means of supplementing their work.

3. Docks, Harbours, and Dockyards

Docks and Harbours.—A growing seaborne traffic necessitates measures of port development to keep pace with, or, better still, to forestall, the increased dock accommodation demanded. Any failure to maintain adequate dock and harbour facilities at the highest degree of efficiency results in delays in transit, damage and deterioration of goods, and economic loss is the consequence. Ports then become the "bottle-necks" of ocean traffic and congestion results. But the rapid growth of new traffic gives rise to an increased demand not only for berths and jetties, but also for better storage facilities, larger and better warehouses, sheds amply provided with rail facilities, and above all for the latest and most expeditious methods of handling cargo efficiently. The question, however, is not so much how to accommodate existing traffic too great for existing capacity, but how to meet the demands which will be made within a few years. Shipbuilders in recent years have been laying down larger keels; for example, the average size of merchant vessels of 100 tons gross and over launched in Great Britain before the War was about 2,500 tons as against 3,000 during the last four years. The shipbuilding programmes of other countries, especially America, show increased construction compared with the corresponding pre-war figures. Hence it is necessary to look ahead and plan for these future requirements, both by the reconstruction and "modernising" of old docks and the construction of new ones. That some of the port authorities are alive to the needs of the times is evident by the carrying out of large development schemes in recent years, for example, the Gladstone system of docks at Liverpool, where the biggest vessels, built or likely to be built in the near future, may be accommodated in ease.

But the port trusts finance their improvement schemes very largely from revenue, and there is a tendency when this declines, as in times of trade and industrial depression, for expenditure on developments to be curtailed. We have already drawn attention in other parts on this Report to the evils of such so-called "economy," but without adequate State assistance the port authorities in many cases are not prepared to undertake the financing of the projects other than from reserves and revenue. It is true that the Development Commissioners assist the smaller port and harbour authorities with grants and loans, but the extent of this assistance is strikingly shown in the seventeenth Annual Report of that body, which states that during the year 1926–7 the grants totalled £18,000 and loans amounted to £16,000.

On the other hand, the French Government, assisted by the Chamber of Commerce and local authorities, have, in recent years, spent 100 to 120 million francs annually on the great ports to improve and equip them to compete with foreign ports; assistance has also been rendered by the State to the smaller ports. Italy has been extending and improving her port works, especially the ports of Genoa, Naples, Trieste, and the new harbour works at Bari. Extension works have been carried out at Antwerp, Ghent, Ostend, and other Belgian ports.

Government Dockyards.—Special problems arise in connection with the industrial establishments maintained by the State for military purposes. A policy of greater economy in armaments might give rise to serious local difficulties, unless the situation that would result was foreseen, and the necessary measures planned in advance. For example, only the Admiralty can decide when a dockyard is no longer needed for naval purposes. But apparently when it was decided to close down the dockyard at Pembroke, it was no one's special duty to consider what was to happen to the town of Pembroke and to the population that had been brought there. It was the existence of the dockyard that had caused Pembroke to expand from a village to a town of 15,000 inhabitants. All the equipment of a town had been created, its roads, its schools, its sanitary system. Assuming that their employment was stable, the great majority of the workmen on the staff had bought their own houses. Suddenly a change of policy puts an end to Pembroke's only industry; the place becomes almost derelict; the houses, acquired by years of thrift and self-denial, become practically unsaleable. Similar consequences would follow from similar action elsewhere, in greater or less degree, according as an establishment was closed or was reduced in scale.

It should be remembered that Government dockyards and arsenals are wholly dependent upon Government orders. Usually there is little opening in the same town for skilled men who are dismissed from those establishments; and many of the workmen are very highly skilled, often trained from their youth as Government apprentices and required to reach an exceptional standard of proficiency. In these circumstances a special obligation rests upon the State.

We are of opinion that when action becomes necessary, it should be based upon two principles.

First, so far as the conditions allow, whatever establishments are maintained by the State should be kept in steady employment. Government dockyards and arsenals, for the reasons that have been given, have an exceptionally strong claim. If, by such tendencies as the reduction of forces on the one hand, or the growing mechanisation of the army on the other, the equipment that is needed changes its character, those establishments ought not to suffer. By a careful adjustment of orders, they ought to be kept as fully employed as possible.

Secondly, the course of future policy, with reference to the size of each establishment, should be carefully surveyed, and the measures to be taken should be definitely laid down in advance and publicly announced. Where it is found necessary to reduce the dockyard or arsenal of a particular town, it should be the duty of the Committee of National Development to endeavour to attract to that town alternative private industries. Instead of leaving derelict important sites, sidings, and buildings, these should be offered to new enterprises. With a population of skilled workmen available on the spot, their houses in being, their municipal and social requirements already met, the place should be more attractive to the founders of a new undertaking than starting afresh in some undeveloped locality. The course we propose in this regard is no more than a special application of our general policy for the preservation and development of the national resources. It is not less necessary to save the towns that exist from being wasted than to promote the growth of new ones where the need arises.

The development of the nation's docks must be regarded from the national point of view. Conflicting claims and interests must be taken into account, but the whole dock system must be the best which can be devised to serve the national interest. We suggest, therefore, that the Committee of National Development should examine the question as a whole and should in all cases, where desirable development is held up by financial difficulties, put forward a scheme to the Board of National Investment.

CHAPTER XXIV

AGRICULTURE, FORESTRY, AND RECLAMATION

THE future of British agriculture is a matter which has received the exhaustive attention of the Liberal Party, both before the War and since. Far-reaching proposals in regard to it have been endorsed by the National Liberal Federation, and there is no need here to go over in detail ground already covered by the Rural Report of the Liberal Land Committee 1923–5.[1]

Our task is to note and to emphasise the vital relationship of those proposals to the problem we are now considering.

1. Agriculture's Intrinsic Importance

Agriculture is still the most important industry in the country. The value of agricultural and horticultural land, including the farmhouses and buildings upon it, has been estimated for the year 1925 at £815,000,000. The working capital employed in agricultural production was at the same time estimated at £365,000,000. The value of the gross output of the land of England and Wales, i.e. that of the agricultural and horticultural produce sold to the non-farming community or consumed in farmers' households, was officially estimated for the year 1925 at £225,000,000. The importance of this figure is illustrated by the value of the net production of some of our other staple industries, as ascertained by the Census of Production in 1924 for Great Britain[2]:

	£ millions
Coal	210
Engineering	117
Cotton spinning and weaving . .	82
Iron and Steel	61

[1] *The Land and the Nation—Rural Report.* (Hodder & Stoughton, 1*s*.)

[2] An actual comparison of the relative value of the output of agriculture and other great industries is not possible: on the one hand, agricultural returns relate only to England and Wales, and the figures of other industries to Great Britain as a whole; on the other, the agricultural figure represents gross output and the other figures net output.

Its importance is no less strikingly shown by the figures of the employment it provides. Even in 1921, despite the heavy decline in agricultural employment in the last fifty years, agriculture gave occupation to 1,232,000 men and boys and 107,000 women, a total, that is, of over 1,300,000 persons.[1] This figure can be compared with the totals of persons employed in 1924 in the great industries, e.g. 1,198,000 in coal, 588,000 in engineering, 517,000 in cotton spinning and weaving, and 303,000 in iron and steel.

Nor does its importance derive only from the amount of the capital employed and the number of persons engaged. It affords employment which contributes to the health and well-being of the nation to a degree altogether out of proportion to the money profit which it returns. It is, therefore, an industry which should peculiarly be an object of national concern and attention, the last industry which ought to be left to its fate with the lazy phrase, "If it is not paying better let it go." It is, of all industries, peculiarly dependent on the creation for it, by the nation as a whole, of the right economic environment.

2. Agriculture and Imports

There is, too, another aspect of the problem of British Agriculture which, and the importance of which, is not sufficiently recognised, namely, that concerned with the balance of trade.

In an Appendix to this chapter [2] will be found statistics of the excess of imports into the United Kingdom in 1924, 1925, and 1926 of food and other agricultural and raw products apparently capable, from a climatic point of view, of being produced within the United Kingdom. There is, of course, room for some difference of opinion as to what precisely should be included in this category. We have tried to take a conservative view. After making all allowances, however, for margin of error, the figures are sufficiently striking.

Taking the average of the three years 1924–6, the total excess of imports under this heading amounts to some £450.0 million per annum (or about twice our home production). Taking some of the details, the three-year average of the excess

[1] Domestic gardeners, included in the Census enumeration under agriculture, are here excluded.

[2] Appendix III, pp. 339–40.

of wheat imports is some £66.0 million, wheat meal and flour £2.5 million, barley £8.5 million, and oats nearly £3.5 million. The corresponding figures for beef, mutton, and lamb are £53.0 million, and pig products £51.5 million. For living cattle, sheep, and swine the figure is £18.5 million, fruit £11.5 million, cheese £14.0 million, eggs £18.5 million, and butter over £48.0 million. Even for potatoes we paid foreign countries, on balance, an average of £4.5 million, and for other vegetables £7.0 million.

Comparison with our staple exports adds significance to these figures. The three-years' average of our exports of machinery of all classes was £46.5 million, or £5.0 million less than our imports of pig products. If we lost all our export trade in machinery but raised all our pigs at home, we should be better off from the point of view of the balance of foreign trade than we are to-day. Again, our total exports of coal, taking here the average only of 1924–5, was £61.0 million, or £5.5 million less than our imports of butter and eggs. The total exports of our greatest export industry, cotton yarns and manufactures (less the corresponding imports of raw cotton), were less than £74.0 million, or approximately equal to our imports of cattle, sheep, and meat.

We do not, of course, suggest that we can ever hope to provide in this country all the food capable, from a climatic point of view, of being produced here. What we do submit is that by the Liberal policy of agricultural reform we might show much improvement on the present situation, and that any such improvement would bring a sorely needed contribution to our balance of trade. The way to meet a quasi-permanent falling off in demand for our exports lies obviously, in part, in less reliance on outside sources of supply. There could be no more effective method of achieving this end than by the home production of a greater proportion of our food and raw material supplies.

3. Agriculture and the Industrial Situation

It will be seen, therefore, that it is of very great economic importance to restore and develop our agriculture by raising its efficiency and productivity, not merely from the point of view of the well-being of those engaged in it, but also from the wider point of view of the industry and employment and general economic position of the country as a whole. The recent World

Economic Conference at Geneva laid stress on the economic interdependence of agriculture and industry.

While this is true of the world as a whole, it is peculiarly true of this country in the situation with which it is at present faced.

A healthy and progressive British agriculture would immensely assist the national situation in three main ways.

In the first place it would ease the competition for employment in the towns. For many years now the cream of the agricultural workers have been drifting into the towns, and by virtue of their superior physique, and possibly their greater docility and will to work, have tended to secure preference over the urban worker, who in consequence has gone to swell the pool of urban unemployment. And incidentally, unemployment of urban workers is worse than that of rural, because the urban worker is, as a rule, entirely dependent upon employment for his means of subsistence, whereas the rural worker can frequently avoid the demoralisation of complete idleness, and at the same time earn at any rate some livelihood by work in his garden or allotment and by intermittent employment of various kinds. To return, however, to our main theme: an increased return to British agriculture would be reflected in higher wages and increased profits and would offer the promise of a better and more secure career on the land. The effect of this would be to check the drift into the towns, and by permitting the absorption on the land of the natural increase of the rural population, to increase its numbers. This would be a real contribution to the unemployment problem, even if the movement did not extend to the reabsorption into agriculture of some proportion of present urban workers born and bred in agricultural surroundings. How far such reabsorption might be anticipated would depend on the relative attractiveness of agriculture to urban industry, and this in turn would depend, in part (but only in part), on the relative financial prospects offered by agriculture, which in turn depend upon matters we have still to discuss.

In the second place, the increased prosperity of the agricultural population, reflected in its increased purchasing power, would stimulate employment in all those other industries which supply the needs of the agricultural community.

In another part of this Report, dealing with the economy of

high wages, we have shown that the wages paid by an employer represent the purchasing power available for the goods sold by other employers. This is a particular instance of this general truth. The greater the real earnings of the agricultural population, the greater will be the prosperity not only of the country towns directly supplying their needs, but also of the industries manufacturing the goods sold there and railways and other transport agencies carrying these goods.

Thirdly, as we have shown, increased agricultural production at home would ease the situation as regards the balance of trade.

Both, therefore, in its immediate and in its more distant effects, an improvement in our agricultural industry will have a very vital bearing on our unemployment problem and on our economic position as a whole.

4. The Present Position of Agriculture

Meantime, it is evident that this vital industry is in a most unsatisfactory condition. Other countries have been overhauling and passing us in yield of crops, in spite of the fact that we now only cultivate the best land, and that British agricultural research is certainly not behind that of the Continent. Agricultural wages are the lowest accorded to any great group of workers, in spite of the very real degree of skill and experience required; and labourers are not being provided with such an opportunity as is provided in other countries for supplementing their incomes by a system of small-holdings that can be attended to partly by the labourer in spare time, and partly by his wife. At the same time farmers, caught by the fall in agricultural prices at a time when great changes are being forced on the industry by the breakdown of the old system of landlord tenancy, are involved in difficulties greater than any that have been experienced in modern times. Landlords themselves are increasingly unable to exercise their historic function of furnishing the industry with adequate capital for permanent work like farm buildings, cottages, and drainage, with the inevitable result that diminished expenditure on their part runs in vicious circle with decreased enterprise on the part of the farmers. Above all, in consequence of these things agriculture declines, home production falls and the rural workers drift into the towns at a time when conditions make it urgently desirable that opposite tendencies should rule.

In a report recently made by Mr. Lange, the Warden of the Smallholders' School, Odense, Denmark, who paid a visit to England to examine the agricultural conditions here, there is the following passage which has a bearing on the situation:

> "From land of far inferior quality and not much above one-quarter in extent as compared with England and Wales (43 against 151) we are able to *export* £56,000,000 worth of agricultural products, while the total *production* of English agriculture is only £225,000,000. (Perhaps it also goes a little way towards explaining why the Danish death-rate is the lowest in the world.)"

To every ten square miles of land used for crops and grass in Great Britain there is an agricultural population of 282 persons. The same area of farm land in Denmark maintains 352, Germany 416, Holland 576, and Belgium no less than 640. Each of these countries brings into some kind of economic use a larger proportion of its total "soil-area." Population on the land varies almost directly as the intensity of its cultivation. Intensive cultivation does not, as is often assumed, simply mean the substitution of market gardening for arable, pasture, or mixed farming. Danish agriculture, for example, is more intensive than English largely because more animals are kept, and arable land is used for stock-breeding. Belgian agriculture, on the other hand, comes much more nearly to what is commonly thought of as intensive cultivation. But in all these other countries the common factor is that the land as a whole carries a much larger number of family farms, that is to say, holdings of a size which can be cultivated normally without reliance on hired labour. This economic division of agricultural land is both the cause and result of more intensive farming. Both it and intensive farming are due fundamentally to the conception that the primary use of land which is not required for building is for the production of wealth, not for amenity. If this conception were restored in our own country, and if the same degree of efficiency in production and marketing were attained in agriculture as are recognised as necessary in the urban industries, we could hope to occupy on our land a population bearing a higher ratio to agricultural area than the 1,330,000 reported at the last Census. If our ratio of persons to agricultural area were as high as in Denmark, this 1,330,000 would become something like 1,700,000; if as high as in Germany, 2,000,000; in Holland, 2,750,000; or in Belgium, well over 3,000,000.

In quoting these figures we must not be taken as suggesting that it is possible in a short time to raise the numbers of our agricultural population to these levels. We state them simply as showing the matter in a new perspective. It is, nevertheless, significant that a country like, say, Denmark, with poorer soil and climatic conditions than we enjoy, should be able to maintain an agricultural population relatively so much greater than ours, though our farmers have at their doors the markets which the Danish farmers serve overseas. Furthermore, wherever the explanation is to be found, it is not in the lower standard of life of the Danish agriculturist, who both in living, in housing, in education, and in culture enjoys a standard which will bear comparison with that enjoyed on farms of comparable size in Great Britain.

But it is not necessary to rely upon illustrations from abroad. Experience shows that whereas in purely rural parishes generally the population has steadily dwindled, it has been maintained, and even increased, where smallholdings on any adequate scale have been established. As an illustration may be taken two groups of parishes, one in Lincolnshire, where the powers given by the Smallholdings Acts have been fully exercised, and one in Suffolk, where they have not. Three parishes in the Lincolnshire area show an increase in population between 1901 and 1921 of 8, 9, and 13 per cent. respectively. Three parishes in the Suffolk area show a decrease in the same period of 21, 23, and 25 per cent. respectively. The Lincolnshire increase has been secured in the face of notorious difficulties, and it is reasonable to expect that a much greater increase would follow from the adoption of the Liberal Land Policy as a whole with its schemes of credit supply, organised marketing, and transport reform based on a form of tenure which ensures good cultivation and gives security to the good farmer. Mr. Lange, whom we have already quoted, gives the parallel experience of Denmark. He says:

> "We generally find that in the course of ten to fifteen years the population increases two to three times wherever a large farm of, say, 500–600 acres is cut up in thirty to forty smaller ones."

Numerous examples can be found in England of cases where enterprising farmers have taken over neglected farms and have doubled or trebled the amount of labour employed in a few years.

The importance of increasing the number of such farmers and the number of such parishes as have here been mentioned stands out against the background of dwindling population in our rural areas at large. County after county may be taken to illustrate the evil. In Oxfordshire, for example, in the period 1871 to 1921 the number of persons living in rural districts remained constant, but the agricultural population declined from 27,000 to 17,000, and the number of agricultural labourers from 21,500 to 10,000. When full allowance is made for any possible changes in census classifications and for the effect of the Education Act of 1870, the decrease in this county, and indeed in every area which has remained mainly agricultural, is alarming.

The census figures for individual villages tell the same tale even more clearly. In Bedfordshire, for example, the parish of Harrold had shrunk from 1,119 in 1861 to 834 in 1921; Riseley from 1,026 to 600; Cranfield from 1,591 to 1,059; Houghton Regis from 2,169 to 1,435. Moreover, with agriculture have dwindled those rural industries which formerly provided alternative or supplementary occupation for families living on the land. The effect of this is seen in its most telling form in a number of villages and little towns which fifty years ago were centres of local importance. In the parish of Cerne Abbas, for example, in Dorsetshire, a population of 1,164 persons in 1871 was in 1911 reduced to only 511. In their local significance such instances of depopulation have probably no precedent since the Black Death, and we know of no parallel in other countries.

It is no answer to say that these dwindling parishes have fallen out of the main stream of national life, and that methods of cultivation have changed. The fact to be faced is that the strength of these villages has been drained away into the overfull reservoir of town labour to cause increased unemployment there, whilst simultaneously there is an actual shortage of labour even in those parishes which thin farming has depopulated. "Not a man can be had to lay a hedge, build a wall, thatch a rick, or even clean a ditch." "Roots are being smothered by weeds; there are few shearers; horses are idle—and this with a million and a quarter men unemployed."

We believe that the vigorous application of the Liberal Land Policy will, in the first instance, stop this flow of workers from the land, and in time make a substantial contribution to the diminution in the number of unemployed in the towns.

The troubles of agriculture are partly due to causes which, we may hope, are temporary. Agriculture is perhaps our leading "unsheltered industry." At the present moment farming is in difficulties all over the world, and the position of our own farmers has been further aggravated by the fall of prices attendant upon the return to the gold standard. In a period of declining prices farming suffers with special severity by reason of the long time-lag in its operations.

But while the situation of British agriculture has been made worse by certain temporary causes arising out of the War and its after-effects, the root causes of the decline, like the decline itself, are of long standing, and their effects are likely not only to persist, but to grow more pronounced, unless special steps are taken to counteract them. This essential fact was recognised by the Liberal Government before the War, and they undertook to deal with the problem by drastic measures.

A policy which aims at the revival of agriculture forms a principal plank of the programme of the Liberal Party. It is not our intention here to repeat in detail the case made in *The Land and the Nation* and other recent Liberal publications for rural land reform. Our task here must be limited to bringing our agricultural policy into its proper relation to our general plan for the adequate and profitable employment of the national resources of capital and men.

In certain fundamental respects the remedy for the present unsatisfactory position of British agriculture is the same as that suggested above in the case of our great export industries, namely the taking of such steps as will secure an increased net return per head of those engaged. This cannot be secured by any arbitrary increase in price. As in the case of the latter industries, its productive efficiency must be improved. The resulting increased product per acre and per head will make possible a proportionately increased return to those engaged, whilst at the same time leading to an increase in the area under cultivation and to an increase in the numbers engaged.

Again, as in the case of industry, this increased productive efficiency will come from better and more advanced methods—more intensive cultivation—and this will call for adequate credit. Credit facilities therefore form an essential part of our proposals.

There is another source from which the agricultural producer, like the industrialist, can draw, but to a much greater extent than the latter. That source is the altogether too wide margin which exists between the price received by the agriculturist and that paid by the ultimate consumer.

In part this margin will be reduced, and the resulting saving be secured to the farmer, by the improvement and cheapening in transport made possible by the adoption of our proposals in regard to roads. This, it should be noted, can be expected to include some appreciable reduction in cost of rail transport, in part due to the competition of road transport, and in part made possible by the large-scale feeding of the railways by that transport. This, however, is only part of the remedy. There will still remain the arbitrary power of the middleman and the altogether unreasonable tribute levied as a result of that power. Fundamental to agricultural regeneration is a great policy of organised marketing, which will at one and the same time secure to the agricultural producer a higher price for the fruits of his toil and enterprise and to the consumer a cheaper and more ample supply of home-produced food.

Finally, an essential foundation for the carrying out of these proposals is the assurance to the farmer of a real security of tenure. Without this, credit facilities will be of only very partial value, while the savings resulting from improved marketing may be appropriated by the landlord.

Any agricultural policy appropriate to our present needs must therefore cover these three things—credit, organised marketing, and security of tenure.

5. Security of Tenure

First in order we put the question of tenure. This matter is dealt with in detail in the Reports of the Land Inquiry Committee and there is no need to repeat that detail here. It is necessary, however, to emphasise that a change in the conditions of land tenure is essential to that restoration and development of our agricultural life which the present situation demands. Unless the cultivator can feel assured that the rewards of the skill and toil and expenditure which he may invest in the land will accrue to him and his, the most skilful and far-reaching schemes of credit and marketing will avail little. We are not discussing this matter now from the point of view of justice, but simply from that of business. It would not be businesslike for a cultivator, for example, to arrange for credit and to invest capital in improving the land so long as he knew that at short notice the resulting improvement in his holding might, to all intents and purposes, be taken from him by an increase in rent or a sale of his land at the new level of value which he had created; any more than it would be businesslike to advance any substantial credit on such poor security. These two things, the raising of rent and the sale of his land at a value which he himself has created, are the twin fears ever before the cultivator. So long as they remain, it is unreasonable to expect him (or his banker) to follow more than a hand-to-mouth policy. Really valuable programmes of improvement, whether in business or in agriculture, must be carried out over a period of years. It is unreasonable and unbusinesslike to expect a farmer to risk toil, thought, and capital on the security of a yearly tenancy. In the old days, even if the farmer was a yearly tenant or a tenant under a short lease, he had in fact a practical freehold. The old landowning families had a high tradition in such matters and were able to respect that tradition. Now, changed conditions and the rapid breaking up of the large family estates have created a fresh sense of insecurity. Recent legislation has given larger rights to compensation for disturbance, but it has not gone to the roots of the trouble. The intrinsic insecurity of annual tenancy is now aggravated by the disintegration of the old system of landlordship. A right to compensation for disturbance is not sufficient to give free play to the incentive towards full cultivation of the land. Moreover, if a farmer buys the freehold of his land, he denudes himself of his floating capital and burdens himself with interest, whilst as security for additional loans he can only offer the poor security of a second mortgage. The inevitable result is the prevalence of poverty-stricken and unenterprising farming just when higher production from the land and larger population on it are for national reasons most urgently required.

It is true that an improvement in land tenure will in itself be insufficient; but it forms an essential foundation to any policy designed to revivify the rural life of the nation. With security of tenure, the good cultivator will be encouraged to develop the full possibilities of his land, both as regards production of food and employment of labour. With the existence of such security, the last excuse of the bad cultivator will be gone and he will have to make way for better men. Security of tenure, then, is the foundation of our proposals.

6. Credit for Agriculture

Our second main proposal relates to the machinery for the supply of agricultural credit. We have already emphasised the importance to agriculture of an abundant flow of new capital. We do not under-estimate the services to agriculture rendered by the Joint Stock Banks. But, on the other hand, we are not blind to the limitations of a banking system constructed primarily and mainly for the needs of urban industry. The decaying landlord system was, in effect, this country's system of agricultural banking. In other countries where landlord tenancy has not been established specific systems of agricultural banks, land banks, or co-operative credit have grown up to place agriculture on something like an economic parity with other industries.

We propose, therefore, that the Board of National Investment should be authorised to advance funds to duly recognised organisations for agricultural credit, whether they take the form of co-operative credit banks, land mortgage banks, or agricultural banks. The time to constitute a sound and adequate system of agricultural credit has certainly come. A variety of experiments should be encouraged. There are three main types of credit to be provided for:

First, *Long Term Credit,* for works of major importance remunerative in the long run, too slow in coming to fruition to be undertaken by tenant farmers and increasingly beyond the scope of landowners.

Secondly, *Trading Credits,* to finance the turnover of stock and crops, and

Thirdly, *Commencing Credit,* to enable new farmers, particularly smallholders and family farmers, to stock and equip their holdings.

Commencing Credit will be peculiarly the charge of the County Agricultural Authorities which the Liberal Land Policy proposes to set up. Pending the formation of such *ad hoc* Agricultural Local Authorities, the Smallholdings Committee of the County Councils, which already have power to grant loans to smallholders established by them, would operate any scheme brought into being. The administration of Long Term Credit would also be the function of the County Agricultural Authorities, which would take over and develop the work of the Lands Improvement Company. County Councils or County Agricultural Authorities would, for the purposes of these credits, be in direct contact with the Board of National Investment. Trading Credits are a different matter. The machinery found most flexible and most reliable for this purpose has in all countries been the Co-operative Credit Association. We propose that further efforts should be made to make Co-operative Credit Banks as important and as successful in this country as they have been elsewhere, and that encouragement should be afforded to the formation of such Banks by County Agricultural Authorities, by local *ad hoc* associations and partly through the formation of subsidiaries for this special purpose by the existing Joint Stock Banks. We doubt whether such institutions, however soundly conceived, would be in a position to appeal successfully on a sufficient scale to the private investor, and therefore we propose further that the Board of National Investment should be authorised to advance funds to all such properly constituted organisations. The terms of these advances would be proportional to the risk involved. For example, to subsidiaries of the "Big Five," or to Local Government authorities with the security of the rates behind them, the charge should be the lowest possible, say under existing conditions 4½ per cent. Such institutions might become in time a substantial element in the whole financial organisation of the country. The alternative would be to create an Agricultural Bank on lines adopted successfully in other countries. The establishment of such a bank, if it were found desirable, would clearly fall within the scope of the Board of National Investment's activities.

7. Marketing

Our third proposal relates to Marketing. The wholesale prices of agricultural produce have stood for years past at a lower level than the wholesale prices of the commodities which the farmer has to buy. This difference in price-level is largely the result of world-causes, which neither the individual farmer nor the Government of this country can control. But the gap between the price that the producer gets for what he has to sell and the price paid by the consumer for those same commodities is unjustifiably wide, and there is immense scope for an improvement in marketing methods which will enable the producer to get for his produce a price which is not only a larger share of the consumer's payment but will cover adequately the legitimate costs of production. The Linlithgow Committee, which made an exhaustive survey of the marketing of home-grown agricultural produce, came to the conclusion that "the spread between the producer's and the consumer's prices is unjustifiably wide" and that "taken as a whole, distributive costs are a far heavier burden than society will permanently consent to bear." It is unnecessary to multiply instances of the producer obtaining a ridiculously small proportion of the retail price of his goods. Milk producers, for example, are in a better position than other producers, inasmuch as a collective bargain has been made on their behalf by the National Farmers' Union, but at the best the producer gets 1*s.* in summer and 1*s.* 4½*d.* in winter for milk which is retailed at 2*s.* and 2*s.* 4*d.* In other cases the milk producer, after paying ¾*d.* a gallon to the purchasing company for collection, gets only 6¼*d.* a gallon for milk which is sold at 6*d.* a quart in the nearest town, that is, at four times the producer's price. The producers of other foodstuffs, by whom or on whose behalf no collective bargain has been made, are at the mercy of forces and processes entirely beyond their control. Of hundreds of extreme cases of hardship to consumers, a few instances may be given here. The first, reported in the House of Commons in May 1927, is of a consignment of 2,250 lb. of cabbages sent from Worcestershire to Covent Garden market; the cabbages were retailed at 1½*d.* apiece; the growers received nothing in return but a debit note for 3*s.* 6*d.* The second may be taken from the Linlithgow Committee's Report: a sale of tomatoes by a British grower, the consumer being charged 1*s.* 3*d.* per lb., and the producer receiving 5*d.* per lb., the cost of distribution accordingly being two-thirds of the consumer's price. To these may be added an instance quoted in the recently published *The Farmer and his Market* by the Land and Nation League: a Malvern grower obtained £3 17*s.* 9*d.* for high-quality dessert apples properly graded and packed, for which the consumer paid £27 6*s.* The cost of transport is an important element in the spread of prices. We note, for example, in another recent publication, *The Economy of a Norfolk Fruit Farm,* 1923–6, published by the University of Cambridge Department of Agriculture, that the agriculturists who are struggling to develop strawberry growing in Norfolk can only send produce at passenger-train rates. It is unnecessary for us to go into the question at length, particularly because the whole question has been handled in a report on the whole marketing question by the Land and Nation League in *The Farmer and his Market.* We would emphasise only that the development of new possibilities of motor transport, running over an improved road system and working in close conjunction with the railways, is so essential to the revival of the life of the countryside that it would be justifiable for the State, in our opinion, to run certain financial risks during an official experimental period. Complementary to these arrangements for distribution from the farm would be those for the supply to the farm of the machinery, artificial manures, and other things required for its needs.

The problem of selling is more difficult. We should like to see Central Selling Organisations set up in every district which would contract with the producer for the purchase of the whole of his output at stated prices or at prices bearing a fixed relation to the prevailing retail price. Our object would be to relieve the producer of all responsibility for bargaining, and, so far as possible, from anxiety as to the course of prices during the season. Co-operative organisations must play a large part in any scheme. The producer, who is inevitably an isolated economic unit, must acquire the power of collective bargaining. But even the power to bargain collectively is not enough. American and other experience tends to prove that there must be some control by the producer or in his interest of the actual process of distribution. The right method, in our view, is to establish business organisations, preferably public concerns, to handle each important group of agricultural commodities. Such bodies could eliminate much of the material and economic waste which at present occurs between the farm and the retail counter, and would, we believe, give the producer a fair and remunerative share of the price which the consumer pays.

As aids of a secondary but none the less important character we suggest that the Post Office should reconsider its charges for extending telephones to country districts with a view to their more general use, so that producers can be in close touch by telephone with collecting and marketing organisations. We suggest also that plans for the electrification of rural areas should be pressed forward wherever possible.

By this means, on the basis of the Liberal Party's proposals as to land tenure, we should hope to create an environment in which the types of intensive cultivation, so successfully pursued elsewhere, could become a leading feature of every part of Great Britain where the soil and other conditions were suitable. With credit facilities, transport facilities, and selling facilities, combined with security of tenure, cost of production would be reduced simultaneously with the securing of an increased proportion of the ultimate price to the consumer. A few years of successful experiment on these lines would cause the agricultural tide to turn. The rural population would cease to decline and begin to grow again, and, as an incidental but exceedingly valuable consequence, the cutting out of the present excessive costs of distribution would bring to the urban populations the fresh agricultural produce of their own countrysides in greater abundance and at a cheaper price. In creating the right conditions for agricultural prosperity lies waiting a great opportunity of adding to the purchasing power of the whole community.

A fact of utmost seriousness in relation to British agriculture is that it will emerge from the present depression with its power of future production impaired, whereas the agriculture of other countries of North-western Europe, thanks to better internal organisation, sounder psychological foundations, and general national organisation on its behalf, will (it may safely be prophesied, on the history of previous depressions) be in a position actually to increase its output. Given equal advantages of soil and climate, a country which has very large and wealthy markets situated close to its agricultural areas should be peculiarly well able to make high farming pay. Our country pre-eminently has that advantage. Almost at the farm gates of Great Britain lie the markets which it is the ambition of agriculturists throughout the world to serve. So far from being handicapped by soil and climate, the British farmer is favoured. Yet the productivity of English land remains stationary, while, thanks to the development of scientific methods, the productivity of other agricultural land in Europe continuously increases. Instead of having fewer persons employed to every hundred acres of agricultural land than other comparable countries, we should have more. The restoration of British agriculture will take time. All the more reason that it should begin at once. The first thing is to stop the drain from country to town. That in itself would do something to mitigate unemployment in the towns by reducing competition of country-bred migrants with town-bred workers.

8. Reclamation and Drainage

> "Hundreds of thousands of acres of what might be valuable and productive land, both above and below high-tide mark, are left derelict for want of the labour and energy necessary to reclaim them from the dominion of river and sea and to bring them under cultivation."

This statement of fact is taken from a leading article in *The Times* of a year ago, and the writer—in a mood which must be induced by any clear-sighted study of the facts—goes on to point to the very different attitude towards wasted land adopted in other countries of North-western Europe, where dry land is deliberately preferred to marsh and lagoons.

> "It is difficult to look across the North Sea to the Zuyder Zee and Haarlem Meer without registering the uncomfortable thought that, in spite of the fact that they have not there our inexhaustible reservoir of unemployed labour from which to draw, they manage to do these things very much better in Holland."

It is startling that Great Britain alone should lack any continuous policy for reclaiming land, or even for preventing land becoming waterlogged and useless. To bring into productive use every acre capable of being farmed at a profit would seem to be a rudimentary principle of national policy throughout the civilised world. Holland at the moment, with its gigantic scheme of colonising the Zuyder Zee, stands out as an example; but this is not a sudden outburst of activity, it is part and parcel of a continuous policy by which, in the last twenty-five years, that country has reclaimed 250,000 acres. To take other examples: Belgium has in the last sixty years reclaimed half a million acres. Denmark, of whose small territory sixty years ago one-fifth was waste, has reclaimed just on one million acres for agriculture and another half a million acres for forest. Italy has in hand the reclamation of no less than 1,750,000 acres. All these countries have profited by the experience of the past and are stimulated by knowledge gained in practice of the essential value of reclamation. In Great Britain, on the other hand, the area of productive land has actually been allowed to decrease. The recent "Census" of agriculture taken by the Ministry of Agriculture reported that in addition to land in want of field-drainage there are over a million acres of English land urgently in need of drainage, and that a further 500,000 acres can be "improved" by drainage.

Another authoritative estimate contained in the Report of the Royal Commission on Land Drainage in England and Wales (December 1927) states that the productive value of no less than 4,362,000 acres of land, that is approximately one-seventh of the total agricultural area, is dependent for its fertility on arterial drainage, and that 1,279,000 acres suffer from flooding caused by defective or obstructed arterial channels. The Report of this same Commission on Drainage, while it calls attention to the serious need for land drainage, to the steady worsening of the position, and to the prospect that under present arrangements more and more land will as the years go on become waterlogged, could come to no more dynamic conclusion than that the arguments in favour of national expenditure upon land drainage are cogent, that in many continental countries the State recognises that it cannot afford to lose through waterlogging a valuable national asset, but that "until the State is prepared to accept due financial obligations, very little progress can be made . . . towards the realisation of the ideal of an efficient system of arterial drainage." The whole argument of this book is to present to the public a practical alternative to so impotent a conclusion.

We believe that much of the land thus lying waste could be reclaimed with every prospect of almost immediate economic return on the expenditure incurred. The reclamation of some of the rest of the land would be a paying proposition in the long run, but arrangements would have to be made to carry the enterprise over the first unproductive years. But in reckoning the cost of reclamation it is of vital importance to take into account not only the expenditure that must be incurred in the actual work of reclamation, but the expenditure which is now being incurred in relief of unemployment. We might add that if Holland had not, over a long term of years, increased the productive area at the disposal of its people, it might well have an unemployment problem of a gravity comparable to our own.

9. Afforestation

To afforestation only a brief reference need be made, as the case for it is very largely contained in what has already been said about reclamation.

Before the War the Royal Commission on Coast Erosion and Afforestation estimated the land in Great Britain which could be afforested at 8,500,000 acres. During the War an immense quantity of timber was cut and not replaced. The Forestry Commission set out in 1919 to plant 150,000 acres in ten years. So far less than 70,000 acres have been planted, and the latest report of the Commissioners indicates that the total area of woodland in the whole country is now less than 3,000,000 acres. Of this total area less than half is reasonably productive; of the rest, 733,000 acres being "coppice of little value, or amenity woodland definitely uneconomic." On the other hand, the experimental work of the Commission, while it has not yet proved whether afforestation on certain kinds of land is an economic proposition, has proved that "large areas formerly considered unplantable may now be afforested with success."

If this tale of neglect were not so familiar it would indeed be startling. France in the last century has added to its afforested areas no less than 3,000,000 acres, that is to say, as much as the whole of the existing woodlands (economic and uneconomic) of this country. Germany in the last fifty years has added a million acres. Denmark has doubled her forest area in the same period. Belgium has very largely increased her forests. We, in fact, have the unhappy distinction of being the only country without a consistent policy of forest preservation and extension. Yet the need for such a policy is at least as strong here as anywhere else. In proportion to the area of land at our disposal, we have the largest and most constant demand for timber. The shortage of the supply of timber throughout the world is a commonplace business experience. We are importing timber products to the value of £40,000,000 to £50,000,000 per annum. The sources of supply throughout the world are diminishing. The demands of other countries upon the forests of the northern hemisphere continue to increase.

The case for a vigorous forest policy is unanswerable. Even if there were no unemployment problem to be faced, the need for a national policy of afforestation would be great. Inertia and the lack of that driving force which it should be the function of the Government to supply in a problem of this magnitude are responsible for our backward condition. Climatically we have all the advantages. Wales has been referred to as having the ideal climate for timber-growing, and yet there are half a million acres of unafforested land in Wales within a few miles of coal-pits which create an incessant demand for pit props, and which now depend almost wholly on timber imported from abroad.

To quote one authority, Sir Herbert Matthews, Secretary of the Central Chamber of Agriculture, speaks of the timber position as being " extremely grave." The process of afforestation provides work. Forest holdings are an admirable type of land settlement. In afforested areas rural industries of the best type may thrive.

10. Rural Industries

Before we conclude this section dealing with agriculture and its sub-heads of Reclamation, Drainage, and Afforestation, we would emphasise that we have in mind not only the work which can be provided immediately by a comprehensive campaign for land betterment, but also the permanent employment which would result from reconditioning the land. A thinly populated and discouraged countryside is in itself a cause of unemployment. A thorough-going policy of draining land now under-used for agriculture would largely increase the amount of food produced and the number of families maintained. The actual work of reclamation would employ for some years a small army of men and, on the land thus redeemed, many families could be settled. The reafforestation of many areas in which the woods have been cut down without consideration for the future will save a number of local industries—some of them rural, some of them carried on in considerable centres of population—from extinction. The afforestation of other areas from which the timber has long since been cleared would bring new local industries into existence and would create alternative and subsidiary employment for smallholders and their families.

The development of rural industries should be in itself an object of national policy. In Germany, since the time of Bismarck, who saw clearly the dangers of over-centralising industry in urban areas, the fostering of rural industries has been a deliberate object of national policy. Other European countries have taken care to preserve those industries which are subsidiary to agriculture, and we believe that even in an age of mass production and mass advertisement there is abundant scope for the redevelopment in this country of crafts and manufactures which depend primarily on local raw materials or serve a specialised need. In this connection has to be considered the provision of cheap electrical power in rural areas, either from the great power stations or, in suitable hilly areas, from locally generated power. The case is obvious and we would refer here only to this interconnection as reinforcing the case for giving charge of the development of our national resources to such a Committee of National Development as we suggest. Concentration of population in and around the coal-pits, mines, and quarries, or, as is happening now, on the fringes of great popular markets such as London, is in the long run detrimental, not only to health, but to production itself.

APPENDIX III

IMPORTS (LESS EXPORTS[1]) INTO UNITED KINGDOM OF MAIN FOOD AND OTHER AGRICULTURAL AND RAW PRODUCTS APPARENTLY OF THE KIND WHICH CAN BE PRODUCED IN THIS COUNTRY

Values—£1,000s

CLASS I

	1924.	1925.	1926.
Group A. Grain and Flour.			
Wheat	68,521	66,899	62,788
Barley	12,051	8,174	5,056
Oats	4,082	3,497	2,849
Maize	16,376	12,177	11,419
Peas, not fresh	1,373	1,297	1,427
Wheatmeal and flour	2,779	930	4,869
	105,182	92,974	88,408
Group B. Feeding-stuffs for Animals.			
Corn offals	2,914	2,264	1,459
Group C. Meat.			
Beef; Mutton and lamb	49,574	57,274	52,497
Pig products	47,045	54,696	52,429
Rabbits, etc.	2,636	2,550	2,101
Poultry and game	1,858	2,404	2,467
	101,113	116,924	109,494
Group D. Animals, living, for Food.			
Cattle	18,890	15,607	13,838
Sheep and lambs	1,741	1,191	1,319
Swine	1,159	613	1,678
	21,790	17,411	16,835

[1] Including re-exports.

APPENDIX III—continued

CLASS I—*continued*

	1924.	1925.	1926.
Group E. Other Food and Drink. Non-Dutiable.			
Butter	47,742	50,038	46,330
Cheese	13,213	14,771	13,541
Eggs—in shell	15,228	16,400	15,292
,, —not in shell	2,524	2,561	2,879
Fish, fresh or frozen, cured or salted, excluding canned	*— 4,143*	*— 3,030*	*— 2,293*
Fruit (capable of growth in United Kingdom) *	11,523	10,100	13,014
Hops	425	230	*— 314*
Milk, condensed, not sweetened	1,104	832	905
Vegetables—Potatoes	5,058	4,406	3,368
,, —Other	6,606	7,474	7,425
	99,280	103,782	100,147
Group F. Other Products. Dutiable.			
Sugar	41,237	31,628	24,445
Milk, condensed, sweetened	4,127	3,609	3,441
	45,364	35,237	27,886
Grand Total, Class I	375,643	368,592	344,229

CLASS II—RAW MATERIALS

	1924.	1925.	1926.
Group E. Wood and timber	49,726	45,031	37,947
Group G. Wool—raw: Sheep and lamb	33,377	34,351	31,263
Group I. Flax and flax tow	4,559	3,405	3,283
Group K. Hides and skins—undressed	6,298	5,601	5,216
Grand Total, Class II	93,960	88,388	77,709
Total, Classes I and II	469,603	456,980	421,938

* Apples, apricots and peaches, cherries, currants, gooseberries, pears, plums, and strawberries.

Compiled from the Annual Statement of the Trade of the United Kingdom, 1926, vol. i.

CHAPTER XXV

THE PROBLEM OF THE COAL INDUSTRY

WE have so far been dealing with the development of industry in general, and have surveyed the possibilities of stimulating national development in various ways with the object of increasing the demand for labour. But there is one industry whose problems are so large and which has in recent years been so disturbing an element in national economic life that it demands separate treatment. It is no exaggeration to say that if the coal industry could be reorganised on an efficient and stable basis, if its surplus workers could be provided for and unrest in the mining areas appeased, we should have gone far to solve our difficulties. Coal is the foundation on which our industrial life has been built up; it still gives employment to one in ten of all the men engaged in industry; it is much the most important single raw material which we produce in the British Isles; and on it depends not merely the older established metallurgical industries such as iron and steel, shipbuilding and engineering, but also the newer electrical and chemical industries which are destined to play a leading rôle in our industrial future. Yet the coal industry has suffered most conspicuously from unemployment and has been the chief battlefield of industrial warfare.

It is not necessary to survey the problems of the coal industry in any detail, for they have been exhaustively examined by the Sankey Commission in 1919, by the Macmillan Committee of 1925, and by the Samuel Commission in 1925-6, as well as by the Committee of Liberals who published *Coal and Power* in 1924 in the attempt to stave off the catastrophe which fell in the following year.

1. Special Problems of the Coal Industry

The industry's problems may be briefly summarised as follows:

The main cause of the present troubles of the coal industry is the expansion of the capacity for coal production throughout the world, the stagnation of world-demand for coal, and the contraction of the market for British coal. Though there has been a great extension of industry throughout the world in the last fifteen years, the world's consumption of coal has remained almost stationary. According to statistics published by the League of Nations, the world's production of coal in 1913 was 1,213,000,000 metric tons. In 1924 it was 1,188,000,000 metric tons, and the production for 1925 was about the same. In the first eight months of 1927 production in twelve countries, which account for over 90 per cent. of the world's output, amounted to roughly 783,000,000 tons. In 1913 Great Britain produced 287,000,000 tons and employed 1,105,000 coal miners. To-day she is producing only at the rate of 250,000,000 to 260,000,000 tons a year, and the number of men enumerated as miners is about 1,200,000, of whom less than a million are in actual employment. The contrast between the present state of the British coal industry and that of the rest of the world is all the more marked when it is realised that in the last eight months of 1927 the production of coal in France, Germany, Belgium, the Saar, and the United States was at a distinctly higher rate than in 1913.

This stagnant condition of the world-output of coal is the result partly of more economical methods of using fuel, partly of the immense development in the use of oil both for firing boilers and in internal-combustion engines, and partly of the increased use of water power and of lignite. No statistics are available to show the effect of economy in the use of coal. The World Power Conference of 1925, however, produced figures showing that at that time water-driven electrical plants developed nearly 10,000,000 h.p., and estimated that further development that might be contemplated amounted to 65,000,000 h.p. In 1914 the gross tonnage of motor-ships was only 234,000 tons and of ships fitted to burn either coal or oil fuel only 1,310,000 tons. In July 1927 these figures had risen to 4,271,000 tons and

18,482,000 tons respectively. In July 1927 the total steam and oil-burning tonnage recorded at Lloyd's were as follows:

	Gross Tons.
Coal-burning only	40,515,000
Motor-ships, and ships burning either oil only, or oil and coal . . .	22,752,000

Again, there has been an immense development in the use of lignite, especially in Germany. It would be easy to produce other figures, but these are ample to substantiate the fundamental fact that coal is losing its old predominance as practically the sole source of power in industry, and has new conditions to face which did not exist before the War.

The difficulties of the British coal industry which arise from the operation of these world-wide factors have been enhanced by special problems peculiar to Great Britain. The long period of control during the War and its abrupt termination in 1921 lowered the standard of efficiency to an extent which in itself increased the cost of coal per ton. Since the War many European countries have pursued the policy of developing national resources so as to become as nearly as possible self-supporting in the production of coal and the generation of power. In Britain itself the export trade in coal has been greatly handicapped in some cases by higher costs, such as those due to increased local rates which were imposed upon it by increases in public expenditure, and those due to the higher wages paid in sheltered industries. The result of all these diverse factors in the export market has been materially to reduce the volume of exports of British coal. Thus whereas exports of coal, coke and manufactured fuel, and bunkers amounted in 1913 to 98,000,000 tons, or more than a third of the national output, in 1925, despite the subsidy, they were only 71,500,000 tons. In 1927, in spite of lower wages and longer hours, they still only amounted to 72,000,000 tons.

The British coal industry has suffered to an unexampled degree from antagonism between the mine-owners and the miners. We need not attempt to assess the degree of responsibility of the two sides. But, speaking broadly, the mine-owners have been reluctant to face the necessity for reorganising the industry to meet new conditions. They have kept alive low-efficiency mines which ought to have ceased production. They have done little to promote amalgamation of mines for production, or, scarcely less important, to create selling combinations which would stabilise prices or enable them to deal with foreign competitors. They have preferred to attempt to maintain the scale of industry by a process of ruthless competition, only possible by forcing the standard of living of the miners to a minimum (Sir Adam Nimmo in the *Observer* for July 24, 1927).

The Miners' Federation has been no wiser. Obsessed by the dogma that nationalisation would solve all difficulties, it has disregarded economic facts and economic law altogether. In 1919, after the Sankey Commission had reported, the Coalition Government made sweeping proposals for nationalising the minerals, for the amalgamation of the mines, and for giving the miners a voice in controlling their own conditions of employment; the men turned the offer down. In 1920 Pit Committees were proposed to be set up under Part II of the Mining Industry Act; and the miners refused to operate them. Later on, when the miners saw their mistake, the owners, who had originally accepted the idea, refused in their turn. In 1921, though the Sankey award on hours and wages was fully conceded, the Federation led the miners into a prolonged strike for the "pool"—a device which, if it had been adopted, must have ended in economic disaster. In 1926, despite the evidence produced by the Samuel Commission and the advice of the Trades Union Congress leaders, it persisted in a calamitous stoppage on a programme economically impracticable unless the liability for an immense and continuing subsidy were imposed on the taxpayer. It has sought to solve the problem not by placing the industry on a sound economic basis but by trying to make the good mines carry the poor ones, and so intensifying those economic burdens from which the industry must be freed if it is ever to recover health.

We have emphasised the mistakes, now obvious to everyone, which have been made in recent years by both owners and miners, but the responsibility which the Government of the day must bear for its contribution towards the difficulties of the coal industry is also grave. The policy which was pursued throughout the spring and summer of 1925 and which culminated in the coal subsidy; the failure to carry out the recommendations of the Samuel Commission; and the weak and irresolute handling of the coal stoppage of 1926 which caused it to last many months longer than need have been the case—these facts can be neither overlooked nor forgotten.

Despite the changed conditions there is nevertheless no reason, in our judgment, for pessimism about the future of the coal-mining industry on a scale suitable to the new conditions, if mine-owners and miners are willing to co-operate intelligently together and if the State will use its ultimate powers with sufficient vigour. The coal industry is in a state of transition. If it is to be in a position to pay good wages and give full-time employment to its workers, and to maintain production at not less, and if possible at more, than the present figures, certain conditions are necessary.

The first is that the producing units of the industry should be reconstituted, so as to secure the highest standard of efficiency and economy in production. This involves, in a large number of cases, the amalgamation of independent collieries. It involves also the closing of a number of poor and inefficient mines.

The second is the remedying of the legitimate grievances of the miners, so as to ensure that close co-operation between employers and employed which is in itself a prime factor in efficient production.

The third is the better organisation of transport and sale.

The fourth is the encouragement of more scientific methods in the utilisation of coal.

In addition it will be necessary to adopt special measures to meet the present emergency that arises from the presence in the industry of an excess of workers.

2. The Labour Scheme of Nationalisation

But before proceeding to formulate the specific measures that are needed for carrying out this policy, it is necessary to consider the alternative that is offered by the Labour Party. This alternative scheme, presented in evidence to the Samuel Commission, was based upon the conclusions of a committee representing the Miners' Federation of Great Britain, the General Council of the Trades Union Congress, the Executive Committee of the Labour Party, and the Executive Committee of the Parliamentary Labour Party. It has since been published in a pamphlet called *Coal and Common Sense,* and was generally approved by a resolution passed in 1926 by the Margate Conference of the Labour Party.

Briefly stated, the scheme proposes—

(*a*) That the minerals, collieries, and plant should be purchased by the State as an unified industry in close association with a State electrical industry.

(*b*) That the ultimate control of the unified coal industry should be vested in a Statutory Power and Transport Commission, whose members would be appointed by the Government and for whom the President of the Board of Trade would answer in Parliament.

(*c*) That the actual administration of the unified industry should be entrusted to a National Coal and Power Production Council operating in large measure through Provincial Councils to be set up in appropriate districts.

(*d*) That the industry so constituted should be self-supporting: that is to say, the interest and sinking fund on the purchase price and other Government loans are to be a "first charge" upon its revenues after paying working expenses and a minimum rate of wages.

(*e*) That proposals for modifications in wages should be discussed between representatives of the workers concerned, the Coal and Power Production Council, and a Consumers' Council, consisting of representatives of employers and workers in the coal- and power-using industries. Local Authorities, Co-operative Societies, and a Coal Export Commission. Where agreement is not reached, the question is to be referred to a special court, who could recommend but not order a solution. The right to strike is preserved.

(*f*) That changes in prices should also be discussed between the Production Council and the Consumers' Council. Where agreement is not reached, prices are to be determined by the President of the Board of Trade or by an independent tribunal appointed by him.

(*g*) That the export trade should be managed by a single Coal Export Commission of three members or a Public Utility Corporation.

(*i*) *Unification and Nationalisation*

The Labour Party proposes that the coal industry should be unified and nationalised. The Labour Party's scheme does indeed include provisions intended to bring about a certain measure of decentralisation; but both the ideas current amongst the miners and the working out of the scheme, if it were ever put into practice, would in fact lead inevitably to unification on a national scale. But national unification is a very different thing from the amalgamation of suitable and neighbouring mines. It does not allow for the enormous diversity of conditions which exists between the various areas, and, in many cases, between mines in the same area. And it would in practice prove impossible to obtain any body of directors capable of coping with the overwhelming complexity of a unified coal industry.

Experience in Germany and elsewhere abundantly enforces that view. The Rhenish-Westphalian Coal Syndicate is often quoted as an example of unification. This Syndicate, in spite of difficulties which have arisen from time to time, has worked efficiently on the whole. But the essence of this Syndicate is that it arises from the special circumstances of the Ruhr district, that it does not comprise coal-fields which lie at a distance, and that it is a cartel for the sale of coal and not a combine for the production of coal. Moreover, no attempt is being made to unify all the coal-mines of Germany into a single trust. Great Britain presents no equivalent to the Ruhr situation. Its coal-fields are widely distributed throughout the whole country, are operated under very different conditions and serve different markets at home and abroad.

Another argument which the Labour Party puts forward for national ownership of the mines is that it would transform the *moral* of the industry, because under private ownership extra effort benefits the shareholders, while under public ownership it would benefit the miner or the consumer. But this contention ignores the fact that substantially the same share of the proceeds will have to be paid to the people who provide the capital, whether they be Government *rentiers* or private shareholders. What practical difference does it make to the working miner to whom that share is paid? And in so far as it is a question of ensuring a more just participation by the miners in the gains of prosperous times that can be secured in other ways.

(ii) *Administrative Problems*

The Labour Party does not propose that the nationalised and unified coal industry should be run by the State, but by a Coal and Power Production Council, assisted by a number of Provincial Councils, and mainly elected by those engaged within the industry itself. The National Coal and Power Production Council would consist of fourteen members and a chairman, of whom six are to be " executive and administrative workers," " six are to be miners and by-product workers," all twelve " elected by their respective organisations largely from the Provincial Councils," while two are to be " representative " of the Power and Transport Commission, and the chairman is to be the Secretary for Mines or his deputy. There are also to be a Consumers' Council with considerable powers in the fixing of prices, an Export Trade Commission, and some other interesting features which need not be summarised here.

This is really the heart of the Labour Party scheme. It implies assent to the arguments against bureaucratic management. It is an attempt to create a system under which those engaged in the industry would manage it and in which the miner himself would have a large and direct voice. But it looks unworkable even at a first glance. In practice it would certainly prove so.

Efficiency in management is what matters most to the miner, to the consumer, and to the owner, whether the owner be the community or the shareholders. But can any system of election from within the industry produce efficient control? Unless election can produce management at least as efficient as the present the result must be dearer coal and more unemployment, or else lower wages, or, as a third alternative, a fresh burden on the taxpayer for making good an annual deficit. Is there any chance of its doing so?

The essence of industrial administration is executive decision. Nobody proposes that engineers or accountants should be elected by the personnel in a business. They are appointed by reason of their professional qualifications, and their record in results actually produced. The controllers of business and industry are, or ought to be, chosen for their business capacity. The only test of this is their success in " getting results " in the shape of those prices, wages, and profits which are necessary to the prosperity, health, and peace of any industry. The real problem in Government-owned, as in private, industry is that of picking directors. When you have found the right directors, the only practical course is to equip them with the right organs through which they can consult workers, consumers, or others who are affected by their actions, and to leave them a free hand, subject to a yearly or half-yearly account of their stewardship to the ultimate owners of the business. How are a million "electors" within the industry to choose such men? Even if candidates of that type are put forward, are they likely to be elected in competition with others who have long been known for their sympathy with the electors' particular point of view? How would the candidates be nominated—by "parties," by Trade Unions, or by individuals? How would the "campaign" for election be conducted, so that the electors should judge of the rival candidates and listen to their rival policies? And as the outcome, is it probable that election would produce just that proportion of administrative experience, financial knowledge, understanding of the needs of industry and labour at home and abroad, which the directors of a nationalised coal industry must possess if they are to have the least chance of making a success of their business? The Labour Party consider that these qualities can be assured by popular election. We are convinced that they cannot.

Once elected, the Council would find its responsibilities shared by a number of Provincial Councils of fourteen members each. Of these it would have nominated two, while six would have been elected, presumably in much the same way as the Coal and Power Council itself, by the manual and manipulative workers, and six by the technical and administrative staffs. In the event of differences of opinion, and differences would be likely to be frequent, which authority would be given the last word? And which would have the greater power to make its decision prevail? It is impossible to conceive a more certain method of producing chaos and inefficiency.

Even if this elective scheme of administration could ever be set on its legs, the plan so oddly labelled "common-sense" comes up against a second insurmountable difficulty. It is an axiom of sound business administration that power and responsibility must go together. The Labour Party's plan completely disregards this axiom. The unfortunate Coal and Power Council, even if it could be efficiently constituted, would find itself saddled with responsibility without power. The coal industry is to be vested in the Power and Transport Commission, which is charged with the duty of "enforcing financial stability," so that the industry will meet the interest and other charges on the coal bonds. If there was a default it could only discharge that duty by taking over the control of the industry itself. Again the Coal and Power Council has no power of final decision as to output or wages or prices, which in the last resort are to be determined after an elaborate process of consultation with the Power and Transport Commission, the Consumers' Council, and other bodies. Yet every practical business man knows that prices are determined not by academic discussions, but by a vast number of different factors, national and international, which alter in force and range from week to week, from day to day, sometimes from hour to hour, and that the output of every mine or business must be adjusted continuously to these factors.

Can it be seriously contended that the method of administration proposed in *Coal and Common Sense* would ever be set in motion, or, if it were set in motion, that it would work even for a month?

(*iii*) *Conclusions*

The truth is that if the coal industry were to be nationalised at all it would have to be administered by a Public Board. The community, after spending some hundreds of millions of pounds in acquiring the industry, could not surrender final control of it to anybody else. It would certainly keep the ultimate responsibility for appointing the management in its own hands, as otherwise it would have surrendered the asset to others to enjoy or destroy. But reasons have already been given for thinking that any attempt to conduct so large an industry, employing 1,000,000 men, as a single unified concern would break down.

In some respects indeed its conduct by the State might involve new obstacles. The real need of the industry is the elimination of the poor mines, the development of new and better mines and the transfer of surplus labour to other industries. These reforms, difficult enough when the losses involved are falling on the private owners, might be almost impossible for a nationalised industry. Strong, and in many cases irresistible, political pressure would be brought to keep open uneconomic mines, for the sake of local miners or traders. It is difficult to conceive anything worse either for the mining industry itself or for the political life of the nation than that the day-to-day industrial problems of an industry employing a million men, who with their wives and dependents would number two million voters, should intrude themselves, as they necessarily would, into every election and many Parliamentary debates.

Finally, it may be asked how nationalisation can help the country to cope with those urgent difficulties, already described, which confront the post-war coal industry? Nationalisation would not diminish the competition of oil or water or other competitive sources of power. It would not lessen the effects of the widespread adoption of methods of economising coal. It would not restrict the coal output of foreign countries, or force an entry for British coal into their markets. On the contrary, by forcing a fundamental change in the organisation of the industry, it would introduce a new element of confusion, and would certainly make more difficult the discovery of solutions for the existing evils.

3. Proposals for Reform

We turn to the four groups of proposals to which we have previously referred.

(a) *Reorganisation*

In order to secure the "rationalisation" of the industry—its conduct by the most efficient units that can be devised and not merely by such as happen to have been evolved haphazard from the conditions of the past—it is essential that the mineral itself, as distinct from the mines and their plant, should be acquired by the State. This measure was recommended by all the various Reports that were the outcome of the Sankey Commission, by the Report also of the Samuel Commission, as well as in *Coal and Power*. The cost, according to the estimate laid before the Samuel Commission by the Chief Valuer to the

Board of Inland Revenue, would be about £100,000,000. The interest and sinking-fund on this sum would be fully covered by the revenue from royalties.

The national mineral estate would then pass under the management of Coal Commissioners. These would be experts; they would form a non-political body; they could make plans maturing over a long period of years.

Exercising the "landlord power," they could direct the development of the industry only to those areas which gave reasonable assurance of being able to produce good and cheap coal, of paying adequate wages, of providing proper housing and other amenities. The Commissioners could actively promote that development of new and modern mines to replace old and out-of-date mines, which is essential to the permanent health of the industry. They could also promote scientific research, in which, despite its vital importance, the mining industry has been, and is still, exceptionally backward. In a decade or two the Coal Commissioners could ensure that the mineral resources of the country were being developed on a coherent and well-considered plan in the best interest of both consumer and worker.

Again, the Coal Commissioners, endowed with suitable powers during the transition period, could produce an immediate effect on conditions in the industry. Impediments to efficiency still continue, in spite of the assistance given by Part I of the Mines (Working Facilities and Support) Act, 1923, and Part II of the Mining Industry Act, 1926, resulting from the ownership of the coal by a multiplicity of owners. The Commissioners could not only sweep away such impediments, but they could also do a great deal more to facilitate such amalgamations and other measures of reorganisation, as they might consider to be in the public interest, than is possible under the provisions of Part I of the Mining Industry Act, 1926. That Act leaves the initiative still remaining in the hands of the coal-owners, who only too often have shown themselves unwilling to move. There is, indeed, no sign of any general movement in the industry towards the formation of more economic units of production; the few amalgamations which have been made in recent years seem sometimes to have been devised at least as much in the interest of the financiers who have promoted them as in the interest of productive efficiency; and the Act of 1926, which was to have given a fresh impulse has so far proved itself almost inoperative.

But if they are to assist effectively in the reorganisation of the industry, the Coal Commissioners must be empowered to deal, in certain cases and subject to proper safeguards, with existing leases. We wholly endorse the proposals on this point made in *Coal and Power* as early as 1924. They were as follows:

> "In regard to existing leases, it shall be competent to any owner or group of owners, or a District Board, or the miners' representatives upon such a Board, to submit to the Commissioners proposals for the amalgamation or grouping of pits for the rectification or rearrangement of boundaries, or for other purposes tending to the more efficient working of the industry. On receiving such proposals, the Coal Commissioners shall institute an inquiry; and if in their judgment a case is made out for the proposed changes, they shall invite the interests concerned to submit a detailed scheme for their approval. The Commissioners shall then have power to make the necessary variations and modifications in the old lease or leases, and to grant new ones, but they shall not impose terms to the detriment of existing lessees without compensation. A new lease once granted, or an old lease once confirmed or revised by the Commissioners, shall not be subject to revision by them except upon the request of the lessees for a period of, say, thirty years."

We would add that power to assist amalgamation is not enough. The great immediate difficulty is the existence in the various districts of the less successful mines, which, by lowering net proceeds, also lower wage-rates and so increase the profits of the more successful mines in the district. We support the Samuel Commission's proposal that these should be excluded from the wage ascertainment. This would mean that they would have to pay the district wages, but that their working results would not be taken into account in fixing the wage-rates. The result would be that wage-rates for the various districts would be set by the most efficient employers and not depressed by the less efficient; and that, as is desirable, the closing of uneconomic mines would be hastened.

(*b*) *Removal of Grievances*

(i) The first step towards the ending of the bitter antagonism that has so long prevailed between employers and employed in the mining industry is to establish a proper system for the discussion of grievances.

In *Coal and Power* it was stated that the "best method of securing the peace and prosperity of the mining industry is to provide for open consultation between miners and mine-owners about the general policy and conditions of the industry, while leaving the executive functions vested in the hands of those who are primarily responsible for the success of mining operations." For this purpose the association of mine-owners and miners at three different points was suggested:

(1) A National Mining Council of, say, 100 members, half representing mine workers and half capital, management, and technical skill, with possibly some representatives of the chief consumers added. This Council would have power to discuss the policy pursued by the Coal Commissioners and to refer matters, on which it disagreed with the Commissioners, to the Minister of Mines for decision; to administer the Miners' Welfare Fund created under Section 20 of the Mining Industry Act of 1920, and amounting to about £1,000,000 a year, and certain other funds; to make suggestions for improving the efficiency of the industry; to receive full statistical information about the condition of the industry; to make recommendations about hours and conditions of labour, the safety of workers, and so on; to discuss matters referred to it by District Boards or the Board of Trade. Full details of its proposed powers are set forth in Paragraphs 81–89 of *Coal and Power.*

(2) District Boards, as provided for under the Minimum Wages Act of 1912 and Part II of the Mining Industry Act of 1920 (which never came into operation), subject to certain detailed modifications set forth in Sections 90 and 91 of *Coal and Power.*

(3) Pit Committees, also as contemplated by the Mining Industry Acts of 1920 and 1926, and by *Coal and Power,* to deal with matters affecting safety, efficiency, disputes, etc.

It will be clear that these three grades of machinery will

confine their activities to consultation as to the general problems of the industry, but will not deal with questions of wages. With all these proposals we entirely concur. The third is in close correspondence with the recommendations for the establishment of Works Councils which we have made in Chapter XVIII.

(ii) With respect to the fixing of wages, wage-problems in the mining industry present exceptional difficulties at all times; and to-day the gloomy outlook of the industry, and the irreconcilable and impracticable attitude of both sides in the controversy, make a satisfactory solution of the problems almost unattainable. We believe that the best course, in these circumstances, would be to initiate a National Wages Board with a neutral element, like that which has been established in the railways. And since mining is certainly to-day, and is likely for some time to remain, a distressed industry, it may even be necessary to give such a Wages Board the definite powers of a Trade Board for the fixation of, at any rate, minimum wage-rates. This would probably soon compel the closing of the less economic mines, and force the nation to face the problem of providing for a huge surplus of labour—a problem which is discussed elsewhere in this Report.

One of the grievances of the miners arises from the fact that, under present practice, the figure of the receipts of the collieries, by which wages are largely regulated, is taken as being the sums entered in the books as the receipts of sales. But a large proportion of the coal is not sold in the open market, but transferred by the colliery to an associated industry or sales agency. It is by no means certain that the transfer price credited to the colliery always corresponds with the true market price. The Royal Commission proposed the adoption of a different and a fairer method for the calculation of values in all such cases, and we are of opinion that that method should be universally applied.

(iii) There are other recommendations in the Report of the Royal Commission which, if adopted, would contribute to the removal of the discontent among the workers. They relate to the improvement of housing; and to the establishment of pithead baths, together with the grant of annual holidays, with pay, whenever the economic condition of the industry shall have sufficiently improved to permit the expenditure. With these recommendations—which are broadly developed or implicit in the recommendations of *Coal and Power*—we also concur.

(*c*) *Transport and Sale*

The information collected by the Samuel Commission shows that between producer and consumer there exists a substantial margin of profit and expenses, which is capable of curtailment. We believe, with the Commission, that the present methods by which coal is distributed are wasteful and capable of considerable improvement.

The necessary reforms are of a technical character, and it is sufficient to say that, so far as they relate to railway transport, they are now being examined by the Standing Committee on Mineral Transport set up by the Ministry of Transport and the Mines Department, in accordance with the Commission's recommendation.

But even more important is the establishment of agencies to act on behalf of large groups of collieries. The Commission advocated an extension of such agencies, and the point was referred to a Departmental Committee on Co-operative Selling in the Coal-mining Industry (the Lewis Committee).

This Committee presented a Majority Report signed by nine members, of whom two made a slight reservation; and also a Minority Report signed by three colliery owners. The following is a summary of the recommendations contained in the Majority Report:

(1) The development of organised marketing in the coal-mining industry is desirable in order to avoid excessive competition, to effect economies and improvements in the marketing of coal, and to help to stabilise the industry.

(2) The present lack of consolidation in the industry is a serious impediment, and the full development and benefits of organised marketing cannot be realised unless the industry can be consolidated, by amalgamations, into a much smaller number of units.

(3) Organised marketing is only immediately practicable in those localities and districts where there is a fairly general desire among the coal-owners to develop it.

(4) The voluntary development of local arrangements—more particularly selling pools—among neighbouring colliery owners is advocated.

(5) District organisations, of wider scope than local arrangement, are the next stage of development. Where in any particular district a fair and equitable scheme for more efficient marketing is supported by a majority of 75 per cent. or more calculated on a tonnage basis, power should be vested in a tribunal to make the scheme compulsory, subject to effective safeguards for the minority.

(6) The co-ordination of district associations will be, ultimately, a desirable development, but can only be justified to the community by the industry effecting and sharing with the consumer economies, not only in the marketing of coal, but in all phases of its production and transport.

(7) The Government is advised to consider the question of revising and clarifying the law on restraint of trade so as to remove the present uncertainty as to the status in law of marketing organisation.

(8) In the export trade, local selling pools and the possibilities of closer co-operation between colliery owners and exporters should be developed.

A reservation recommends that the voluntary principle be at first given a full trial for a limited period, after which the Board of Trade should have power to impose a compulsory scheme. The Minority Report consists of a lengthy exposition of the doctrine of unrestricted competition.

In our view, it is necessary to avoid excessive competition between collieries not merely to prevent prices from falling to an unproductive level, but to stave off the over-production which has of late become characteristic of the industry, and is directly the cause of unremunerative prices. As the Majority Report puts it:—

> "at present the industry can have no choice of policy. It is powerless to frame any policy or to help itself in times of depression, when unregulated production on a falling demand tends to result in unremunerative prices."

We strongly support the general proposals put forward in the Majority Report of the Lewis Committee, and we are of opinion that if, after a reasonable lapse of time, it is found that co-operative selling agencies have not in fact been created, it may be necessary to consider the application of some form of compulsion.

With respect to retail distribution, we consider that it is clearly desirable that those municipalities which wish to do so should be empowered to engage in the retail sale of coal. If a few enterprising town councils undertook this service and conducted it with success, a considerable reduction in the price to the consumer might be effected.

(*d*) *Utilisation of Coal*

It is this sphere that offers the largest scope for the measures which will raise the coal-mining industry from the slough in which it now finds itself. The more scientific use of coal, the full exploitation of every one of its valuable constituents, the utilisation of grades that have hitherto been regarded as little better than waste, the efficient preparation of the products for the market—here lies, in the long run, the best hope for the future. But here again the measures that are practicable, and that offer an opportunity to the State to be of assistance to the industry, raise questions of a highly technical character. It indicates no lack on our part of appreciation of the importance of these matters if we do no more than refer our readers to the various reports already quoted, in which an adequate treatment will be found.

4. The Surplus Workers

We reach, finally, the pressing, but difficult, problem of the redundant workers.

When everything possible has been done to increase the efficiency of the coal-mining industry, to concentrate employment, and to reduce costs, there is little doubt that we shall still have to deal with a large surplus of labour in the coal-mining industry.

This conclusion is based upon our view of its future. The attitude of the coal-owners throughout recent years has been that the curve of British coal production would continue to rise in the future as it did before the War; and that 300,000,000 tons is the normal figure from which the upward movement might be expected to start. If this were a sound view, there would be no problem. But the facts and figures given at the outset of this chapter show that, as a result of substitutes for coal and economy in its use, the industrial activity of the world is increasing rapidly while its consumption of coal, except in America, is standing still. Secondly, with the development of new mining areas in various parts of the world, there is a tendency to diminish the importance of British coal. Thirdly, the use of oil in ships has hit chiefly that section of the world coal market which is supplied by Great Britain. While therefore we may expect the volume of international trade to increase, we cannot confidently look for a rapid return of our coal exports to the high peak reached in 1913, nor can we expect that, even if British trade in general steadily regains prosperity, there will be any marked increase in the home consumption of coal. Judging from recent figures (excluding the strike period), the annual home-consumption of coal has been in the neighbourhood of 180,000,000 tons per year; if the steel industry resumes something like full working, the total will rise to 190–195,000,000 tons.

Exports of coal, coke, and manufactured fuel, and coal shipped for the use of steamers engaged in foreign trade, in recent years have varied between 71,500,000 and 84,500,000, the latter figure being reached in 1924, when Germany was still affected by the occupation of the Ruhr. 75,000,000 tons would represent comparative prosperity for the export districts. This means an output of 255–260,000,000 tons a year, with a possible increase to about 270,000,000, as against nearly 290,000,000 in 1913. The latter tonnage was produced by 1,105,000 miners, and, if we are to regain our competitive position, it is essential that output per head should be at least as great as in 1913. The output we have suggested, therefore, should be obtained by less than a million miners. The number actually on the Register in recent years has fallen from 1,260,000 in 1924 to 1,228,000 in 1926 and to 1,199,000 in July 1927 (the latest figures available), but still shows a surplus over the number required of about 200,000. This figure agrees closely with the numbers wholly or temporarily unemployed in the year 1927, which in the first eleven months numbered 222,000.

The difficulty of dealing with this situation is complicated by the fact that certain areas are already offering, and will to an increasing extent continue to offer, more employment, while others are reducing employment to a greater degree. If the men thrown out in the latter districts could be drafted to the former, it would at least prevent the problem getting worse. This was definitely recommended by the Samuel Commission, which proposed that miners should be moved from one district to another before outside labour was recruited. The Mining Industry Act of 1926 gives the Ministry of Labour power to deal with recruitment of persons over the age of eighteen, and the Minister has recently negotiated an agreement with the Mining Association which provides for a voluntary undertaking by mine owners to limit employment to those engaged in mining before April 30, 1926.

We do not think that any stronger measures which would bar a man who has already been engaged in the industry from taking part in it would be justified. Any attempt by the State to interfere with the liberty of choice of workers by those responsible for carrying on an industry, or the right of a man to obtain employment if he can in any occupation, is a serious encroachment upon individual rights, and is only to be justified in very grave conditions.

In the special circumstances of the case, however, the State should use its utmost endeavours to draw off or make alternative provision for as many as possible of the surplus miners. This question is urgent. The existence of 200,000 unemployed men in the coal industry is not merely a grave social problem in itself, but it is a drag on miners' wages, encourages short time, is an inducement to keep open uneconomic pits which ought to be closed, and generally tends to delay a sound reorganisation of the industry. Its repercussions are not, however, limited to the mining industry itself, for it hinders the adoption of measures for the improvement of our whole system of unemployment insurance.

We therefore propose that the Committee of National Development proposed in Chapter XXI should be assigned in the first instance the task of planning and directing a series of measures for dealing with this problem.[1] It is essential that the

[1] As these pages are passing through the press, it is announced that the Government are about to appoint a small Industrial Transference Board with some of the objects that are advocated here. But apparently the powers of this Commission are to be very restricted, and it remains to be seen whether the Board will be able to make any real impression upon the problem.

task of dealing with surplus mining labour should be under the supervision of the Committee of National Development, since the problems involved will touch a number of Government Departments and only some central body can effect the necessary co-ordination. The measures proposed fall under three heads:

(*a*) Limitation of recruiting.
(*b*) Pensioning of older workers.
(*c*) Transfer of existing workers into other industries.

(*a*) *Limitation of Recruiting.*—We have already referred to the voluntary agreement recently made under the Act of 1926. It should be the first duty of the Committee to review arrangements of this kind and to ensure that they are as effective as circumstances permit. In particular, the conditions of recruitment in each area need to be considered in relation to the circumstances of other areas. For example, areas in which new pits are being sunk should not recruit, as has been the tendency in the past, from local labour outside the industry, but should draw exclusively upon the reserve of unemployed in areas where the industry is overmanned. It should be the duty of the Committee to facilitate transfer in these cases by every means possible, and to take such action as is feasible to ensure that lack of housing facilities does not stand in the way of a transfer of labour on a considerable scale where such is necessary.

But in addition to these voluntary arrangements, there should be a compulsory scheme of limitation on new entrants. Even in the year ending June 1927 there were about 40,000 new entrants into the industry—of whom an unknown proportion, however, were juveniles. New entrants, other than juveniles, should be prohibited; and steps should also be taken to limit the entry of juveniles. A certain number of juveniles are, of course, essential in every continuing industry; but the number in the coal industry should not be as large as in recent years.

(*b*) *Pensioning Older Workers.*—The Census of 1921 showed nearly 6 per cent. of the coal-miners in England and Wales were over sixty years of age, and 10½ per cent. over fifty-five. If this percentage is applicable to Great Britain, it means that there are now about 70,000 miners over sixty. This estimate is broadly confirmed by a recent official estimate, according to which the total number of men over sixty years of age now employed in coal-mining, including both employed and unemployed, is about 78,000, of whom about 13,000 belong to such classes as craftsmen, clerks, etc. (*Hansard,* December 6, 1927).

We suggest that a special pension scheme should be worked out for the benefit of men who have now reached the age of sixty, and who are prepared to leave the industry and to undertake not to return it. Even where they find other employment, they should still be allowed to draw their pensions. Against the cost of such a scheme should be set the present expenditure upon unemployment benefit in the cases of these men. When they reach the age of sixty-five, and draw the contributory old-age pension, the charge should be reduced by the amount of that pension, only the difference being payable as part of the special pension scheme; and at seventy the ordinary pension provisions would operate and the special scheme would cease.

(*c*) *Transfer of Existing Workers into Other Industries.*—Limitations on recruitment at one end and the acceleration of retirements at the other, whilst capable of effecting a great deal in three or four years, will nevertheless scarcely operate fast enough to solve by themselves the problem of the surplus workers. We shall still be left with a substantial number of miners in the prime of life who ought, if possible, to be transferred into other industries.

The means of effecting this are: (i) by offering them special inducements to find for themselves a berth elsewhere, and (ii) by assisting them with training schemes, etc. We believe in utilising method (ii) as fully as possible, but we are a little doubtful whether the absolute number which can be successfully handled in this way will be very large. We are therefore in favour of a substantial offer under (i).

(i) We propose that any miner, who has been unemployed for a specified period, and who will voluntarily bind himself not to seek employment in the mining industry for a period of not less than five years, should receive a special unemployment allowance (to be charged on the Exchequer and not on the Unemployment Fund), with a view to giving him time and opportunity to leave the mining areas and find himself work elsewhere. It would, of course, be necessary, to prevent evasions, that this plan should be coupled with arrangements for the limitation of recruitment.

The actual amount of the special allowance would need to be most carefully considered. But we suggest that it might be 35*s.* a week for a period of three months, followed by 25*s.* for a further period of three months.

(ii) Financial assistance should be given for the training of miners in other occupations and for the purchase of tools and equipment for their new trade, and a grant, where necessary, for transferring the families of married miners to their new place of occupation. Suitable emigration schemes should also be devised and possibly combined with training schemes.

We are dealing elsewhere (Chapter XXVII) with the experimental training-centres established by the Ministry of Labour. The Committee should arrange to set up such training-centres in mining areas, designed to meet the special requirements of unemployed miners for whom openings in other occupations appear to be available. The activities of these centres should obviously be related to such schemes for land settlement, emigration, or transfer to other industrial occupations as the Committee might have in view.

The most suitable alternative employment is perhaps to be found in agriculture, since a large proportion of the men drawn into the mining industry come from agricultural districts. Experience of the schemes for placing ex-Service men on the land shows that only a proportion of men who have been engaged in other occupations prove suitable for agricultural work and take permanent root, and on any such schemes the State must for a while be prepared to lose money. But that loss must in any case be balanced against the cost that would otherwise be incurred in providing unemployment benefit. Where, therefore, facilities for transfer to agriculture or other suitable industries are arranged, it would be legitimate to strengthen the conditions under which a man may refuse alternative employment without forfeiting benefit. The State cannot indefinitely pension adult workers whose occupation has permanently gone, or leave it to the option of the recipients to decide whether the alternative work offered is suitable or not.

We are of opinion that a contribution towards the expenses of the above schemes, and also for other purposes, should be required from the royalty owners. We recommend that when the mineral is acquired by the State, a levy should be made for the benefit of those who have laboured in the industry, and should be collected in the form of a deduction from the purchase price.

It is true that special taxes have already been levied upon mining royalties under the Budget of 1909 and the more recent Mining Industry Act, but, in our judgment, there is a just case for a further substantial contribution from this source in the special situation in which the industry is now placed. While the royalty owners have in no way shared in the creation of the wealth produced by the coal-mining industry, nor in the risks incurred, they have continued to draw their incomes as a first charge upon it. Moreover, while in these circumstances, and particularly in view of the hazards of the miner's life, there has always been a strong moral obligation on the royalty owner to use some part of his receipts for the benefit of those labouring in the industry, that obligation has been widely (though not universally) disregarded. Indeed, except in Scotland, the royalty owner, as such, has not even contributed to the burden of the rates. We consider, therefore, that now, when the industry is experiencing the greatest adversity in its history, when those who have borne the burden of financing and administering the collieries are confronted with serious losses, and when miners who have given their best years to the industry are faced with low wages and permanent unemployment, the royalty owners should bear their share.

There should therefore be deducted from the full value of the compensation to be paid by the State a further substantial contribution. This should be used first for facilitating the carrying out of the scheme which has been outlined above for meeting the present inevitable displacement of labour, by contributing to the cost of training and transfer of displaced miners and to the provision of pensions for the older men. For the rest the funds should be used for the general improvement of the amenities of the mining areas.

The question of unemployment is closely connected with that of the hours of labour. Before the War, the miners were working a so-called eight-hour day which was legally established by the Act of 1908. Under an amendment inserted by the House of Lords, however, one winding-time had been permanently added to this period. The men were therefore below ground on the average for 8½ hours. Following upon the Report of the Sankey Commission, the statutory period was reduced in 1919 by one hour. During the stoppage of 1926 the Government passed through Parliament a Bill which repealed this provision and allowed the various districts to fix their own hours within the limits that had prevailed before the Sankey Commission. The position now is that a nominal eight-hour day is worked in the districts of Scotland, South Wales, Lancashire, Cheshire, North and South Staffs and Salop, South Derby, Leicester, Cannock Chase and Warwick, and certain smaller areas, and a nominal 7½-hours day in Northumberland and Durham (for hewers), Yorkshire, Derbyshire, and Kent. An average addition of half an hour, in respect of the winding-time, must be made all round to arrive at the actual time that the men are below ground. As a consequence, the majority of the British miners are now working longer hours than the miners in any European country. This country, which used to pride itself upon being the pioneer in shortening the hours of underground labour, now finds itself the least advanced of all, a hindrance, instead of an example, to the rest.

Undoubtedly the extension of hours imposed on the men in 1926 has tended to increase the number of unemployed. Fewer men are needed to produce the present total output. On the other hand, it has increased the output per man by about 14½ per cent. If, in the present condition of the industry, the hours were restored to their previous level, either a fresh charge would be laid upon the industry, since a larger number of men would be required to raise the same tonnage, or else the miners, who are paid by the ton, would earn in the shorter day an even lower wage than now. It is, of course, the miners themselves who are most affected by the choice to be made. Although it is to the general interest that they should enjoy the fullest leisure that is practicable, if they found that the restoration of the pre-stoppage hours involved a further reduction of their earnings they might themselves prefer further to postpone that measure until the industry had been brought to a more prosperous position.

It needs no argument to show that the shortening of hours would be greatly facilitated if it were effected simultaneously in all countries with competing coalfields. The Miners' Trade

Unions throughout Europe have been striving towards this object for many years, and any steps which can be taken in that direction, under the auspices of the International Labour Office of the League of Nations, should receive the active support of the British Government.

CHAPTER XXVI

IMPERIAL DEVELOPMENT

IT is often contended that by means of an enlightened policy of imperial development we might find within the British Empire full compensation for our trade-losses in the rest of the world. And it is certainly true that any expansion of Empire markets is (other things being equal) more advantageous to us than a corresponding development elsewhere, because the Empire populations buy more of our goods per head than the corresponding populations in other parts of the world.[1] To do everything in our power to encourage the development of Empire resources is therefore as much our interest as it is our duty, in view of the responsibilities we have assumed.

1. Empire Trade

But it is necessary to guard against exaggeration. The view quoted in the first sentence of this chapter is, in fact, a dangerous over-statement. Valuable as the Empire-markets are, their capacity for any greatly increased absorption of British goods is limited, in the case of the Dominions by their

[1] The value of exports of produce and manufactures of the United Kingdom during 1926–7 per head of population of the importing country was:

	£	s.	d.
New Zealand	14	16	5
Australia	9	19	6
South Africa	3	19	7
Canada	2	16	1
India	0	4	11

as against:

	s.	d.
France	9	3
Germany	9	1
United States of America	7	9
Italy	4	8
Russia		9

Extracted from Hansard, December 1, 1927.

small population, and in the case of India and Africa by their low purchasing-power per head. For these reasons, our trade with the Empire forms little more than one-third of our external trade. The following table shows, for 1925, i.e. the most recent representative year, how our trade is shared between the Empire and foreign countries:

TABLE 31

DISTRIBUTION OF THE EXTERNAL TRADE OF THE UNITED KINGDOM, 1925

Millions of £

	The Empire.				*Foreign Countries.**	*Grand Total.*
	The Dominions.	*India.*	*Rest of Empire.*	*Total.*		
Net imports from .	223·3	64·7	53·8	341·8	824·9	1,167
Exports † to . .	183·1	86·1	65·9	335·1	438·3	773
Re-exports ‡ to .	20·8	1·2	4·3	26·3	127·7	154
Total foreign trade .	427·2	152·0	124·0	703·2	1,390·9	2,094
Percentage of grand total . . .	20	7	6	33	67	100

Compiled from the Annual Statement of Trade of the United Kingdom, 1926, vol. i.

It appears from this table that our external trade falls into three approximately equal sections: (1) with the Empire, (2) with Europe, and (3) with foreign countries outside Europe; and that while the Empire takes less than half of our exports, and less than one-fifth of our re-exports, it supplies us with not much more than one-quarter of our imports.

We hold a very strong position in most of the Empire

* In our trade with foreign countries, the share of Europe (excluding British Possessions) is given below:

	Per cent.
Imports from Europe	50
Exports to Europe	46
Re-exports to Europe	71

† Of the produce of the United Kingdom.

‡ Of imported merchandise, whether consigned from the Dominions or foreign countries.

markets, thanks in part to the preferences which the Dominions accord to us, and still more to the influence of sentiment and of long-established trade connections—an influence which operates in India and the Crown Colonies as well as in the Dominions.

TABLE 32
UNITED KINGDOM'S SHARE IN THE EXTERNAL TRADE OF THE EMPIRE

Year.	*Percentages of Total Exports consigned to the United Kingdom from—*				*Percentages of Total Imports received from the United Kingdom by—*			
	The Dominions.	*India.*	*Rest of Empire.*	*Total Empire.*	*The Dominions.*	*India.*	*Rest of Empire.*	*Total Empire*
	Per cent.	*Per cent.*	*Per cent.*	*Per cent.*	*Per cent.*	*Per cent.*	*Per cent.*	*Per cent.*
1895 . .	72	32	30	49	60	66	23	52
1913 . .	59	24	30	41	38	63	25	42
1923 . .	48	24	25	36	37	54	24	38

Compiled from the latest available Statistical Abstracts for the several British Oversea Dominions and Protectorates.

This table shows the strength of our position. But it also shows that our proportion of Empire trade has strikingly diminished during the last thirty years, especially in the Dominions, in spite of the preferences they have accorded to us. This is the natural result of the development of the export trade of other countries, notably America, which inevitably dominates the trade of Canada and shows a growing strength in the trade of the Pacific.

2. Opportunities and Limitations

It is inconceivable, in view of these facts, that there should be a development of Empire trade so rapid and on so large a scale as to balance any serious and rapid decline in that two-thirds of our trade which is carried on with the rest of the world. This would be true even under a system of complete free trade within the Empire. It is yet more true in view of the determination of the Dominions and (in a less degree) of India to pursue a policy of self-sufficiency, and to build up their own manufactures behind tariff-walls which are (in the case of the Dominions) only a little less high against us than against our foreign competitors.

To trust for the improvement of our trade position wholly or mainly to Empire development is therefore to ensure disappointment. And a policy which would deliberately raise barriers in the way of our trade with the rest of the world in order to increase our trade with the Empire would not only be ruinous to ourselves; it would, by further impoverishing us, disable us from contributing as much as we might otherwise do to imperial development.

These considerations do not, however, alter the fact that the Empire presents opportunities for development of vast potentiality, which it is both our duty and our interest to utilise to the utmost of our power. No policy of national revival would be other than incomplete if it did not give a high place to this task; a task which is peculiarly incumbent upon Liberals, seeing that the Liberal Party may justly claim to have been responsible for the most important stages in the development of the Empire's modern form, as a commonwealth of co-operating peoples. The notion that Liberalism has been indifferent to the well-being of the Empire is a gross distortion of history, which rests exclusively upon the fact that Liberals have never believed that either the prosperity or the unity of the Empire can safely be made to depend upon fiscal bonds.

The problem of imperial development has, however, been rendered far more acute by the very economic difficulties which make it at this moment doubly urgent and important; and careful study of the problem has become more needful than ever lest we should waste our diminished resources. It is not, indeed, possible to examine it here with any fullness of detail. Any adequate treatment of a subject so vast and various would demand a volume in itself; and we touch upon it here only in outline. The problem will be clearer if we consider separately the widely different needs and claims of the variant types or classes of communities included within the Empire. Though the classification is rough and not exhaustive, it will be convenient to consider in turn three different groups: (1) the self-governing Dominions; (2) the vast and populous Empire of India (which includes four out of every five subjects of the Crown); and (3) the Crown Colonies in the West Indies and elsewhere, and the backward tropical lands, mainly in Africa.

3. The Self-governing Dominions

Though the Dominions include 59 per cent. of the area of the Empire, they contain only 6 per cent. of its population. Huge, thinly-peopled, and under-developed lands, their chief needs are (*a*) population, (*b*) a stream of capital for development, (*c*) markets for their products, and (*d*) the most effective possible communications with the main centres of civilisation. All these needs we have in the past mainly provided, and the provision of them has been our vital contribution to the growth of the Dominions. In regard to communications, the work still mainly lies with us; and it is our business to see that the new forms of communication, by air and by wireless, are developed as rapidly and efficiently as possible. But in regard to the needs of population and capital, the difficulty is now greater than it has ever been; and therefore the need of studying these problems so as to make the best possible use of our diminished resources is greater than ever.

Emigration

Hitherto the population of the Dominions has been mainly, and in the case of Australia and New Zealand almost wholly, drawn from our surplus. From the time of Gibbon Wakefield to the creation of the Empire Settlement Board, we have wrought out one scheme after another for the encouragement of Empire migration: without these schemes, lands so distant as Australia and New Zealand could never have been peopled. We have a large apparent surplus at the moment, in our army of unemployed. But few of the unemployed are of the type needed by the Dominions; any real revival of trade would quickly do away with the surplus; and our shrinking birth-rate makes it possible that in a few years (probably by 1940) our population will cease to increase.

Moreover, the United States still draws a high proportion of the available emigrants, both because it is nearer and because it offers more immediate prospects of employment than most of the Dominions. In spite of the post-war American restrictions on emigration, this still remains true, as the following table shows:

TABLE 33

EMIGRATION OF BRITISH SUBJECTS FROM GREAT BRITAIN

Seven-year Periods.	*To British North America.**	*To Australia and New Zealand.*	*To British South Africa*	*To Other Parts of Empire.*	*To U.S.A.*	*To Other Foreign Countries.*	*Total.*
1900–6	387,000	105,000	213,000	63,000	853,000	43,000	1,664,000
1907–13	1,043,000	397,000	175,000	131,000	877,000	114,000	2,737,000
1920–6	664,000	392,000	164,000	195,000	475,000	114,000	2,004,000
Total	2,094,000	894,000	552,000	389,000	2,205,000	271,000	6,405,000

* A substantial but undefinable proportion of these emigrants have subsequently passed over the frontier into the United States.

Compiled from the Statistical Abstracts for the United Kingdom and from the Board of Trade Journal, March 17, 1927.

If, therefore, the Dominions are to be in the future peopled by the British stock, it is important that the process should be accelerated while there is still a surplus; the more so as this would be a material contribution to the problem of unemployment. What can we do to help?

(*a*) We can make known the opportunities that are open, give advice and guidance, and provide assistance towards the cost of passage. This we are already doing through the Empire Settlement Board; doubtless its methods can be developed and improved. But in the existing condition of our finances there are narrow limits to the financial assistance which we can afford to offer, especially as we have in any case to bear the training and maintenance of the emigrant from birth to the moment of emigration, while he will become a source of revenue to his new country from the moment when he is fairly planted. In these circumstances it is reasonable to expect that the Dominions, which are far more prosperous than we are, and which ultimately stand to gain by immigration, should give more aid than they have hitherto done, by organising or creating opportunities for the settler, and seeing that he is helped through the difficult period of settlement. In the early days of colonisation the cost of migration was in the main defrayed by the sale of colonial lands, then controlled by the Crown. Some equivalent means of helping emigration must somehow be devised if the short-lived opportunity before us is to be used; and only the Dominions can devise it.

(*b*) We can provide a more effective system of training (i) for boys and girls whose parents may be willing to seek a new career for them, and (ii) for unemployed young men and women, as a condition of unemployment relief. The training should be such as will fit them among other careers for life on the land, either at home or in the Dominions. We have elsewhere made suggestions on this head (see Chapter XXVII, p. 399). But a systematic policy of Empire migration can only be made possible by co-operation between the Dominions and this country, on an ampler scale than is now practised; and it should be an aim of Liberal policy to do everything possible to organise and stimulate such co-operation.

Supply of Capital

We have long provided capital on a very large scale and at a very low rate for Dominion development, by the device of giving the rank of trustee securities to the stock issued by Dominion or Colonial governments. In Table 34 on p. 374 will be found a detailed analysis of all new capital applications for the past six years and for the average of the three pre-war years. The very high figures for the Empire are unquestionably due in a large degree to the trustee privilege. These figures show that by far the largest part of our overseas investments are used for imperial development.

The grant of Trustee status to approved investments overseas has been a contribution of immense value, which has not only enabled the Dominions and Colonies to borrow at a low rate, but has in many cases given to public utilities owned by Dominion or Colonial Governments real advantages in comparison with similar utilities, privately or municipally owned, in this country. This privilege, which has been far more advantageous to the Dominions than any system of preference could be, will, we hope, be continued. But, as we have already pointed out (Chapter III), we no longer have so large a surplus for external investment as we used to have, and we need a larger proportion of the available capital for home development. We have suggested above (Chapter IX), in the Board of National Investment, a

TABLE 34

BRITISH INVESTMENTS OVERSEAS

(000s *omitted*)

Destination.	*Average* 1911–13	1922	1923	1924	1925	1926	1927
	£	£	£	£	£	£	£
British Empire .	68,065	74,924	92,723	72,277	60,920	53,174	99,812
U.S.A. and Dependencies .	24,413	nil	nil	60	600	500	3,947
Central and South America . . .	44,376	19,916	7,608	3,768	7,035	23,599	21,679
Far East . . .	9,568	6,138	20,006	14,496	1,035	7,442	1,060
Europe . . .	15,104	29,179	17,140	34,112	7,606	16,892	21,775
	161,526	130,157	137,477	124,713	77,196	101,607	148,283

Extracted from "The Economist."

means of centralising the available funds and of ensuring that they are employed to the best advantage. Yet it is unlikely that we shall be able, in the near future, to provide capital for Dominion needs as freely as in the past. This makes it the more important that the capital which is available for these purposes should be wisely guided into channels which, while beneficial to the Dominions, will also more directly encourage British trade with them. If, as we have suggested (Chapter XIX), there is, under proper regulation, a considerable development of popular investment trusts for small savings, this is likely to provide an additional and new source of supply for Dominion and Colonial needs.

Fiscal Preference

The Dominions also want access to markets, especially for the foodstuffs and the raw materials which are their principal exports. As ours are the most valuable markets in the world, they would naturally desire a preferential position in them, such as would enable them to undersell countries with lower standards of living; and they feel that this would be only a fair return for the preferences they afford to us. But there is this difference between the preference accorded to us by the Dominions and the preference asked from us, that while the granting of a preference by the Dominions involves no departure from the policy of self-sufficiency which they have adopted, the preference we should have to give would involve a radical departure from our accepted policy, and would necessitate the setting up of barriers against two-thirds of our customers. Again, the preferences given by the Dominions involve no increase of the cost of living of their people, but possibly a diminution; the preference we should have to give would involve a serious increase in the cost of living, the more so as the only commodities upon which a really useful preference could be granted are foodstuffs and raw materials. Any large system of preferential duties likely to be effective for the purposes desired by the Dominions would have the unhappy effect of making the Empire appear burdensome to the poorest classes in this country, and might impoverish us to such an extent as would disable us from doing what we can now do for imperial development. Moreover, such a system would be mutual only in the case of the Dominions; it would not be applicable to India, which shows no readiness to adopt any general system of preferences; and it would be impossible to enforce a system of preferences in our favour in the Crown Colonies and Protectorates, seeing that our control of these vast regions is only endured by the world as a whole because the traders of all nations are admitted to them on equal terms. For these reasons, while desiring to use every means of encouraging imperial development, we are compelled to discard this means as being at once impracticable and likely to do more harm than good.

4. India

India presents at once one of the greatest potential markets in the world and one of the most valuable sources of supply for a great variety of products. It must be enormously to our advantage to encourage the growth of Indian prosperity and of Indian trade. India's chief need is an increase of the purchasing power of her vast but poverty-stricken population; it has been said that if every Indian ryot could afford one additional *dhoti* a year, all the mills of Lancashire would have to work full time to meet the demand; and anything which adds to the gross income of India adds to the trade of the world, and particularly of this country. At present India is endeavouring to achieve this end by stimulating manufactures, behind a protective tariff, at the expense of the immense and impoverished agricultural classes who form the vast majority of the Indian population, thus diminishing their purchasing power.

For the increase of Indian prosperity, a great expansion of capital investment for the equipment of the country with scientific means of production is required. In the past we have supplied the bulk of this capital; but the excited opinion of Indian nationalism regards the interest on these investments as a "drain" on the country. We can no longer supply new capital on the same scale as formerly. But India herself possesses enough capital to render possible a great development, if her people could only learn to abandon the agelong habit—born of insecurity—of hoarding wealth in the form of buried bullion, instead of using it productively. A recent inquiry carried out by an American Commission even suggests that the amount of the precious metals stored in India is equal to that held by the United States; but in India this wealth is immobilised and rendered sterile by the habit of hoarding. Before India can learn to use her available wealth for productive purposes, three things are necessary: an acceptable and sound system of deposit banking; political security together with the allaying of racial strife; and practical education. These are all governmental problems, for the right solution of which we still have our share of direct responsibility; and it is equally a governmental problem to alleviate political unrest and to calm the racial animosities which have in recent years done so much to disturb trade and to retard economic development. A liberal, conciliatory, and imaginative policy in the purely political sphere, and a vigorous use of the power of Government to bring about economic advance, are the primary needs of India to-day; and the use for these ends of the power we still wield must form the greatest contribution we can make to the development of Indian prosperity, which in its turn would contribute not only to our prosperity, but to that of the world's.

5. The Crown Colonies

The vast and almost undeveloped tropical lands, inhabited by simple and primitive peoples, which have been brought within the Empire mainly within the last fifty years, constitute that part of the Empire over which we exercise the most direct authority, and for the development of which, because of their very backwardness, our responsibility is heaviest. They can yield, in abundance, essential materials for commerce, notably rubber, vegetable oils, and (perhaps, in the event, the most important of all) a supply of raw cotton, which might render us less dependent upon America, and stabilise the extremely fluctuating prices of that crop, which constitute one of the peculiar difficulties of the cotton industry. They will also provide great and growing markets, as their primitive inhabitants acquire new tastes and wants, and find in the production of raw materials the wealth wherewith to satisfy them. The primary need of these lands is capital wherewith to open them up and make their resources available by roads, railways, and steamboats. Capital is also required to foster new industries, especially cotton growing. For many purposes sufficient capital will be provided by the normal processes of the new issue market; rubber companies, for example, are not likely to lack support. But for those purposes which cannot be expected to yield an immediate return, such as the construction of roads fit for motor transport, Government action is indispensable; and we think that the Board of National Investment should facilitate substantial loans to the colonial administrations. A share of the increased values given to these lands by such improvements should be obtained, by means of betterment taxes, both as a security for loans and as an aid to further development.

Another primary need of these undeveloped lands is organised research in regard to their economic resources and problems, their sanitary needs, and their social and linguistic characteristics, together with the provision of effective training for administrators, traders, and educators. This is an obligation which falls primarily upon the controlling Government. A very modest expenditure in this direction would be repaid a hundredfold by the results of a more scientific development.

Finally, it is indispensable that the native populations over whom we have assumed control should be justly and generously treated, safeguarded against exploitation, and secured in the possession of their lands. There is a strong temptation to accelerate development by large concessions to exploiting companies, which proceed to extrude the native workers from their lands, and to turn them into mere labourers for a paltry pittance. There are cases in which what is called the "plantation" system may be justified, but its extension has to be watched with care: it may yield a more rapid return to the investor at home, but in the long run it does not make for the prosperity either of the colony or of the ruling country; and the slower and more laborious process of teaching the natives to make the best use of their own lands is demanded by justice and in the long run is better for trade. A disinherited and discontented native population, dragooned into working under open or veiled compulsion for foreign exploiters, is unlikely to supply so good a market for British goods as a contented population producing from their own lands crops which trade needs, and which they can exchange for the products of British factories. The contrast between the methods which have unhappily been pursued in Kenya and the more enlightened and liberal policy adopted in Nigeria has many lessons. The only sound course of development in these lands is to define as its first object the contentment and well-being of the native population.

CHAPTER XXVII

THE RISING GENERATION: ITS EDUCATION AND EMPLOYMENT

THE "efficiency," to use the word in its narrower sense, of industry must, in the long run, be largely determined by the training it gives to its recruits. Its real effectiveness in producing material wealth and in satisfying human needs must, even more certainly in the long run, depend on the opportunities it offers to the children who enter its ranks on leaving school.

1. Schools and Efficiency

To examine in close detail the methods by which British boys and girls are trained and placed in industry would involve a survey of the whole educational system which we do not propose to attempt. But we wish to indicate in this chapter some points in which an improvement of the present arrangements is urgently necessary, and to make certain recommendations to which we attach considerable importance. The whole subject demands fuller consideration than we can give to it here, for, apart from its involving questions which go to the root of social contentment and political stability, the competitive power of great industrial countries will, we believe, in the near future turn largely on the soundness of their educational system and the use to which the product of that system is put in the office, the market-place, and the factory.

To technical and commercial education considerable attention has been given in recent years in many countries. In Germany, and the more progressive of the States of the U.S.A., to instance two only of our most prominent industrial competitors, more rapid and consistent educational progress has been made since the War than in this country, particularly in the extension of education over the whole adolescent period. Here, there is a growing uneasiness, but little practical progress to record. Recent studies of the problem, such as the Reports of the Malcolm Committee [1] and of the Hadow Committee [1] are timely in that they have begun to prepare the public mind for that step forward that will be the more effective the sooner it is taken.

2. Dimensions of the Problem

Before discussing policy, the general position with regard to the numbers of juvenile workers, the existing machinery for advising and placing boys and girls in work, and the main facts with regard to apprenticeship and training, continued education, and the hours of juvenile labour must be briefly set out. In the last year for which figures are available (1924–5), 714,312 children left the public elementary schools of England and Wales. Of this total, 88,101 left in order to attend secondary schools or other full-time educational institutions. The number leaving the elementary schools at fourteen to enter employment on becoming totally exempt from school attendance was 539,514. Leavers from the secondary schools, technical, commercial, domestic, and art schools number not less than 100,000 per annum. The intake of industry in the year may therefore be put at approximately 600,000 boys and girls in England and Wales. In Scotland the total intake may be estimated (as the statistics are defective) at 75,000 per annum.

These figures are not wholly consistent with the figures of juveniles [2] available for employment, which in 1926 were given as 2,190,000 for England and Wales, and 248,300 for Scotland. But owing to the continued fall in the birth-rate and the accentuation of this fall during the War, the total both of school leavers and of occupied juveniles will substantially decrease during the next few years. The best estimate of this decrease shows that the lowest point will be reached in 1933, when the total is expected to be 1,556,000 in England and Wales, and in Scotland 201,700. After 1933 the number will rise again, but not to its present level. Unless there is a radical change in the birth-rate, industry

[1] I.e. *Report of the Committee on Education and Industry* (1926, 1s. 6d.), and *The Education of the Adolescent* (1926, 2s.). Both published by H.M. Stationery Office.

[2] I.e. boys and girls exempt from school attendance and under eighteen years of age.

will not again in our times have at its disposal as many juveniles as it has now.

3. Juvenile Unemployment

The amount of juvenile unemployment was serious in the years 1922–4; it has diminished since that date. During 1926 the average monthly number of boys and girls registered at the Employment Exchanges and Bureaux as wanting work was 37,874 and 38,866 respectively, a total of 76,740. But it must be emphasised that these figures represent only the boys and girls who register for employment, and, as the young worker under sixteen, not being eligible for Unemployment Insurance benefit, very often for that reason does not register, and as for various reasons a number of youngsters over sixteen also do not register, the published figures represent only a portion of the actual amount of unemployment. The figures are mainly useful as giving some indication of fluctuations from time to time, and of those industries or areas where juvenile unemployment is particularly severe.

The position at the present time may be summarised by saying that over the country as a whole employment is good for boys and girls under sixteen, better for them than for adults; but not good even for them in the necessitous areas; that many boys and girls are thrown out of work as they near the age of eighteen; and that there is a tendency for a new blind-alley gap to be created at sixteen. In many parts of the country the demand for young boys and girls leaving school at fourteen is to-day actually greater than the supply.

A " Sample Investigation " carried out in June and July 1925 by the Ministry of Labour into " the Personal Circumstances and Industrial History " of 6,000 boys and girls registered for employment provides valuable data. It showed that unemployment then was intermittent rather than continuous. It found no indication of there being a large class of boys and girls who had markedly deteriorated as a result of continued unemployment. " But," it added, " there is a residue of difficult cases which, in themselves, constitute a problem of the first magnitude."

The finding here quoted suggests that any policy for treating the evil of juvenile unemployment must have regard to the fact that the youngsters most likely to suffer are those who are physically the weakest and mentally the most backward. The effect of unemployment during the formative years of adolescence on social and industrial *moral* is incalculable. Enforced idleness during youth is the royal road to adult unemployability, particularly in the atmosphere of discouragement which besets the "necessitous areas."

4. Treatment of Juvenile Unemployment

Juvenile unemployment was not a social problem of any magnitude before the War, with the important exception that the lives of many young workers were dislocated at about the age of eighteen by the termination of those many jobs which were termed "blind-alley occupations" and that a spell of unemployment, often of considerable length, then ensued. The absorption of juveniles into munition work made it evident at the end of the War that there would be unemployment among juveniles of all ages, and with this in view Juvenile Unemployment Centres were established after the Armistice to provide boys and girls awaiting fresh employment with some education and supervision. The primary purpose of these centres was to prevent deterioration. Attendance was made a condition of receiving donation under the Out-of-work Donation scheme, which was in force between November 1918 and November 1919. Another scheme of Juvenile Unemployment Centres was put in force under the Unemployment Insurance Act of 1920; and in 1922, when the seriousness of the problem came to be more generally recognised, a special effort was made to increase the number of the centres. According to the latest return (October 1926), there were 80 Unemployment Centres actually at work in the areas of 30 Educational Authorities. Where the centres exist, attendance for a minimum of fifteen hours weekly is made a condition of the payment to boys and girls under eighteen of unemployment benefit. The cost of administering the centres under the different schemes has been borne in varying proportions by Local Education Authorities and the Exchequer.

This simple outline is enough to show that there is a problem of Juvenile Unemployment which requires close attention, but that its treatment so far has been discontinuous and vacillating.

It should, in our view, be regarded less as part of the general problem of Unemployment as of that of Juvenile Employment.

5. Careers and Blind Alleys

(a) *Apprenticeship and Training*

The Ministry of Labour's Sample Inquiry referred to above showed that the first situations actually taken should be classified as follows:

Apprenticeships	5 per cent.
Prospects of Training. . .	25.8 ,, ,,
No training	54.1 ,, ,,
Casual or Seasonal . . .	15.1 ,, ,,

On the other hand, the Balfour Committee estimates that skilled industry can absorb 80,000 boys a year, about half of them at the age of fifteen or sixteen, and give them some sort of systematic training.

(b) *Openings and Blind Alleys*

Opportunities of apprenticeship or training vary widely in different districts. In London over 50 per cent. of the boys leaving school each year enter "conveyancing of men, goods, and messages." That means in most cases messenger work, an occupation in which the privileges of physical exercise wholly outweigh the opportunities of training. But the Ministry of Labour reported last year that there had been some reluctance, especially in London, on the part of boys to take those jobs which are definitely labelled "blind alley" by public opinion; it would seem that the continued effort made in the schools to persuade boys when they leave school to think, not of the biggest shilling, but of their future is beginning to have effect. On the other hand, the Ministry also reports that in some districts where employment for juveniles was good there was a shortage of suitable boys to fill better-class vacancies.

(c) Methods of Engagement

The Exchanges and Bureaux [1] in 1926 filled 220,000 vacancies out of 266,000 vacancies notified to them. Only 12.4 per cent. of first placings were made through Exchanges or Bureaux. Twenty-five per cent. were made through relatives or friends, and just on 60 per cent. were "unaided." The full meaning of "unaided" in this context will be realised by anyone who has talked to boys on leaving school about their future prospects, or has seen them wandering in the morning through the streets looking for the sign "Boy Wanted."

Further figures from the Sample Inquiry may be quoted in this connection. Thirty-seven per cent. of the boys and 25 per cent. of the girls were in the highest class of employability, and 25 per cent. of the boys and 24 per cent. of the girls in the lowest class. There were more boys and girls of the best type than there were situations of the best type, though there was in general "a substantial correspondence" between the type of boy and the type of job. But of the very worst jobs of all, namely, the casual and seasonal jobs, 18.4 per cent. were filled by boys of the best type and 14.2 per cent. by girls of the best type. Of the boys and girls who had held four, five, six or more situations, "a comparatively high proportion of the boys and a comparatively low proportion of the girls were of the best type." Finally, the worse the type of first situations obtained the longer was the total period of unemployment.

(d) Continued Education and Training

The Sample Inquiry showed that 15 per cent. of the boys and girls were continuing their education, at evening schools for the most part. A recent return by the London County Council shows that 75.16 per cent. of the children who left school in the period under examination had not received any continued education since leaving school, and that 67.5 per cent. had not belonged to any club, social or educational institution.

We may illustrate the facts here indicated by some results of

[1] The Juvenile Employment Exchanges are maintained by the Ministry of Labour under the Labour Exchange Act, 1909; the Choice of Employment Bureaux by Local Education Authorities under the Choice of Employment Act, 1910.

an intensive study made by Sir Wyndham Deedes of the after-school life of the boys and girls leaving a group of schools in Bethnal Green. Of the jobs recorded in this inquiry, 10.5 per cent. of the boys' and 5 per cent. of the girls' were apprenticeships of some sort; but the majority of jobs, taken on leaving school or entered within the next two years, provided no training whatever. One per cent. of the boys and 5 per cent. of the girls had stayed at school after the statutory school-leaving age; 17.5 per cent. of the boys and 32.5 per cent. of the girls had enrolled at evening institutes but had given up attendance; 13.5 per cent. of the boys and 6.5 of the girls were attending evening institutes at the time of the Inquiry (June 1927); 11 per cent. of the boys and 14.5 per cent. of the girls had belonged to a club or juvenile organisation of some kind; 28 per cent. of the boys and 25 per cent. of the girls were still members of juvenile organisations at the time of the Inquiry. The hours being worked by very many of these Bethnal Green youngsters made attendance at evening schools or clubs difficult or impossible.

To the question of hours we shall return after touching on the training which industry gives or can be expected to give.

6. Education by Employers

Apprenticeship has special importance, partly intrinsic and partly arising from prevalent misconceptions on its scope and its utility. At one time its revival was advocated as a means by which the young worker would be assured of training, "have a trade in his hands," and continue his education. Apprenticeship Committees and Skilled Employment Associations were set up in many places, but it soon became apparent that the revival of apprenticeship on anything like a general scale was out of the question, and that in any case apprenticeship is not a cure under modern conditions for blind-alley employment. The field of apprenticeship has been drastically restricted, for one reason, among many, that machinery has made long experience and close training in craftsmanship to a large extent unnecessary. Experience during the War proved that even in many of the most jealously guarded crafts "skill" could under modern conditions be very rapidly acquired. None the less there remain a few industries, notably engineering, printing, and the building trades, in which access to skilled employment can scarcely be obtained except by the channel of apprenticeship. It follows that "Industrial Training" must be understood as aiming at special skill in particular processes only for a few of the entrants into industry, and for the majority at the development of manual dexterity, mental alertness, and adaptability.

The Post Office a few years before the War was rightly criticised for taking on a large number of boys and discharging them without training at the "blind-alley" age. It then became within its own sphere a model employer of juveniles. The number of boy messengers is limited by that for which adult employment can be found. The general education of the boys throughout the age of adolescence is continued. A considerable variety of adult employment, ranging from the pedestrian postman to the higher flights of technicians, is open to them. Some private firms also provide admirable educational facilities for their young workpeople. But they are mainly firms which have many apprentices and take particular care of their specialised education. There are not many firms which regard the education of its young workers generally as part of their duty to society and to their own self-interest.

While we are convinced that general education must be continued throughout adolescence, we do not maintain that it is the duty of employers generally to provide that education. We suggest rather that juveniles who are at work should be employed under conditions which will enable them to profit by what the educational system of the country provides for them.

7. Hours of Work

The possibility of training and education, to say nothing of the well-being of juveniles generally, is intimately connected with the hours of labour. The scandal of long hours worked by women and children in the early days of the industrial revolution roused the conscience of the country to intervene and to regulate the conditions of their employment. The present situation may be shortly summarised:

1. In textile factories there is a permissible maximum week of 66 hours including meals or 55½ hours exclusive of meals.

2. In other factories and workshops a permissible maximum of 68 hours including meals or 60 hours exclusive of meals.

3. In shops there is a permissible maximum of 74 hours including meals. There are statutory provisions regarding meals, which appear to permit of a maximum working week of 65½ hours exclusive of meals. In practice, the working week must almost certainly be shorter, owing to statutory provisions regarding time of closing.

The limitations now established have been arrived at by a series of steps taken with respect to employment in particular types of occupation. There is still no regulation of the hours of young workers:

(*a*) In offices, warehouses, etc.

(*b*) As messenger boys, van boys, and in similar capacities.

(*c*) In domestic service, including hotels, clubs, etc.

(*d*) In agriculture, although in practice the regulations of the Wages Committee appear to keep the juveniles' working week at the same length as that of adults.

The industries for which "permissible maxima" have been enacted are, generally speaking, those in which wages agreements have still further reduced the hours of work. The "unregulated" boy and girl occupations are among those in which for the most part wages agreements are inoperative.

Some attempt has been made to deal with these "unregulated" boy and girl occupations. A Departmental Committee on the Hours and Conditions of Employment of Van Boys and Warehouse Boys, which reported in 1913, found that the hours of van boys in certain trades were sometimes excessively long, and recommended that they should be regulated by means of by-laws administered by the Local Authorities, and that a weekly limit of 70 hours, inclusive of meal-times, should be fixed, the meal-times to be not less than 1½ hours per day. Somewhat similar recommendations were made with regard to warehouse boys. No action has been taken as a result of this Committee's recommendation—although it attracted considerable attention at the time—except in so far as the Employment of Young Persons Act of 1920 prohibits the night employment of young persons in mines and quarries, constructional work, transport, and industries.[1]

Not only the number of hours worked, but the times of starting and finishing, are of importance in their bearing on education and training. A pre-war inquiry laid down that, if attendance at evening schools was to be physically possible, the maximum hours of employment (including meal-times) should be not more than 58 hours per week. But it pointed out that a 58-hour week, although it made attendance at an evening school physically possible, often left the juvenile so tired that he or she was incapable of profiting by attendance at an evening school. It suggested that a maximum of 48 hours per week (including meal-times) should be enforced if proper advantage was to be taken of the evening school.

It is notorious to those in touch with young workers that the hours of a large proportion are still much in excess of a 48-hour week. The facts brought out by the Inquiry in Bethnal Green, to which we have already referred, may be taken as fairly representative of a large section of young London workers. The sample taken was of 200 boys and 200 girls who left school at Christmas 1924 and Easter 1925. Their age would, therefore, be in no case more than 16 years 9 months, or less than 16 years 4 months. Table 35 on page 389 gives an analysis of the hours worked in all the jobs concerned (omitting those in which hours varied weekly or seasonably).

This table does not include four jobs which even in this context invite particular attention. In the first, a van boy was working up to 78 hours per week. In the second a boy was working in a garage from 8 in the morning to any hour up to midnight every weekday. In the third a boy (also in a garage) was working from 7.45 a.m. to 10 p.m. each week-

[1] By the Factory and Workshop Act of 1901 and the Shops Acts of 1912 and 1913 young persons are persons between the ages of fourteen and eighteen. By the Children Act of 1908 a young person is a person between the ages of fourteen and sixteen. By all these Acts a child is a person under fourteen. By the Education Act of 1918, incorporated in the Education Act of 1921, a person is a child so long as he is under statutory obligation to receive elementary education, i.e. at present up to the end of the school term in which his fourteenth birthday falls, and a young person is a person between the age at which childhood ends and the eighteenth birthday. It will be seen that a person between sixteen and eighteen may be a young person for the purposes of Factory Acts, etc., but not a young person under the Children Act.

TABLE 35

HOURS WORKED BY JUVENILES (BETHNAL GREEN INQUIRY)

*Hours Worked.**	*Boys.*	*Girls.*
44 and under	3	5
Over 44 and up to 46	5	1
,, 46 ,, ,, ,, 48	6	13
Total with hours 48 or less	14	19
Percentage	*4·8*	*6*
Over 48 and up to 50	38	51
,, 50 ,, ,, ,, 54	95	143
,, 54 ,, ,, ,, 58	94	77
Total with hours 58 or less	241	290
Percentage	*83·1*	*93·9*
Over 58 and up to 62	29	16
,, 62 ,, ,, ,, 66	11	3
,, 66 ,, ,, ,, 72	6	—
,, 72 ,, ,, ,, 74	3	—
Grand Total	290	309

* Inclusive of meal-times.

Compiled from Inquiry quoted in text.

day. In the fourth, a boy in a fish-shop, whose day started some time between 8 and 9 in the morning, continued till 10 p.m. for six days a week and on the seventh day worked from 9 in the morning till 12 or 1 p.m.; that is, he worked 81 hours a week as a minimum. The information on hours of work in this sample Bethnal Green inquiry was obtained from the young workers themselves and their parents; information so obtained is subject to a certain margin of error, but that error is not by any means always in the direction of exaggeration. Many, but not all, of the jobs were in "unregulated" occupations, and it is evident that the problem is partly how protective legislation already in existence can be enforced, and partly whether the existing law does in fact protect the young person from exploitation and permit his continued education.

That these instances of excessive working hours are not peculiar to London is indicated by the results of another small Inquiry undertaken for us in a parish in the Home Counties with a well-to-do residential population. Many boys leaving school in this parish go as errand boys to the local tradesmen, and the working hours (including meal-times) per week of the representative number of boys examined include the following:

(*a*) Age 16, with baker—67 hours per week.
(*b*) Age 16, with grocer—73 hours per week.
(*c*) Age 17, with milkman—82 hours per week (5 a.m. to 5 p.m. six days; 5 a.m. to 3.30 p.m. on Sunday).

These small sample investigations illustrate in their special areas what is a fact for the country generally—namely, that many boys and girls work hours which effectively forbid any kind of continued education and to a very large extent deny them any opportunity of organised games or wholesome recreation.

8. Present Usefulness and Future Value

In the light of such facts as are contained in the preceding paragraphs it is impossible to contend that we are making the most of the nation's human resources. We may quote the searching questions with which the Lewis Committee [1] summed up its reference:

"Can the age of adolescence be brought out of the purview of economic exploitation and into that of the social conscience? Can the conception of the juvenile as primarily a little wage-earner be replaced by the conception of the juvenile as primarily the workman and the citizen in training? Can it be established that the educational purpose is to be the dominating one, without as well as within the school doors, during those formative years between twelve and eighteen?"

The Lewis Committee perhaps had their minds sharpened to a sense of human values by the War. It is clear from the simple statement given above of what happened to children who left school eight years after the War, that they have not yet been brought into the purview of the social conscience, that seven out of ten of them are still subject to economic exploitation, that the educational purpose is not dominant, and that the conception of the juvenile as primarily the citizen in training has not yet been accepted.

[1] *The Departmental Committee on Juvenile Education in Relation to Employment after the War.*

9. Principles of Policy

No form of waste is more harmful than the deterioration which too often takes place in young workers between the ages of fourteen and eighteen. That deterioration is due partly to the nature of the work which youngsters are often taken on to perform while they are cut off from the stimulus of further education, and partly to the innumerable repressions and denials of opportunity inflicted on the youth of our industrial centres by their environment. Fundamentally it springs from continued failure to define what industry requires of youth and what youth may rightly demand of industry.

Employers sometimes complain that the schools do not provide them with the employees they require. It is obvious from the terms in which this complaint is made that it is often due to a belief that the purpose of the schools is to turn out finished industrial or commercial products at the age of fourteen. But that in fact is not the purpose of the schools, and no child of fourteen is, for any purpose, a finished product. On the other hand, "educationists" sometimes draw an unreal distinction between life and livelihood, and between living and occupation.

Happily the educationist and the industrialist are drawing more closely together. There are fewer employers every year who expect the elementary schools to give a vocational training. Agreement is in sight on the principle that education must be organised so that, in the words of the Hadow Report, it may "develop more fully . . . the powers . . . of the great mass of boys and girls whose character and intelligence will determine the quality of national life during the next quarter of a century."

Liberals have always abhorred the "factory-fodder" theory of child-labour. Standing as it does for the freedom of the human spirit, Liberalism holds that the purpose of education is not to provide industry with amenable or even efficient human material, but to form and strengthen character, to create interests which will occupy and dignify leisure, to strengthen the mind against incitements and to arouse it to incentives, and at the same time to put the means of livelihood within reach of the human personality thus educated. The permeation of the national mind by this view is, in itself, responsible for much of the present dissatisfaction with the chaotic methods of industrial recruitment which are responsible for many misfits, much inefficiency, and much discontent.

10. Raising the School Age

By the provision of free places in secondary schools and of scholarships, a ladder to the University has been erected; but the manifest waste of much potential ability, the need in industry for character and brains, and the example of other countries, all point to the need for doing much more than has yet been done. The ascent is still too toilsome and precipitous even for the minority. For the majority the chance of further education depends upon raising the school age and on providing continuation schools for the whole body of juvenile workers.

The Report of the Hadow Committee brings the proposal for raising the school age into the sphere of practical politics. Its conclusion is that: "The course of wisdom . . . would be to pass legislation fixing the age of fifteen as that up to which attendance at school will become obligatory, after the lapse of five years from the date of this Report—that is, from the beginning of the school year 1932."

The case for raising the school age to fifteen is, in brief, that the extra year of school life, enacted as part of a scheme for the reorganisation of elementary education into primary and post-primary periods, will enormously increase the effectiveness of our whole educational system, that a child starting work at fifteen is in the long run of greater value to industry than one who starts at fourteen, and, to quote the Majority Report of the Poor-Law Commission of 1909, that young persons must be protected "against the demoralisation of character arising from premature entry into industry."

The opposition is based on several grounds. Many employers resist any proposal which would decrease the supply of the cheapest labour. Parents are very often anxious to realise the potential earning power of their children as early as possible. There is at present a shortage of suitable teachers for older pupils, and, although the diminishing child-population of the country tends to make vacant many school places, new buildings would be required in a number of areas, and the annual expenditure on Education would be swollen.

11. Continued Education

The proposal to provide Continued Education up to eighteen (or to sixteen) is sometimes regarded as an alternative to raising the school age. The two policies in reality deal with different aspects of the same problem and they are certainly not in conflict. The continuance of part-time education up to the age of eighteen was the policy adopted in the Fisher Education Act of 1918. The principle laid down by the Lewis Committee that boys and girls up to the age of eighteen were to be regarded by the State as primarily "citizens in training," was definitely adopted in the Act, which provided for attendance at Continuation Schools in the day-time for 320 hours in the year. The scheme was actually put into operation in London and a few other areas; it has been maintained in Rugby; but the wave of "Economy" and the industrial depression which followed the boom of 1922 destroyed at its commencement what was intended to be a permanent advance in national education.

We believe that no system of Education can be satisfactory if it does not provide for the age of adolescence; that the present lack of physical, mental, moral, and social training during the 14—18-year period prejudices our future as a nation, and that it is as much to the interest of employers that the educational needs of their juvenile workers should be met, as it is to that of the nation to meet the rightful demands which industry makes on the schools.

12. The Objective

In our view, the evils which at present beset juvenile employment and the chaos in which the arrangements for entry into industry are now involved are so overwhelming, and the results likely to follow a really adequate handling of a problem so promising, that the school age should be raised and part-time continued education provided as soon as the necessary machinery can be erected and set to work. Half a century's educational progress has step by step raised the age of entering industry to fourteen. But no well-to-do parent to-day cuts off his child at fourteen from educational influence and direction, and it seems to us that democracy must continue to push forward the threshold of employment until childhood in the family of a weekly wage-earner is allowed to be as long as it is in the families of the well-to-do. If the child in one class is too young at fourteen to be cut off from education, so is the child in another. Parents' narrowness of means must not be the main factor in deciding the length of their children's school-life. So long as it is, equality of educational opportunity is denied and industry is deprived of potential brain-power.

Expenditure on education ought to be a highly remunerative investment. Waste in that expenditure comes not from paying teachers adequate salaries or from providing schools adequately equipped, but from tolerating squalid environment for the schools and from launching their output on the world in such conditions that ten years' education is forgotten in two. Economy in relation to education means scrupulous prevention of administrative waste and thorough provision for the needs and capacities both of the average and of the exceptional child. The objective of educational policy is clear. It is that all children should be in attendance at school up to the age of sixteen; that the places available in secondary schools should be proportionate to the number of children in all classes of the population capable of benefiting from specialised or more prolonged teaching; that part-time education should be continued up to the age of eighteen; and that the arrangements by which children are placed in employment should be, not the present chaos of half-measures and cross-purposes, but a businesslike system by which the Education Authorities themselves will respond to the needs of industry while exercising their proper responsibility for the rising generation.

13. Recommendations

As the step which should be taken now towards that objective we suggest an advance along different but co-ordinated lines:

(1) That the number of secondary school places should be increased throughout the country in accordance with a definite programme, particular attention being paid in the first instance to those areas where the provision is notoriously inadequate and to the cases where the poverty of parents prevents children who win free places taking them up.[1]

[1] As we have said at the beginning of this chapter, it is not our intention to discuss the educational question proper. For this reason we put our first

(2) That every Local Education Authority should be under a statutory obligation to provide by the beginning of 1932 sufficient accommodation in the elementary schools [1] and also sufficient day continuation school accommodation, to give every child in their area an effective choice between whole-time education up to the age of fifteen or part-time day continuation schooling up to the age of sixteen.

(3) That, after a term of years long enough to arrange for the necessary accommodation and for training teachers specially qualified for adolescent education (this period should, we think, be one of five or seven years), daytime continuation school accommodation should be provided for all boys and girls up to the age of eighteen.

(4) That it should be the statutory duty of Local Education Authorities to provide training for all unemployed boys and girls up to the age of eighteen. This training should be an extension of the work done in the day continuation schools, and out-of-work allowances should be payable conditional on attendance at the full course of unemployment training provided.

(5) That in all areas the work of placing young people in employment and advising them on the choice of a career should be the duty of an Employment Committee set up by the Local Education Authority and advised by the Ministry of Labour.

recommendation in very general terms. What have to be remedied are two gross discrepancies: the first between the practice of different Local Education Authorities, the second the handicap imposed on scholarship children in the poorer areas. Merely to illustrate the facts we may quote from the most recent examination of the problem—*Social Progress and Education Waste* (Kenneth Lindsay: Routledge)—that 9·5 per cent. of the children leaving elementary schools go to secondary schools, one-third of them being exempt from fees; that 1 in 1,000 of them reaches the University; that the percentage of the ten- to eleven-year-olds who pass from primary to secondary schools was 27·1 per cent. in Bradford, but only 6·4 per cent. in London, 7·3 per cent. in Warrington, and 8·4 per cent. in Oxfordshire; that the proportion of children from seven well-to-do London boroughs winning scholarships was four times as high as that in seven poorer boroughs; and that while 26·9 per cent. of the pupils in secondary schools were the children of wholesale and retail traders, 20·5 per cent. were the children of skilled, and 3·2 per cent. the children of unskilled workmen. We give these figures merely to illustrate an argument which lies mainly outside our field, though it must enter it at this point.

[1] We are purposely not entering into the Hadow Committee's proposal to divide the elementary school period into primary and post-primary. The phrase "elementary education" is used throughout this chapter on the assumption that the primary and post-primary system will, in fact, be instituted at an early date.

We have already said sufficient to explain the purport of the first four recommendations above. A word must be added on the fifth. We have said nothing in this Report except by inference on the present division by areas of responsibility between Juvenile Employment Committees maintained by the Ministry of Labour and Choice of Employment Committees maintained by the Local Education Authorities. Nor do we wish to enter into this vexed question, except to point out that by an Order in Council made operative in September 1927, the Choice of Employment Committees are placed under the general authority not of the Board of Education but of the Ministry of Labour. It may be that in this way an administrative solution may be found of the industrial-education dilemma. The working of the expedient must be watched from this point of view. What must be emphasised is that the conception of the juvenile as primarily a citizen in training can only be realised by placing the responsibility for his welfare on the Educational Authority. The Ministry of Labour's function, therefore, with respect to juvenile as distinct from adult employment, must be to advise in the discharge of this responsibility.

14. Time for Adjustment

The policy proposed in the last section will necessitate certain changes in industry. Changes are in any case inevitable. As we have already pointed out, industry in the next five or six years will have to adjust itself to a substantial decrease in the number of young persons available for employment. That in any case will mean that some work which is now done by juveniles will be done by adults. It may mean the abandonment of certain processes and possibly even the loss of certain trades. But we do not believe that in anything but the very short run, industry benefits from displacing adult workers by successive relays of young boys and girls. And we do not believe that industry will be crippled, or even seriously handicapped, by being compelled (as it is about to be compelled simply by the fall in the birth-rate) to devise ways and means of employing adults rather than children. The adjustment will necessarily to a large extent take the form of technical and managerial improvements. Against any difficulties caused by the shortage of juvenile labour must be set a consequent reduction in the rate of adult unemployment and a general improvement in the standard of labour available.

We should add perhaps at this point that we think the proposals made by the Malcolm Committee for setting up a National Advisory Council for Juvenile Employment and for instituting a system of working certificates are steps in the right direction. But we hold with conviction that a longer stride forward must be made now in that steady and rapid advance on the objective of educational policy indicated in Section 13.

15. Training in Industry

If the policy we suggest is carried out, the responsibility of employers as such for training and education will be diminished. We do not think that much progress can be made by attempting to insist on industry educating its own young workpeople. Continued Education should recognise fully and generously the provision by certain firms, either of general education or more often of specialised technical education for youngsters in their employ. But education is primarily a matter for educationists, not industrialists. The State has a right to insist that an employer should not employ a young person for more than a limited number of hours per week, and that he should release that young person for certain hours in the week to enable him or her to attend a Continuation School. Where apprenticeship persists, technical schools of all grades should work in the closest co-operation with employers. But what Industry requires to-day is not merely a limited number of workers with highly specialised knowledge and skill, but a vast number of alert, intelligent, adaptable, fit, and willing workers. It follows that "training for industry" means a method of increasing general alertness and intelligence and of giving all working youngsters that adaptability that comes of wider knowledge, those opportunities of physical training peculiarly needed when the physique of manhood is being formed, and "social education," which means essentially a grounding in the principles of civics and economics without which willing membership of the industrial, as of the social and political, unit can hardly be expected.

16. Blind-Alley Employment

If Industry could devise methods by which it would itself train all its young recruits, or even offer them fair prospects of adult livelihood, the nation might be content with a less thorough policy than that we propose with the object of ensuring that the care given to the nation's childhood shall not be wasted by ignoring the special needs and difficulties of adolescence. But it is evident that blind-alley employment results from the nature of modern industry and particularly from modern sub-division of labour. There are some few industries in which the number of juveniles employed could be kept in due proportion to adult workers. But any attempt to secure a balance in such industries would be made ineffective by the existence not only of trades which employ a disproportionately large number of juveniles, e.g. in operating automatic machines, but of those in which the heaviness or difficulty of the work to be done necessitates the employment wholly or mainly of adults. The coming shortage of juvenile labour creates an opportunity of putting an end to the least desirable types of boy and girl labour. The Local Education Authorities, as they take over the responsibility for adolescent education and employment, will be able to abolish casual employment for juveniles, and to favour entry into jobs with prospects.

But, as we have said, blind-alley employment cannot be got rid of altogether. Its persistence means that there will always be a considerable number of boys and girls between the ages of seventeen and twenty-one, and sometimes even at the age of sixteen, who will be squeezed out of juvenile employment without being able at once to obtain adult employment. Even before the War the duration of unemployment at the end of the blind-alley gap was often serious. Youths tramped the streets in vain looking for work (and in those days the great majority of them were not eligible for Unemployment Benefit) for three months, six months, a year, or even two years. The result was confessedly disastrous. Under present conditions both the number of those suffering from blind-alley unemployment and its duration have increased—in some areas very largely increased. In some industrial centres there is a disquietingly high percentage of registered unskilled workers between the ages of eighteen and twenty-five. Moreover, boys who have been in blind alleys are nearly always unskilled. The proposals for National Development contained in other chapters of this Book will, we hope, provide work for scores of thousands of adults, and we recommend that in the organisation of this work special arrangements should be made for employing those suffering from blind-alley employment. Moreover, Training Centres would be of particular value for such youths and young men. From them some would graduate for work on the land at home or abroad. Others would go back to the towns strengthened and reinvigorated for adult employment at a crucial turn of their lives.

17. Training Centres

The four Training Centres already established by the Ministry of Labour have, we think, proved their value. It is time that the experience gained should be applied. The total capacity of the present centres is for less than 1,500 men. We suggest that non-residential centres should be established on lines similar to those at Wallsend and Birmingham in all the urban areas where unemployment is most severe; and that there should be a considerable increase in the number of residential centres in order to provide training on the land for youths and young men suffering from blind-alley unemployment. Trainees at the end of their course of instruction would be free to decide whether to look for an opening on the land at home, to settle overseas, or to return home to look for industrial employment. The purpose of the training, that is, would be partly remedial; it would aim at preventing the marked deterioration that too often takes place in a prolonged break between juvenile and adult employment. But it would also do something to restore that mobility of labour between town and country which has been checked not only by the lowness of agricultural wages, but by the creation of a purely urban habit of mind. The constant allegation that "the unemployed" refuse work on the land has been exploded time and again; and we hope that openings for employment on the land, at reasonable wages and with fair prospects of attaining independence, will be considerably increased as the Liberal Land Policy gets to work. In any case, the position of Britain as the centre of a great Empire, demanding in every part men with knowledge of the land and some love of it, makes it imperative that something should be done to correct the disparity between the number of settlers required and the number of land workers available. We are dealing with Training Centres in this section of our Report because, while they will provide training for young men of all ages, we think that they should not exclude boys of under eighteen who are not yet able to obtain adult employment. It is obvious that their establishment and direction would be in the hands of the Ministry of Labour.

18. Rural Industry

We are not suggesting that large numbers of town-bred boys can be induced to leave their accustomed pavements for work as farm-labourers. We would provide for training on the land partly for its own sake, partly for the sake of the Empire, and partly for those few town-bred boys in whose minds the idea of getting back to the country somehow survives. But the problem of the country-bred boy and girl is in itself important.

In any properly balanced community a number of countrymen and countrywomen will go to the towns. But their migration should be an overflow, not a running leak. The country itself should offer a career to the country-bred boy. Agriculture must offer opportunities of independence sufficient to outweigh the attractions of town-life before the distinctively rural problem of entry into industry can be solved. That means in effect a great increase in the number of small-holdings and family farms, and freedom of movement from wage-earning on the land to use of the land. No spirited boy will, if he can avoid it, commit himself for life to an employment in which his prospects are limited to a wage of 30*s.* or 32*s.* per week. The task of those who are responsible for guiding entry into agriculture is obviously governed by the opportunities which agriculture offers in their areas. But whether the surplus of country-bred juveniles be the natural surplus or the present excessive surplus, the entry of rural children into industry should be properly guided and developed. Some County Councils, notably Kent and Leicestershire, have paid special attention to the problem, and we note with particular interest the attempt being made by the Kent County Council to revive apprenticeship in agriculture and the setting up in the Romney district of a Winter School on the lines of the Danish High Schools.

Another important task undertaken by County Council Choice of Employment Agencies is to make arrangements for the after-care of boys and girls in the towns where they go to work. The difficulties of setting up satisfactory machinery in thinly populated scattered rural areas are obvious. It is impossible to establish Juvenile Employment Exchanges in every village. On the other hand, an effective system of advice, placing, and after-care can be worked through the village schools. This is one of the facts among many which persuades us that whatever part the Ministry of Labour plays in relation to Juvenile Employment, the Education Authorities must be mainly responsible.

19. Limitation of Hours

The very important question of hours of juvenile labour remains for treatment. The figures we have given indicate that a large number of young boys and girls are still employed for a number of hours per week which make impossible any kind of continued education.

It is an ironical comment on the Washington Convention, which aims at making the principle of an 8-hour day and a 48-hour week operate in industry throughout the world, that Great Britain, although it has accepted that principle in practice without actually ratifying the Convention, still permits boys' and girls' working-weeks of 60, 70, or more hours. It seems to us imperative that juveniles as such should be protected from over-long hours at work irrespective of the kinds of occupation in which they are employed, and that the limitation of hours should be imposed by Parliament. To make it a permissive subject of local bye-laws, as is proposed in a Bill recently introduced in the House of Lords, would create highly undesirable local inequalities. We suggest that the maximum working week for any young worker up to the age of eighteen should be 48 hours inclusive of meal-times and of the time given to continued education, and that the normal working day should lie between seven in the morning and six in the evening. That would mean an average full working day of less than nine hours with the evenings left free for recreation and education. In agriculture the hours of commencing and finishing work should be rather more elastic, and also in domestic service of certain kinds. But exemptions should be very sparingly given. The general prohibition of juvenile employment after six in the evening would do more than anything else to stop the present evasions of the law.

Trades which would "suffer"—if the word may be so misused—would include a number of shops, hotels, and clubs. The productive industries, apart from their giving time off for continuation schooling, would not be seriously affected. As we have pointed out, the supply of juvenile workers is decreasing fast and will continue to decrease in the next six years, and after that will rise slowly to a level lower than that at present existing. That means a considerable measure of reorganisation in industry and commerce, and the disappearance of certain types of boy and girl labour. The occupations which should be closed to juveniles first should be those which exploit present willingness at the cost of future fitness. The reorganisation forced on industry by the fall in the birth-rate must be governed by the consideration that an immediate shortage of juveniles means a coming shortage of adults.

20. Conclusion

The reforms we have outlined in this chapter may be described primarily as industrial, or primarily as educational. It is of the nature of the problem that either description is equally correct. The young worker occupies debatable ground. The educationist, who at his best represents the interest of the nation in the future of the race, claims him [1] as his charge. The industrialist, who at his worst allows present profit to blind him to future earning power, has in reality the best of reasons for allowing the educationist's claim. There was a time when colliery proprietors and cotton spinners thought that prosperity would vanish if little children were no longer allowed to pull a truck underground or doff a frame. That state of mind has gone, happily beyond recall. The belief that maturity in the children

[1] Or "her." The lack of a pronoun of common gender handicaps us throughout this Chapter. "Boy" must be taken as including "girl" wherever the context permits, and "he" as including "she."

of the working classes is reached at the age of fourteen is going.

The reforms we have put forward,—whether they affect the school-leaving age, the continuation of education throughout the dangerous and difficult years of adolescence, the methods of advising children on leaving school and of placing them in work, or the limitation of juvenile hours of labour—are inter-dependent. They are based on the conviction that the future of British industry depends on the quality as well as on the quantity of the goods it can produce, and that the quality of our industrial production rests first and last on our ability as a nation to give its children scope and freedom for the development of their natural endowments. The recommendations we make in this Chapter are not shaped simply by educational considerations; nor do they proceed from a sentimental or even humane desire to do justice to the youngsters who are in industry but are powerless themselves to control the conditions of their employment. They represent an attempt to see from the national point of view the solution of a problem in which the present to a peculiar extent governs the future.

BOOK 5

NATIONAL FINANCE

ARGUMENT OF BOOK 5

Unemployment is partly attributable to monetary causes and the eccentricities of post-war European currencies. There are grounds for believing that monetary phenomena have always played a large part in fluctuations of trade activity than used to be recognised. The return to the gold standard sets limits to the control over these phenomena that can be exercised by national action. But something more may be achieved by international action. Close co-operation between Central Banks is, therefore, desirable. The national character of the Bank of England should be emphasised by fixing its dividend at the present rate, surplus profits being retained by the Bank for national purposes. More detailed figures and additional information should be made public on the lines followed by the United States Federal Reserve system. The note-issues of the Treasury and Bank of England should be amalgamated, but only after full and public discussion of the future principles of regulation.

The system of national accounting in the Budget should be so reformed as to enable Parliament to control expenditure and ensure economy with full knowledge of the facts.

The area of possible economies is mainly confined to the War Departments. But an ill-devised system of taxation may inflict avoidable damage upon industry. Thus direct taxation has now reached a point which necessitates the closest scrutiny of all properly reducible national expenditure; this does not include judicious outlay upon social betterment, since wise social expenditure contributes to industrial efficiency. Besides, taxation is in one aspect an effective instrument for the just redistribution of wealth.

The system of local rating is far more injurious to industry than national taxation, raising production costs, bearing more heavily on the more depressed industries, and burdening the worker out of proportion to the burden imposed on his wealthy neighbour. The relief of rates is by far the most pressing of financial reforms. With a view to the reduction of this burden, liability for outdoor relief to the able-bodied poor should be transferred from Local Authorities to the State; expenditure on roads should be so redistributed as to throw a larger proportion on the Road Fund; the system of grants-in-aid should be extended; rates should be transferred, as far as possible, from buildings and improvements to site values; and rating areas should be drastically revised with a view to a more equal distribution of the burden of rates. The possibility of further reforming the rating system by the graduation of rates for the relief of the less wealthy classes of ratepayers on lines analogous to those already adopted for income-tax is also suggested.

CHAPTER XXVIII

CURRENCY AND BANKING

I. The Monetary Factor

(i) *Inflation*

NO survey of the conditions and problems of industry can be complete without reference to the important part which monetary factors play in the ups and downs of trade. The vagaries of European currencies since the Armistice have provided us with a series of fresh and vivid illustrations of the far-reaching effects which currency derangements can exert on economic life. The experience of one country after another has made the features of the process of inflation familiar, almost stereotyped, phenomena. Prices rise slowly at first, but with a gathering momentum; they rise generally, but most unevenly, wholesale prices outstripping retail, the prices of goods that enter into foreign trade rising most of all. There is a state of feverish business activity, with little or no unemployment, with, for some time, even an appearance of general prosperity. But the appearance soon proves to be illusory. The feverish business activity is seen to be inefficient and most wasteful activity, with speculative cleverness at a premium, and solid work and enterprise at a discount. There is a fungoid growth of unnecessary intermediary operations, and a decline in genuine productive effort. The country's products are exchanged for the products of other countries on absurdly disadvantageous terms. A redistribution of wealth is effected, more revolutionary than the most revolutionary of Governments would deliberately enact, yet of a kind to increase rather than diminish the inequalities of wealth. The public servants, and the professional classes, and the *rentiers* are pulled down; and the profiteer and the speculator are exalted in their place. Such are the characteristics of inflation, which have been profusely illustrated by the post-war history of Europe.

(ii) *Deflation*

The post-war period has been almost equally prolific of object-lessons in the opposite process of deflation; and the characteristics of deflation, though less spectacular, are no less clearly marked: falling prices, and again unevenly falling prices; a falling-off in general demand; depression and unemployment. Attempts on the part of the employers to get wages down; resistance from the side of the workers; conflict and chaos and loss. Profound disharmonies are set up by the process between the prices and wage-rates in different groups of trades. In " unsheltered " industries exposed to foreign competition the fall in prices is inexorable; the employers accordingly are inexorable in their demands for lower wages, and the workers are unable to resist. In " sheltered " trades, on the other hand, the pressure is less severe; the wage-rates of the workers and the selling prices of the products are lowered comparatively little. An obstinate maladjustment is thus set up, which weakens the country's competing power in foreign markets. The incongruous spectacle is exhibited of the most dignified and difficult trades, as regards business enterprise and manual skill alike, offering the most inferior rewards.

Just as feverish activity is the leading characteristic of inflation, so the leading characteristics of deflation are prolonged depression and *malaise*; and the medical parallel holds at least so far, that it is probably unavoidable that a fever of inflation should be succeeded by a period of subnormal business temperature. In the case of several European countries, however, the malady has been aggravated by the desire to " revalorise " the currency (i.e. to raise its exchange-value) before " stabilising " it. This process of revalorisation, which may be likened to the once fashionable medical policy of " bleeding," is infallibly accompanied, whenever undertaken, by severe trade depression. In extreme cases, no room for doubt exists as to the relationship of cause to effect. No one, for example, can fail to connect the business depression which overtook Italy in 1927 with Signor Mussolini's policy of revalorising the lira. In our case, the return to the gold standard at the pre-war parity has undoubtedly involved a strain, about the precise degree of which opinion differs. In the opinion of some of us it has been a major cause of our immediate difficulties.

Others of us consider that its disadvantages have been outweighed by advantages to trade resulting from the restoration of stability in the international exchanges and by giving a general stimulus to European recovery.

2. The "Trade Cycle"

The influence of monetary factors is thus seen at work in the movements of trade and prices in post-war Europe; and the question arises whether they may not have played a larger part than it has hitherto been usual to assign to them in the more moderate fluctuations of trade and prices which occurred normally, with a curious rhythmic regularity, before the War. It is certainly noteworthy that the world-wide character of trade booms on the one hand, and trade depressions on the other, which were so prominent a feature of the pre-war "trade cycle," disappeared with the disappearance of the common gold basis which had hitherto linked together the currency systems of most of the world. It has not been true since the Armistice, as it used to be true before the War, that the course of trade activity has been broadly similar in Britain, in continental countries, in America, and in the Far East. On the other hand, there has been a remarkable correspondence in each country between its course of trade activity and the particular monetary policy which it has chosen to pursue. Countries which have been inflating their currencies have experienced, at least in the initial stages, the hectic fevers of a boom; countries which have been deflating their currencies have undergone the *malaise* of trade depression; while a remarkable steadiness of trade conditions has been noticeable in the United States, where, under the new Federal Reserve system, the experiment has been more or less consciously pursued since 1923 of regulating the supply of credit so as to keep trade and prices on an even keel. The American experiment, indeed, is of great interest. Though the evidence is as yet far from conclusive, it is permissible to hope that it may prove to be within the power of a wise monetary policy to diminish materially those wide fluctuations in general trade activity which led periodically to unemployment on an extensive scale. Failing this, the return of the world to a common gold basis may be expected to bring with it a recurrence of something resembling the pre-war "trade cycle."

Our existing unemployment in Great Britain, however, can scarcely be represented as being the result of a cyclical depression, properly so called. It is mainly due to a loss of export trade. This loss is attributable in part, as we have already argued, to general impediments in the way of the world's commerce, and to other causes having no connection with monetary policy. In part, however, it is attributable to causes with a monetary origin—namely, to the added difficulties of competing with our foreign rivals arising out of the maladjustment between "sheltered" and "unsheltered" prices which has been left behind by wartime inflation and subsequent deflation, a part of which was afterwards stereotyped by the return to the gold standard at the pre-war parity. Here, however, a complete monetary remedy is no longer open. We have returned to a gold standard on the basis of the pre-war gold parity; and however our views may differ as to the wisdom of that step, its reversal is deemed to be impracticable. We cannot therefore seek for a remedy of the existing disparities in wage-levels in an alteration of the parity of exchange.

It is none the less important to safeguard, in so far as we are able, against the possibility of the occurrence of a fresh general trade depression, which might undo all our efforts to solve the existing problem. We regard this possibility as a serious danger, in view of our basic monetary conditions. It is pertinent, therefore, to consider what safeguards against it are available.

3. The Case for International Co-operation

Having placed our currency once more on a gold basis, the limits are fairly narrow to what can prudently be done within the sphere of national policy. The freedom of action of the Bank of England in regulating the volume of credit is necessarily limited by the necessity of protecting its gold reserves against a heavy external drain. The monetary conditions prevailing in this country are thus largely at the mercy of the policies which other gold-standard countries choose to pursue. This consideration emphasises the importance of the project, approved by the Genoa Conference in 1922, of international co-operation between Central Banks for preventing undue fluctuations in the purchasing power of gold. The gold standard has the advantage of supplying the readiest means of securing stable foreign exchange-rates between different countries—a condition of great importance for international investment and of convenience to international trade. But stable foreign exchange-rates are not enough. A steady, healthy development of trade requires, as an indispensable condition, the utmost possible stability in the purchasing-power of money. It is, indeed, implicit in our use of money at all as the intermediary by which commodities and services are exchanged, that we regard it as possessing a stable, reliable purchasing-power. It is implicit in the idea of a Standard of Value that the value of the standard should be definite. If these expectations are disappointed, it is not therefore surprising that the working of the economic system should be thrown out of gear.

But there is no reason why these expectations should be realised, if in each country which adopts gold as its basis of its currency the Central Bank devotes its energies to maintaining exchange-stability, regarding the value of gold as outside its control, and makes no attempt to control this value by mutual co-operation. On the contrary, it is possible, under such conditions, as past experience has shown, for the value of money to undergo a radical change within a comparatively brief space of years, either downwards or upwards, entailing all the disagreeable consequences of inflation or deflation. We have no security, moreover, failing a measure of international co-operation, that the value of money may not change much more considerably in the future—and with more damaging effects to industry—than it has done in the past. We attach, therefore, great importance to the Genoa project of international co-operation.

The practice of consultation between Central Banks has in fact developed considerably in recent years. This practice of consultation should be continued and extended. At present, however, it is shrouded in an atmosphere of impenetrable secrecy. We believe that the practice of issuing from time to time public statements of policy would strengthen business confidence and hasten the evolution of banking methods by facilitating informed criticism. The concealment of important facts is indeed in itself a serious obstacle to the creation of stability and confidence, on account of the doubts and uncertainties which it occasions.

In any case it is very desirable that there should be more formal international discussion of the objectives of monetary policy either in the form of the Conference of Central Banks suggested at Genoa, or in some other form. Actual measures of collaboration between Central Banks must be a matter of day-to-day administration; but monetary policy in general is a different matter.

4. The Bank of England

It is further desirable, in our judgment, that the control of our credit system, which is wielded by the Bank of England in virtue of its position as our Central Bank, should be exercised more deliberately and systematically than hitherto, with a view to the maintenance of steady trade conditions. The power of the Bank of England in this direction is, as we have said, limited by the necessity of maintaining the foreign exchanges and thus safeguarding the gold reserve. But these limits still leave it a useful margin of discretion. We are not in agreement with those who would nationalise the Bank of England, much less our banking system as a whole. On the contrary, we regard the Bank of England as an admirable specimen of the "semi-socialised" institutions which represent, in our view, the true line of development. But it ought to become part of the recognised duties of the Bank of England to regulate the volume of credit, so far as possible, with a view to the maintenance of steady trade conditions.

We are clear that for this purpose the Bank of England should in essentials be retained in its present form. But in the last resort ultimate responsibility for a sound currency and credit system must rest upon the State. If this vital responsibility is to be entrusted to the Bank of England, it should be made evident that the Bank is a national institution, as indeed it is already in all but form and name, and not a piece of private property and private enterprise such as it actually was in its early days. If this can be made clear, it will indeed strengthen the Bank, by freeing it from criticism on the ground that it represents a narrow class rather than the whole community, or that it is operating in the interests of private shareholders and is therefore capable of being influenced by their special interests. With this object in view we make the following suggestions as to the formal constitution of the Bank of England, but we do not contemplate that these changes would in themselves make any very material change in its actual means of operation; for it is the aims and objects of the Bank rather than its position or its powers which need modification.

(1) The dividends to the shareholders of the Bank should be fixed permanently at their present figure, which figure should, however, be guaranteed by the whole assets of the Bank. The surplus profits should normally be retained within the Bank, as they are now, and used to increase its financial strength. In the last resort, however, any surplus profits which were not required for this purpose should belong to the Treasury. We attach great importance to the financial strength of the Bank of England, and we think that the policy of further strengthening it would be facilitated by the removal of any suggestion that the great profits of its privileged position are being accumulated for the ultimate benefit of private persons.

(2) The Court of Directors, which is at present an unwieldy body, should be substantially reduced in size, and the method of appointment and the qualifications of directors reconsidered.

(3) The recent practice, by which the Governor has held office for much longer than the old term of two years, should be formally approved, the term of office being fixed at five years, renewable for a further five years.

(4) The co-operation between the Treasury and the Bank of England, which has inevitably become much closer than it was in pre-war years, should be expressly provided for in the inner Management of the Bank.

5. The Note Issue

We share the general opinion that the Currency Note Issue and the Bank of England Note Issue should be, sooner or later, amalgamated into a single issue on a revised basis.

The effective volume of our currency is regulated at present by the terms of a Treasury minute, which, apart from a substantial inflow of gold, allow only a very slight margin for possible expansion. The maximum volume of currency at present admissible would, therefore, be insufficient to sustain any considerable expansion in trade and in employment; so that an incipient revival of trade might be brought up sharply against the obstacle of credit restriction.

Apart, however, from the volume of the currency, the principles governing the gold reserve to be held against it should be reconsidered. Formerly this reserve was held partly against the contingency of a foreign drain and partly against the contingency of a drain into the internal circulation. Now that gold sovereigns no longer circulate, the latter contingency cannot arise. The whole of our gold reserves are held, therefore, for external purposes. This change of conditions should be deliberately recognised with a view to immobilising as little gold as possible and to rendering the maximum proportion of our stock available to meet an external drain or other international emergencies. At present out of a total gold holding of about £150,000,000, only some £35,000,000 is available to meet contingencies, the balance of £115,000,000 being totally immobilised except in the event of the internal note issue being contracted, a contraction which it may be impossible or undesirable to bring about at the moment when the gold is required for use abroad.

Thus there are sufficient grounds to justify the demand, voiced by Mr. McKenna and others, for a public inquiry into the future regulation of the Note Issue. We consider that it is indispensable that the change should not be made until the matter has been fully and publicly debated.

6. Publicity in Finance

We have referred above to the vital need for full enlightenment of the public as to monetary, credit, and exchange policy, and for open discussion of the problems involved in the amalgamation of the note issues. There is the same need for publicity over the whole field of banking. As in industry, so in finance, full knowledge of the essential facts and public discussion of the policy are the only remedies for suspicion and the only safeguards against hostile criticism. Both the Bank of England and British Banks generally lag far behind corresponding institutions in the United States in respect of publicity. The statement made by George Norman, a former Director of the Bank of England, before the Bank Inquiry Committee of 1832 that "generally the Bank will suffer more from ignorance than knowledge; even under the present system its affairs are not absolutely secret," is even more true to-day than it was almost a century ago, and it applies not to the Bank of England alone but also to the whole of the British banking system.

In our opinion, the Bank of England should give far greater publicity than at present to the principal monetary transactions for which it is responsible. The existing form of accounts, which was drawn up over a century ago, is altogether inadequate for modern needs. For a proper understanding of the policy of the Bank, detailed figures prepared in the light of contemporary requirements are essential. In addition we consider that the Bank of England might well follow the path blazed by the Federal Reserve Board and give general indications of its monetary and credit policy from time to time, of the objectives it is pursuing, and of the means by which it hopes to attain its ends. We are convinced that such publicity, far from doing harm, would actually strengthen the position of the Bank and would give confidence and assurance to responsible financial and banking authorities.

In the case of the Joint Stock Banks, their published statements should be made on a uniform plan, and should be more comprehensive and more detailed. The common practice of "window-dressing" the published statements by making them refer to the figures of specially selected days instead of the daily averages should be made illegal. Furthermore, the Banks should make a return of the aggregate of the sums transferred by cheque to and from individual accounts—a figure which has become important with the decline in the number of banks and the consequent shrinkage in the proportion of cheques passing through the various clearing-houses.

These changes and the fuller discussion of banking policy, together with the other reforms set forth above, would remove ignorance, cure suspicion, and generally create popular understanding and confidence in the part played by the monetary and banking system in the economic life of the nation.

CHAPTER XXIX

REFORM OF THE NATIONAL ACCOUNTS

I. The Case for Reform

ECONOMY in the Public Services, as we shall argue later, is of the first importance. The greater the part which these services are expected to play in the national life, the more important it becomes. The problem of efficient administration is to get good value, and economy in expenditure is one-half of this task. But the present way of setting forth the Budget and the National Accounts is ill-adapted for bringing to notice the degree of economy practised. The items where economy is of the essence of efficiency are swamped by items where a reduction of expenditure is either impossible or undesirable. The result is that the demand for economy in administration is hopelessly mixed up in the public mind with the quite different demand for a reduction of expenditure through the State ceasing to fulfil functions or provide services. A business can diminish its gross outgoings either by handling the same turnover of goods more cheaply or by turning over less goods. The first is economy; the second is restriction of output. These are obviously totally different things. The items of the National Budget, however, are set forth in such a way that what correspond to these two things are frequently confused. We never know when a publicist demands economy whether he is calling on the State to do its business more economically or to slow down altogether one or more of the businesses which it carries on; whether the call is for less expenditure on overhead or for less turnover. The fact that in the case of the State there is often no exact criterion of "good value," whether from warships or from schools, renders the distinction inevitably less clear-cut than in the case (e.g.) of electrical supply, where no one is likely to make a confusion between a reduction of expenditure due to producing current more cheaply and one due to producing less current. This makes it all the more necessary that the national accounts should be kept in such a form as to make everything as clear as possible.

2. The Obsolete Character of the Budget

Let us remind the reader what the Budget is. It remains what a hundred years ago most accounts were, a purely *Cash Account,* namely, a statement of actual cash receipts and actual cash outgoings between specified dates. It permits no distinction between capital items and current items. It makes no allowance for liabilities or debts incurred but not discharged, or for assets or income accrued but not collected. For example, the yield of the income-tax is not the amount of tax accrued and due within the year, but the amount collected and paid into the Exchequer during the period. Thus it is at the mercy of the accidents of the actual dates of payment and of the fluctuating pressure, voluntary or fortuitous, of the tax authorities. Since income-tax and super-tax are collected near the end of the financial year, the above irrelevant factors may enrich or impoverish a given year's revenue at the expense, or for the benefit, of the following year by many millions.

Whilst, however, the existing form of the Budget itself concedes nothing to the modern conceptions of a Balance Sheet and of a Capital Account, nevertheless the consequences of following this method completely would be in modern conditions so inconvenient, and indeed absurd, that it has been increasingly modified in recent practice by establishing separate funds outside the Exchequer. Some capital expenses (e.g. for the Post Office) are entered in the weekly published accounts "below the line" (i.e. are not paid for out of revenue account); some assets and overdrafts are accumulated in separate funds (e.g. in the case of the Insurance Funds and, hitherto, of the Road Fund); and some current receipts are also thus separately accumulated in the first instance and are then paid over to the Exchequer, not as they accrue, but at irregular intervals. All this is done, however, not according to any single plan, but as the result of a gradual evolution and of historical causes. In consequence the Budget Statement is exceedingly ill-adapted for disclosing the true financial position of the country as it emerges from the year's activities. Moreover, the practice of not paying all receipts into the Exchequer as they accrue, but at irregular intervals (which intervals can be lengthened or diminished at the discretion of the Chancellor of the Exchequer), has had the result of further increasing the extent to which the published Budget results can be rigged. In recent times the actual results have probably been variable in any given year to the extent of at least £10,000,000 to £20,000,000, to suit the book of the Chancellor of the Exchequer for the time being. Apart from the public hen-roosts which Mr. Churchill has raided, it is impossible for an outsider to estimate what private hen-roosts inside the Treasury he has also helped himself to. At any rate, the Finance Accounts show the following items brought to account in the last two years which do not belong in any way to the Revenue levied and accrued in these years. Previous Chancellors of the Exchequer have also done the like in varying degrees.

	1925–6.	1926–7.
	£	£
Anticipation of Brewers' payments	—	5,000,000
Transfer from Road Fund	—	7,000,000
Excess Profits Duty and Munitions Levy	2,000,000	4,500,000
Corporation Profits Tax	11,670,000	3,970,000
Sale of British Dye-stuffs Corporation Shares	600,000	—
Agricultural Credits, Surrender of Balances	400,000	15,000
Payment for Herrings supplied in 1919	488,000	—
Disposals and Liquidation Commission	7,194,000	3,108,000
Shipping Liquidation Commission	3,807,000	3,716,000
Enemy Debts Surplus	8,000,000	5,500,000
War Risks Insurance	1,706,000	367,000
Food Commission Surplus	1,000,000	1,000,000
Railway War Agreements Liquidation	850,000	753,000
Sale of British Corn Bureau, Bucharest	160,000	160,000
Transfer from Bankruptcy and Companies Winding-up (Fees) Account	—	473,000
Transfer from Navy, Army, and Air Force Insurance Fund	—	1,100,000
Repayment of Advances for Damage by Enemy Action	84,000	140,000
Pre-Moratorium Bills	500,000	50,000
Sugar Commission Surplus	100,000	40,000
Allied Governments Suspense Accounts Balances Surrendered	615,000	5,674,000
Repayment of Loans to other Governments	135,000	35,000
Taken from Balances of Revenue Departments, etc.	815,000	4,644,000
	£40,124,000	£47,245,000

It is impossible to deduce from Mr. Churchill's Budget Statement at what the corresponding figure for 1927–8 should be estimated—but it is certainly substantial; and in the absence of this figure the House of Commons cannot form a judgment as to its financial soundness or otherwise.

The preceding table is not complete, and there are probably some compensating items of which account should be taken on the side of expenditure. Our point is, however, precisely this, that Parliament and the country can have at present no idea as to the extent to which a Chancellor of the Exchequer is helping himself out by bringing previously existing assets into account. We should consider a private enterprise which showed its accounts in this shape as unbusinesslike and unsound.

An extreme instance of the practice of the Treasury to take account only of liabilities which have been discharged in cash has been recently disclosed by the Colwyn Committee in the case of interest accruing on National Savings Certificates. As is well known, the interest on these certificates is not paid to the holders year by year as it accrues, but in a lump sum when the certificate is finally redeemed. The Treasury, therefore, bring the interest into account only when it is paid out on the redemption of the bonds, with the result that the interest accrued on these certificates in the course of a year may exceed the sum brought to account in the Budget by as much as £10,000,000 to £20,000,000, and (eventually) *vice versa.* For example, in 1926–7 the interest accrued during the year on Savings Certificates exceeded the sum debited to the Budget by nearly £12,000,000. Further, the accumulated interest belonging to previous years, not yet provided for but requiring provision in some subsequent budget, amounted on March 31, 1927, to £121,000,000.

We believe that the recent inability of the House of Commons to control expenditure and to ensure economy in the right places is largely due to the unintelligibility of the National Accounts, through which no one but a Treasury expert can find his way securely. The first reform, therefore, is to secure uniformity, simplicity, and correspondence to the relevant facts in their form of presentation.

3. Constructive Proposals

With this object in view we venture to suggest a tentative outline of the kind of reform we have in view. Our suggestions are necessarily tentative because no one outside the Government Service can possess the expert knowledge required for drawing up the best possible classification.

The Budget should fall into three parts:

(I) *Cash Account* (i.e. Cash Receipts and Payments on Income Account).

(II) *Income Account* (i.e. Income and Expenditure (accrued) as distinct from cash received and paid).

(III) *Capital Account.*

Part (I)—the Cash Account—would be much as at present, i.e. a statement of cash receipts and outgoings within the financial year, except that all items deemed to be on capital account would be transferred to Part (III), to which also the proceeds of the annual Sinking Fund, which would appear as an outgoing in Part (I), would be transferred; and that trading departments would be brought to account net, instead of gross.

Part (II)—the Income Account—would involve an estimate by the Revenue Authorities (realised errors in these estimates being brought to account in subsequent years) as to the difference between the income accrued and the income paid over to the Exchequer within the year, and by the spending departments as to any increase or decrease during the year in the amount of liabilities properly belonging to the year in question, incurred but not discharged. This need not prevent the spreading of certain kinds of expenditure over more than one year in suitable cases, where this is specifically authorised. Adjustments would also be made in this place for variations in the amount of Departmental non-voted balances ("Deposit Accounts") and for any transfers into or out of the Cash Account in respect of Appropriated Funds on which the Exchequer has normally had no claim (e.g. the Local Taxation Account, the Development Fund, and the Road Fund). Thus it would be the Income Account, rather than the Cash Account, which would show the true Surplus or Deficit on the year.

Part (III)—the Capital Account—to which we attach great importance, would be worked in close connection with the programme of the Board of National Investment (see above, p. 111). Into it would be paid the annual Sinking Fund and all budgetary receipts on capital account. These receipts, together with other receipts of a capital character accruing in the hands of the Central Government, including the proceeds of loans and repayments, the nature of which has been further particularised above (pp. 104–7), would be administered by the Board of National Investment; which Board would charge against it all expenditure of a capital nature by any Government Department, a corresponding item being brought into the outgoings of that Department for interest and depreciation in subsequent years, and also the various loans and advances for new capital developments outlined above (pp. 112–3). Each year the equivalent of the Sinking Fund and of the budgetary receipts on capital account would be written off the Dead-weight Debt, which amount would either have been paid off or converted into productive debt, Part (I) being in either case relieved for the future of the interest on the amount thus written off.

It is a further defect in the National Accounts as now presented that they afford no indication of our *total* expenditure on Social Services. Some of these (e.g. education) are paid for partly out of taxes and partly out of rates; others (e.g. social insurance) partly out of taxes and partly out of compulsory contributions. In the aggregate about one-eleventh of the national income is spent upon these services, and this proportion is likely to increase. It seems essential, therefore, that this expenditure should be set forth intelligibly in any summary statement of the nation's finances. The most satisfactory way of doing this would be the inclusion in the National Accounts of a Social Services Budget. Herein public expenditures on Health, Pensions, Public Assistance, Unemployment, and Education, and the sources from which the corresponding revenues—whether the National Budget, local rates, or individual contributions—are derived, should be clearly and simply set forth. It would also be desirable to present in summary form a capital account under some of these headings. Even a brief conspectus of the National Accounts should show (e.g.) the accumulated funds of the Approved Societies, the balance (or debit) of the Unemployment Fund, and the capital value of school premises which are the property of public bodies.

Lastly, there are certain re-classifications of the Budget headings which we recommend in the interests of intelligibility and sound policy. The existing classification, though lately somewhat improved, has grown up under historical influences and does not meet present needs. It provides safeguards which are no longer necessary, and omits those which are. The costs of administration cannot be easily disentangled, and the picture presented is exceedingly confused.

It would be a task of great detail to put the matter straight. We suggest, however, that it should be gone into anew and brought up-to-date in accordance with modern developments. As we have already recommended, all capital items should be excluded and the results of Trading Services should be brought in *net*. The aim should be, we think, to arrive at main headings more or less as follows:

1. The interest on the Dead-weight Debt.
2. The Sinking Fund.
3. National Defence (including normal non-effective charges).
4. War Pensions.
5. National Civil Administration.
   - (i) Law and Justice.
   - (ii) Revenue.
   - (iii) Social Services.
   - (iv) Foreign and Colonial.
   - (v) General Administration.
6. Social Services: (A) Relief and Insurance.
   - (i) Old Age.
   - (ii) Sickness.
   - (iii) Unemployment.

   (B) Constructive.
   - (i) Education, Science and Art.
   - (ii) Information.
   - (iii) Public Health.
8. Trading Services and Subsidies (net).
9. Miscellaneous.

The cost of administration of the Social Services should not be amalgamated with their grants and constructive expenditure but separately stated under 5 (iii). The various headings under (3) and (5) should be charged with interest and depreciation on their buildings and with superannuation payments to their retired personnel, so that each item would be, so far as possible, self-contained. The amount of any credits brought in from Trading Services should be determined on the same principles as the dividend of a conservatively-managed private enterprise.

We doubt if the existing distinction between Consolidated Fund Services and Supply Services is in accordance with present needs. It is worth considering whether some items now voted in Supply should not be transferred to the Consolidated Fund and *vice versa.* At the same time, the powers of the House of Commons in finance and the mode in which it exercises them should be transformed into something more real and effective than the existing Estimates and Public Accounts Committees.

Nothing, in our opinion, stands in the way of a rational programme of economy so much as the confusion of the National Accounts. No one outside the Civil Service can thread his way through them. Intelligibility of the accounts is an indispensable first step towards restoring to the House of Commons the effective exercise of its prerogative of criticism.

These reforms would lay the foundation of sound, honest, and intelligible national finance. They would render impossible for the future the manœuvres which have disfigured Mr. Churchill's Budgets. Temporary embarrassments on revenue account would no longer stand in the way of necessary capital developments. The House of Commons and the public would know exactly how we stood. And the true figure of what we were saving out of the current year's revenue for the discharge of the Dead-weight Debt would be plainly apparent; whereas during the past two or three years, in spite of the flourishes of the Chancellor's trumpet, this true figure would probably prove, if one could accurately ascertain it, to be less than nothing at all.

CHAPTER XXX

THE BURDEN OF NATIONAL TAXATION

1. Taxation and National Economy

OUR total national income is estimated to be about £4,000 millions per annum. Of this sum, something like a fifth passes every year through the hands of the State, is collected by it partly in such forms as Post Office revenue, but mainly in the form of taxation, and is expended on a variety of objects—interest on the National Debt, defence, social expenditure, and general administration. It is obvious that a transaction of this magnitude must exert an influence of the first importance upon our industrial life. It is, therefore, a necessary condition of the pursuit by the State of a wise policy towards industry that our system of Public Finance should be soundly conceived and adapted to the needs of the industrial situation. The higher the level of taxation and of Government expenditure, the more important does it become to avoid unnecessary expenditure, and to reduce administrative costs to the minimum consistent with efficiency. The machinery of Government is vast and complex, and in the nature of the case cannot be subjected to the simple, rough-and-ready business test of profit and loss, so that failing an atmosphere of constant vigilance, waste and extravagance are certain to creep in.

We need, therefore, an atmosphere of informed criticism and of pressure towards economy. At the same time, our object will not be best attained by concentrating on the aggregate figure of money expended by the Government, to the neglect of how it is expended and how it is raised, or by extending an impartial anathema to any increase in Government expenditure, regardless of whether it represents wasteful administration, an adventurous policy of building a capital-ship base at Singapore, or an eccentric coal subsidy; or, on the other hand, the promotion of public health and education, the relief of local rates, or a commercially remunerative increase in the turnover of the Post Office and Telephones. Not only does such an undiscriminating attitude lead almost inevitably to disillusionment; it is a positive and very serious obstacle in the way of so overhauling our fiscal system as to relieve industry from the burdens which press most seriously upon it. It is useless to talk vaguely about reducing expenditure without having any clear idea in what direction reductions can in practice be made.

More than half of the colossal amount now raised by taxation is paid out as interest on or amortisation of the National Debt. A reduction here must depend upon the possibility of conversions to lower rates of interest; and this in turn depends upon the credit of the State and upon the extent of national savings. General financial conditions may in the course of time render possible reductions under this head of no inconsiderable figure. Another large portion—nearly one-tenth—is devoted to War Pensions; a charge which is gradually decreasing without the need, and indeed without the possibility, of specific action by the State. The contributions to the expenditure of Local Authorities on education, housing, and police are not susceptible of reduction, nor are the sums spent on Old Age Pensions or on National Insurance. Economies may be found possible in the general expenditure upon the Civil Service, but it is not likely to amount in the aggregate to any figure that would appreciably lighten the general burden of taxation. The principal field for immediate economies is in the vast expenditure upon defence, which involved last year a charge upon the taxpayers of not far short of £120 millions.

Before the War we were engaged in the greatest armaments race that the world has ever seen, and we were spending the colossal sum of £78 millions on defence. To-day the immediate threat of war has been removed, yet we are spending above 50 per cent. more than before the War. Mr. Churchill recently claimed that this was moderate, seeing that it did not represent appreciably more than the increase in prices. But such a statement is an astounding confession to make to a country overburdened with taxation, for it indicates that we are arming ourselves as vigorously and on the same scale as in 1913. If we are to shoulder this burden in perpetuity, it means that, so far as the burden of armaments is concerned, the War was fought in vain.

There is no automatic standard of reasonableness in this connection; but we may find comparatively firm ground if we regard our expenditure on defence as an insurance premium incurred to enable us to live our lives in peace and consider what rate of premium we have paid for this privilege in the past. During the last quarter of the nineteenth century we were in no imminent danger of war. It is estimated that in 1875 our national income was £1,200 millions. Our defence expenditure was £25 millions—a premium of 2 per cent. In 1913 our national income had grown to £2,250 millions; but our defence expenditure was £78 millions. The premium had jumped to 3½ per cent. To-day it is still 3 per cent., though we see no reason for regarding this country as in greater peril than in the last quarter of the nineteenth century. Even if we leave aside the influence of the League of Nations, and merely aim at getting back to the 2 per cent. premium of forty years ago, we should reduce defence expenditure by one-third from £120 millions to £80 millions.[1]

We may look at the matter from another point of view and compare our record in this matter with that of other countries. The figures in Table 36 show the defence expenditure of six principal Powers before the War and to-day. Although the totals are not strictly comparable, one country with another, because of widely different methods of accounting, within the same country they are generally comparable. The latest figures have been recalculated from actual expenditure after allowing for the rise of prices which has taken place in each country. They show that only in the United States, Japan, and Great Britain are the present figures at all comparable with their previous expenditure.

We conclude, therefore, that in the case of our War Departments a substantial reduction of expenditure should be possible, but that in other departments the amount of practicable economy is not likely to be large.

2. The Effects of Taxation upon Industry

It is sometimes supposed that taxation diminishes the aggregate purchasing power of the community, and that its main harm

[1] Vide *Economist* Budget Supplement, April 11, 1925, p. 10.

TABLE 36

EXPENDITURE ON ARMAMENTS (IN PRE-WAR VALUES)

(In millions of £s)

Country.	1913–14.	1926–7.
Great Britain and Northern Ireland	77·1	83·6
France	72·0	36·0
Germany *	94·5	23·2
Italy	44·3	26·9
Japan	19·2	24·7
U.S.A.	61·8	77·3

The 1913-14 figures relate to the then existing areas of the respective countries; the 1926-7 figures to the present areas.

* The 1926-7 figure for Germany assumes the Index number of wholesale prices to have been as in Britain, viz. 147.

Extracted from "The Economics of Armaments," by Major J. W. Hills, M.P., The Banker, November 1927, p. 399. *Major Hills's figures for* 1913–14 *were "supplied by the Secretariat of the League of Nations," and those for* 1926–7 *were taken from The Armaments Year Book,* 1927.

lies in this. But this notion ignores the fact that the State proceeds to spend the money which it obtains by taxation; and, except in the case of obligatory external payments such as the interest on the American debt, the aggregate purchasing power of the community is not directly diminished by the transaction. It is its direction, not its amount, which has been changed.

The injuries caused to industry by high taxation arise in other ways. Taxation may be so imposed as to discourage desirable enterprise. It may make it unprofitable for a business to undertake operations which, apart from the taxation, would have shown a profit. It may discourage social habits, on the prevalence of which industrial progress depends; for example, it may check the habit of saving and thus diminish the supply of available new capital. It may fall so unevenly upon different kinds of industry as to divert productive effort from the most economic into less economic channels. In the case, especially, of indirect taxation, it may increase the cost of living. In such ways as these, faulty finance may truly be said to affect the purchasing power of the nation, for purchasing power ultimately depends upon producing power.

The amount of the damage done mainly depends, therefore,

on the ways in which revenue is spent and on the system by which it is raised; and a bad tax, even though it yields a comparatively trifling revenue, may do much more harm to industry than a well-conceived tax which brings in a larger sum. At the same time the disadvantages even of a well-conceived tax tend to increase progressively as its *rate* increases. For example, we regard the principle of the British income-tax as sound, and in relation to the revenue it raises the harm which it does to industry is remarkably small.[1] None the less it involves inevitably incidental anomalies and deterrents which, while comparatively negligible when its level was about 1*s.* in the £, are an altogether more formidable affair at a standard rate of 4*s.* It follows that the larger the revenue which the State must raise, the more must it either have recourse to bad taxes or raise good taxes to the point at which their incidental defects become serious objections.

In actual fact the handicaps which our system of direct taxation places on industry are sufficiently great to warrant the strongest and most unceasing pressure towards economical administration and the reduction of armaments. They are sufficiently great to raise the standard of scrutiny which it is proper to apply to all proposals for additional expenditure, whether in the field of social reform or elsewhere. But they are not so great, in our opinion, as to justify calling a halt in the development of wisely conceived policies of education, public health, and social reform. There is no more foolish form of apparent hard-headedness than to describe such expenditure as extravagance or waste, as though it were on all-fours with the profligate use of material or the employment of an unnecessarily large number of clerks to discharge the duties of an office.

Substantial revenue is also raised by indirect taxes, of which the most important are those on drink, tobacco, tea, and sugar. While some of these taxes represent a substantial burden on the poor and increase the cost of living, they are not open to serious objection from the purely industrial standpoint.

3. Taxation and Social Expenditure

The quality of a nation's population is the most vital of all elements in industrial efficiency; and few factors within the con-

[1] This also is the view taken in the Colwyn Report.

trol of statesmanship play so large a part in determining the industrial quality of a people as its standards of education and public health. Even from the narrowest industrial standpoint, we believe that we have got exceedingly good value for the public money expended on these objects over the last fifty years, and that it would be a short-sighted policy to-day to cut it down or to hold it rigidly in check.

There is, moreover, another consideration which must be taken into account, particularly when we turn to more general forms of social expenditure, such as Old Age Pensions. Social expenditure on the one hand, and the graduated taxation of wealth on the other, may be regarded as the two component elements of a policy which would go far towards modifying the distribution of wealth. It is not sufficiently recognised how largely the real distribution of wealth has already been transformed by the development of this policy during the past twenty or thirty years. The income of a very rich man is halved by the operation of income-tax and super-tax alone. When he dies, a substantial proportion, even up to 40 per cent., of his capital fortune is taken by the State. For the most part, unfortunately, this taxation has been imposed to finance not social expenditure but war, preparation for war, and the debt entailed by war; and accordingly it has only done a small part of what it might have done under more fortunate international conditions to raise working-class standards. None the less, it is estimated that the benefits which the average working-class family derives from the multifarious forms of public expenditure are equivalent to an addition of about 12½ per cent.[1] to their income. And the fact that these benefits largely take the form of the provision of services like education, the cash value of which is not easily assessed, does not detract from their real importance.

Now, in so far as the taxation which is raised to defray social expenditure is really prejudicial to industrial activity we pay a price for the improved distribution of wealth in the shape of diminished productivity and diminished aggregate wealth. Clearly a point comes at which it is not worth while to pay this price, and there is nothing to be said for a policy which would impoverish the rich without serving, on balance, to improve the

[1] 14·7 per cent. of employers' contributions to insurance funds are taken into account. See p. 245.

condition of the poor. None the less, a more equal distribution of wealth is so important, it is indeed so imperative to move steadily and manifestly in this direction if we are to build up a truly democratic society, secure against the evil passions and subversive dangers of class-hatred, that we must be careful not to discard on inadequate or ill-considered grounds a policy which makes for a better distribution of wealth.

A man who insists that taxation (meaning, as a rule, direct taxation) must at all costs be reduced, and that, if necessary for this purpose, social expenditure must be curtailed, is apt to do so with a light heart. He imagines that he is talking the language of unimpeachable virtue, and that he has on his side the immaculate if austere angels of high principle and sound finance. He has no suspicion that the course he is advocating is *prima facie* so reactionary that a special obligation rests on him to make good his case. But that is the real position. The man who would curtail social expenditure is advocating a more unequal distribution of wealth. He has his arguments no doubt. But, that being the issue, does not a heavy responsibility rest on him to show that the injury done by high taxation is as great as he alleges? And must we not scrutinise his arguments as closely as he would have us scrutinise the expenditure?

Approaching the subject from this angle, we hold that our system of national taxation is in the main well conceived. We regard our principal direct taxes—the income-tax, the super-tax, the death-duties—as efficient taxes. We agree with the Colwyn Committee that there is not much substance in many of the objections brought against these taxes from the industrial standpoint, and that the objection of most substance is their tendency to diminish the volume of saving. To a large extent this is attributable to the very fact that they make for a more equal distribution of wealth. And in so far as this is so we must look for our remedy in the development of the saving habit among persons of smaller means.

CHAPTER XXXI

REFORM OF THE RATING SYSTEM

1. The Disastrous Effects of the Present System

(a) *On Industry and Business*

ON the test of the injury done to industry it is our system of local rating, much more than our national taxation, which is open to severe criticism. Rates, except in so far as they are expended on services directly beneficial to the rate-payer, operate as a heavy *ad valorem* tax on houses, on factory buildings, on fixed capital equipment generally. For poor-relief, public health, education, and other objects of local expenditure we exact contributions from our industries, not in proportion to the profits they make, but in proportion to the amount of fixed capital which they employ. This is an extraordinarily vicious principle; so vicious that we should hardly tolerate it if immemorial usage did not blind our eyes to its significance. It penalises enterprise and capital development. It puts a premium on doing things in ways which require only a small plant to the detriment of ways which require a large one.

A business must pay its rates whether it earns any profits or not; it must therefore include an allowance for rates in the prices which it charges. Thus rates, unlike income-tax, enter directly into the costs of production, raising the cost of living, and diminishing the competitive power of our industries. Our industrial leaders are constantly asserting, and with truth, that local rates are now, by reason of their effect on selling price, a serious handicap to our exports.

Rates are now so heavy—the average rate in the £ of assessable value [1] has approximately doubled since 1913 (6*s.* 8¾*d.* in

[1] The value of lands and buildings has not risen since the War in proportion to the increase in the cost of living, with the result that on the average assessable value did not increase between 1913–14 and 1926–7 by more than about 20 per cent.

1913–14 and 12*s*. 5½*d*. in 1926–7),[1] that the objections to them on the ground of the vicious principle they embody are of great practical importance. Not only are rates heavy; their burden is spread most unequally between different industries and districts. The depression of the exporting industries during the last few years has led to abnormally heavy expenditure on poor-relief, and correspondingly heavy rates in those districts where the exporting industries are centred. Thus the very industries which are the worst hit and have the greatest difficulties to overcome are by reason of the vicious incidence of rating subjected to the heaviest deterrents. In just those districts where there is the most unemployment, and where it is therefore most desirable that new industries should be established, a special discouragement is extended to any manufacturer who is looking out for a site for a new works.

The Report of the Balfour Committee on Industry and Trade has published some striking examples. For instance (figures given by the President of the Crucible Steel Makers' Association):

Cost of rates per ton of crucible steel on actual output:

June 30, 1914 . . 3*s*. per ton
June 30, 1924 . . 21*s*. per ton

Cost per ton if working full capacity:

June 30, 1924 . . 6*s*. 8*d*. per ton

This example well illustrates the radical defect of local rates as a tax on industry, that the greater the difficulties of a trade, the heavier is the burden per unit of output.

In his Presidential Address before the Incorporated Accountants' Conference (September 29, 1927), Mr. Thomas Keens quoted the following figures, supplied to him by incorporated accountants, relating to shipbuilding and coal-mining:

1. In a particular shipbuilding yard the rates per vessel built in 1913 were £268, in 1926 £3,182, and the corresponding figures per ton dead-weight were 8½*d*. and 7*s*. 5*d*.

[1] Rates collected in 1913-14 amounted to £1 18*s*. 11*d*. per head of population and in 1926–7 to £4 2*s*.

2. In a second case the total rates per vessel built in 1912–13 were £89 5*s.* with a total rate dead-weight per ton of 3*d.*, and in 1922–3 the figures were £2,161 and 5*s.* 6½*d.*

3. In another yard the rates per vessel in 1914 were £246, or 6¾*d.* per ton; in 1924–5 the figures were £1,850 per vessel, or 4*s.* 6¼*d.* per ton.

4. In coal-mining in the year 1925–6 the cost of rates per ton varied in different parts of the country from 1*d.* to 6*d.* per ton.

In the case of cotton spinning, the Chairman of Joshua Hoyle & Sons has stated (November 1927) that in their case rates have increased from 7*s.* pre-war to 14*s.*, 15*s.*, and 17*s.* in the £, whilst at the same time their mills have been assessed at 100 per cent. on their pre-war value; nor is any abatement allowed when these mills are working short time. It is easy to see what a heavy burden this means per lb. of yarn spun in present conditions.

In the case of iron, coal, and steel, the burden of local rates at present and as compared with pre-war, may be seen in Table 37 on p. 436.

Doubtless these instances are mostly extreme cases due to part-time working of plant situated in a necessitous area. There are many types of industry on which the burden of rates is relatively trifling. But it is the inequality in the incidence of the burden and the tendency of rates at the present time to fall most heavily, as between industries, on those which are least able to bear them, which constitute the most formidable indictment of the system.

Nor is such inequality limited to the field of industry. Rates are also divided most unequally between shopkeepers, financial institutions, and professional men, to the great detriment of the first-named. Rates on lands and premises grew up historically at a time when the ownership or occupation of lands and premises was the best rough-and-ready test of capacity to pay. But at the present time our rating system, regarded as an attempt at measuring either capacity to pay or benefit received, may be said, within the field of industry, agriculture, and business, to have broken down entirely.

To relieve enterprise, therefore, from these burdens and in-

TABLE 37

LOCAL RATES—EFFECT ON COST OF PRODUCTION

(*Figures supplied by a prominent N.E. Coast Iron, Coal, and Steel Company*)

	Rates per ton.	*Selling Price per ton.*	*Per cent.*
Coal.	*s. d.*	*s. d.*	
June 1914 . . .	2	12 0 f.o.b.	1·39
June 1927 :			
On plant 15–20 years old	9·8	13 0 ,,	6·28
On modern plant . .	9·8	13 0 ,,	6·28
Coke.			
June 1914 . . .	3·6	14 6 at ovens	2·07
June 1927 :			
On plant 15–20 years old	1 6·5	14 6 ,,	10·63
On modern plant . .	1 5·6	14 6 ,,	10·11
Pig Iron.			
June 1914 . . .	6·5	60 0 ,,	·90
June 1927 :			
On plant 15–20 years old	2 4·3	70 0	3·37
On modern plant . .	2 1·7	70 0	3·06
Steel Plates.			
June 1914 . . .	1 8·2	120 0 d/d N.E. Coast	1·40
June 1927 :			
On plant 15–20 years old	6 3	162 6 ,, ,,	3·80
On modern plant . .	4 0·6	162 6 ,, ,,	2·49
Steel Angles			
June 1914 . . .	1 7·9	115 0	1·44
June 1927 :			
On plant 15–20 years old	5 10·5	152 6	3·85
On modern plant . .	4 2·5	152 6	2·76

N.B.—The rates as shown for each article are cumulative, i.e. they include the rates paid on the previous articles made by the same company, which are its raw materials. The 1927 assessments have been fixed since the slump set in, but are considered too high and may be the subject of appeal.

equalities, or at least to mitigate them, is the most pressing task of financial statesmanship.

(*b*) *The Burden on the Working Classes*

Nor is it only on industry that the burden of rates falls injuriously. The incidence of rates on individuals and families is even more unjust. In the case of the working man with a large family the rates may consume nearly 10 per cent. of his income, if his children are to be housed with the barest minimum of decency. In the case of the rich man they will usually amount to less than 1 per cent. of income. So far from being graded in accordance with ability to pay, rates press most heavily on those least able to bear them.

It is evident that a policy of reducing the income-tax, whilst at the same time increasing the burdens of the ratepayer, is a most potent method for transferring burdens from the rich to the poor. Yet this has been in fact the policy of Mr. Churchill. In 1925 he took 6*d*. off the income-tax. In 1926, in order to avoid raising the income-tax to its previous figure, various expenses were thrust off the National Exchequer on to the rates. In particular the tightening-up of the regulations with regard to granting Unemployment Insurance benefit and to providing grants in aid of schemes of work for the unemployed involved an increase in expenditure from rates, which, in Manchester alone, came to £1,500 a week, or the equivalent of a 3*d*. rate. "Economies" which took the form of shifting burdens with respect to the tuberculous war-pensioners from the taxpayer to the ratepayer and similar measures by the President of the Board of Education brought the total increase of Manchester rates in the single year, 1926, due to "economy" by the Chancellor of the Exchequer, to 5.22*d*. in the £. This year the same misguided policy has been continued by raiding the Road Fund for the benefit of the Exchequer, instead of using its abundance to diminish road-expenditure from the rates, and by the provisions of the Unemployment Insurance Bill which is before Parliament as we write.

We think that a reversal of this reactionary policy and a far-reaching reform of our rating system, with a view to the mitigation of the anomalies and injustices which we have here set forth, should be a leading feature of the programme of the Liberal Party.

2. How Rates are Spent

In the year ending March 31, 1925 (the last year for which detailed figures are available), the net expenditure of Local Authorities in England and Wales [1] on income account (i.e.

[1] All the figures given above relate to England and Wales only, since we have not been able to obtain comparable figures for Scotland. Detailed figures for Scotland have not been published for any year later than 1919–20. Probably about 10 per cent. should be added to the above figures to obtain the total for Great Britain as a whole.

TABLE 38

LOCAL AUTHORITIES, ENGLAND AND WALES—NET EXPENDITURE 1924–5

(*In millions of £s*)

	Exchequer Grants.	*Rates.*	*Total.*
(1) Education	38·68	31·64	70·32
(2) Public Libraries	—	1·39	1·39
Totals of (1) and (2) . .	38·68	33·03	71·71
(3) Maternity and Child Welfare .	·65	·70	1·35
(4) Tuberculosis and Venereal Diseases	1·85	1·27	3·12
(5) Lunacy and Mental Deficiency .	1·43	5·83	7·26
Totals of (3) to (5) . .	3·93	7·80	11·73
(6) Housing and Town Planning .	7·49	1·29	8·78
(7) Relief of the Poor . . .	1·20	28·56	29·76
Totals of (1) to (7) . .	51·30	70·68	121·98
(8) Highways and Bridges . .	12·98	30·51	43·49
(9) Sewage and Refuse Services .	·30	13·77	14·07
(10) Hospital and Medical Services	·44	5·56	6·00
(11) Public Parks, Baths, etc. .	·19	3·90	4·09
(12) Water-supply . . .	·06	·57	·63
(13) Cemeteries	·01	·40	·41
Totals of (9) to (13) . .	1·00	24·20	25·20
(14) Police and Police Stations .	9·09	9·03	18·12
(15) Administration of Justice .	·02	·62	·64
(16) Fire Brigades	·01	1·77	1·78
Totals of (14) to (16) . .	9·12	11·42	20·54
(17) Other specific services . .	1·66 ‡	5·70	7·36
(18) General administrative expenses and unallocated . . .	—	12·93	12·93
Grand totals . . .	76·06 *‡	153·08 †§	229·15 †§

* Excluding Exchequer grants referred to in the next footnote.

† Including Exchequer grants totalling £5·36 millions, and fees, tolls, rents, etc., totalling £5·34 millions, which were not allocated to any one service.

‡ Including about £124,000 for Exchequer grants to trading services showing a surplus.

§ Net figure after deducting about £2,350,000 surplus on certain trading services.

Compiled from Eighth Annual Report of the Ministry of Health, 1926–7 [*Cmd.* 2938 *of* 1927], p. 227.

after deducting receipts in respect of income-earning services) was roughly £229,000,000, of which rather more than one-third (36 per cent.) was paid for from Exchequer Grants and the balance out of local rates. The main headings are given in Table 38 on p. 438.

The percentages of the rates received in 1924–5 spent on the principal groups of local expenditure were as follows:

TABLE 39

LOCAL AUTHORITIES—PROPORTIONATE EXPENDITURE OUT OF RATES ON VARIOUS SERVICES, 1924–5

	Per cent.	
Education (including Libraries)	21·2	
Other Health Services ; Lunacy and Mental Deficiency	5·0	
Housing and Town Planning	0·8	
Relief of the Poor	18·4	
		45·4
Highways and Bridges (excluding Lighting)		19·6
Sewage and Refuse Services and Preventive Health Services	15·6	
Administration of Justice, Police, Fire Brigades	7·4	
Miscellaneous	3·7	
General Administrative Expenses, etc.	8·3	
		35·0
Total		100·0

Extracted from the Eighth Annual Report of the Ministry of Health, 1926–7, p. 109.

Broadly speaking, we might describe Education, "other" Health Services, Housing, and Poor Relief as *Social Services*. These amounted in 1924–5 to 45.4 per cent. of the whole. Highways and Bridges (19.6 per cent.) are mainly a central, as distinguished from a local, service. The rest (35 per cent.) may be called Local *Administrative Services*.

The total rates collected rose from £142,000,000 in 1924–5 to £147,500,000 in 1925–6 and £159,500,000 in 1926–7. The increase of £12,000,000 in 1926–7 over the previous year was mainly due to the extra expenditure imposed on Boards of Guardians as a result of the general strike and the coal trade dispute. The actual outgoings, however, payable out of the rates were another £9,000,000 higher than this, the excess being discharged by temporary borrowings.

That every effort should be made to secure that the ratepayers receive full value for their expenditure is obvious. This can only be achieved by a close control, by the Local Authorities who are responsible, over the estimates and disbursements. We come now to proposals for relieving the burden of the rates and the inequities of its distribution along lines which aim at preserving the existing incentives to local responsibility.

3. Proposals for Immediate Reform

The evils of the present rating system mainly arise from extending a method which probably achieves rough justice and reasonable efficiency as a means of providing for Local Administrative Services to an increasing volume of Social Services and to the greatly increased expenditure on roads necessitated by new methods of transport which are more and more a central, rather than a local, service. Reform must come, therefore, from disentangling the three types of service. When this has been done, we can then redistribute the burden between local and central taxation and between different categories of ratepayers, to the great advantage both of justice and of efficiency.

Our proposals fall under two main heads. We shall first deal with the readjustment of burdens as between rates and taxes, which can be carried out comparatively easily. We shall then turn to consider certain highly desirable reforms in the assessment and collection of local rates, some of which will involve difficult and complex changes.

4. The Readjustment of Rates and Taxes

(1) *The Burden of Unemployment a National Responsibility.*—There can be no doubt that the aggravation of the evils of the rating system which has characterised the last few years has been primarily due to so substantial a part of the burden of supporting the families of the able-bodied poor, in other words, of the unemployed having been thrown on to the Poor Law. The Poor Law, whilst it has more than once drifted into such responsibilities, was never designed to deal with problems of protracted unemployment due to national causes, and the attempt to make it fulfil such functions is largely responsible for its present difficulties and failures.

Moreover, it is important that such relief as can be afforded by the Exchequer should go in the first instance to the necessitous areas, and that these areas should be aided out of proportion to the relief to those areas which are not suffering from similar burdens.

A beginning has been made in the policy of treating unemployment as a national responsibility by the system of State Insurance. But we are convinced, for the reasons given above and for other reasons to follow, that the time has now come to go further, and for the State to take over from Local Authorities and administer itself the whole system of out-relief to the able-bodied poor. This could then be co-ordinated with the existing machinery for administering Unemployment Insurance, which is already centrally administered. There would also be the advantage of relieving the political pressure which has been brought to bear on certain notorious Boards of Guardians to give very high rates of out-relief. At the same time a substantial burden which is mainly due to national causes would be removed from the rates.

We believe that considerable incidental advantages would be gained from this reform. At present legislation in respect of unemployment is largely concerned, in effect, with deciding what part of the burden shall fall on the Insurance Fund and what part shall be borne locally. Thus any stiffening up of the conditions of the Insurance Fund, which may be very desirable in itself and indeed necessary if the proper principles of insurance are to be observed, has at present the effect of breaking down the Poor Law system at the same time that the Insurance system is strengthened. The real question should be how far the charges arising out of unemployment and the burden of relieving the families of the unemployed represent an insurable risk which it is proper to charge on the Insurance Fund, and how far they represent exceptional and abnormal outgoings due to national causes not contemplated by the Insurance scheme which should be shouldered as a national responsibility and paid for by the Exchequer. We hope, therefore, that the reform we recommend will not only relieve the burden of rates where relief is most needed, but will also allow a great improvement in our methods of handling unemployment as a whole.

(2) *Roads and Road Fund.*—We think that the division of

the expenditure on roads, both classified and unclassified, between the Local Authorities and the Exchequer should be reconsidered, with a view to throwing a much larger proportion than at present on an augmented Road Fund. All the principal roads of the country now serve a far wider public than the inhabitants of the particular locality through which a road passes. The coming of motor traffic has made it impossible to regard any roads in the country as existing simply to serve local needs. We believe that greater efficiency, as well as a relief of the rates, could be secured by increasing central responsibility for the development and maintenance of the roads. That part of the expenditure on roads, especially in towns, which ought to remain a local service, might reasonably be incorporated with what we have called Local Administrative Services.

On the basis of distribution by which the Road Fund contributes 50 per cent. to the maintenance and improvement of Class I roads, 25 per cent. to that of Class II roads (33 per cent. as from 1927–8), and nothing to unclassified roads, the position in 1926–7 may be estimated as is shown in Table 40. It should be noted, however, that as exact figures are not available, this table represents only an estimate, though the best that can be made on existing data.

TABLE 40

PRESENT EXPENDITURE ON ROADS IN GREAT BRITAIN, 1926–7

(In millions of £s)

	Road Fund.	*Local Authorities.*	*Total.*
Class I Roads	11½ *	9½	21
Class II Roads	4	12	16
Unclassified Roads	2½ †	15½	18
	18	37	55

* This is slightly more than 50 per cent. of the total, because expenditure on certain main trunk roads, in respect of which a higher percentage is payable out of the Road Fund, is also included.

† Estimated special grants in respect of rural roads.

Compiled from the Annual Reports on the Road Fund and of the Ministry of Health.

We recommend that in future an augmented Road Fund should bear 75 per cent. of the cost of Class I roads, 50 per cent. of Class II roads, and 35 per cent. of the unclassified roads. On the basis of our estimate of the 1926–7 figures, expenditure would then be distributed as follows:

TABLE 41

PROPOSED REDISTRIBUTION OF EXPENDITURE ON ROADS

(*In millions of £s*)

	Road Fund.	*Local Authorities.*	*Total.*
Class I Roads	15¾	5¼	21
Class II Roads	8	8	16
Unclassified Roads	6¼	11¾	18
	30	25	55

Except in the case of the great trunk roads of the country, which probably ought in any case to be taken over by the Central Road Authority, such a proposal need not involve any new administrative machinery. At present it is not uncommon for County Councils to arrange with District Councils for the latter to undertake the maintenance of main roads passing through their districts, at the cost of the County Councils. Similarly, the Ministry of Transport, or its successor, could often arrange for the actual work of maintenance, in respect of the traffic routes for which central funds had assumed the main financial responsibility, to be carried out locally as heretofore.

(3) *Grants in Aid—Local.*—Generally speaking, the present rating system is a very inexpedient method of paying for Social Services. Since many Social Services are best administered locally, a sufficient part of the charge must remain on the rates to secure local efficiency and responsibility. The present distribution of the burden of local expenditure between local rates and grants in aid from the Central Government is, however, often arbitrary.

The principle of transferring a portion of the cost of locally administered Services to national taxation has been already recognised, and has been adopted in recent years on an increasing scale. At the present time, grants of 50 per cent. of the cost are given in the case of infant welfare work and tuberculosis work, and grants averaging over 50 per cent. for education. The grants have had the advantage of relieving the rates, while there has remained on the Local Authority sufficient responsibility to ensure economical administration. Further, the control gained by the Government owing to its power to withhold the grant has been of great benefit in screwing up laggard Local Authorities to a higher standard of efficiency, and of securing economy all round.

We regard, therefore, the general principle of grants in aid of local Services as a proved success, and believe that they could be extended in such a way as to transfer a further substantial burden from rates to taxes without undermining local responsibility.

It will not be difficult to find further items suitable for transfer, once an extension of the principle is admitted; for a very large part of local expenditure on Social Services is already virtually outside the discretion of local bodies and is prescribed by Acts of Parliament or by administrative direction from Whitehall. We do not enter here into the difficult and technical questions of the choice in particular cases between block grants and percentage grants.

We anticipate that under these three proposals not less than a third of the present burden of the rates [1]—say £50,000,000 per annum, or £55,000,000 including Scotland—would be found suitable, under one head or another, for transfer to the Central Exchequer. It would, of course, be difficult or impossible, both on financial and on administrative grounds, for so considerable a reform to be carried out in a single year. A Chancellor of the Exchequer should aim, we think, at removing from the rates the responsibility for supporting the families of the unemployed with the least possible delay. The other transferences proposed should be coupled with, and made the opportunity for securing, certain other fundamental reforms in our rating system outlined below.

We should add that steps might be necessary to secure that the various reliefs recommended above should accrue to the occupier, and not to the landlord. In the long run the introduction of the principle of rating site-values should prove an important safeguard. But to meet the immediate problem it would be necessary to make certain express provisions.

[1] We are assuming that the 1926 rate of expenditure was abnormal, and that the existing expenditure from the rates in England and Wales is £150,000,000 in round figures.

5. The Reform of the Rating System

(1) *The Rating of Site Values.*—A very substantial alleviation of the burden imposed by the present system of rating both upon industry and upon working-class housing can be obtained by transferring to the site value of land a fair share of the rates now imposed upon the composite value of the land and the buildings which it carries, and usually paid by the occupier, whether owner or tenant. The existing assessment is based upon the letting value of the whole hereditament, and does not discriminate between that part of the value which is due to the buildings and that part which is due to the site. The value of the site results mainly from the presence and activity of the community, and is therefore a peculiarly suitable subject for taxation for the needs of the community. Yet the owner of the site, where potential wealth is increased by every improvement, is not called upon to make any direct contribution; and he may actually find it financially advantageous to leave his land undeveloped, or to place obstacles in the way of the healthy development of industry or of housing, because the burden of rates is charged upon the actual yield of the site, and not upon its real value, and is, in any case, usually paid not by the landlord but by the tenant. We believe this arrangement to be fundamentally unjust; and we are satisfied that a redistribution of burdens such as would place a fair share upon site values would form a very solid contribution to the relief of industry, besides helping towards a more healthy and economical solution of the housing problem, which is itself an obstacle in the way of industrial revival.

This reform has long been an accepted element in Liberal policy. The arguments in its favour are set out in *Towns and the Land,* and we need not elaborate them here.

We recommend that the principles embodied in Sir John Simon's Rating of Land Values Bill of 1924 should at once be put into operation, and that Rating Authorities in towns and urban districts should be empowered to assess separately the value of every site and of the buildings and other capital equipment standing upon it. The value of the site should be taken as being the price which it would fetch if sold as an unencumbered site in the open market, whether occupied or unoccupied at the date of assessment, and the basis of assessment should be computed at 5 per cent. of this capital value. A gradually increasing portion of the burden of rates should thus be transferred from buildings and improvements to the unimproved value of sites.

(2) *Compounded Rates.*—We think it important that in all cases where rates are "compounded," i.e. are paid by the landlord and included in the rent of a tenement, it should be obligatory upon the landlord to present in his demand-note a clear statement of the amount charged respectively for rent and for rates. This seems to us to be desirable for two reasons: first, in order to bring out the real incidence of rates; and secondly, in order to bring home to the tenant how much he is actually paying for the upkeep of social and administrative services, and thus to give him a clearer sense of his civic responsibilities. This would be especially necessary under any system of site-value rating, as a means of showing how far these rates were passed on to the occupant.

(3) *Rating Areas.*—At present our Local Government is a mass of anomalies and intricacies due to long-past historical origins. Overlapping, inefficiency, complications, and inequity exist everywhere, due to the variety of local government areas and to their failure to correspond to the facts and necessities of to-day. Yet local jealousies and local interests are so strong that it is exceedingly difficult to secure the needed reforms and rearrangements—particularly because in any redistribution certain areas are bound to lose, as probably in equity they ought, in order that others may gain. It is obvious that any attempt to average out burdens must in some cases leave them heavier than they were.

We are strongly of the opinion, therefore, that a change which will have the effect of greatly reducing the aggregate of local burdens should be made the opportunity for carrying through a thorough-going reform of Local Government areas. In the case of the Administrative Services in particular, efficiency and convenience of operation may require the definition of new areas, which should probably be County or Regional Areas for some purposes, and should preserve something like the existing district, municipal, and parish autonomy for others.

The evils arising from the unequal distribution of the burden of rates could be sensibly diminished by increasing the rating area in the case of most of the social services to an area not less than that of a County or County Borough. The Education Rate already approximates to a County Rate. It is probable that the Poor Rate should also be averaged in future over County Areas, as indeed was proposed under the earlier version of the present proposals of the Ministry of Health but abandoned subsequently in face of local opposition.

We must not enter further in this report into an exceedingly complicated problem. But we think that this is pre-eminently a case where one reform can be made the opportunity for another.

(4) *Differentiation and Graduation of Rates.*—We have argued above that the evils of the rating system are at their worst in the case of industrial, agricultural, and business lands and premises, and of working-class dwellings. It would, therefore, be desirable, if it were practicable, to concentrate as much of the relief as can be afforded by the Central Exchequer on these classes of ratepayers. We should like, that is to say, to introduce into our rating system, as we have done in the case of our income-tax system, measures of differentiation and graduation.

In this connection we think it worth while to outline briefly some interesting suggestions, as to the practicability of which we have found it difficult to form a final opinion without more detailed knowledge than is at our disposal. The suggestions are as follows.

The eventual effect of the above proposals would be to reduce the total expenditure from rates in England and Wales to about £100,000,000 per annum. The balance of expenditure thus remaining on the rates is capable of classification into the two broad categories of Social Services and Administrative Services. If the division were to be made on some such lines as indicated above, it would probably be found that Social Services would be responsible for about one-third of the total, and Administrative Services for about two-thirds. There might then be instituted, corresponding to the two sets of services, the levy of two distinct rates which might be termed the Administrative Rate and the Social Rate respectively. The Administrative Rate would be levied as at present over the rateable value of all lands and premises, though the existing basis of assessment, which is in some respects illogical and unwise, might be revised in detail. The burden of the Social Rate, on the other hand, might be distributed between different categories of ratepayers according to some principle of capacity to pay and other relevant considerations.

It has also been suggested that an element of graduation according to rateable value might be introduced, either by partial relief to certain classes of dwelling-houses or by a higher rate where the capacity to pay is greater. The existing principles of our rating system go back to a period before the principle of progressive taxation had been seriously introduced into our fiscal system. The introduction of a distinction between the Social Rate and the Administrative Rate would, however, greatly facilitate the introduction of principles of differentiation and graduation. The extent and degree of the relief which would thus be given is, however, a question of facts and figures of a more detailed character than we have before us.

If such a system of differentiation and graduation were to work smoothly as between different local areas, it would be necessary to levy the Social Rate over an area sufficiently large to enable a reasonably representative average to be struck over different classes of ratepayers. For this reason it would have to be considered whether the two rates should not also be distinct in respect of the districts over which they are levied. That is to say the Administrative Rates might be levied over strictly local areas as at present, whilst the Social Rate would be partly or wholly a county rate. Thus the feasibility of introducing a separate Social Rate would partly depend on the success of the reform of Local Government areas recommended above.

6. Conclusion

The rating system of this country is at present a jungle of anomalies, complications, and historical survivals into the details of which it is rash for anyone to enter but a Ministry of Health expert. For this reason any such scheme as the above must be susceptible of considerable amendment and improvement in details. But we have no doubt as to the character of the evils to be remedied or as to the main lines along which a remedy can alone be found.

It will be seen that our financial programme would consist

in treating the burden of national and local expenditure as a whole, and in regarding the latter as having a more urgent claim for relief than the former, out of whatever free resources the Chancellor of the Exchequer may obtain, as the result of a steady policy of disarmament, a reform of inheritance duties, or the natural elasticity of the revenue as the country recovers once more a normal rate of progress. It makes no difference to tax-payers as a whole whether they pay a given sum in local taxes or in national taxes. But since our system of national taxation is much more efficiently devised than our system of local taxation, it is better that the relief which can be afforded to tax-payers should affect local taxes first.

SUMMARY OF CONCLUSIONS

BOOK 1

THE CONDITION OF BRITISH INDUSTRY

THE range of subjects which we have covered in this Report is large. The problems of British industry are many and various; and a wise industrial policy must be correspondingly many-sided. We have not attempted to emulate the simple comprehensiveness with which extremists of the left and right sum up these problems in a single phrase—telling us either that the State should cease to meddle with industry, or that the capitalist system should be replaced by "Socialism." Such phrases are always attractive to certain minds. Yet it is noticeable that their attractiveness is now very much on the decline. Nor is the explanation far to seek. Real problems have emerged, serious, indeed urgent, which demand attention. And no one trying to deal with a real problem has ever found the smallest assistance either in the platitudes of inaction or in the grandiose formula of revolutionary change.

We have started out with a careful survey of the facts of the industrial situation. The broad picture which presents itself is one of long-continued adversity in our leading exporting industries, contrasting sharply with considerable expansion and prosperity elsewhere. The general forces making for economic progress have not ceased to operate. Human intelligence is still restlessly at work. New inventions are made, machinery is constantly becoming more efficient, the technique of business undergoes a corresponding process of improvement; our expenditure on education and public health and social services has not been without effect in raising the efficiency of the population; and all these forces make powerfully for increased productivity. They have been just about strong enough—or nearly so—to cancel out against both the diminished hours of work and the waste arising from unemployment and idle plant in the exporting industries. And, since the leisure and freedom from undue fatigue which results from moderate hours of work constitute one of the most important elements in human welfare, it is fair to say that, as a people, we have still been making progress on the whole, despite all our post-war economic difficulties.

But this fact is no excuse for complacency. On the contrary, when we remember the immense growth in prosperity which each decade in the nineteenth century showed over the preceding decade, or when we reflect on the rapid strides forward that are being made to-day in the United States, the small, doubtful progress which has been achieved here since the Armistice is disappointing and disquieting. These comparisons supply the measure of what we have lost by the depression of the export industries, of what we stand to lose in future unless the difficulties which face them are overcome. For the past seven years the condition of these industries—coal, iron and steel, shipbuilding, textiles—the chief contributors to our development during the nineteenth century, has been profoundly unsatisfactory, whether we have regard to the volume of trade and of employment, or to the wages and profits which they have afforded to those engaged in them. Moreover, while the outlook for some of these industries is improving, the difficulties of others, and among them the most important, namely coal and cotton, are becoming increasingly acute. The troubles of the export industries have acted as a brake on our general economic progress. They render its continuance precarious. They have persisted too long to entitle us to dismiss them with facile expressions of hope that better days may be in store.

In part, we believe that our loss of foreign trade is due to the growth of general impediments to world commerce. Our first industrial need is, therefore, a wise international policy which will secure peace and promote intercourse between nations. But that is not the whole story. The nineteenth century has passed away; and we have to adapt ourselves to the conditions of the twentieth. We acquired a long start in the application of steam to manufacture. During the nineteenth century we derived immense advantage from the momentum of that long start. The momentum is now nearly spent, and we are beginning to feel its disadvantages. In many of our leading, old-established industries the organisation is too deeply embedded in nineteenth-century grooves. The essential weakness is not national, it does not lie in obsolete plant or in an antiquated lay-out of coal-mines. It is, rather, psychological. It lies in a stubborn adherence to outworn methods, ideas, traditions, resulting in a general organisation of industry which fails to pass the test of twentieth-century conditions. Nor is it only business organisation in the narrow sense that is at fault. Our industrial efficiency is gravely impaired by unsatisfactory relations between employers and employed, bursting out every now and then into wasteful conflict.

But we have not only to adapt to new conditions the structure of some of our industries, we must be ready also to re-adapt the whole structure of our economic life. We must not continue to wait passively for something to happen which shall restore the peculiar balance of our pre-war industrial life. Rather should we extract compensation for the troubles of our export industries by turning our attention to what we have too long neglected—the development of our home resources. We should seize the opportunity to press on with housing, road construction, electricity, and the regeneration of agriculture and our rural life. These are the broad conclusions to which our survey leads us.

BOOK 2

THE ORGANISATION OF BUSINESS

CHAPTER VI

THE PUBLIC CONCERN

1. *Individualism and Socialism.*—Individualism is an unrivalled method for (i) the decentralisation of decisions, (ii) as a means of discovering the most effective from amongst the possible alternatives, and (iii) as a method of measuring the comparative efficiency, not only of methods, but of individuals.

Nevertheless, (i) where undertakings of great national importance require large amounts of capital, yet may fail to attract private enterprise on an adequate scale, perhaps because of the necessity of limiting profits, or (ii) where conditions of monopoly render unregulated private enterprise dangerous, or (iii) where the private shareholder has ceased to perform a useful function, there must be room for what we have called the Public Concern.

Public Concerns of one kind or another, of which the leading examples are enumerated in the text, already cover so vast a field that the supposed choice between Individualism and Socialism is largely an obsolete issue. An examination of the existing types of Public Concerns shows that the Socialist would gain nothing by assimilating to a single theoretical model a diversity developed by experience to meet actual situations. On the other hand, it would be quite impossible to scrap the elaborate legislation enacted by Governments of every political complexion and hand over our public utilities and railway system to the operation of uncontrolled Individualism. There is therefore no question of principle at stake, but only one of degree, of expediency, and of method. The important practical issues are the correct delimitation of the field of the Public Concern, and, above all, a thorough overhauling of the methods of running those Public Concerns which already exist.

2. *The Nationalisation of Industry.*—If this means direct State trading, we are opposed to it. The best method of conducting large undertakings owned by the Government and run in the public interest is by means of an *ad hoc* Public Board analogous to a Joint Stock Company, in which the capital is owned and the directors appointed by the State.

3. *Municipal Trading.*—We are in favour of local public ownership of local public utilities, but we doubt whether the right forms of organisation and the right geographical units have yet been attained. Here also we favour the development of *ad hoc* Public Boards, the executive and administrative Boards of which would correspond to the boards of directors of private concerns, the Local Authorities corresponding to the shareholders.

4. *The Organisation of Public Boards.*

(i) The method of appointing the Executive Authority of Public Boards should be reformed, business and technical efficiency being aimed at rather than the representation of interests.

(ii) We need to build up an attractive career for business administration open to all the talents. A regular service should be recruited for Public Boards, with a cadre and a pension scheme, with room for rapid promotion and satisfactory prizes. To cover the case of Public Boards subject to Municipal and other Local Authorities, a body might be set up similar to the Civil Service Commission.

(iii) A proper system of accounting, distinguishing on sound principles between expenditure on capital and on current account, should be introduced into all Public Boards, and the system should be as uniform as possible, to facilitate comparisons.

5. *The Field of Operation of Public Concerns.*—We do not wish at the present stage greatly to enlarge the existing field of operation of Public Concerns. The next step is to bring those which exist up to date, to improve the position and prospects of their officials, and to get their capital accounts into order. But some further extension of the field of Public Concerns will probably be indicated as desirable year by year in the future, as in the past. For example, we favour a new Road Board with wider jurisdiction and larger resources. We also favour a single Public

Board to control every section of the transport system of the London area. We think that Public Boards dealing with the supply of electricity should be considerably developed. We are not satisfied with the present position of the Railways, but we think that some further experience should be gained before modifying the recent Railway Act.

CHAPTER VII

THE JOINT STOCK COMPANY

The important practical distinctions are:

(i) Between those Companies which have passed out of the effective control of their shareholders and those which are still controlled by them; and

(ii) Between those Companies against whom competition from new-comers is likely to be ineffective and those which are still subject to normal competitive conditions.

Where neither diffused ownership nor monopolistic tendencies are present, there is no need to interfere materially with the existing state of affairs. Our proposals are directed to the problems arising from diffused ownership and monopolistic tendencies.

1. *Publicity of Accounts and Responsibility of Auditors.*—We make far-reaching and drastic proposals, the details of which are given in the text, for securing the effective publicity of accounts in the case of all Public Companies, and for enlarging the responsibilities of the Auditor and strengthening his position.

2. *Directors.*—We make recommendations dealing with the publicity of remuneration of directors, the question of their dealing in the shares of their own companies, and of their superannuation. In certain types of companies of widely diffused ownership, directorships are in fact the pocket boroughs of the present days, but in the main we must depend for improvement on the leaders of the business world becoming more alive to the dangers of present methods and to the importance of increased efficiency in this respect.

3. *Supervisory Councils.*—We suggest that the right line of evolution in the case of companies of diffused ownership is towards a system by which, in addition to the board of directors consisting of the active management of the concern, with a few

outside persons with technical qualifications, a Supervisory Council would represent the shareholders, and in some cases the employees.

Chapter VIII

Trusts and Trade Associations

1. *The Problem of Monopoly.*—The instinctive public distrust of monopolies is well founded, because it is competition which has passed on to the consuming public, in the form of low prices, the results of industrial and economic progress. It is, however, useless to-day to attempt to restore the old conditions of competition, which often involved waste of effort and prevented full advantage being taken of large-scale production. In modern conditions some degree of monopoly is, in an increasing number of industries, inevitable, and even quite often desirable in the interests of efficiency. The progression from purely private Individualistic enterprises to the Public Concern is a gradual one. We must try to find room for large-scale semi-monopolistic private concerns. A monopoly, held in check by its vulnerability against concerted action by consumers, may serve the public well and offer many of the advantages of free competition simultaneously with the economies of concentration. But publicity is the necessary condition for the right use by the consumer of his ultimate weapons.

2. We recommend, therefore, that large Public Companies controlling more than 50 per cent. of a product within Great Britain should be registered as a Public Corporation and should be subjected to specially stringent provisions of publicity.

(i) It should be subject to inspection by the Board of Trade, with power to the latter to report.

(ii) In the event of abuses coming to light, the procedure of investigation and control recommended by the Committee on Trusts should be followed, including the establishment of a Trust Tribunal.

3. *International Cartels.*—International Cartels should not be indiscriminately attacked. But they are capable of developing into dangerous monopolies, and should be closely watched. The best remedy against the abuse of such agreements is, as in the case of National Agreements, full publicity.

4. *Trade Associations.*—Where a Trade Association comprises more than 50 per cent. of a trade or industry it should, generally speaking, be incorporated and be subjected to special rules as to publicity and the preparation of statistics. On the other hand, since cases may arise where a small minority of any industry may legitimately be required to conform to the rules which the majority have imposed on themselves, we recommend that, in special cases and subject to special safeguards, an Incorporated Trade Association should be allowed to apply for the Association rules to be enforced throughout the industry.

Chapter IX

The National Savings

1. *The Present Situation.*—The aggregate new savings of the country are estimated at about £500,000,000 annually. The manner in which, and the channels through which, this sum is invested are analysed in detail. A doubt is expressed whether the existing machinery for investment necessarily preserves the correct balance between expenditure on Transport and Public Utilities at home and loans for similar purposes overseas. Our constructive proposals are based on the assumption that the first and most important use of our National Savings should be in the development and expansion of Transport Facilities, Public Utilities, Industries, Housing, and Agricultural Equipment at home.

2. *A Board of National Investment.*—It is recommended that there should be established a Board of National Investment which should take over the present functions of the National Debt Commissioners and certain other bodies. All capital resources accruing in the hands of Government Departments should be pooled in the hands of this Board, and out of the pool there should be financed new capital expenditure by Public Boards and other official bodies. It is proposed that the whole of the capital expenditure which is being currently incurred under some form or another of Public Authority should be reviewed annually, that the funds available for such purposes should be pooled, and that no desirable development should be postponed so long as savings are available to finance it.

The Board of National Investment, in drawing up its programme, would have regard to the resources flowing into the pool, to the state of the investment market, to the urgency and importance of the demands upon it for advances, and to the state of employment. It should also pay special attention to the provision of bonds of a type suitable to the small investor.

We believe that without any encroachment on the legitimate field of private enterprise, the Board of National Investment might become a factor of great importance in the development of the national resources.

Chapter X

An Economic General Staff

We propose, as an essential instrument of better and wiser government in modern conditions, the establishment of an Economic General Staff closely associated with the Prime Minister and the Cabinet, and at the same time with principal Economic Departments of State, with duties in general terms as follows:

(1) To engage in continuous study of current economic problems affecting national policy and the development of industry and commerce.

(2) To co-ordinate and, where necessary, to complete statistical and other information required by the Government and by Parliament.

(3) To act on its own initiative in calling the attention of the Cabinet (or the Committee of Economic Policy suggested below) to important tendencies and changes at home or abroad.

(4) To suggest to the Government plans for solving fundamental economic difficulties, such, for instance, as measures for stabilising trade conditions, avoiding unemployment, and developing national resources.

It is also suggested that a Standing Committee of the Cabinet should be set up, called the Committee of Economic Policy, to which the Chief of the Economic General Staff should act as Secretary.

With the Committee of Economic Policy and the Economic General Staff the executive Government would be far better equipped for handling and foreseeing the complex economic problems of modern administration.

Chapter XI

Business Statistics

The improvement of economic information is necessary for wise intervention or guidance by the State. But it is not less necessary for the efficient functioning of individual enterprise. We believe that secrecy in business is one of the greatest factors of inefficiency in British economic life to-day.

We therefore recommend uncompromising measures against the withholding of facts, and in particular a far-reaching extension and development of the Government Statistical Service along the lines indicated in the text.

Increased resources of money and staff should be placed at the disposal of Government Departments for the purpose of strengthening their statistical organisation.

The Census of Production, instead of being taken at long intervals, should be in operation continuously. The figures collected should be made readily available.

The Stationery Office should revert to its practice of selling official publications at prime cost.

The Economic General Staff should keep an eye on the completeness and co-ordination of the statistical information collected and on the prevention of overlapping.

As much use as possible should be made of the assistance of Trade Associations and of auditors and accountants acting through their Institute.

Chapter XII

Business Efficiency

Whilst there is some inefficiency in individual businesses in face of the more complex and difficult problems of the present day, especially in the case of old-established enterprises, the more striking opportunities for improvement probably relate, not so much to the affairs of individual businesses, as to the general problems of industry as a whole.

Examples are quoted in three leading industries, namely coal, steel, and milling. It may be possible to aid the solution of some of the problems by better education and increased information. But in the main the remedy must necessarily lie with industry itself.

Proposals are made in connection with training and education, and for the development of right methods.

The heading under which there is perhaps most reason to doubt the efficiency of our existing organisation is that of marketing. Doubts are cast on the suitability of our traditional merchanting system to the altered conditions of international competition in the modern age. It is held to be not without significance that those industries which are now finding it most difficult to hold their own are the old-established industries in which the nineteenth-century merchanting system has struck its deepest roots. The difficulties of introducing better marketing methods are admitted, but the conclusion is drawn that some of our industries could do much to improve the efficiency of their marketing.

BOOK 3

INDUSTRIAL RELATIONS

Chapter XIII

The Causes of Industrial Discontent

The existence of widespread discontent among the workers is a principal cause of industrial inefficiency and an obstacle to prosperity. It shows itself (*a*) in the growing scale and cost of industrial disputes, and (*b*) in constant friction and, in some cases, restriction of output.

This discontent is due to legitimate grievances and aspirations. In particular, workpeople feel—

(*a*) that they are treated rather as tools than as partners in production, and that they do not enjoy in industry a standing corresponding with their standing as free citizens;

(*b*) that the distribution of the wealth they help to create is carried out on principles to which they are not parties, and leads to a cleavage between a small owning and directing class and a large working class.

It must be a primary aim of industrial policy to remove the causes of this discontent. This does not involve any revolutionary reconstruction of our social order. The course of industrial evolution already points in this direction.

Chapter XIV

Collective Bargaining

The regulation of industrial relations and the distribution of the product of industry are now carried on mainly by the process of "collective bargaining" between organised bodies of employers and workpeople. In this process the "third party" in industry (the managerial and technical staffs) have hitherto taken no direct part.

Analysis shows that, on the scale on which we know it, this process is a very recent development. Hitherto it has been mainly confined to an endless tug-of-war regarding wages and conditions, and it has led to costly and wasteful conflicts. But it is capable of being developed into a system of "joint ascertainment" of what is just, practicable, and advantageous to the industry and to the community.

In some industries (e.g. cotton, iron and steel, boots and shoes, and the railway service) there has been a remarkable development in this direction, and some of these industries have been very successful in avoiding strife.

Trade Unions and Employers' Associations, though they wield immense power over the life of the nation, are very incompletely recognised by law. We recommend (1) that a Commission should be appointed, including Trade Union representatives, to examine the whole question of Trade Union law; and (2) that the same knowledge should be made available regarding Employers' Associations as is already made available regarding Trade Unions.

Chapter XV

The State and Industry

The State, since it exists to secure peace, justice, and liberty for its citizens, has necessarily been compelled to intervene in industrial relations.

It has directly intervened, by legislation, (*a*) in the regulation of conditions (Factory Acts), (*b*) in the determination of the hours of labour (various Acts), and (*c*) more recently, in the fixation of wage-rates, through the Trade Boards—a Liberal invention.

The Trade Board system has shown the value (*a*) of a neutral element in discussions, and (*b*) of legally enforceable powers as a substitute for enforcement by strike or lock-out.

The State has also encouraged the growth of peaceful self-government in industry by devising the Whitley system of Joint Industrial Councils, which have gone beyond bargaining to co-operation in the pursuit of efficiency. But this system has had only a limited degree of success in a few industries, mainly owing to the lack of enforceable powers.

The State has undertaken the work of conciliation, and has set up the Ministry of Labour to deal with all these problems. It has also set up a system of voluntary arbitration, culminating in the Industrial Court, which has, within its limits, achieved a high degree of success.

Encouraged by this success, some have urged the establishment of a system of compulsory arbitration for the settlement of industrial disputes. We are satisfied that such a system would be unworkable in this country, and that it might discourage the growth of co-operative self-government, which is the true aim of industrial policy (see pp. 179–180).

Chapter XVI

The Remuneration of the Worker

The maintenance of the highest practicable level of wages is the common interest of the community, the workers, and the employers.

This depends primarily upon efficiency in production. While the Trade Unions have contributed notably to the improvement of conditions, analysis shows that wages advanced most rapidly when our productive power was growing fastest, though the Trade Unions were then weak; and that the rate of advance slowed down when our relative efficiency in production decreased, though the Trade Unions were then strong and belligerent.

There is therefore far more to be gained by labour through co-operation than through conflict. But this involves two things: (*a*) full knowledge of the financial facts in order to ensure that the highest practicable rates are fixed and that capital does not take more than its share; and (*b*) the establishment of a wage-system which will be felt to be just.

There are three elements in a just wage-system: (*a*) a *minimum* below which no worker should fall; (*b*) *standard* wages corresponding to the skill and effort required from the worker; (*c*) a variable element (*profit-sharing*) dependent upon the prosperity of the concern in which the worker is employed.

Minimum Wage.—It is impracticable to fix a universal national minimum. We therefore recommend that every properly constituted negotiating body should be empowered under proper safeguards to fix a legally enforceable minimum for its industry.

We consider that some system of family allowances would provide a means of meeting more adequately the needs of the workers. Recognising the difficulties of this device, we recommend that every negotiating body should be urged to consider whether and how such a system could be applied in its industry.

Standard Wages.—The principle that reward should be proportionate to skill and effort can often be best met by a system of piece-work, fellowship-bonus on time-rates, or other methods of payment by results. But no such system can work well unless it is based upon consent and open consultation whenever revision of rates is necessary.

Serious disparities have arisen since the War between the wages paid for occupations of corresponding skill in different industries. These will only ultimately be remedied by an improvement of the rates in depressed industries as and when trade revives. But we recommend that the Council of Industry (see below) should watch the movements of wages in various trades, and should direct the attention of negotiating bodies to undesirable disparities.

Profit-sharing.—We desire to see a wide extension of suitable forms of profit-sharing. The primary purpose of such a system should be neither to encourage greater output nor to increase the earnings of the workers, though these results should incidentally follow; but to define the principles upon which the wealth created by a concern is divided and to give assurance that these principles are observed.

In order to secure this object it is essential (*a*) that the basis of any scheme should be clearly defined and legally secured; (*b*) that the participants should have access to adequate knowledge of the financial facts; (*c*) that the freedom of the workers should be in no way impaired.

It is not possible to enforce generally any single scheme of profit-sharing, since every scheme must be adjusted to the conditions of the concern adopting it. But we recommend (*a*) that certain types of large-scale concerns should be required to adopt schemes; and (*b*) that the Council of Industry should work out schemes of various types, and should urge negotiating bodies to consider what types would be suitable for their industry.

Chapter XVII

A Programme of Industrial Co-operation

It is the aim of Liberal Policy to bring about the establishment, in every industry, of a representative regulating body, including both employers and workers, for the consideration of common interests, and endowed with the power of obtaining, under proper safeguards, legal sanction for their agreements.

This involves (*a*) the improvement of existing negotiating machinery; (*b*) the provision of adequate knowledge of the financial facts; and (*c*) the provision of better machinery for central guidance, particularly by the creation of a Ministry of Industry, including the powers of the present Ministry of Labour, and of a representative Council of Industry working in close association with the Ministry.

Negotiating Bodies.—It is desirable that negotiating bodies should include a neutral element, without the power to vote except when legal powers are sought; and also in many cases representative of managerial and technical staffs for consultative purposes on subjects other than wage-negotiations. But as this involves considerable departure from existing practice, the question of the invitation of such members and of the conditions under which they are to act should be left to the negotiating bodies themselves.

Any difficulties affecting the demarcation between organised industries should, when necessary, be referred to the Council of Industry.

Trade Boards.—We recommend that the Trade Board system should be extended to all industries insufficiently organised to be able to make and keep general agreements; that such Trade Boards should, as now, be constituted by the Ministry, and should have power to fix minimum wage-rates enforceable by criminal process; that in the fixation of wage-rates above the minimum and of other conditions neutral members of Trade Boards should be entitled to speak, but not to vote, unless legal enforcement was sought; that in such cases enforcement should be by way of civil, not criminal, process; and that all regulations for which legal force is sought should be laid before the Council of Industry for review before being endorsed or disallowed by the Ministry.

Joint Industrial Councils.—Joint Industrial Councils should be encouraged to include in their membership (*a*) a neutral element, and (*b*), where appropriate, representatives of technical and managerial staffs; but this should be at their discretion. We recommend that the Council of Industry should maintain a panel of persons suitable for appointment as neutral members, or, alternatively, should approve persons nominated by the Councils.

We recommend that Joint Industrial Councils should be empowered to obtain legal sanction for their agreements subject to the following conditions:

(*a*) the proposal for which legal sanction is sought should have been supported by a majority on both sides;

(*b*) any sections of the industry not represented on the Council should have been given an opportunity of presenting their views;

(*c*) neutral members should have taken part in the discussion and voting;

(*d*) the Council should be able to show, in making application for the enforcement of wage-rates or conditions, that undesirably low wage-rates or bad conditions are prevalent in some sections of the industry; and that the rates or conditions proposed to be enforced are not markedly above or below those ruling for occupations of corresponding skill in other industries.

Applications for legal sanction should be laid before the Council of Industry for report, together with any criticisms which may have been made, reasonable opportunity having been given for such criticisms. After receiving a report from the Council, the Ministry of Industry should be empowered to issue an Order which, after lying on the table in both Houses of Parliament for a defined period, should have the force of law.

Other Negotiating Bodies.—In industries where neither Trade Boards nor Joint Industrial Councils exist, the Ministry and Council of Industry should strive to bring suitable machinery into existence.

(*a*) In highly organised industries which have already

developed satisfactory negotiating machinery, no attempt should be made to interfere with this machinery, but these industries should be urged also to establish the machinery of organised discussion on the lines of the Joint Industrial Councils, with power to obtain legal enforceability for their decisions.

(*b*) In less organised industries the establishment or revival of Joint Industrial Councils should be stimulated; or, where the organisation on both sides is weak, Trade Boards should be instituted with the advice of the Council of Industry.

Essential Public Services.—With a view to the protection of the public and the smooth working of industry, it is necessary that special safeguards should be taken against interruptions in the essential public services, provided that the ultimate right to strike or to lock out should not be impaired.

For this purpose we recommend:

(*a*) that the Council of Industry should schedule the essential services, and should request the negotiating bodies in each scheduled industry to submit a scheme providing (i) a satisfactory system of negotiation, and (ii) adequate guarantees for its full utilisation;

(*b*) that in these cases the system of negotiation should include a reference for report to an impartial inquiry, no strike or lock-out to be valid until the report of the inquiry had been published;

(*c*) that the guarantees might take one or more of the following forms: (i) the organisation of the workers in the service concerned on an establishment basis; (ii) appointments for a term of a month or three months, with penalties for breach of contract; (iii) the deposit of forfeitable pledges on either side; (iv) a provision that the privileges of the Trades Disputes Act, 1906, should not apply in the case of stoppages declared before the whole machinery of negotiation had been utilised;

(*d*) that in the event of no scheme, or an unsatisfactory scheme, being submitted by the industry concerned, the Council of Industry should itself draw up a scheme for submission to and enactment by Parliament.

Provision of Knowledge.—We recommend that it should be

the duty of the Ministry of Industry, acting in conjunction with the Economic General Staff (see above, pp. 117 ff.), to equip all negotiating bodies with adequate knowledge of the financial facts affecting their industries.

Ministry of Industry.—We recommend that the Ministry of Labour should be reconstructed under the name of the Ministry of Industry, taking over the powers of the Home Office under the Factory Acts and Compensation Acts, the Mines Department of the Board of Trade, and such other functions as may be necessary to bring within the purview of a single ministry all the relations between the State and the organised bodies of employers and workpeople.

We also recommend that the Ministry, thus reconstructed, should undertake the duty of advising and stimulating the various industries towards co-operative action in the pursuit of efficiency.

Council of Industry.—We recommend the establishment of a representative Council of Industry, of workable size, in close association with the Ministry of Industry. It should include nine representatives of employers and nine of workers together with six appointed by the Ministry. The members should be appointed for three years, one-third of each category retiring each year, and being eligible for reappointment. The Council should meet at frequent and regular intervals.

The Council should—

(i) report on all applications for compulsory powers, whether from Trade Boards or other bodies;

(ii) keep under continuous review the development of consultative machinery in the various industries;

(iii) keep under continuous review the movement of wage-rates and direct the attention of negotiating bodies to undesirable disparities;

(iv) present an annual report on these subjects, which should be published;

(v) give preliminary consideration to measures affecting industry proposed to be introduced in Parliament;

(vi) generally advise the Minister of Industry on all matters referred to it by him.

The institution of the Council of Industry should not stand in the way of the subsequent establishment of a larger National Industrial Council, when such a step seemed desirable.

Chapter XVIII

The Status of the Worker

It is even more important to create the machinery of organised co-operation in the individual factory or workshop than in national negotiating bodies. But this must be done (*a*) without impairing the necessary authority and prerogatives of management, which would be fatal to efficiency, and (*b*) without conflicting with the agreements or decisions of national or district negotiating bodies. Anything which can be accurately described as " workers' control " is therefore out of the question.

The representation of workers upon boards of directors is of little value, unless either (*a*) the workers have an established right to a share of residual profits, or (*b*) the functions of direction have been divided as suggested above (p. 91), in which case workers might advantageously be represented upon a Supervisory Council.

We regard it as important that there should be permanent, regular, and established methods of consultation in every factory and workshop of substantial size. We therefore recommend that it should be a legal obligation upon every concern employing fifty or more workpeople, or, alternatively, upon every concern falling under the Factory or Workshops Acts, to establish a Works Council.

The Works Council should include representatives of every important grade or group within the concern, from the managing chiefs downwards, and it should meet at regular intervals.

Its functions should be in the main consultative, except that its assent should be necessary for works rules; in the event of a failure of agreement on rules, there should be a reference if possible to a district negotiating body, with an ultimate appeal to the Ministry of Industry.

Every workman should receive, in print or writing, a statement of the conditions of his employment, including the conditions on which he may be discharged.

The rules should provide safeguards against arbitrary dismissal, without prejudice to the ultimate authority of management, and should provide suitable modes of ensuring that the discharged workman shall be able to state his case to a higher authority if discharged (*a*) for a moral offence or (*b*) for incompetence, and an assurance of some consultation before men are selected for discharge on the ground of shortage of work.

The Works Council should annually receive a statement upon the financial condition of the concern as full as would be offered to the shareholders, together with an explanation of its trade prospects. It should also be fully consulted in regard to all welfare work, and on schemes for profit-sharing or ownership-sharing.

Chapter XIX

The Diffusion of Ownership

The existing distribution of the ownership of property or capital in this country is so grossly unequal as to constitute a social danger, and to give substance to the complaint that the nation is divided into a small owning class and a large working class.

It is essential that every possible means should be taken to amend this evil, by bringing about a more general diffusion of ownership.

The distribution of wealth has been substantially affected by the use of progressive taxation to defray the cost of the social services. But this has affected income rather than capital. It has, however, helped to bring about an increase of popular saving, though not on a sufficient scale to balance the decrease in investments by the rich.

A firm handling of the rights of bequest and inheritance would contribute to a solution of the problem; but we make no detailed proposals on this subject, which lies outside our reference.

The chief hope of improvement lies in the wider diffusion of new capital as it is created, (*a*) by the setting aside of reserves within industry, (*b*) by private saving.

It is by the creation of reserves that the major part of industrial capital is provided. This is all now assumed to be the property of the existing shareholders. We consider that after existing capital has received an adequate return, the balance ought to be shared with the employees, and that it is best shared in the form of capital allotments, which create new ownerships.

We recommend that the Council of Industry should do everything in its power to stimulate distributions of this kind, which are already adopted by various concerns.

In order to encourage widespread popular saving and investment it is necessary that the banking habit should be greatly extended. We recommend that the stamp duty on cheques for small amounts (which is a strong deterrent) should be either abolished or reduced to ½*d.*

Instalment sales of stock by trading companies to their employees present some dangers, but they stimulate popular investment, and should be encouraged subject to reasonable safeguards which should be devised by the Ministry of Industry or the Board of Trade.

Instalment sales of stock to customers, especially by public utility companies, afford another useful method of overcoming the difficulty experienced by the small investor in buying stocks.

We have elsewhere recommended that the Board of National Investment should use all practicable means of enabling small investors to purchase Government stock with the minimum of trouble.

The growth of investment trusts presents a means of enabling the small investor to distribute his risks and to obtain a better return than he can obtain on Government securities. There is room for a popular type of investment trust, with a limit to the individual investment, the dividends not being subject to deduction at the source. Such a system should, however, be carefully regulated, without involving the State in any guarantee.

The concurrent pursuit of all these methods should (especially if or when prosperity returns) render possible a rapid expansion of popular investment, and a wide diffusion of ownership; thus enabling the savings of the million progressively to take the place of the unspent surplus of the very rich, placing industry upon a much wider foundation, and bridging the gulf between the owning class and the working class.

BOOK 4

NATIONAL DEVELOPMENT

CHAPTER XX

UNEMPLOYMENT

Unemployment is the gravest of our social maladies, and its deplorable results point to fundamental defects in our social order.

It is necessary to distinguish between (*a*) *normal* unemployment, due to trade fluctuations, seasonal changes, etc., and (*b*) *abnormal* employment such as we have suffered from since the War, especially in the export trades.

Normal unemployment can be tempered by a wise regulation of monetary policy and by forethought in the distribution of orders. It can be alleviated by a system of social insurance, such as has been already wrought out, the risks being calculable, and therefore insurable.

Abnormal employment ought not to be dealt with by a straining of the insurance system, or by poor-relief. The results of the attempt to deal with it in this way have been (*a*) to impair the insurance system and to impose an unfair burden upon many industries; (*b*) to break down the poor-law, especially in distressed areas.

We later recommend (Chapter XXXI) that the State should assume direct responsibility for the relief of the able-bodied unemployed. This would render possible the restoration of the Unemployment Insurance Scheme to a sound actuarial basis, and would make it practicable so to revise the scheme as to facilitate the mobility of labour instead of discouraging it—a result highly important at the present time.

But other methods must be used to relieve the heavy load of abnormal unemployment.

Chapter XXI

A Programme of National Development

The only sound way of dealing with unemployment is vigorous action to redress the balance of our national economic life. Means of achieving greater efficiency and effective co-operation (discussed in Books 2 and 3) will contribute towards this end, but they are not enough.

The existence of a large unemployed labour force should be utilised for the purpose of reconditioning the nation's capital equipment. It is false economy to withhold the capital outlay necessary for this purpose.

There is an ample supply of capital for this purpose, provided that it is rightly guided; even to-day the nation is creating new capital at the rate of £500 millions a year. It is sheer waste to avoid using a part of this capital for the purpose of utilising our labour resources in the improvement of our national equipment.

We propose that a large programme of national development should be undertaken, and that, since it would impinge upon several departments of State, it should be placed under the control of a Committee of the Privy Council, directly responsible to the Prime Minister, and to be known as the Committee of National Development.

The Board of National Investment (p. 111) should organise the means of financing this policy.

Chapter XXII

Roads and Housing

A revolution in transport is being effected by the rapid development of road-borne motor traffic. This necessitates a bold reconstruction of our road system, the cost of which cannot be faced by the existing local road authorities. Failure to meet this need handicaps industry and cripples agricultural revival.

We propose that a large programme of road construction should be undertaken, as an indispensable means of equipping the nation for its work and at the same time relieving unemployment.

This programme should be financed (*a*) by restoring the growing revenues of the Road Fund to the purpose for which they were designed, and, if necessary, by raising a loan on the security of these revenues; (*b*) by levying betterment taxes on land directly benefited by these works.

Besides improving the competitive power of the nation, and providing a large amount of employment, such a programme would bring about a better distribution of population and directly contribute to the solution of the problems of housing and slum clearance.

Bad housing being a primary cause of inefficiency and a heavy charge on the social services, we recommend a continuous and comprehensive policy of housing and slum clearance as part of the programme of national development.

To carry out this policy on a systematic plan, regional authorities should be established, as advocated in *Towns and the Land,* and they should receive financial assistance, during the period that works of improvement are maturing, from the Board of National Investment.

New industrial towns of the garden city type should be created, planned from the outset for health and efficiency; and under proper safeguards the Board of National Investment should be empowered to guarantee the interest on bonds issued, under its approval, for such purposes.

Chapter XXIII

Electricity, Waterways, and Docks

A steady and rapid improvement of our electrical supply is necessary for the increase of our competitive power. We have fallen behind other nations in the equipment of our industry with this kind of power. An ill-advised parsimony in this sphere would be mere folly.

The Act of 1926 marks a step forward, but it has defects. In any case, the Central Electricity Board ought to be supported by the constant and steady backing of Government through the Committee of National Development.

Our canal system has largely been allowed to go derelict, while continental nations have been showing great energy in developing this cheap method of transport. Little or nothing has been done to give effect to the recommendations of the Canal Commission of 1906, or the Departmental Committee of 1920.

We recommend that this work should be vigorously pushed forward by the Committee of National Development, the canals being brought, in seven groups, under the control of public trusts.

The maintenance of docks and harbours in a state of the highest efficiency, and with foresight of future needs, is essential for our sea-borne trade. Development is often impeded by a shortage of the revenues of port authorities. The Committee of National Development should keep these needs under review, and should facilitate financial assistance to port authorities where this is necessary.

Chapter XXIV

Agriculture, Forestry, and Reclamation

A revival of British agriculture, which is still the greatest industry in the country, would not only help to relieve unemployment, but would greatly improve our general economic position, (*a*) by increasing the purchasing power of the home market, and (*b*) by its influence upon the balance of trade in diminishing the import of foodstuffs and timber.

A far-reaching policy aimed at these ends has already been adopted by the Liberal Party. It has three main elements: (*a*) a reform of land-tenure, designed to give greater security to the cultivator and opportunities of access to land for the labourer; (*b*) facilities for credit, which should be assisted by the Board of National Investment; (*c*) improved marketing conditions, which would be closely connected with the development of transport.

We recommend that the Committee of National Development should make the pressing forward of this policy of revival one of its main tasks.

Hundreds of thousands of acres of British land, which could be reclaimed by drainage, are left derelict. Great Britain is the only country in Western Europe which has no continuous policy for reclaiming land, or preventing it from becoming waterlogged. We recommend that the working out of such a policy, and the provision of the necessary capital, should be one of the tasks of the Committee of National Development.

While we import between £40 and £50 millions' worth of timber, and while we have millions of acres suitable for afforestation, we are showing immeasurably less energy than France, Germany, Denmark, and Belgium in this field. We recommend that the work now being done by the Forestry Commission should be extended and enlarged under the direction of the Committee of National Development.

The development of rural industries should be an object of national policy, especially as electric power becomes more readily available. This would help to solve the problem of unemployment, and also to bring about a healthier distribution of population.

Chapter XXV

The Problem of the Coal Industry

The situation of the coal industry forms the gravest feature in our national outlook. We have analysed the causes of this situation, and the mistakes of policy on the part of mine-owners, miners, and the Government which have contributed to bring it about.

We have also analysed the proposals of the Labour Party for dealing with the problem by the nationalisation of the industry, and conclude that these proposals are quite unworkable, and would make the situation worse.

The mineral royalties should be acquired by the State, and placed under the administration of an expert body of Coal Commissioners, who should use the landlord power to facilitate the reorganisation of the industry.

The Commissioners should encourage and facilitate amalgamations where these were likely to produce increased efficiency; but purely financial amalgamations, which have in some cases done harm to the industry, should be prevented.

The method of wage-ascertainment should be improved by the exclusion of small pits from the district ascertainments. This would hasten the closing of uneconomic pits. It should also be ensured that all coal transferred by a colliery to an associated concern or a selling agency should be credited at the market price.

A full system of conciliation and co-operation, including pit-committees, district boards, and a national mining council, should be set up.

A National Wages Board, with neutral members, similar to that on the railways, should be created; if necessary it should be endowed with Trade Board powers.

Selling agencies to act on behalf of large groups of collieries, and other means of improved marketing, should be introduced. Those municipalities which wish to do so should be empowered to engage in the retail sale of coal.

Every assistance should be given by the State to research in the utilisation of coal.

There is a surplus of about 200,000 miners who have to be provided for. The difficult problem of transferring this large body of labour should be the special care of the Committee of National Development. Recruitment of new labour in mines should be restricted. Older workers in the industry should be given an opportunity of withdrawing from it on a pension. Financial aid should be given for the training of miners for new occupations, for the provision of tools, and for the transfer of their families.

A contribution towards the cost of these schemes should be required from royalty owners, a deduction being made from the price paid to them when the State acquires the royalties.

Chapter XXVI

Imperial Development

The peoples of the Empire buy more of our goods per head than the corresponding peoples of other countries. It is therefore our interest, as well as our duty, to do everything possible for the development of the Empire.

Our trade with the Empire constitutes about one-third of our total external trade. It is impossible for us to adopt any method of Empire development which would involve placing barriers in the way of the other two-thirds of our trade.

The needs of different parts of the Empire vary widely, and must be separately studied.

The *Dominions,* which include 6 per cent. of the population of the Empire, need (1) population, (2) capital, (3) markets, and (4) communications. We have hitherto mainly supplied all these needs, but in the circumstances of to-day the difficulty of doing so is greatly increased.

In view of the declining rate of increase of our population, it is important that emigration should be systematically encouraged, but the effective co-operation of the Dominions is necessary for this purpose.

We still use the greater part of our exported capital for imperial development, and this is greatly encouraged by the privilege of having their stocks treated as trustee securities which the Empire Governments enjoy. In view of the stringency of capital supply and our needs for home development, the use of British capital for these purposes ought to be supervised by the Board of National Investment.

We cannot adopt any effective system of preferences without greatly increasing the cost of living of our people, and putting obstacles in the way of our foreign trade; moreover, such a system would mainly benefit the Dominions, not India or the other parts of the Empire.

The needs of *India* are peace, the allaying of racial discord, and an increase of the prosperity of her impoverished masses. She needs also a better banking system to overcome the sterilising of her capital by hoarding. A liberal political policy, and courage in economic development under the ægis of Government, are the best ways of meeting these needs.

The tropical colonies, which can supply many essential needs of industry, require to be opened up by the construction of roads and railways. As this can only be done by Government action, the Board of National Investment should facilitate loans for such purposes.

More attention should be given to research and training regarding the conditions and problems of these colonies.

It is essential that a liberal policy should be pursued regarding native rights, and that exploitation should be prevented.

Chapter XXVII

The Rising Generation

It is essential to national efficiency that there should be a great improvement in the arrangements by which boys and girls are placed in industry and trained for their life-careers.

Juvenile unemployment is not now a serious problem; nor is it likely to become so, owing to the decrease in the number of juveniles available for employment due to our shrinking birth-rate. But adolescent unemployment, resulting often from lack of training and from blind-alley occupations, presents real difficulties.

We regard it as fundamental to social, political, and industrial progress that the young worker should be treated primarily as a citizen and worker in training; he should not be exploited because he is cheap.

A marked deterioration takes place in many young workers between leaving school and becoming adult. It is essential in the national interest that this process should be stopped.

The objective of educational policy, to be achieved as conditions permit, should be to extend the school-leaving age to sixteen; to provide an adequate number of secondary-school places; to make part-time continued education statutory up to eighteen; and to set up efficient arrangements for getting the school product into suitable employment.

In the meanwhile, it should be made obligatory upon every Local Educational Authority to give every child in its area an effective choice between (*a*) whole-time education up to fifteen or (*b*) part-time education up to sixteen.

Local Education Authorities should provide training for all unemployed boys and girls up to eighteen. The training should be connected with the work done in day-continuation schools, and an out-of-work allowance should be paid on the condition of attendance.

The work of placing young people in employment and of advising them on the choice of career should be entrusted to the Education Authorities, with the advice of the Ministry of Industry.

Special provision should be made for youths and young men

employed in blind-alley occupations. The residential and non-residential training centres already established experimentally should be increased in number, and their curriculum should be developed. Special attention should be given to training for work on the land, with a view both to Empire settlement and to agricultural revival at home.

While the hours of work for adults have been generally reduced, there are many instances in which juvenile and adolescent workers are required to work for very long hours, sometimes reaching seventy or even eighty a week. The maximum working week for workers under eighteen should be fixed by law at forty-eight hours; and to make this provision effective, juvenile employment should in general be prohibited after 6 p.m.

BOOK 5

NATIONAL FINANCE

Chapter XXVIII

Currency and Banking

Inflation and Deflation.—The disastrous effects on business both of inflation and of deflation are analysed and illustrated. In extreme cases no room for doubt exists as to the relationship of cause to effect. In the case of Great Britain the return to the gold standard at the pre-war parity has involved a strain, about the degree of which opinion differs.

International Co-operation.—Failing improved methods of monetary control, the return of the world to a common gold basis may be expected to bring with it a recurrence of something resembling the pre-war trade cycle. Having placed our currency once more on a gold basis, the limits are fairly narrow to what can prudently be done within the sphere of national policy. We attach, therefore, great importance to the Genoa project of international co-operation. The practice of consultation between the Governors of Central Banks should be continued and extended. But more open methods should be employed, since an atmosphere of secrecy is in itself an obstacle to the creation of stability and of confidence.

The Bank of England.—It should be part of the recognised duty of the Bank of England to regulate the volume of credit with a view to the maintenance of steady trade conditions.

The formal constitution of the Bank of England should be so modified as to emphasise further its character as a national institution.

(i) The dividends to the shareholders of the Bank should be fixed permanently at their present figure.

(ii) The Court of Directors should be reduced in size, and the method of appointment and qualifications of directors reconsidered.

(iii) The term of office of the Governor should be fixed at five years, renewable for a further five years.

(iv) Co-operation between the Treasury and the Bank of England should be expressly provided for in the inner management of the Bank.

The Note Issue.—We share the general opinion that the currency note issue and the Bank of England note issue should be sooner or later amalgamated on a revised basis. This revised basis should expressly aim at immobilising as little gold as possible, and at rendering the maximum proportion of our stock available to meet an external strain and other international emergencies.

We recommend that there should be a public inquiry into the future regulation of the note issue, and that a change should only be made after the matter has been fully and publicly debated.

Publicity.—There is need for greater publicity throughout the whole field of finance. Suggestions are made in this connection as to the information that should be furnished both by the Bank of England and by the Joint Stock Banks.

Chapter XXIX

Reform of the National Accounts

The present method of setting forth the Budget and the National Accounts is ill adapted for bringing to notice the degree of economy practised in the public service.

The Budget is a purely cash account and permits no distinction between capital items and current items, with the result that the Budget revenue in any given year can be manipulated on a large scale to suit the book of the Chancellor of the Exchequer for the time being. Illustrations are given of the scale on which items have been brought to account in the Budget which are not part of the revenue of the year.

A reform of the national accounts is necessary for intelligent criticism by the House of Commons and to secure economy in the right places.

We therefore recommend that the Budget should be divided in future, into the Cash Account, the Income Account, and the Capital Account, as to which details are given in the text.

The National Accounts should also afford particulars of our total expenditure on social services, showing how far they are met out of taxes, how far out of rates, and how far from individual contributions.

There should also be a reclassification of the leading headings of expenditure, and the existing distinction between Consolidated Fund Services and Supply Services should be revised.

With these reforms the House of Commons and the public would know exactly how we stand, which at present is difficult or impossible.

It is probable that the true figure saved out of the current year's revenue for the discharge of the dead-weight debt has been during the last two or three years less than nothing.

Chapter XXX

The Burden of National Taxation

Taxation and National Economy.—A fifth of the national income passes every year through the hands of the State. The higher the level of taxation for Government expenditure, the more important does it become that there should be an atmosphere of informed criticism and of pressure towards economy. Nevertheless, an undiscriminating attitude towards all kinds of expenditure alike will do more harm than good. It is useless to talk vaguely about reducing expenditure without any clear idea in what direction reductions can be made.

The principal field for immediate economies is in the vast expenditure upon defence. We conclude that in the case of our War Departments a substantial reduction of expenditure, possibly amounting to one-third, i.e. £40 millions, should be aimed at, but in other directions the amount of practicable economy is not likely to be large.

The Effects of Taxation upon Industry.—The handicaps which our system of direct taxation places on industry are sufficiently great to raise the standard of scrutiny which it is proper to apply to all proposals for additional expenditure. But they are not so great as to justify calling a halt in the development of education, public health, and social reform.

Education and Social Expenditure.—Even from the narrowest industrial standpoint, we have got good value for the public money expended on education and public health over the last fifty years. It would be a short-sighted policy to-day to cut it down or hold it rigidly in check.

Moreover, social expenditure on the one hand and the graduated taxation of wealth on the other are the two component elements of a policy which goes far towards modifying the distribution of wealth.

Approaching the subject from this angle, we hold that our system of national taxation is in the main well conceived.

Chapter XXXI

Reform of the Rating System

Our system of local rating is far more injurious to industry than our system of national taxation. Rates enter directly into the cost of production, they fall most heavily on industrially depressed areas, and they are based on the vicious principle that industries and businesses should contribute to local expenditure in proportion, not to profits made, but to the amount of fixed capital employed. Again, local rates are assessed inequitably as between individuals; they fall far more heavily on the poor man than on the rich.

Nearly half (45.4 per cent.) of the total sum raised by local rates is spent on Social Services, one-fifth (19.6 per cent.) on roads and bridges, and the remainder (35 per cent.) on Local Administrative Services. Reform must come by disentangling these three types of services and then redistributing the burdens they respectively impose. Under this head our proposals fall into two parts:

(*i*) *Immediate Reforms*

(*a*) The relief of the ablebodied poor should be transferred from Local Authorities to the State and co-ordinated with the existing machinery for administering Unemployment Insurance.

(*b*) A substantial part of the expenditure on roads which is at present borne by Local Authorities should be transferred to an augmented Road Fund.

(*c*) The present system of grants-in-aid, which is in many respects highly advantageous, should be extended.

Under these three heads, we anticipate that one-third of the present burden of local rates—say £55,000,000 a year in Great Britain—would be found suitable, under one head or another, for transfer to the Central Exchequer. Steps should, of course, be taken to ensure that the relief thus gained should accrue, not to the landlord, but to the occupier.

(*ii*) *Further Reforms*

In addition to the above there are other reforms which should be undertaken:

(*a*) An alleviation of the burden imposed by the present system of rating might be obtained by the rating of Site Values.

(*b*) A reform long overdue is the reorganisation of rating areas.

(*c*) So far as practicable, it is desirable to concentrate relief on industrial, agricultural, and business lands and premises, and on working-class dwellings. With this end in view, the possibility of differentiating the administrative from the social services should be considered, with separate administrative and social rates, and graduation of the latter in accordance with some test of capacity to pay.

The rating system of this country is at present a jungle of anomalies, complications, and historical survivals. The system of national taxation is much more efficiently devised. We therefore consider it better to give such relief as can be afforded to local rates rather than to national taxes.

INDEX

References in italics are to the Summary of Conclusions.

J

N

Q

R

S

T

U

Printed in Great Britain
by Lewis Reprints Ltd,
London and Tonbridge